THE END OF AMERICAN INNOCENCE

A STUDY OF THE

FIRST YEARS OF OUR OWN TIME

1912-1917

BY

Henry F. May

COLUMBIA UNIVERSITY PRESS
NEW YORK

TO

HENRY NASH SMITH

COLUMBIA UNIVERSITY PRESS MORNINGSIDE EDITION 1992

Columbia University Press
New York Chichester, West Sussex

Morningside Edition with new preface

Library of Congress Cataloging-in-Publication Data
May, Henry Farnham, 1915–
The end of American innocence : a study of the first years of our own time, 1912–1917 / by Henry F. May.—Columbia University Press Morningside ed.
p. cm.
Originally published: New York : Knopf, 1959.
Includes bibliographical references (p.) and index.
ISBN 0-231-09652-6 (alk. paper)—ISBN 0-231-09653-4 (pbk. : alk. paper)
1. United States—Intellectual life—20th century. 2. United States—Civilization—1865–1918. I. Title.
E169.1.M496 1993
973—dc20 93-33225
CIP

Casebound editions of Columbia University Press books are printed on permanent and durable acid-free paper

Printed in the United States of America

c 10 9 8 7 6 5 4 3 2 1
p 10 9 8 7 6 5 4 3 2 1

The present age is a critical one and interesting to live in. The civilization characteristic of Christendom has not yet disappeared, yet another civilization has begun to take its place.

George Santayana, 1913

Contents

Foreword to the Morningside Edition

By David A. Hollinger

When *The End of American Innocence* was published in 1959, professional historians rarely addressed the writings of philosophers and novelists and were not inclined to see such writings as parts of a single discourse shared with presidents and political agitators. Yet here was a book that began with William Howard Taft and ended with Woodrow Wilson, attended closely to William James and Sherwood Anderson, and travelled comfortably from the *Saturday Evening Post* to the most radical and fly-by-night of the "little magazines" produced in Greenwich Village. Henry F. May found that these diverse voices were addressing some of the same questions and were thus participants in a sprawling, but ultimately quite coherent conversation about the nature of American civilization. The writers and thinkers normally studied by professors of literature and philosophy were here cast alongside politicians and publicists as characters in a single story, told by a bona-fide historian.

In the 1990's, intellectual history is routinely counted as one of the standard specialties for historians, and "cultural studies" is widespread throughout the humanities. No one is surprised when a historian addresses an even broader range of sources than May did. Nor is anyone surprised when professors of English return the favor by going well beyond canonical texts to scrutinize both popular fiction, the reformer's tracts, and the presidential speeches that were once left to historians. But at the end of the 1950's, the sense that *The End of*

American Innocence was a truly distinctive triumph of the historian's craft was registered across the spectrum of professional and popular magazines, from *The American Historical Review* to *Vogue*.[1]

Although this book is often remembered as one in a series of "fifties books" that consolidated the position of American intellectual history as a professional specialty, very few of these famous books were written by people who had been trained as historians, and who themselves directed Ph.D. dissertations in departments of history. The two most creative and influential of these authors, Perry Miller and Henry Nash Smith, were professors of English.[2] So, too, was R. W. B. Lewis, author of *The American Adam*.[3] Morton White, whose *Social Thought in America: The Revolt Against Formalism* predated *The End of American Innocence* by a decade and was destined to co-habit with it in countless footnotes of the 1960's and 1970's, was a professor of philosophy.[4] The most widely cited work of "consensus history," *The Liberal Tradition in America*, was written by a professor of political science,

[1] "The Best of the Best," *Vogue*, April 1, 1960. The *American Historical Review*'s appreciative reviewer was C. Vann Woodward; see *AHR* LXV (1960), 637–638. Intellectual history was already a presence in the professional study of the history of the United States, but primarily through three textbooks: Ralph Henry Gabriel, *The Course of American Democratic Thought: An Intellectual History Since 1815* (New York, 1940); Merle Curti, *The Growth of American Thought* (New York, 1943); Henry Steele Commager, *The American Mind: An Interpretation of American Thought and Culture Since the 1880's* (New Haven, 1950). None of these widely acclaimed works had the monographic focus and sharpness of argument that helped to distinguish *The End of American Innocence*.

[2] Perry Miller's most respected work of the 1950's was *The New England Mind: From Colony to Province* (Cambridge, Mass., 1953). Henry Nash Smith's greatest impact on historians was achieved through *Virgin Land: The American West as Symbol and Myth* (Cambridge, Mass., 1950). Miller was among May's graduate teachers at Harvard, and Smith among May's colleagues at Berkeley. May dedicated *The End of American Innocence* to Smith, and later wrote a sensitive and probing account of Smith's early career: "The Rough Road to *Virgin Land*," in May's *The Divided Heart: Essays on Protestantism and the Enlightenment in America* (New York, 1991), 33–60.

[3] R. W. B. Lewis, *The American Adam: Innocence, Tragedy, and Tradition in the Nineteenth Century* (Chicago, 1955).

[4] Morton White, *Social Thought in America: The Revolt Against Formalism* (Cambridge, Mass., 1949; later editions, 1957 and 1976). It should be noted here that philosophers had been the chief carriers of the tradition of scholarship known in the 1930's and 1940's as "the history of ideas," especially as institutionalized in *The Journal of the History of Ideas* founded in 1940 by the philosopher, Arthur O. Lovejoy, and managed by another philosopher, Philip P. Wiener.

Louis Hartz.[5] Within the discipline of history, then, *The End of American Innocence* loomed especially large. The book's role in establishing a genre of scholarship in the study of the American past was comparable to that played in the historiography of modern Europe by a work of comparable scope addressed to the same period, and published at almost the same moment: *Consciousness and Society: The Reorientation of European Social Thought*, 1890–1930, by H. Stuart Hughes.[6] Hughes and May were not the only contemporary exemplars of the study of intellectual history,[7] but the simultaneous appearance of these two sophisticated, commanding books by respected historians at Harvard and Berkeley had a telling effect in the historical profession. Hughes and May helped to make history departments safe for ideas.[8]

On the occasion of the reissuing of *The End of American Innocence* thirty-four years later, three questions demand special attention. Exactly what did this book argue? How does it stand in relation to more than three decades of subsequent scholarship? And in what terms are we to interpret this book as a historical artifact, as a product of its own time and place?

[5] Louis Hart, *The Liberal Tradition in America: An Interpretation of American Political Thought Since the Revolution* (New York, 1955).

[6] H. Stuart Hughes, *Consciousness and Society: The Reorientation of European Social Thought*, 1890–1930 (New York, 1958). For an appraisal of this work in relation to recent methodological trends in intellectual history, see Paul Robinson, "H. Stuart Hughes and Intellectual History: The State of the Discipline," *Intellectual History Newsletter* IX (1987), 29–35.

[7] For a fuller account of the development of intellectual history as a specialty, see Robert Allan Skotheim, *American Intellectual Histories and Historians* (Princeton, 1966), and John Higham, "Introduction," in John Higham and Paul Conkin, eds., *New Directions in American Intellectual History* (Baltimore, 1979), xi–xix. For European intellectual history before and after Hughes, see Martin Jay, "European Intellectual History and the Specter of Multi-culturalism," *Salmagundi* # 96 (Fall 1992), 21–26.

[8] At Berkeley, May produced a steady stream of doctoral students in American intellectual history until his retirement in 1980. Many of these worked on eighteenth and early-nineteenth century topics, connected to May's *The Enlightenment in America* (New York, 1976). But a number of others wrote dissertations within the orbit of *The End of American Innocence* that later became books. Among these books were Samuel Haber, *Efficiency and Uplift: Scientific Management in the Progressive Era* (Chicago, 1964); Laurence R. Veysey, *The Emergence of the American University* (Chicago, 1965); William L. O'Neill, *Divorce in the Progressive Era* (New Haven, 1967); Nathan G. Hale, Jr., *Freud and the Americans* (New York, 1971); David A. Hollinger, *Morris R. Cohen and the Scientific Ideal* (Cambridge, Mass., 1975); and Peter Frederick, *Knights of the Golden Rule* (Lexington, Ky., 1976).

The argument of *The End of American Innocence* is best understood in two parts. One is a claim about the entirety of the intellectual history of the educated middle class of the United States from the late nineteenth century to the 1950's: that this history has been characterized by a crucial transition coded by the word "innocence." On the innocent side of this great divide is a confident and cheerful sensibility, characterized above all by an "absence of guilt and doubt and the complexity that goes with them." Specifically, this old, "genteel tradition"—May relied heavily on this notion of George Santayana's—consisted of three core doctrines: (1) "the certainty and universality of moral values," (2) "the inevitability, particularly in America, of progress," and (3) "the importance of traditional literary culture." [9] On the post-innocent side of the divide is something less clearly defined, but consisting at least of the honest confrontation with doubt and complexity vital to the self-image of most "modern" intellectuals. *The End of American Innocence* is thus a narrative of spiritual maturation in which the subject—"America"—comes to terms with complications and responsibilities to which it had once been oblivious, sometimes willfully so. This part of the argument amounts to a highly particular construction of the familiar, but much debated transition, victorian-to-modern.

The second part of the argument has to do with the dynamics of the transition. "It was the war" runs an old cliché. *The End of American Innocence* is written explicitly against this facile belief in the explanatory omnipotence of the war. But this book also counters, more subtly, another common explanation: that the old edifice was brought down by the critical force of the intellectual giants of the age, Nietzsche and his fellows in Europe, and, in America, William and Henry James, Henry Adams, Theodore Dreiser, John Dewey, H. L. Mencken, Charles Beard, and Thorstein Veblen, among others. May treats both the war and the great minds in relation to a movement he dates from 1912 and calls "the innocent rebellion." This insurgency of young American intellectuals displayed "exuberant innovation, cheerful mysticism, insistent spontaneity, and certainty that everything was turning out su-

[9] May, *Innocence*, 6, 393.

perbly,"[10] and thus partook, in its glib and irreverent way, of the very "innocence" worn more soberly by the "custodians of culture." What the "innocent rebellion" did was to popularize in more cheerful, less threatening tones some of the subversive ideas developed by the "older insurgents and invaders," May's term for the tougher, gloomier critics we now remember as the giants of the age. The coming of the war in 1914 deeply shocked the "custodians," who, by identifying the Allied cause with their own increasingly shrill, rigid formulations of "morality, progress, and culture," escalated a dialectical conflict with the young intellectuals. Woodrow Wilson took the nation into war as a defense of the traditional values, while Randolph Bourne, "the nearly official voice of the rebellion,"[11] condemned both the war and its ideological justification. After Versailles, the "custodians" had lost much of the cultural capital invested in the Allied cause, and the outlook of the "rebels" was ripe for more vigorous development in the 1920's by the aging Mencken and Dewey and by such newer voices as Ernest Hemingway and Joseph Wood Krutch. Hence World War I emerges from May's analysis as vital, but in the terms set by the cultural war already underway between 1912 and 1917. The ideas of the major intellectuals emerge as vital, too, but on ground prepared for their reception in the twenties by the lighter, "innocent" rebellion of the teens.

How does all this look, after more than thirty years of additional scholarship? My task in addressing this question is made easier by Joan Shelley Rubin and Christopher Wilson, authors of two well-informed appraisals published in 1990. Rubin supports May's essential insights into the character and historic function of the "innocent rebellion." She also stresses the continuities between May's approach and "new cultural history" of our own era, with its reading of behavior—such as the testimonial dinner for William Dean Howells with which *The End of American Innocence* begins—for its symbolic meaning. Within this strongly sympathetic retrospective, Rubin comments on four features

[10] May, *Innocence*, 393.
[11] May, *Innocence*, 197.

of the book "that bear rethinking in the light of subsequent developments." [12]

Of women there are not nearly enough in this book, Rubin points out. "Feminism and the effort to restructure gender relations, limited in May's treatment to brief mention of Emma Goldman, Margaret Sanger, and Elsie Clews Parsons, do not assume the centrality most of us would now insist they deserve." A second element emphasized by more recent scholarship is "consumer culture." How might "the language of freedom and fulfillment" undergirding the rebellion have been "susceptible to appropriation by advertising," Rubin asks. Third, does not May's attitude toward some of the young intellectuals of the teens now look somewhat patronizing? A recent study by Casey Blake detailing the critique of industrial capitalism mounted by Bourne and other *Seven Arts* critics, Rubin observes, makes it difficult to accept May's characterization of these critics as "somewhat superficial." Finally, Rubin believes May left the impression of too sharp a break and underestimated the persistence of the genteel tradition into the 1920's. Rubin cites the careers of Henry Seidel Canby and John Erskine as examples of a "middlebrow culture" that flourished even until the 1940's and perpetuated "the familiar touchstones of the genteel tradition while accommodating the values of a consumer society." [13]

[12] Joan Shelley Rubin, "In Retrospect: Henry F. May's *The End of American Innocence,*" *Reviews in American History* XVIII (March 1990), 143.

[13] Rubin, "Retrospect," 144–145. The work of Casey Blake cited by Rubin is *Beloved Community: The Cultural Criticism of Randolph Bourne, Van Wyck Brooks, Waldo Frank & Lewis Mumford* (Chapel Hill, 1990). The interest in "consumer culture" mentioned by Rubin has been pursued in a host of works, prominent among which is Richard Wightman Fox and T. J. Jackson Lears, eds., *The Culture of Consumption: Critical Essays in American History, 1880–1980* (New York, 1983). Feminism and the effort to restructure gender relations in this period have been the subject of numerous studies, two of the most influential of which are David Kennedy, *Birth Control in America: The Career of Margaret Sanger* (New Haven, 1970), and Rosalind Rosenberg, *Beyond Separate Spheres: Intellectual Roots of Modern Feminism* (New Haven, 1982). In a book of Rubin's own, *The Making of Middlebrow Culture* (Chapel Hill, 1992), Rubin has developed carefully her argument concerning the perpetuation of the genteel tradition in certain discursive spaces of the 1920's, 1930's, and 1940's. For the insistence that catholic thought constitutes yet another sphere in which this cultural tradition persisted, see William M. Halsey, *The Survival of American Innocence: Catholicism in an Era of Disillusionment, 1920–1940* (Notre Dame, Ind., 1980). The complaint that

Wilson shares Rubin's appreciation for May's having developed "an investigative strategy that was a real achievement," manifest especially in the "ethnographic present of 1912" created in the early chapters of the book. But Wilson observes that scholars today would want "to know more about audience reception" of the books and articles that were the sources for May's study. Where Wilson feels the greatest need to get beyond the limits of May's achievement is in confronting the extent to which the world of public expression studied by May was in fact a "marketplace": *The End of American Innocence* can be construed as a study in "what thoughts produce in the marketplace." This construal can enable us to see that "the pressure" with which May's "innocent rebels" came to terms was "not only a disembodied tradition, but the institutionalizing, professionalizing tendencies of the marketplace." Wilson reminds us that the testimonial dinner for Howells attended by President Taft was, after all, a promotional event organized by a publisher intent on packaging Howells for public consumption at a good price. Wilson notes May's recognition that the private Howells was more complicated than Howells the public symbol, but Wilson wants to reopen "the border" May closed "between private and public," in order to investigate more fully what drove behavior in the public realm.[14]

The comments of Rubin and Wilson can be supplemented by the observation that the bulk of the relevant scholarship since 1959 divides into two parts which reflect the two dimensions of May's argument as set forth above. One group of studies has focused on the cultural warfare of the teens, especially the activities of radical intellectuals and artists. Another has been directed at an arena of larger scale and has sought to clarify either Victorianism or Modernism, or the vaunted transition from one to another.

May rendered the "end" of American innocence too decisively has always been the most commonly expressed criticism of *The End of American Innocence.*

[14] Christopher Wilson, "Coming to Terms with *The End of American Innocence,*" *Intellectual History Newsletter* XII (1990), 33–37. Wilson himself is the author of the most important study of the literary marketplace of the period, *The Labor of Words: Literary Professionalism in the Progressive Era* (Athens, Ga., 1985).

Most of the works on what May called "the innocent rebellion" acknowledge the classical status of May's interpretation, but affect little of his reserve and prefer to designate this episode, "the little renaissance." [15] It has proved difficult to resist the charms of the men and women who created the Armory show, brought the Paterson Strike to Madison Square Garden, gathered at Provincetown and in Mabel Dodge's salon, wrote for *The Masses* and *Seven Arts*, discovered Freud and Bergson when they were still fresh, started *Poetry* and took over *The Dial*, marched with Big Bill Haywood, and opposed American entry into World War I. These remarkable people continue to inspire a host of increasingly detailed, largely sympathetic studies, well represented within the covers of a collection entitled *1915, The Cultural Moment.*[16] Some of these studies, by detaching the creative work of the young intellectuals from the very general, abstract terms of doctrinal conflict emphasized by May, discover artistic innovations of historical significance. This is the case, for example, with Rebecca Zurier's study of the graphics done for *The Masses.*[17] May paid scant attention to the early phases of "the Harlem Renaissance," a movement of young intellectuals now seen as a major episode in American history. However, one of the leading studies of it by Nathan Irvin Huggins draws upon May's analysis of the white milieu surrounding the creative work of New York's black intellectuals.[18] The most striking point of difference between May's treatment of the young intellectuals and that of recent scholarship concerns neither blacks nor women, but a single white male: Bourne. Although May depicted Bourne as more compli-

[15] Arthur Wertheim, *The New York Little Renaissance: Iconoclasm, Modernism, and Nationalism in American Culture, 1908–1917* (New York, 1976). See also Martin Green, *New York, 1913* (New York, 1988); Leslie Fishbein, *Rebels in Bohemia: The Radicals of THE MASSES, 1911–1917* (Chapel Hill, 1982); Edward Abrahams, *The Lyrical Left: Randolph Bourne, Alfred Stieglitz, and the Origins of Cultural Radicalism in America* (Charlottesville, Va., 1986).

[16] Adele Heller and Lois Rudnick, eds., *1915, The Cultural Moment: The New Politics, the New Woman, the New Psychology, the New Art, and the New Theatre in America* (New Brunswick, N. J., 1991).

[17] Rebecca Zurier, *Art for The Masses: A Radical Magazine and Its Graphics, 1911–1917* (Philadelphia, 1988).

[18] Nathan Irvin Huggins, *Harlem Renaissance* (New York, 1971).

cated than his fellow rebels, May was willing to characterize Bourne and Van Wyck Brooks as "not great critics; what they said mattered less than what they were," which was "openers of doors." [19] This evaluation, if proclaimed today of Brooks, would raise few eyebrows, but as applied to the most remembered of Dewey's critics and the author of "Trans-National America"—one of the most cited essays in the multiculturalist debates of the 1990's—is more at odds with today's conventional wisdom than perhaps any judgment offered in *The End of American Innocence.*

In the meantime, "Victorianism" and "Modernism" have become more prominent on the agenda of American historians. This intensification of interest is reflected in *Victorian America,* edited by Daniel Walker Howe, and *Modernist Culture in America,* edited by Daniel Joseph Singal. [20] Both of these collections of commissioned essays began as special issues of *American Quarterly* designed to encourage historians to explore analytic categories earlier associated primarily with literary scholarship and the history of the arts. May's influence on both is evident. Yet the role May's formulations now play in the historiographies of Victorianism and of Modernism are not equal. *The End of American Innocence* offered a much more firmly etched account of the old "innocence," after all, than of the post-innocence May dealt with in only the most general of terms. It is May's nuanced reconstruction of genteel culture as visible in American public discourse in 1912 and his vivid account of the reactionary tendencies in that culture called forth by the crisis of World War I that continue to inform contemporary scholarship the most actively. [21] If May's depiction of the proto-modernism of the "innocent rebels" has provoked repeated and diverse reconsiderations within a scholarly discourse still largely framed by *The*

[19] May, *Innocence,* 329.

[20] Daniel Walker Howe, ed., *Victorian America* (Philadelphia, 1976); Daniel Joseph Singal, *Modernist Culture in America* (Belmont, Calif., 1991).

[21] See, for example, May's influence on the treatment of genteel culture in late-nineteenth-century New York City in Thomas Bender, *New York Intellect: A History of Intellectual Life in New York City, From 1750 to the Beginnings of Our Own Time* (New York, 1987), 206–222.

End of American Innocence, his portrait of the "custodians of culture" remains authoritative.[22]

May's construction of the twentieth century as a transition from innocent confidence and good cheer to sophisticated doubt and complexity is invoked episodically in recent scholarship, but is rarely a point around which argumentation revolves. The most sustained effort to develop May's specific version of the Victorian-to-Modern transition has been Singal's *The War Within*, interpreting a distinctive group of American intellectuals: white Southerners deeply socialized into the genteel culture May described so well.[23] Studies of other intellectuals sometimes take for granted that a transition of this sort has taken place, but are more immediately directed at other transitions, including from a producer's culture to a consumer's culture, from individualism to communitarianism, from sexism to feminism, from provincialism to cosmopolitanism, from racism to anti-racism, and from Eurocentrism to multiculturalism. "Divide studies," moreover, do not exhaust the prodigious literature on modern American intellectual history, much of which tells stories not of grand transitions but of continuing projects, conflicts, and dilemmas. The narrative of progress from childlike innocence to mature doubt has not so much disappeared as receded into an indefinite background.[24]

May's engagement with this narrative was far from idiosyncratic for American intellectuals of his generation. Recognition of the generational intensity of this engagement can bring us to the last of our three

[22] May's special gift for analyzing the genteel culture of late-nineteenth and early-twentieth century America is evident, once again, in his most recent publication, issued as a pamphlet by the University of California, *Three Faces of Berkeley: Conflicting Ideologies in the Wheeler Era* (Berkeley, 1993).

[23] Daniel Joseph Singal, *The War Within: From Victorian to Modernist Thought in the South*, 1919–1945 (Chapel Hill, 1982).

[24] Some of the concerns behind this narrative animate Christopher Lasch's vision of American history as a site for a grand struggle between a "progressive optimism" associated with the Enlightenment resting "on a denial of the natural limits on human power and freedom," and a "populist or petty-bourgeois" tradition exemplified by Reinhold Niebuhr projecting hope within a "sense of limits." See Lasch, *The True and Only Heaven: Progress and Its Critics* (New York, 1991), 530. For an illuminating analysis of this book and of Lasch's career in relation to the careers of historians and critics who flourished in the 1950's, see Louis Menand, "Man of the People," *New York Review of Books*, April 11, 1991, 39–44.

questions, how we might interpret *The End of American Innocence* as an artifact of its time and place? Here, May's autobiographical writings are pertinent. In *Coming to Terms,* May reveals that his own father was profoundly a man of the genteel tradition, in whose den in the 1920's the young Henry May—born in 1915—could see "small plaster busts of Shakespeare and Daniel Webster, and a full-length plaster statue of Thackeray." [25] *Coming to Terms* does not describe the actual writing of *The End of American Innocence,* but this deliberate, searching account of May's youth and early career can be read as the story of May's travelling of the road to that task. Much of the *Coming to Terms* is, in fact, a loving and ambivalent study of May's obliquely innocent father and his milieu. Although May's experience with his father is a highly individual step along the road to *The End of American Innocence,* some of the other steps May took in tandem with a number of his own contemporaries. Among these were an attraction to Marxism in the 1930's and 1940s, a rejection of it in the 1950's, and a simultaneous attraction to the political and religious ideas of the theologian, Reinhold Niebuhr. May's appreciation for Niebuhr, acknowledged both in *Coming to Terms* and in a brief autobiographical sketch introducing a collection of essays,[26] helps explain the preoccupation with "innocence" that renders *The End of American Innocence* a firm and instructive witness to a distinctive historical moment.

That moment is marked by the conviction that it is an enormous spiritual and psychological triumph to recognize tragedy, irony, and paradox as among life's common features, and to accept, as permanent conditions, moral ambiguity and humanity's lack of perfection. American intellectuals at midcentury were neither the first nor the last people to attain these insights. But it may be that these intellectuals had to struggle harder to attain them because, as many insisted at the time, the men and women from whom they had tried to learn—various

[25] Henry F. May, *Coming to Terms: A Study in Memory and History* (Berkeley, 1987), 6; see also, 163–165.

[26] May, *Coming to Terms,* 304–305; May, *Divided Heart,* 9. The most relevant of Niebuhr's writings are *The Children of Light and the Children of Darkness* (New York, 1944), and *The Irony of American History* (New York, 1952). For May's current perspective on Niebuhr, see *Divided Heart,* 61–72.

Victorians, Progressives, and Communists—proved insufficiently grounded in them. In 1960 Daniel Bell described this mid-century generation—Bell's own—as "twice-born," made prematurely wise by the cataclysmic events of the century, finding "wisdom in pessimism, evil, tragedy, and despair." Although Bell located "the loss of innocence" primarily in the 1930's and connected it more directly to disillusion with Stalin, he, like May, was massively invested in a generational self-conception that yielded a master narrative of historical progress from naive progressivism to mature uncertainty.[27]

"Youth's a kind of infirmity," said an apparently sagacious character in *By Love Possessed*, James Gould Cozzens's novel of 1957.[28] The remark exemplified the somewhat indulgent, avuncular stance many reflective men and women of the period affected toward those impetuous, self-righteous, cheerful souls who, for all their charm and verve, just didn't understand what life was about. This celebration of judicious maturity did not have to become smug nor authorize a politics of acquiescence, but it could do both, and sometimes did. Amid his own study of American innocence, R. W. B. Lewis was moved to complain that an impulse in contemporary culture which began admirably "as an able corrective to the claims of innocence in America" had declined into a "cult of original sin." [29] But if the Niebuhrian sensibility of heightened responsibilities and diminished expectations could invite parody, it also inspired some of the most creative energies of the generation. This sensibility is visible in some of the era's best novels, including Robert Penn Warren's *All the King's Men*, J. D. Salinger's *Catcher in the Rye*, and Cozzens's great novel of 1948, *Guard of Honor*, perhaps its most carefully designed literary expression.[30]

The End of American Innocence, too, is a work of literary art. Much of its capacity to survive "the fifties" derives from May's writerly voice in which critical detachment is constantly and carefully balanced against

[27] Daniel Bell, *The End of Ideology: On the Exhaustion of Political Ideas in the Fifties* (Cambridge, Mass., 1988; originally published 1960), 300, 302.

[28] James Gould Cozzens, *By Love Possessed* (New York, 1957), 6.

[29] Lewis, *Adam*, 196.

[30] Robert Penn Warren, *All the King's Men* (New York, 1946); J. D. Salinger, *Catcher in the Rye* (New York, 1951); James Gould Cozzens, *Guard of Honor* (New York, 1948).

empathetic identification with diverse, and sometimes suspicious characters. The historians, critics, and novelists of May's generation were at their best when divided against themselves and eager to express what they took to be a wisdom special to their generation but worried that this wisdom would authorize a complacent, more-mature-than-thou invidiousness. This strictness of conscience is displayed throughout *The End of American Innocence*, where it informs May's discerning encapsulations of the ideas and temperament of a host of individuals—H. L. Mencken, Stuart Sherman, William James, and Charles W. Eliot, among others. These critical portraits, even more than the general arguments with which they are connected in the text, render *The End of American Innocence* a classic, an artifact of an honest struggle with the tensions of the author's own time as well as with those experienced by his immediate cultural ancestors.

Berkeley, California David A. Hollinger
July 1993

DAVID A. HOLLINGER is Professor of History at the University of California, Berkeley. He is the author of *Morris R. Cohen and the Scientific Ideal* (1975) and *In the American Province: Studies in the History and Historiography of Ideas* (1985), and is the co-editor, with Charles Capper, of *The American Intellectual Tradition* (2nd. ed., 1993).

Introduction

Everybody knows that at some point in the twentieth century America went through a cultural revolution. One has only to glance at the family photograph album, or to pick up a book or magazine dated, say, 1907, to find oneself in a completely vanished world. On one side of some historical boundary lies the America of Theodore Roosevelt and William Jennings Bryan, of Chautauqua and Billy Sunday and municipal crusades, a world so foreign, so seemingly simple, that we sometimes tend, foolishly enough, to find it comical. On the other side of the barrier lies our own time, a time of fearful issues and drastic divisions, a time surely including the Jazz Age, the great depression, the New Deal, and the atom bomb. Clearly on one side of this line lie Booth Tarkington and O. Henry and the American Winston Churchill, and also, we should not forget, Henry James. Clearly on our side lie Ernest Hemingway, Thomas Stearns Eliot, and also the writers of television advertising. At some point, if not an instantaneous upheaval, there must have been a notable quickening of the pace of change, a period when things began to move so fast that the past, from then on, looked static.

Most people place the dividing line at the end of the First World War and for this reason, partly, the postwar decade fascinates the present generation. Current romantic accounts make the twenties a period of hectic gaiety and financial irresponsibility, which it was. Slightly more searching inquiries emphasize the desperate seriousness of the expatriate intellectuals, the paradoxically fervent complacency of business, the struggle between the creeds of Greenwich Village and the *Saturday Evening Post.* The twenties were the period of beginnings, the time when social scientists and psychologists announced a brave new world, when technological accomplishment fixed a new image of America in the eyes of jealous Europe, when Henry L. Mencken created a new language to castigate the bourgeoisie and the Young Intellectuals found new reasons for rejecting the whole of American culture.

These tendencies are so various and contradictory that few historians have tried seriously to explain them all at once. The postwar period has been treated usually as *either* the period of the new literature or that of Babbittry and isolation, *either* the peak of pragmatic and experimental philosophy or the betrayal of American progressivism. Whatever is being explained, one fact helps a great deal with the explanation: this was a postwar period. America's first major foreign war, with its devastating outcome in frustration and bitterness, explains the period's rejection of the past.

There is, of course, much truth in this as in most popular myths. The First World War was, clearly, an enormous experience for this peaceful and optimistic country. It is part of my purpose to suggest some of the content of this experience. Yet when one looks closely at the period just *before* the war, expecting to find the peaceful and stable America of later reminiscence, one becomes puzzled. On the official surface, it is true, reigns an almost intolerable placidity and complacency. Yet if one pokes through the surface almost anywhere, one finds the beginnings of the later revolution in nearly all its variety, excitement, and potential destructiveness. One finds, for instance, every one of the tendencies associated with the twenties which I have just mentioned.

We know, when we stop to think about it, that the period just before the war seemed to many a time of beginnings, that people were always talking about the New Freedom or the new poetry or even the new woman. Students of the American past realize that some of the best little magazines of revolt flourished before 1917, that Carl Sandburg and Ezra Pound and Sherwood Anderson were being published, that John Dewey and Thorstein Veblen had done much of their most important work, that some Americans were beginning to hear the names of Freud and even Einstein. Historians of law, of social science, of poetry, of popular music, of painting have all presented the second decade of the century as a time of drastic innovation. Even the general accounts usually mention some of these areas of change. Yet, a few pages further on, general accounts often point out that in 1917 America went to war for such formal nineteenth-century concepts as neutrality and freedom of the seas, under the leadership of an old-fashioned idealist and a master of old-fashioned rhetoric. And when they come to the twenties, most writers are unable to resist the temptations of simplicity: postwar changes in manners and morals and ideas are attributed to the war.

Some of these paradoxes are, of course, more apparent than real. We do not have to choose between the two pictures of prewar America: the end of Victorian calm and the beginning of cultural revolution. Both of these pictures are true. In the years we are going to examine, the few years just before the impact of war on America, we are uniquely able to look at both pictures at once. We can see the massive walls of nineteenth-century America still apparently intact, and then turn our spotlight on many different kinds of people cheerfully laying dynamite in the hidden cracks. It is my hope that a concentrated but fairly wide-ranging study of this short period, of its thought and literature and politics, may tell us something about the old America and something about the beginnings of our own time.

Part of the difficulty in doing this is that it demands a departure from the dominant tendency among American historians. Ever since the period we are talking about, when Charles A. Beard did his early and most important work, most of the ablest American historians have taken for granted the central importance in our history of rather simple socio-economic causes and motives. This tendency has had its advantages and disadvantages. It has added greatly to our understanding of much of American politics. It has, however, almost cut off historians from communication with students of literature, who have moved in an opposite direction.

For our immediate purpose, for instance, a socio-economic interpretation would make it easy to conclude that the war caused a revolution in thought and mores. It would make it harder, on the other hand, to understand how this revolution got started in a period of prosperity, comparative class harmony, and international peace. Of course the prewar period was a time of urbanization and technological change, but so had been every decade at least since the 1850's.

Instead of starting with economics or technology, I am starting here with general ideas. Let me make it clear at once that this does not imply any rigid intellectualist theory of history. I am not saying that people are guided in their lives by philosophical propositions to which they consciously subscribe. I am not denying the importance for history either of daily work or of sudden catastrophic experiences like the outbreak of war. I am arguing only that something called tradition plays a very large part in the way people deal either with daily routine or with catastrophe. What I am calling tradition centers in assumptions of value, however inarticulate, which have been inherited from the past.

These assumptions constitute what William James, the central thinker of the early twentieth century, called philosophy:

> For the philosophy which is so important in each of us is not a technical matter; it is our more or less dumb sense of what life honestly and deeply means. It is only partly got from books. It is our individual way of just seeing and feeling the total push and pressure of the cosmos.[1]

It is in philosophy in this sense that I have tried to center this

[1] William James: *Pragmatism* (New York, 1907), p. 4.

book. The sense of what life means was what was stable in prewar America, and it was this that was beginning to change. Technology had its large part in this change, as did city life. So did the work of abstract scientific thinkers and dead European poets whose names most Americans did not know. The change started in America to affect small groups of people directly. Soon, I hope to show, its indirect effects spread through the whole society.

In dealing with this change and its spread, I have concentrated on those areas of American life in which general ideas were most clearly expressed. I have given most attention to literature and politics, then as in most periods, I think, the most important and revealing means of American self-expression. It has been one of my main objects to bring together the diverging insights from these two areas. I have given some attention also to philosophy strictly so called, to popular science, psychology, social science, and education. Historians of somewhat different training might have given much more emphasis to such fields as architecture, music, or painting, without, I suspect, coming to very different conclusions.

Most writers who have recently dealt with aspects of this great change in the intellectual climate have passed judgment upon it. In certain quarters it has become fashionable to denounce as irresponsible, almost treasonable, the rebellious intellectuals who led the way toward modern American literature. In other quarters it is still the custom to talk about the breakup of idealist philosophy or traditional education as the overthrowing of the dead past, the opening of doors to the future, a process not only heroic but almost without cost.

In the long run, I suppose, one's attitude toward the beginning of the contemporary period depends on one's prediction of its outcome. Since my emotions about the current scene are divided, my interpretation of the past is divided also. It is not hard, retrospectively, to find the standard American culture of 1900 or 1912 seriously inadequate. Neither intellectual nor social orders are likely to be overthrown unless they *are* inadequate. Yet revolution, and this kind of revolution in particular, has its cost. I have tried to understand both conservatives and radicals. My major purpose has been to show the size and complexity and some of the meaning of the change, and not to draw up a balance sheet of gains and losses.

If this book helps the reader to understand the revolution that got under way by 1917, it may make it easier for him to live through it, or even, in some small area, to influence its outcome. I take it for granted that this cultural revolution is still going on.

Acknowledgments

Thanks are due Professor Kenneth Stampp, Professor Carl Bridenbaugh, Mr. Nathan Hale, Professor Daniel Aaron, Professor Henry Bamford Parkes, and Mr. Alfred Knopf for critical readings of all or part of my manuscript. The Social Science Research Council provided funds for a summer research trip at an early stage in my work, and the Institute of Social Sciences at the University of California has furnished funds for typing and research assistance in the last few years. Two research assistants, Samuel Haber and Charles Morrissey, have been extremely helpful during the past two summers. The staff of the University of California Library has been extraordinarily flexible and long-suffering. Both Mr. and Mrs. Alfred A. Knopf have contributed to my understanding of tendencies in publishing, and still more to my general impression of the New York scene during the years their work was beginning. Needless to say, neither they nor any other informant has any responsibility for the opinions I express.

My seminar at the University of California has been working on tendencies in this period for several years, and many students have contributed both ideas and information on various topics covered here. I should like to mention particularly Lucille Birnbaum, Philip A. Elwood, David Grimsted, Samuel Haber, Nathaniel Huggins, James P. Kindregan, Lynn Marshall, Frederick Matthews, Charles T. Morrissey, and William L. O'Neill; but this list is by no means exhaustive.

Acknowledgments

My wife has collaborated in my work in many ways. Still more impressive, she has lived with this book and with me during the period of its writing.

In my dedication, which is entirely without permission, I mean to express appreciation for help of many kinds given generously over many years. I also want to repay a small portion of the debt all students of American civilization owe Professor Smith. I am sure that he will disagree with many of my evaluations and conclusions; this seems to me to make the dedication all the more fitting.

PART ONE

The Nineteenth Century Intact (1912)

1

A Link with the Past

On March 3, 1912, President William Howard Taft made a special trip from Washington to New York to attend a dinner in honor of William Dean Howells. The dinner was given by Howells's publisher, Colonel George Harvey of the great house of Harper. It was the seventy-fifth birthday of the dean of American letters—or rather it was not exactly, because the celebration had been moved to accommodate the crowded presidential schedule. Taft was both a cultivated and a genial man, and doubtless he was glad to get away for an evening from the Senate, the unkind attacks of the progressive press, and the developing feud with Theodore Roosevelt. Yet for any president to go literally out of his way for a writer is a rare event, and Taft meant all that his gesture implied. To the President, as to most literate Americans, Howells was not only the greatest living American writer, but something more than that—a valuable national possession, a link with a hallowed tradition, and, in the simple and confident language of the Progressive Era, a "force for good."

A wide segment of American leadership (though by no means the whole range of American life) was represented by the four hundred invited guests. As one would expect at a dinner for a man of Howells's progressive social opinions, there was an assortment of reformers—Ida M. Tarbell the muckraking journalist, Herbert Croly the liberal nationalist, and Oswald Garrison Villard, half patrician and half reformer pacifist. All these guests undoubtedly mixed on terms of ease and even cordiality with such others as Charles Francis Adams, Ogden Mills Reid, and Admiral Alfred Thayer Mahan. As a matter of course the editors of the still powerful serious magazines attended, and there was a sprinkling of university presidents. Writers of rank like Winston Churchill, the best-selling novelist, were joined by a few writers of promise, like James Branch Cabell. Most of the diners were Anglo-Saxon, but George Sylvester Viereck represented the German-Americans and Abraham Cahan the Eastern European Jews, the most articulate section of the new immigration. Cabell, from Virginia, was balanced by Mary Austin, the chief literary spokesman of the unknown, romantic Southwest. Gratifyingly, as the *New York Times* front-page account remarked: "Nearly everyone in the hall knew everyone else."

The President's speech, like nearly all the others, paid an obviously genuine tribute to Howells's novels but stressed still more his consistent service to the important and related ideals of "refinement and morality." [1] Few if any of those present would have questioned the importance or the relevance of either, though Thomas Hardy and Henry James, who sent letters, praised Howells's literary art in rather different terms. On the whole the speakers, putting aside the passions of a particularly tense campaign year, reflected an appropriate optimism about the state of the nation and its literature under Taft's and Howells's respective leaderships.

Colonel Harvey, the host and toastmaster, who still supported Woodrow Wilson despite their recent falling-out, paid a graceful and nonpartisan tribute to President Taft's love of literature and service to international peace. The guest of honor, too, was associated with this last cause, and Harvey praised Howells for a recent stand against the obsolete sentiment, "my country, right or wrong." Howells had, Harvey reminded his audience, recently expressed a sounder view in a public letter:

> When our country is wrong she is worse than other countries when they are wrong, because she has more light than other countries, and we ought somehow to make her feel that we are sorry and ashamed for her.

[1] *New York Times*, March 3, 1912, p. 1. Other quotations in this chapter are from this account unless they are otherwise identified. Throughout the book, footnotes are used only for direct quotations or occasionally for particular facts which seem to need documentation. For sources used, see the Bibliographical Note at the end.

In the complacent chorus, a keen ear might occasionally have detected a defensive note. Churchill, speaking for the novelists of America, congratulated Howells on standing for the purity of the English language against the menace of "polyglot corrupters," and for keeping himself clean against "the muddy tide of commercialism, of materialism, which has swept over our country, and which is leaving its stain on other dignified professions besides our own."

Certainly the guest of honor in his own speech voiced no such worries, and combined reverence for the past with a robust optimism. He had, Howells pointed out, known all of those "in whom the story of American literature sums itself" except four: Cooper, Irving, Poe, and Prescott. As he named the rest of the firmly established canon his audience must indeed have felt the presence of tradition incarnate: Howells's acquaintance had included Hawthorne, Emerson, Whitman, Longfellow, Holmes, Whittier, Lowell, Bryant, Bancroft, Motley, Harriet Beecher Stowe, Julia Ward Howe, Artemus Ward, Mark Twain, Francis Parkman, and John Fiske. Yet even after listing these revered names, Howells refused, as he always had refused, to disparage the present or the future. If not as many of our novelists, playwrights, and poets in 1912 reached the very height of greatness as in the past, there were more writers of a modest excellence: "It is the high average which reigns in this as in all American things." Modern writers, turning from the cloisters to the forum and even the market place, were reflecting modern life, when all humanity was moving into the light of democracy.

The press, commenting enthusiastically on the dinner, sometimes mentioned in passing that Howells had not always been beyond controversy. He had once been widely accused of insisting on the humdrum detail as against the ennobling ideal as the proper material for literature. He had even, a few papers remembered either with praise or depreciation, been a defender of anarchists and a spokesman of a sort of Christian Socialism. The *Saturday Evening Post*, always contemptuous of literary categories, recalled that there used to be some complicated argument about realism and romanticism, and that Howells had once been considered "a terribly wrong sort of person." Now, however, the *Post* agreed with everybody else that Howells was a man to be proud of, "always courageous, always sincere, always and invariably kind." [2]

As the *Post* and Taft both implied, Howells at seventy-five was more than just a critic or a novelist. Doubtless Colonel Harvey's reasons for giving the dinner included a desire to advertise a valuable Harper property, but it took more than that to pull together this particular four hundred. They did not come solely to pay tribute to Howells's literary gift, which many of them realized had long since passed its peak. They would not all have agreed either with his critical or political opinions, or even with his most quoted dictum, that the smiling aspects of life were the more American and the sum of hardship and injustice in this country small. This statement, often contradicted in detail by Howells's own vision of American society, was more nearly true in 1912 than it had been in 1886 when first pronounced. Yet it would have been thought unduly rosy by some of the guests, and so obvious as not to be worth commemorating by others. The dinner was really a testimonial to the unity, excellence, and continuity of American nineteenth-century civilization. Most of the speeches and press comments pledged the country's allegiance to three central doctrines of that civilization. These were first, the certainty and universality of moral values; second, the inevitability, particularly in America, of progress; and third, the importance of traditional literary culture. The last, especially, was sometimes praised in a slightly defensive tone. Many of the diners assembled at Sherry's knew that some Americans valued one of these doctrines more than the rest, and even that a few misguided young people, usually through the effect of European corruption, defiantly rejected all three. This was all the more reason for honoring Howells, since these three major American commitments were almost perfectly summed up in his long career.

Whatever his inner doubts and fears, and later critics have shown that they were many, Howells had long demanded of literature

[2] *Saturday Evening Post,* March 6, 1912, p. 26.

truth to life, he had always insisted that real truth and moral goodness were identical, and he had always held that politics and literature were both amenable to moral judgment. He had always believed that American civilization was treading a sure path, whatever the momentary failures, toward moral and material improvement. Not without qualms, he had believed that the basic decisions about this forward movement could best be made by the whole people. Yet he had taken it for granted that men of education and ability and even of inherited tradition had some special responsibility for maintaining standards. These were the doctrines on which the dinner guests of 1912 agreed and in which they placed their faith.

The future was to show that they had chosen in Howells a more appropriate symbol than they realized: their choice was to be confirmed by those who rejected all they stood for. As early as 1917 Alexander Harvey, a young critic, in a confused and curious book about Howells, was to call him at once the supreme literary artist in English and also head of the "sissy school" of criticism. Our new knowledge of the unconscious, said this young critic of 1917, had made Howells's kind of realism obsolete. Yet Howells deserved to be admired; he had triumphed over almost insuperable obstacles:

> . . . What if Howells be a native American of Anglo-Saxon origin? Homer was blind. Coleridge was a slave to opium. Poe drank.[3]

From 1917 on, Howells rapidly became a symbol, not of American unity, but of a rejected past. In 1919 H. L. Mencken explained the standing of "The Dean" only by the deplorable American habit of judging writers not as artists but as Christian men. Finally in 1930 Sinclair Lewis, in 1912 a young romantic poet but by now the leading realistic novelist of the day, referred to Howells in his famous and fighting Nobel Prize speech. Howells's code, said Lewis, had been dominant up to 1914 and was still not completely dead in 1930. It was the code of professors and universities and the

[3] Alexander Harvey: *William Dean Howells* (New York, 1917), p. 271.

National Academy of Arts and Letters. In case this did not define it clearly enough, it was the code of "a pious old maid whose greatest delight is to have tea at the vicarage." [4]

It seems hardly necessary to point out that this judgment, like that of 1912, made Howells a less interesting and complex figure than he had actually been. He had, after all, been stirred by the same writers that had stimulated Lewis's generation—by Tolstoy and Dostoevsky and Flaubert among many others. He had fought for the shocking subjects and methods of Zola and Stephen Crane. Like many of the great optimists of his day, he found it harder than most people realized to maintain his cheerful serenity. In private, he fought his own continuing battles: we are startled to find him writing to his dear friend Henry James a few days after the birthday dinner:

> It was all, all wrong and unfit; but nobody apparently knew it, not even I till that ghastly waking hour of the night when hell opens to us.[5]

But neither the triumphant guests at Colonel Harvey's dinner nor the iconoclastic critics of later years were interested in the inner Howells. What they were talking about was a public symbol, and Howells meant the same thing to both groups: the dominance of a single, old, traditional set of doctrines over American life, politics, and art. This set of doctrines, unquestioned by most of the diners at Sherry's and most other articulate Americans, was already under attack in a few quarters and would soon be publicly torn apart.

[4] H. L. Mencken: *Prejudices, First Series* (New York, 1919), p. 52. *New York Times*, December 13, 1930, p. 12.

[5] Howells to James, March 17, 1912, in Mildred Howells, ed.: *Life in Letters of William Dean Howells* (New York, 1928), II, 317.

II

Practical Idealism

The men who met in 1912 to honor Howells took for granted that they and most of their countrymen shared a view of life. Part of their confidence in this set of beliefs arose from the fact that it had survived a series of challenges; however insipid the American credo of 1912 seemed to the next decade, we must remember that it had lived through the nineteenth century. This century, and particularly its second half, was by no means the smug Victorian calm created by the mythology of the 1920's. The old men of 1912 had come to consciousness in the midst of a devastating and revolutionary civil war. Their mental as well as the country's physical landscape had been drastically changed by rapid industrialization. Ever since the announcement of the Darwinian hypothesis, the moral cosmos had been subject to a succession of earthquake shocks. Yet, with some difficulty, the main tenets of traditional American faith had managed to adapt and survive. It is not surprising that they seemed proof against anything.

The first and central article of faith in the national credo was, as it always had been, the reality, certainty, and eternity of moral values. Words like truth, justice, patriotism, unselfishness, and decency were used constantly, without embarrassment, and ordinarily without any suggestion that their meaning might be only of a time and place. This central commitment entailed several corollaries, often stated and still more often taken for granted. First, most Americans were still certain that moral judgments applied with equal sureness in literature, art, politics, and all other areas. Second, it seemed clear that such judgments could be and must be applied not only to the conduct of individuals but also to the doings of trusts and labor unions, cities and nations. Finally, and this was perhaps the most often stated corollary of all, the United States, as the leader in moral progress, had a special responsibility for moral judgment, even of herself.

A history of moralism would come close to being a history of American thought. For Jonathan Edwards and his heirs, the morality of the universe had depended on the exertion of God's will, and had demanded the damnation of most men. As this gloomy view succumbed to the European enlightenment and the American environment, universal morality itself had grown no less secure. For Jefferson, for instance, it had been a matter of self-evident natural law, confirmed by man's innate moral sense. For Emerson, the moral meaning of the universe had been something that all men could find by looking either inward or outward through the eyes of the spirit. For the drier academic pundits of the early nineteenth century, morality had been demonstrable through logic; it was necessary to thought, we could not help believing it, so it must be true. Materialism and skepticism were the discredited notions of a few heathen Greeks and dissolute Frenchmen.

Then, in the middle of the century, evolutionary science had raised a new set of specters. The discoveries of Darwin's generation challenged far more than orthodox Christianity; they inescapably suggested the distressing outlines of a mechanistic universe. Not only man himself, but life as a whole, even the existence of the planet and the solar system were apparently to be explained by chemical-physical processes which had little to do with traditional ideas of purpose or destiny. Instead of the eternal skies or the eternal rocks there were only eternal atoms, indivisible units of matter whose nature was much in doubt, endlessly combining and recombining. A deadly fear of mechanistic materialism lay in back of the intense doubts and hard-won affirmations of the great Victorian sages. This was the enemy that young Americans as well as young Englishmen of the late nineteenth century had to wrestle with as their ancestors had wrestled with sin.

In the desperate, usually victorious late-nineteenth-century battle with despair, two modes of argument had proved useful. The first of these was the method of idealism, the reassertion of the old doctrine that reality is that which is known, that nothing exists without mind, that everything therefore in the long run is idea. Idealism in the strictest sense was, after all, very old in the country of Edwards and Emerson, and it was still defending its last ditches in the philosophy departments.

In 1911 at Berkeley, California, George Santayana had pinned on American idealism an epithet that was to be endlessly used and abused by the generation then in college in its attack against nineteenth-century culture: the Genteel Tradition. According to Santayana, idealism had lost the passionate intensity of Puritanism or the glowing romantic faith of Emerson. Instead of being popular sages and teachers, American idealist philosophers had become professors. Turning like all nineteenth-century professors to the great academic homeland, they had found in Germany valuable allies. First they had relied on Kant to help them restrict science to the important but limited and dependent sphere of phenomena. More recently they had turned instead to Hegel, and argued, mostly with each other, that all things were infinite spirit, all opposites eventually the same. By 1912 the academic philosophers, including Josiah Royce, Santayana's favorite opponent, were completely out of touch with the busy, practical American mind. Philosophy had become an elegant pastime instead of a guide to life.

Insofar as his argument was restricted to academic idealism, Santayana was probably right. Yet one should remember, as Santayana himself always did, that for all his marvelous clarity he saw America from the outside. What he had learned of the country, moreover, had been learned in New England. The history of American thought was more than a decline from Edwards to Emerson to Royce. Academic idealism and ruthless, mindless practicality were not the sole options open in 1911.

The second method of sustaining universal morality, more important than the method of idealism, was the method of evolution. When the middle-class American of 1912 wanted cosmic reassurance, he seldom turned to the academic philosophers. He turned instead to the spokesmen of liberal religion and popular science, who had long since driven a tunnel through the Victorian doubt and met each other in the middle. As soon as evolution was formulated, some people saw the possibility of making it the mainstay instead of the enemy of moralism. To those who knew the cruel processes of biological evolution at first hand, to Darwin and Huxley for instance, it might be difficult to moralize nature, but many nonscientists were equal to the task. It was no coincidence that liberal America, even more enthusiastically than England, gave a prophet's mantle to Herbert Spencer, the most optimistic of the great Victorians. Spencer's formulation of the laws of steady progression from the incoherent to the coherent, from the indefinite to the definite, fit the American habit of mind as well as the American social system. Out of struggle and chaos emerged law, out of brutal competition self-regulation and even the rule of love. A number of Americans like John Fiske, greatly increasing the theistic and optimistic component in Spencer's system, made it a new version of the unfolding moral law.

For some time before the work of Spencer or Fiske, American religion itself had been evolving. Instead of an inscrutable Sovereign whose purposes must be accepted rather than grasped, God had become for many first a constitutional monarch, and then a vast indwelling force in the universe. Evolution had not only become compatible with God, it had almost become God.

In 1912 the characteristic American religion of the articulate and up-to-date middle class was the Social Gospel. In this view God's method included not only biological evolution but economic and political progress. According to Lyman Abbott, the aged but powerful editor of the *Outlook*, who had been through the long battles over evolution and the Social Gospel in his youth, the Divine methods included law, commerce, and education.

In its extreme form, the Social Gospel taught that evolution under Divine guidance would eventuate in the coming of Christ's kingdom. This phrase did not connote anything apocalyptic or miraculous. The true work of Christ had been misstated and obscured; it consisted of providing humanity with a method and example for its own progressive salvation. This salvation, in America, was well under way. On June 29, 1912, *Collier's*, starting a series of articles on prominent ministers, quoted the aged Washington Gladden, himself once a lonely battler for progressive Christianity and now "The First Citizen of Columbus," in a prayer delivered in his church on a recent Sunday:

> Lord, we believe Thou art as near to us as Thou hast ever been to any people in any age.[1]

Social Christianity, a massive and varied movement by 1912, was by no means always as smug as this prayer implies. Evil, even if it meant the vestiges of the brute in man or of selfishness in society, might still be hard to overcome. Yet all believers in liberal and social Christianity believed that it could be beaten, and all thought social improvement relevant to this great purpose. This faith, so hard today for either Christians or non-Christians to grasp, had in its own terms accomplished a lot of good. No set of doctrines has ever impelled more people to help their neighbors, to clean up slums and build schools and playgrounds. Perhaps even more important, Social Christianity helped many people to bear the trials of life with confidence in the unfolding purposes of God.

Yet the Social Gospel, like all versions of the 1912 credo, had two great limitations. First, it remained the view of the middle class. It had failed in its campaign to convert the immigrant urban masses. Moreover, millions of native Protestants rejected it as a cowardly distortion of Bible truth. There were already signs, fatally neglected by liberal Christian leaders, of a religious counterrevolution.

Second, in bringing together religion and history the Social Gospel made each dependent on the other. Trials and tribulations could be borne as long as it was believable that mankind was basically improving. If this belief were ever shaken—an event almost

[1] Clark MacFarlane: "Washington Gladden, The First Citizen of Columbus," *Collier's*, January 29, 1912, p. 24.

unthinkable in the world of the Howells dinner—religion would be shaken with it.

Most Americans in 1912 did not argue about the essential morality of the universe—they assumed it. If argument was necessary, they turned not to philosophy or theology but to the plain lesson of current events. A phrase used over and over by Americans commenting on America, usually with a delighted air of having discovered the exact phrase, was "practical idealism." This did not have much to do with the idealism of the schools. Yet such an authority as Josiah Royce approved the use of the term "idealism" to mean a general allegiance to large ideals, and believed that in this sense it pervaded American life.[2]

Here Royce was shrewder than Santayana. Certainly the average American of 1912 considered himself an idealist, and meant by this a man who believed in unseen goals and standards. He also considered himself a realist, which meant to him a practical man who took account of difficulties. To Santayana a man who concerned himself every day with such things as industrial or medical invention or the spread of democratic political institutions could not be much interested in an ideal order. To the average American, if we can judge him from what he read and heard, these things were themselves the principal supports for belief in ideal norms. The main guarantee of universal morality was neither in the mind of God nor in argument nor in tradition, but in the unfolding American future.

Within the large, vague limits of practical idealism it was possible to be mostly practical or mostly idealistic as long as one maintained some touch with both qualities. Thomas A. Edison was certainly a major prophet of material progress, though his pronouncements were not yet as crass as they became in the twenties. At the beginning of 1912 Edison was asked by the Hearst press to name the major events of the past year. Most of his list was taken up by such concrete improvements as the discovery of the salvarsan cure or cur-

[2] Josiah Royce: *Race Questions, Provincialism, and Other American Problems* (New York, 1908), p. 130.

rent developments in "aerial navigation." At the head of his list, however, he put an event in the field of politics, with a future and rather an abstract significance, the revolution in China.[3]

Here he was in close agreement with most of the current press. No event of the period was subject to more incessant moral interpretation. In the hierarchy of nations, clearly headed by the United States, with England close behind and Protestant, progressive Germany probably next, China had a peculiar and special place. Poverty, autocracy, and heathenism put her toward the bottom, but many Americans had long cherished hopes for her redemption and been fascinated by some distant vision of inscrutable Oriental wisdom. Now, the establishment of a federal Chinese republic opened vast visions of hope: expanded American trade, increased influence for missionaries and Chinese graduates of American colleges, even the regeneration of all Asia. That continent might even, the most excited commentators ventured, leap ahead of Europe—that is, become more quickly more like America. Only a minority argued that long and slow evolution was imperative before good institutions could be accommodated to a bad tradition.

Other observers of the twentieth-century scene drew their greatest comfort from what seemed, despite some warnings to the contrary, the increasing prospect for world peace. In a symposium in the December 1911 *World's Work*, only a few of the leading citizens who had been asked for their opinion thought that man's nature made war ultimately ineradicable.[4] Most thought that war in the future would take place only in backward countries (it was going on at the moment in Tripoli). For the great civilized powers it was no longer economically practical, and at the same time advancing moral education was rendering it impossible.

Civil disturbance was rife in 1911 and 1912 in many countries. In Portugal a king had been expelled; in England great strikes were in progress; Budapest, Vienna, and many French cities were seeing socialist riots. These incidents, however painful, were like the Chi-

[3] *San Francisco Examiner*, January 3, 1912, p. 1.
[4] *World's Work*, XXIII (1911–12), 157–64.

nese revolution, milestones of progress. In the United States social and political change was occurring in a more peaceful manner. Citizens might differ about particular laws or movements, but it was very hard not to see the Progressive Era as a whole as another proof of moral evolution. To the novelist Winston Churchill, writing in the January *Atlantic*, the wave of reform apparently reaching a climax in 1912 was itself a proof that America had always been idealist. "Truths," he said, "are eternal,—the expression of them may change from age to age." The past would be explained by the future:

> We are beginning to understand, at the dawning of the twentieth century, that there is still a higher, more Christian conception of government to come, and that our Declaration was but a step toward it.[5]

The "smiling realism" which Churchill's own novels embodied and which Howells had brought to critical triumph was the exact literary version of practical idealism. This was what gave it, and Howells, their special place. Like the Social Gospel movement in religion, a movement in which Howells himself had taken much interest, cheerful realism had had to fight its way. In the strife-torn, graft-ridden years of the late nineteenth century, industrial society had understandably seemed to literary men an enemy, not a subject. Edmund Clarence Stedman, one of Howells's predecessors as semiofficial dean of American letters, had said that science itself was forever an enemy of poetry. The function of literature was to lift us above the sordid details of modern life.

Howells, fighting the battle of realism steadily and bravely, had gradually won. Attacks on his doctrine had become fewer, and some of the old novelist's former opponents attended his 1912 birthday party. It had become clear to all, especially since the brief spectacular vogue of the brutal naturalism of Crane and Norris, that Howells's realism was not like Zola's. It was really a typically

[5] Winston Churchill: "Modern Government and Christianity," *Atlantic Monthly*, CXII (1912), 19.

American mixture of things and spirit, of practical accuracy and, in a loose sense, idealism. "In the whole range of fiction," said a typical Howells dictum,

> we know of no *true* picture of life—that is, of human nature,—which is not also a masterpiece of literature, full of divine and natural beauty. It may have no touch or tint of this special civilization or of that; it had *better* have this local color well ascertained; but the truth is deeper and finer than aspects, and if the book is true to what men and women know of one another's souls it will be true enough, and it will be great and beautiful.[6]

Once Howells had managed to find truth and beauty in Crane or Maupassant but now, an old and unwell man, he found them in less difficult form in the political novels of Brand Whitlock or Winston Churchill. In 1914 he chose Kathleen Norris for special praise in a hopeful article on current fiction in the *North American Review*. She had brought into fiction a new subject—the poor and rich of San Francisco. This was a subject as strange to "us (shall I say?) cultivated Americans" as the subjects of the great Russians.

> . . . She is of such high courage that she makes you feel this beauty in an Irish undertaker's family, the like of which has not happened since Dickens dared it. Her art is always art for truth's sake and goodness's sake, and mostly for hope's sake.[7]

The greatest spokesman of practical idealism in America in 1912, overwhelmingly the most interesting figure to people and press, was neither a Social Gospel minister nor a Howellsian writer, but a man who had many friends in both these camps, Theodore Roosevelt. Some of his friends were worried about the ethics of a few of his recent acts, and deplored the tone of his quarrel with Taft. Yet Roosevelt was far more than a political figure; his freely expressed

[6] Howells: *Criticism and Fiction* (New York, 1891), p. 101.

[7] Howells: "A Number of Interesting Novels," *North American Review*, CC (1914), 912.

views on art and science and religion were still authoritative for many, and they were invariably moral. In 1911, just before his political plunge, he delivered in Berkeley, California, under the auspices of the Pacific School of Religion, a series of lectures on "Realizable Ideals." While it was our duty, our most important duty, to maintain high standards of morality and conduct, Roosevelt robustly insisted that we should keep our ideals within range of realization. We should not, for instance, scorn material wealth, but use it for ideal ends. At the end of his last lecture the ex-President, moved by the approval of his large audience, struck a note of sincere humility:

> Of course, what I have to say is simple because the great facts of life are simple: and I am speaking to you, my fellow citizens, my fellow Americans, whom I trust and in whom I believe, about the elemental needs that are common to all of us, and vital to all of us.
>
> A cultivated and intellectual paper once complained that my speeches lacked subtlety. So they do! I think that the command or entreaty to clean living and decent politics should no more be subtle than a command in battle should be subtle.[8]

Far more than most periods of American history, more than any since the Civil War, the early twentieth century was a time of sureness and unity, at least on the surface of American life. Even the past had begun to change for the better. People looking back on the nineteenth century tended to forget the labor wars and agrarian rebellions. Radicalism, like religious doubt, had been converted into progress. Looking back, the *Outlook* in 1912 said of the nineteenth century that "our electric lights do not dim its glorious sunburst of genius, and most of our legislation and organization for social justice are experiments in pursuit of its ideals." [9]

When we consider the evidence before them, we can hardly

[8] Roosevelt: *Realizable Ideals* (San Francisco, 1912), p. 125.
[9] *Outlook,* March 2, 1912, p. 490.

blame the dignitaries assembled at the Howells dinner for their optimism. Religion, history, and current politics all seemed to bear out both the eternal verities and their relevance to the problems of today. In the nineteenth century, some Americans and many Europeans had waged a desperate struggle to sustain these verities by philosophical argument. Now it seemed safer to rely on common facts. Experience, not finespun theory, was the best proof that the universe was moral. Yet experience, as the older Americans of 1912 had learned and forgotten, has a way of catching up with optimists.

III

A Nobler Future

The second article of the dominant American faith was a belief in progress, and the most crucial task for American thinkers was to reconcile a belief in eternal moral truth with the belief in the desirability of change. In the long run this was to prove, as many Victorians had suspected, the weak point in the nineteenth-century faith. In 1912, though, the link between moralism and progress seemed not only firm but inevitable. Good was eternal, but yet developing. The progress of the world was the chief proof of its underlying goodness; the eternal moral truths pointed out a direction for social change.

Progress could have two meanings. In the broadest sense, the belief that the world was getting better, it was accepted in 1912 by the overwhelming majority. Americans who considered themselves political conservatives often believed in the nineteenth-century version of progress. Herbert Spencer and his many American disciples, mixing together evolution and classical economics, had demonstrated that universal improvement was inevitable. Since this was so, interference would be absurd and wicked: labor unions and settlement work and social legislation would simply jam the works. William Graham Sumner, who had taught this tough and simple doctrine at Yale for a generation, had died only two years earlier, denouncing to the end the drift toward sentimental humanitarianism. In 1916 Spencer's *Man Against the State* was republished with an introduction by four distinguished American conservatives: Senators Elihu Root and Henry Cabot Lodge, ex-President Taft, and Nicholas Murray Butler, president of Columbia University.

But this kind of belief in progress was losing its hold; most people who used the word in 1912 meant something other than the inevitable drift upward. They meant an evolution in which men took a hand, a conscious effort to reach a better world which could be glimpsed, or at least imagined, in the future. Progressives in this sense, the progressives who gave the era its name, agreed with their opponents that progress was natural—even almost inevitable—but they wanted to speed it up. Most of the political differences among Americans in this age of political conflict reflected no difference in ideology more basic than this.

In politics the early twentieth century was a period of consensus, also of combat, and this apparent paradox has puzzled many historians. The Progressive Era was full of prophetic denunciations and last stands for righteousness. Boodlers were driven from city halls, railroad rings from state capitals, powerful conservative senators were toppled like mighty oaks. Concrete products of reform were visible to many in the shape of better parks, playgrounds, and prisons. Important institutions, including even the Federal Constitution, were altered. All this political change seemed to many people in the period to reflect still more important social change; progressives constantly argued that the industrial way of life was making our institutions obsolete. One might expect this much change to produce strain and tension. Yet few historians, looking back from the perspective of the mid-twentieth century, find the Progressive Era a period of serious maladjustment. Most find it, instead, a period of general agreement and confidence.

What seems a paradox is partly a failure of imagination: in some ways it is easier to understand the remote past than the deceptive world of 1912, so familiar and yet so different from our own. Reading the denunciations and calls to battle, we are likely to overestimate the depth of the period's controversies. Then we are likely to make the opposite error: to take to task the proponents of the New Freedom or the New Nationalism because they proposed no really fundamental solution to the problems of modern society. Few leaders of the Progressive Era believed that modern society needed a major overhaul. It is easy to misread the statements made by leading Progressives, because we take for granted a degree of doubt or disagreement which they did not imagine. When Wilson or Roosevelt talked, as both did, about this great experiment in democracy, they did not mean that the country was a risky venture which might or might not succeed. They meant that it was appropriate, under new conditions, to use exciting new methods in moving toward the goals we had always seen clearly ahead. The distinction between changing methods and stable goals was obvious; it did not need to be explained.

In most of the dominant varieties of progressivism there was, as Richard Hofstadter and others have seen, some element of actual conservatism or even, in the sense of return to the past, reaction. The Social Gospel, one of the most important sources of progressivism, called people to make a new application of the Mosaic code or the familiar New Testament ethic. Henry George's proposal for a single tax, perhaps the most effective piece of American social analysis, offered a way to correct a major piece of injustice which had occurred in the past, the private appropriation of the fruits of social progress. Once the grip of the landlord was broken, the original, progressive movement of society could be resumed. In nearly every American reform theory of the late nineteenth century, when the dominant progressives had grown up, some such purpose of restoration was stated. We must get rid of the recent despoilers and go back to the ideals of the founders. We must drive the money-changers out of the temple; the temple itself is perfectly sound.

Most progressives found evil as easy to define as good. It was incarnate in extreme inequality, political corruption, and ruthless power. And this cheerful period was not too cheerful: there was plenty of all these forms of darkness to provide challenge to the bringers of light.

A long succession of settlement workers and social investigators had found, in America, kinds of poverty that could not easily be defended as desirable incentives to effort. In 1904 Robert Hunter had found ten million Americans living below the level of subsistence. Most wage-earners lived so close to the poverty line that they could be pushed over it at any moment by illness or by industrial accidents, in which America led the world. The tubercular nine-year-old in the southern cotton mill, the garment worker burned to death in the factory fire were quite real and provided plenty of scope for indignation. Such things, to the American middle class, were horrifying in a way in which Chinese famines or, for that matter, the greater horrors of the European mid-twentieth century could never be. When the muckrakers brought them to light, cruelty and misery seemed a disgrace to America and the twentieth century. They were the product, not of any innate evil either in human nature or modern society, but of the corrupt power of a few. These few were the enemy. Powerful and corrupt individuals had perverted the country's institutions and dammed for their own benefit the rivers of progress.

The first job for reformers was victory, and the first weapon was the spotlight. Once the enemies were exposed, the people could deal with them. This second stage, of course, raised more difficult problems. Progressives in power were never able to decide how to deal with the most conspicuous enemy, corporate power. Some clung to the really deep conservatism of the trust-busters, the hope of destroying giant combinations as Jackson had destroyed the Second Bank. Others, trying to find some place in traditional democracy for regulated big business, found themselves grappling with disturbing and complex questions. As late as 1912, however, most people could at least agree on a minimum program: immoral actions on the part of big interests were at least as immoral as similar actions by individuals and must be punished or prevented. Above all, the trusts and the bankers must be prevented from wrapping their tentacles around the sacred institutions of government, prevented by an uprising of decent people.

The pattern was presented most literally by the progressive novel, one of the simplest literary genres that ever existed. The young lawyer, usually of sound family, went into politics to help the people. Suddenly, perhaps when he was offered a bribe, he realized that there was a system. Challenging the powerful and sinister bosses, he fought relentlessly until, in a final climactic convention scene with the crowds cheering and the heroine waiting just off stage with brimming eyes, the bosses went down to defeat. This story is easy to laugh at, and it never, of course, represented the whole of reality. But in the Progressive Era if the story was not drawn from life, life sometimes seemed to be drawn from it. The young La Follette defying the attempted bribers, the quiet college president from Princeton beating the professionals at their own game, a mayor here and a governor there looked a lot like the heroes of Brand Whitlock or Winston Churchill.

To people living in the mid-twentieth century, this picture, either in fiction or history, looks much too simple. Lincoln Steffens demonstrated, for his own and also for our generation, the futility of throwing the rascals out. Historians writing in and after the New Deal period, a time of deeper-going change, have emphasized the fragility of much early twentieth-century reform. It has become easy to patronize and diminish the simple moralistic fervor of the Progressive Era.

We are not concerned here with the concrete accomplishments of progressivism, which were not inconsiderable. What we are concerned with is the continuing experience of triumph, which helped men to overcome their doubts and sustain their central beliefs. Triumph, we should remember, seldom seemed easy. The enemy was powerful enough to provide a genuine challenge. The silk-hatted and paunchy villains of the progressive cartoons represented real and formidable people, who held power and did not want to let it go. Financiers were shocked and angry at what they considered ignorant attacks on valuable and necessary institutions; old-guard senators were quite sure that power naturally belonged to those who knew how to use it. Reformers had to face vilification and boycott and blackmail; the odds seemed against them, and yet, again and again, the underdog won. The effect was exhilarating and reassuring, and the process was closely related to the deep-seated moral agreement. Once it had been demonstrated that corruption existed, hardly anybody said either that it didn't matter or that nothing could be done. And every city cleaned up, every ring exposed was another proof of the unfolding morality of the modern world.

❧

Just as it is possible, and today rather easy, to underestimate the kind of progressivism that dominated the early twentieth century, it is possible to overestimate it. Academic historians sometimes tend to make the former error; liberal politicians are liable to make the latter. If the progressive leaders, constantly invoked in editorials and political oratory, were to come again, they would not prove satisfactory to their descendants. They offer few answers to our most pressing questions, and even in their own time, they often ignored the most difficult problems raised by their own victories.

A question continually raised by socialists and others was that of the limits of regulation. At what point would government action, undertaken to eliminate corrupt power and check brutal exploitation, begin seriously to sap the vitality of the competitive system, a system which most progressives were laboring to protect or restore? Partly because it was continually asked by the conservative press, many progressives regarded this as a false question. The paralysis of incentive did not seem a very serious menace when one was fighting hard for a small income tax; the menace of bureaucracy did not loom very large when one was laboring unsuccessfully for the end of child labor. Yet the long-range problems of state power and fundamental economic change were discussed so often by radicals and conservatives that they must have been lodged in the back of many people's minds. In a few years, revolution abroad and wartime regimentation at home were suddenly to make them much more acute.

A still more distressing question for American democrats today was raised less often: the question of the quality of leadership in democratic society. In 1912 few political critics found reason to suggest that democracy might fail to choose the best leaders; this suggestion was usually relegated to the Federalist past. The dangers, in modern society, of sudden waves of popular emotion did not seem real until 1917. Only a few critics of American literary culture were seriously concerned about any possible decline of popular taste; these few, as we will see, were found at the two extremes of literary opinion, among the most conservative and the most radical minorities. Democracy, in short, seemed a simpler matter than it had in the days of Madison or Tocqueville. Too few of its friends dealt honestly with its abiding problems.

One reason many progressives did not worry about the problem of leadership was because they constantly assumed that they themselves and people like them would continue, automatically, to lead. Class and racial exclusiveness are, to modern critics, the most obvious faults of the progressive leaders. When they said, as they constantly did, that power must be taken away from the bosses and given back to the people, the word *people* did not mean everybody. It did not mean, for instance, the people who had given the power to the bosses in the first place or allowed them to take it. It meant the sound people, under the right leadership. *McClure's* in 1912 appealed for confidence in "the huge array of hard-working, sober, intelligent men who, actuated by the most laudable sort of ambition, desire to climb from the precarious position of employees to the more secure position of owners or part-owners of industry." [1] These were Wilson's "men on the make"; these were the people who would defeat the interests.

How big a group was this progressive constituency? Certainly many important groups were left out. Big business was clearly on the other side of the barrier. So, for many progressives, was organized labor, which seemed to have abandoned the effort to achieve ownership status. Labor, which after all had its own organizations, was often regarded by progressives as one of the special interests among which the good citizens must preserve a balance. Farmers were sometimes included in the progressive army, sometimes regarded benevolently as a chronic, slightly anachronistic, "problem."

[1] *McClure's*, XL (1912–13), 120.

The limits were by no means entirely economic. Obviously Negroes were not among those for whom opportunity must be preserved; their road was blocked not by corrupt interests but by a caste system. Most progressives brought themselves, not without some twinges of conscience, to acquiesce in this system and put the greatest American injustice out of their minds; it did not fit their pattern of thought. History, science, and social science helped them as we will see; there was no lack of demonstration that Negro equality was impossible. Only a small minority of progressives, many of them heirs of the abolitionist tradition, worried much about "the man farthest down."

Immigrants raised a slightly more difficult question. Progressives differed as to whether immigrants, particularly recent immigrants, could share in the restoration of democracy. Many of them were skeptical; the progressive program often included not only the overthrow of immigrant bosses but the restriction of immigration. Others took the more generous, but patronizing view, that immigrants could, with patience and understanding, be lifted up. One of the deepest assumptions in the progressive version of history was that in the universal march of progress, the Anglo-Saxons were way in front.

This assumption, frankly stated by many otherwise generous and democratic men, seemed at the time to rest on broader foundations than mere racial snobbery. It was closely linked to the progressive interpretation of the nineteenth century, the century of England and America. It was proved not only by American accomplishments, but by the long list of English Reform Bills and Factory Acts, even (though here many progressives were strangely ambivalent) by British industrial and imperial might. More often than we remember, Anglo-Saxon leadership in progress was accepted by non-Anglo-Saxons; many a discontented youth growing up in Poland or Hungary fervently admired John Stuart Mill or Macaulay, Jefferson or Henry George.

Underlying these unsolved and potentially divisive problems, problems of economic goals or political methods or racial limits, were still more dangerous questions regarding fundamental purposes and values. Most Americans in the Progressive Era believed that institutions and methods needed to be changed but that ultimate values and goals could be taken for granted. A few thought and said that ultimate values and goals were unnecessary, but in most cases this meant that they believed so deeply in a consensus on these matters that they could not imagine a serious challenge. Yet many thinkers in Europe and a few in America had, in the last two generations, been sinking their mines and tunnels through the superficial levels of American agreement down to deeper strata. Heartily swinging their progressive pickaxes, they had pierced through the Constitution and marriage and private property, penetrating finally the bedrock of moral consensus.

Only a minority had gone that deep: most progressives agreed with most other Americans that right and wrong were the most important categories, that all good citizens knew one from the other, and that when a choice between them was pointed out the people would act. Whatever challenged this set of assumptions was genuinely revolutionary. Suppose, for instance, that people were to ask whether corruption really mattered, or whether good government made men happier, or whether a future of ordered peace and prosperity really satisfied human needs. If such questions were to be asked seriously and often, the whole progressive movement might collapse.

Though most Americans did not know it, such questions had actually been raised. For some time a few moral radicals had been proclaiming basically heretical views. As we will see, a considerable minority of young people was beginning to find the new kind of question at least stimulating. Moralistic progressivism, like the whole nineteenth-century culture on which it rested, was a fundamentally unstable compound. It called for questioning ideas and institutions, yet it rested itself on values that must not be questioned. Inevitably, a few dissenters began to push through this limitation.

This radical rebellion within progressivism has led to a good deal of confusion in interpreting the period. A few articulate doubters, actually representing as yet comparatively small groups, have sometimes been taken to be representative of this whole confident age. In the long run the doubters were extremely important, but their ideas were not typical of progressivism; they were a departure from it. The most sweeping and thorough of the pragmatic or relativistic thinkers, men like Charles A. Beard or Thorstein Veblen, were halfway out of the majority progressive camp. Moral radicals like Lincoln Steffens, young innovators like Walter Lippmann were moving close to revolution against the main assumptions of the Progressive Era.

The progressives who demonstrably spoke to the majority, the writers of best-sellers, the editors of popular magazines, the men elected to national office did not question the wide and slightly vague consensus which held together moral certainty and progressive change. As long as this combination held together, isolated heretics could have little lasting effect. Slowly, from 1912 to 1917, and very rapidly thereafter, the consensus faded and the real dissenters began to be heard.

The Progressive Era may be defined as the time when people wanted to make a number of sharp changes because they were so confident in the basic rightness of things as they were. It may be defined as the time in which the leaders of the people believed in their own mission and also in democracy, and in which they were able to get the support, most of the time, of a majority of active citizens. It may be defined still better as the time when eternal morality and progress seemed to be joined together. The hinge which joined them was the central and most vulnerable point in the American credo of the early twentieth century.

IV

Custodians of Culture

The third article of the standard American credo, the belief in culture, was weaker than the other two. We can think of the three as a triptych, an altarpiece made of three pictures, framed in gold and hinged together. In the center, of course, is moralism, painted in the bold and sure colors used by Roosevelt or Lyman Abbott. On the left, joined to the center by a rivet that keeps coming apart, is progress. On the right, a little smaller and dimmer if one looks closely, is culture. In the revolution we are talking about, when the mob broke in it smashed the right-hand panel most thoroughly. The others did not look the same without it.

Culture, to most Americans in 1912, did not mean what it was beginning to mean to anthropologists, the sum of a particular area's customs and institutions. It was not so much a way of describing how people behaved as an idea of how they ought to behave and did not. More specifically, culture in America meant a particular part of the heritage from the European past, including polite manners, respect for traditional learning, appreciation of the arts, and above all an informed and devoted love of standard literature. Standard usually meant British: culture might imply a vague knowledge of the classical and Renaissance tradition, but for the most part it was something that had come via England. This was part of the trouble; Americans for a long time had wanted to construct their own tradition, yet the European and English past was the only past that was available.

Culture was not, most of its defenders insisted, the enemy of progress and democracy but rather their necessary complement. Millions seemed to agree that literary tradition, particularly, had some role for them. The consumers of culture with no vested interest in it, the eager listener to a Chautauqua lecture on Shakespeare, the promoter of the Browning club in the raw mining town, the subscriber to an encyclopedia who hoped his children would somehow acquire something he did not have were not, except in caricature, ridiculous figures.

It is easier to laugh at the professional custodians of culture, a group of men, mostly elderly, who were quite sure that they had the precious commodity and also that it was their special duty to dispense it. The dangers of being a custodian of culture were great. One could easily come to identify all that made life valuable with one's own stock of knowledge. One might confuse the preservation of culture with the preservation of one's own status. Yet not all the custodians of culture made these mistakes to the same degree. Many must be given at least the credit due sincerity and public spirit. Perhaps, looking back from long after their downfall, one can grant that their function, whether or not they performed it adequately, was potentially an important one. Perhaps we are less certain than were the young rebels of 1912 that we can get along without the past.

The custodians of culture were neither an aristocracy nor a plutocracy, though some money in one's background was necessary to membership. They were in fact a group without any exact analogue in other periods and countries. They belonged consciously to the middle class, and yet recognized nothing above them. They demanded few outward tokens of recognition, but were quite conscious of their own identity. Most of them sincerely accepted political democracy and believed in progress, and most, not all, thought America superior to Europe. Yet the importance of Europe, and particularly of England, was the basis of their conception of their own role.

America, the custodians of culture hoped, might reproduce all that was good in English civilization without its grossness and cruelty. It could learn from the English prophets of culture, particularly from certain great Victorians who were still, to educated Americans, part of the immediate background. Carlyle and Ruskin and Morris, Newman and Arnold and many others had themselves been concerned, to different degrees, about the problems of culture in democratic and industrial times. Some of them had addressed special words of warning to America. Their books, their doubts and fears, their religious questions and cultural answers were part of the basic equipment of the American custodian.

Each of the English questioners had both a conservative and an insurrectionary influence in America. Ruskin, for instance, was still opening the eyes of young Americans to the shortcomings of industrial capitalism; he powerfully affected Carl Sandburg in Galesburg, Vachel Lindsay in Springfield, Van Wyck Brooks at Harvard, George Cram Cook and Susan Glaspell in Davenport, Iowa. A version of the influence of Ruskin and Morris was spread by Elbert Hubbard and his imitators, with their crafts and aphorisms. The teachings of Morris, with other ingredients, produced such communities as Arden, Delaware, where in 1912 men and women worked in wrought iron and leather, danced dutifully on the village green, and listened to lectures on socialism, anarchism, and the culture of the future. From Victorian discontent, often profound but nearly always effortful, some young people moved on. They could move, from Ruskin for instance, in two directions, either into more radical socialism or toward the dangerous doctrine of art for its own sake.

The custodians of culture, of course, wanted to convert Philistines rather than to destroy them. For them the most usable of all English prophets was Matthew Arnold, who was neither a socialist nor an irresponsible aesthete but a democrat and a progressive, eager to point out American flaws because he thought America supremely important. American society, Arnold had said, was admirably healthy and prosperous and moral, but it suffered from the faults corresponding to these great virtues. Populated entirely by middle-class Philistines, America lacked the richness English society derived from the classes above and below this group, the barbarous but generous aristocracy and even the tough, brutal populace. To save America from Philistinism, the saving remnant must devote itself to the study and preaching of perfection. Vulgarity must be subjected to a cool and constant criticism; a heroic struggle must be waged for better newspapers and better schools.

Arnold's advice, irritating to some Americans, seemed to a few the sum of wisdom. The American Arnoldians sometimes failed to see that the program had suffered a serious loss in crossing the ocean. Some of the traditions which Arnold valued most were not alive in America; the saving graces were different ones. Sometimes, translated too literally, Arnold's program became in America a program to preserve those things which had never existed. This explains, in part, why some American followers of Arnold, despite their moral earnestness, relapsed eventually into a distinguished and congenial despair.

Many of the most vigorous promoters of culture drew their doctrines not from the English but from old American sources. Some of the custodians, as well as some of their most violent assailants, linked the defense of culture to Puritanism. This linking was not entirely incorrect. Since the days of John Winthrop, the Calvinist tradition had produced people who were conscious of a burden which they had not sought but could not lay down, a responsibility toward the majority quite independent of majority approval. The Puritans, of course, had not valued culture for its own sake, but they had taken it seriously. In the other major source of early American tradition, the political thought of the Enlightenment, there were many references to the special responsibility of the well educated. The Fathers had tried to write this into the Constitution. Both Jefferson and John Adams had believed it essential to develop a class of liberally educated natural aristocrats. None of these old ideas of the importance of culture had persisted unchanged into the twentieth century, but none had vanished quite without trace.

Facing the problems of transmitting culture to a country which wanted it and yet looked at it askance, some of the custodians found their job a hard one. Most of them faced the task manfully. Emerson had announced in stirring and unforgettable words that the American scholar must never seek sanctuary but must work to "cheer, to raise and to guide men," even though this might seem to bring a "state of virtual hostility" between him and society. In the long run, the majority of the custodians believed, progress and culture would lie down together like the lion and the lamb. Yet some had become weary waiting. The custodians of culture were divided into two unequal groups, the cheerful and the gloomy.

The smaller, less optimistic segment was likely to be made up of those closest to polite English or European skepticism. For those who had lost the Puritan's inner warrant for his duty, who found their strength not in the Word but in words, their home not in the City of God, but in London or Paris, America could be a discouraging pupil. It was too large, too noisy and dirty and disorderly, and in 1912 Europe still provided a superbly orderly alternative. A good-sized circle of well-to-do Americans actually lived abroad. This was not yet a matter for defensive manifestoes; in some circles living abroad a good deal of the time seemed only sensible. Yet there was a connection between the older travelers and the new crop of intellectual exiles that was beginning to appear, the important generation that lay between James and Hemingway.

Henry James is clearly the most obvious specimen of the older Europeanized American, but he is too complicated a figure to serve as an example of the more gloomy kind of custodian. For one thing, he was a creator and not a transmitter, and for another his position on the future of America was divided and individual. Emerging from the optimistic center of American nineteenth-century thought, James had spent much of his life in Europe, trying to define his agonized relation to his own country. On his return in 1906 on a curious voyage of adventure, a daring rediscovery of his native land, James found as before a puzzling combination of chaos and uniformity, above all a distressing lack of developed pattern, of clear paths for taste and conduct. Even the scenery of the Atlantic seaboard seemed to him dreary and wasteful; even the New England village, still unreached by the modern highway, with its white spire and green common yet intact served as an example of American formlessness. Yet James knew too much of Europe not to respect the United States. At times he was exhilarated by the gigantic, the fascinating experiment in getting along without tradition, and like the Victorian critics, he paid tribute to "the standard, ah! the very high standard of sensibility and propriety." [1] For twenty years, James had been out of touch with most of his old American audience, and yet he was not alienated *enough* to be among the major patrons of the coming revolt.

The best examples of the two types of American transmitters of nineteenth-century culture are two cousins, Charles Eliot Norton and Charles William Eliot. Norton, editor, Harvard professor, translator of Dante, was perhaps the most important late-nineteenth-century arbiter of elegant American taste. A full member of the top Victorian circle, in his youth he had been first convinced, then somewhat dismayed, by the utilitarians. John Stuart Mill had reassured him, by allowing beauty an important place among useful qualities, but Norton was too acute to find this altogether satisfactory. He had remained liberal in politics, moving from early antislavery to civil service and tariff reform. He had remained also, like his English friends, worried about the future of art.

Part of Norton's separation from the hearty, callous America of the late nineteenth century had come precisely from his mid-nineteenth-century commitments. Like other liberals of his vintage, he had been outraged by the Spanish-American War and its Philippine aftermath. Though he remained moral to the core, he was a courageous nineteenth-century agnostic and could not accept the too-easy compromises of popular liberal religion. As he put it, most of his countrymen seemed to him still to believe in their hearts in the Ptolemaic system, which put not only the world but man in the center of the universe. Representing a different past than Howells, he told Howells that he could not see a way toward righteousness and culture through equality.[2]

Yet nobody was more devoted, more outraged at European op-

[1] James: *The American Scene* (New York, 1907), p. 25.

[2] Norton: *Letters* (2 Vols., Boston, 1913), II, 326; Howells: "Charles Eliot Norton," *North American Review*, CXVIII (1910), 836–48.

pression, more willing to serve democracy if he could. Norton had died four years before 1912, but his memory was green. For half a century his house at Shady Hill had been a center of civilization; dozens of autobiographies attest his talent for manners, his gift for the exquisite gesture, the unobtrusive gift of the first edition to exactly the right person, the word of discriminating praise at the right time. Generations of Harvard students had learned something of Ruskin's love of Italian art, at a time when instruction in this field hardly existed. Norton brought them into touch with a world in which Dante was greater than Tennyson. Like others of the sadder group of custodians of culture, he preserved but also undermined conventional taste. The line from Norton to T. S. Eliot was, as we will see, unbroken.

Norton's cousin and academic chief, Charles W. Eliot, the eldest of elder statesmen, was like Norton, Howells, and many other leading custodians of early twentieth-century culture, a ghost of the eighteen-seventies. He was not, however, like his cousin a ghost of Ruskinian aestheticism but of its opposite, the majority Victorian faith in moralized science and benevolent, expanding industry. As many of his contemporaries had noticed, this university-builder resembled the best of the captains of industry in his views and achievements. Eliot had retired from the Harvard presidency in 1908 but was still, at seventy-eight, a major national figure and for a decade to come a prolific magazine writer on many subjects.

In 1904, as he often had, Eliot told the Harvard students that a gentleman, a natural leader, was by definition both a democrat and a "vigorous doer." [3] For leaders who were both of these, his nineteenth-century world of political democracy and unrestricted competition offered a clear welcome. As far as he could see, this world still existed. He was still denouncing the restrictive tendencies of labor unions, still preaching popular education in both science and literature. His five-foot shelf, designed to bring culture to the

[3] William Allan Neilson: *Charles W. Eliot, The Man and His Beliefs* (2 Vols., New York, 1926), II, 542.

average busy man, had drawn some caustic comment, but in 1912 it was being praised editorially by the *Saturday Evening Post.*

❧

Eliot had always been confident that American society had the strength and virtue necessary to absorb foreign stocks. This was one of the major issues that divided the two groups of custodians. Henry James, in this respect one of the doubters, had found a trip to Ellis Island a profound shock; he could not get over, let alone accept, the "claim of the alien, however immeasurably alien, to share in one's supreme relation."[4] Quite a few of the custodians had doubted whether the United States, still struggling to know itself, could survive the flood of Eastern and Southern Europeans. In the eighties Thomas Bailey Aldrich had lashed the barbarian hordes in verse and in the nineties the Immigration Restriction League had been founded with a charter membership of five Harvard men. Proponents of a literacy test for immigrants had rallied repeatedly around Henry Cabot Lodge, the "scholar in politics."

Yet the early twentieth century, in many ways the interlude of stability, had brought a decline in hostility to immigrants. The extremes of antiforeign demagogy, moreover, had never been approved by the custodians. Baiting Negroes and Chinese and even Catholics was associated with muckerism. Faint vestiges remained of the abolitionist concern for oppressed races, especially those which offered no real competition for status. Solid economic interests in manufacturing communities still favored a wide-open door.

In 1912, even among the gloomy minority of the custodians, hysteria was rare. Immigration was a part of a general decline: Italians, Slavs, and Jews were not much more menacing than Philistines. Among the cheerful custodians, some, like Eliot and Howells,

[4] James: *American Scene,* p. 4.

were confident, others took a middle position between hope and fear. Almost none questioned the hierarchy of peoples; the Anglo-Saxon's mission was to lead and help. Perhaps the task of helping the immigrants already here might be made a little easier by cutting down the flow. By hard work, most of the newcomers could probably be led toward the light. This patronizing tone must have been almost as hard to take as hostility; it is difficult for modern readers to realize that it was well-intentioned.

George E. Woodberry, the Columbia poet, has been used by some historians as an example of upper-class racism. He would have been surprised. In 1901 one finds him, with the utmost good will, writing to a Jewish friend who has just been elected a member of the board of governors of the Columbia Club. The friend must behave with restraint and tact, and above all avoid undue partisanship. Apparently the friend, doubtless appreciating the good intentions, remained a friend. In 1912 Woodberry gave a series of lectures which commented seriously on the current alarms about the swamping of the white race, and managed to face even this prospect with an attitude of *noblesse oblige*. It might be, he said, that the old English stock and even the white race had been elected by God to sacrifice itself, and in disappearing, to humanize mankind.[5]

Nobody was more consciously and proudly an heir of Puritan tradition than Barrett Wendell of Harvard. In 1913 he wrote in a letter that immigrants "however worthy" brought other than American traditions with them, and were not Americans until these had "faded into dim knowledge of whence a family came." Generally, he thought, this took a hundred years. Yet one of Wendell's intimate friends was the philosopher Horace Kallen, later the chief proponent of a diverse multinational culture in America. The two were able to discuss their deeply opposed racial theories with politeness and mutual benefit, a phenomenon which is not easy to imagine in the tenser America of the next decade. Wendell liked and admired Mary Antin, polite Boston's favorite immigrant,

[5] G. E. Woodberry: *Selected Letters* (Boston, 1933), pp. 26–9; and *The Torch: Eight Lectures on Race Power in Literature* (New York, 1912), p. 6.

whose autobiography, serialized in the *Atlantic Monthly* in 1912, discusses with appreciation her first admission to Beacon Street. To Wendell, the Antins, who lived in a section of the city once inhabited by Wendells, were a "miracle."[6] This attitude, with its almost intolerable generosity, was that of Wendell's kind in its last days of confidence.

For those who intended to fight and win the great battle for culture in democracy, the main battleground was clearly education. Ever since the time of Jackson or before, many Americans had attacked traditional humanistic education as snobbish, unless, and out of keeping with the modern age. Recently John Dewey and many other theorists were questioning on philosophic grounds the whole conception of transmitting intact any kind of inheritance from the past.

The attackers of various kinds were winning battles, but they had not yet won the war. Tradition had on its side not only inertia but determined advocates. Such a progressive thinker as William James, for instance, had seen the duty of the colleges in about the same terms as Arnold. In his much-reprinted address on "The Social Value of the College-Bred," delivered three years before his death in 1910, James had made it quite clear that he repudiated any narrow and deliberately exclusive definition of culture. Yet he was no moral or aesthetic equalitarian; the fundamental job of the college, absolutely vital for the survival of democracy itself, was to teach discrimination. The college graduate, James said, must be exposed to what is excellent until he learned to "smell" the difference between the first-rate and the mediocre.[7] If the colleges did not carry out this function, James told his audience, it would be taken over by some new teacher like the popular magazines, and

[6] M. A. De W. Howe: *Barrett Wendell and His Letters* (Boston, 1924), pp. 254, 282.
[7] William James: *Memories and Studies* (London, 1911), p. 315.

it is worth noting that he published this address not in the *Atlantic* but in the muckraking *McClure's*.

This goal, of teaching students to recognize the best by exposing them to it directly, was still fairly widely accepted, but the colleges did not agree as they once had on what was the best. The old, simple curriculum of the early nineteenth century, based on ancient languages and the accepted truths of moral philosophy, had everywhere disappeared. The requirement of Greek and even Latin was cracking. The next line of defense, still defended but not easily, was discipline in writing English; nobody was more conscious of fighting disintegration than the hard-pressed readers of themes. In the few great universities a concern for undergraduate teaching seemed to be giving ground to intense and sometimes quantitative scholarship—James was one of many who had pointed with dislike to the spreading tentacles of "the Ph.D. Octopus." The small Eastern colleges, in this heyday of Alma Mater, were fighting to protect all educational function from being lost in the all-important social and athletic competition. The state universities were a strange, vital mixture of classical discipline, literary uplift, social pioneering, and agriculture.

At least the colleges were not ignored; they were constantly attacked and defended in the popular press. They were accused on the one hand of snobbery and extreme traditionalism, on the other of commercialism, low standards, and a neglect of the humanities. It was the traditional Eastern institutions that attracted the most attention; a crisis like Wilson's fight for reform at Princeton was a national sensation. Through the colleges they still dominated and their partial influence in the rest, the custodians of culture maintained some of their strongest remaining positions. Yet some of the centers of tradition were also major centers of rebellion, a paradox we will have to look at closely.

In the schools, where the stakes were greatest, the attack was more vigorous but the defense less confused. High schools, as the educational insurgents continually pointed out, were still dominated by existing, even by fading, standards of college admission.

Soon this would become quite impossible; the schools were just on the eve of their greatest growth. In 1910 about half the high-school students were taking Latin. A quarter took German, the next most popular language. History and literature were still rapidly growing subjects; economics, art, and bookkeeping had not yet appeared in the curriculum.[8]

President Eliot, one of the most vigorous advocates of change in the curriculum, spoke not for the really drastic kind of innovation but, as always, for the standards of mid-nineteenth-century liberalism. Sound economic truths were clearly needed, he thought, in our turbulent times, and there was much to be said for household arts, the use of tools, and music. At the top of his list, however, came the sciences.[9]

Here Eliot differed from the more conservative custodians; he agreed with them however in another doctrine, the importance of teaching manners. American manners had long been a special sore point to conservative patriots, partly because of a series of British home thrusts. Some highly conservative figures, among them Brander Matthews and Agnes Repplier, argued that American manners were different, rather than inferior. Few doubted, however, that some sort of manners needed to be taught. As Eliot saw it, manners meant primarily good will and kindness, but there were certain skills in expressing these qualities that needed to be learned. Teaching manners was, he indicated, part of the struggle against "objectionable social groups," which included new immigrants and the smart set.[1]

The hardiness of tradition in much high-school education is suggested by John Franklin Brown's *The American High School,* a well-known conservative account published in 1909. Constant attention and respect for authority were fundamental; all subjects must be studied in terms of rules and principles. Literature, art, his-

[8] *Recent Social Trends* (2 Vols. New York, 1931), I, 331.

[9] Eliot: "Present Problems of Education," *Educational Review,* XLVII (1914), 243–4.

[1] Eliot: "Democracy and Manners," *Century,* LXXXIII (1911–12), 173–8.

tory, and science must all be taught with a view to inculcating the higher ideals of the race:

> In no case should either the course of study or the spirit of the work in the high school be such as to subordinate the culture ideal to any other.

And as for manners:

> The rule of the school is "Be a gentleman, a lady. . . ." [2]

Perhaps the most crucial subject for the schools, important to the defenders both of morality and culture, was the national history. Ever since William Bradford, New England historians had taught that America was established by providential intervention. In the mid-nineteenth century, following Spencer and Buckle, some Americans like John W. Draper and Andrew D. White had substituted evolution for God; history became the working-out of freedom according to natural law.

By 1912 the ideas and practice of the younger historians were changing fast. Many of them had been deeply affected by Professor Frederick Jackson Turner, who traced American ideals not to Plymouth Rock but to the frontier. Some students of Turner went on to the conclusion that men's thoughts are shaped by the social environment rather than by moral tradition, but Turner's message was not always interpreted this way. Turner himself was, after all, both a moralist and a synthesizer. A large number of young historians had ceased to think of themselves either as moral instructors or as transmitters of tradition. They were, instead, scientific specialists, looking for detailed answers to limited questions. A smaller group, radically progressive, were making history itself into a tool to attack all kinds of traditionalism.

Yet the view of American history as the transmission of Protestant ideals and Anglo-Saxon culture still had its militant defenders. In 1907 Albert Bushnell Hart gave to the final volume of *The American Nation*, the most ambitious survey yet attempted, the re-

[2] Brown: *The American High School* (New York, 1909), p. 300.

vealing title *National Ideals Historically Traced.* The text made clear whose ideals were meant: "The Puritans have furnished 'the little leaven that leavens the whole lump.' "[3]

Hart's whole book argued the question whether this leaven could survive the immigrant flood, the disappointing failure of the Negro to justify his liberators, and the mounting corruption of public life. On the whole, Hart was optimistic; despite these problems, there were reasons for hope, among them the survival of an ethical religion and a sturdy public opinion.

In 1913 E. D. Adams of Stanford published a specific defense of *The Power of Ideals in American History* against the growth of historic materialism. In 1912 the annual address of the president of the American Historical Association, though it quoted James Harvey Robinson's *The New History* and approved the use of the social sciences by historians, amounted to a powerful defense of traditional views. History, whatever else it was, had to be literature, and still more, moral inspiration.

> The greatest historian should also be a great moralist. It is no proof of impartiality to treat wickedness and goodness as on the same level. . . .[4]

Coming from Theodore Roosevelt, these words must have impressed the most skeptical of the assembled historians.

In the public schools, where most Americans received their indoctrination in the national tradition, history still taught the lessons of morality and culture. The state legislatures, given to prescribing large tasks for teachers, often in these years required them to teach at once, as a natural combination, history, patriotism, and morality. In their own discussions in this period of peace and progress, organizations of teachers tended to stress the problem of inculcating love of country without encouraging nationalist pride or a taste for

[3] Hart: *National Ideals,* p. 46.

[4] Roosevelt: "History as Literature," *American Historical Review,* XVIII (1912–13), 473–89.

war. Manuals telling how to teach history, already a large library, put the general purposes still more simply:

> My teacher of history should increase my capacity for real happiness, and sharpen my appreciation for all things beautiful and for all persons noble and honorable. He should help me to see that righteousness exalts a nation, and that sin not only is a reproach to any people, but has also been the downfall of great empires.[5]

When one gets to the actual product of all this high purpose, the elementary textbook, one finds rather less moralizing and more simple factual statement than one might expect. Nonetheless, the story itself had its lessons. First came the settlement of the colonies, for moral and political freedom, and then the struggle for liberty in 1776. The great leaders of the early Republic were succeeded by Jackson, who introduced a difficult problem, not usually pursued very far. His methods were crude and violent, yet he represented the plain people of the West, who on basic issues, if properly led, were always sound. The books moved on quickly to the great climax. Since nationwide adoptions were important to publishers, the Civil War was presented as a careful balance of right on both sides, and the Reconstruction as an unqualified disaster. In a couple of crowded chapters leading up to "our own time," the problems of bosses, a clearly inferior immigration, and union violence (disapproved, of course, by most workingmen) were given sober attention. Hope was restored by the election of a new and better type of leader, by rising living standards, but still more by the spread of culture.

> *Education.*—All our material advantages would be worth little without a moral and intelligent people to make a proper use of them. For this reason the United States has been among the foremost countries of the world in educating its citizens.[6]

[5] John W. Wayland: *How to Teach American History* (New York, 1914), p. 43.

[6] Wilbur F. Gordy: *A History of the United States for Schools* (New York, 1903), p. 441.

The outlook, if we all worked hard, was one of qualified and sober confidence. In a song which school children were beginning to sing, written in the panic year 1893, they expressed some of their elders' hopes and fears about the nation:

> America! America! God mend thine ev'ry flaw,
> Confirm thy soul in self-control,
> Thy liberty in law.

Yet children, and nearly everybody else, took for granted also a more familiar and wholehearted version of the national mission:

> Humanity with all its fears,
> With all its hopes of future years,
> Is hanging breathless on thy fate.

To make up for the depressing character of the later period, many school histories added a last chapter surveying the Republic's literary achievement which, while it might or might not be the equal of England's, was a sure source of pride. It was more than this. It represented the chief hope for linking together the three strands of the national credo, of saving a culture which was both moral and progressive. It is for this reason that the list of writers remembered by Howells in 1912 was, to the custodian of culture, the very center of the national heritage, and its revision one of the main tasks of cultural insurrection.

The two contrasting virtues most often assigned to American writers in the many school handbooks on American literature were "power" and "art," or sometimes "strength" and "refinement." The greatest writers had both. Most had more of one than the other, but all must have a little of each to be taken seriously. These two attributes corresponded closely to the twin traditions of morality and culture.

Franklin, for instance, was somewhat deficient in moral strength, but he wrote excellently in a simple manner. Emerson combined the two qualities better than anybody else. Whittier was a strong and thoroughly national poet, Hawthorne gifted but too dark, finespun, and mysterious. Longfellow and Lowell deserved much respect, Lowell in part as a public man, yet neither was quite strong enough to merit the highest praise. Poe, of course, had only refinement and no strength at all; his work lacked completely the quality Howells had required of literature, fidelity to the beauties of common life.

Melville, to the coming age almost a singlehanded savior of American letters, was not so much depreciated as ignored. William B. Cairns, who gave him more space than most, thought that an interest in "abstruse philosophy" had caused his style, after the first sea stories, to undergo "a complete and disastrous change" by the time of *Moby Dick*. On the other hand W. C. Lawton, a Greek Professor who had published in 1902 an *Introduction to American Literature*, had evidently stopped reading before this development:

> He holds his own beside Cooper and Marryat, and boy readers, at least, will need no introduction to him. Nor will their enjoyment ever be alloyed by a Puritanic moral, or mystical double meaning.[7]

With Whitman and Mark Twain, one entered a more difficult area. Most writers did not any longer assume, with Barrett Wendell, that American literature came almost entirely from New England. The Knickerbocker school and the Southern and Western local colorists helped at least to make American letters national. These two major writers were usually treated, though Whitman was a New Yorker, as expressions of the Western spirit. The problem raised was much the same as that raised by Jackson for the historians: the West was strong, but crude. Whitman and Twain were, like Jackson, on the whole winning their battles.

Mark Twain, once an exciting but somewhat vulgar entertainer, had been transformed by Howells and others into the Grand Old Man of American letters before his death in 1910. His humor, they

[7] William B. Cairns: A *History of American Literature* (New York, 1912), p. 369; Lawton: *Introduction to American Literature* (New York, 1902), p. 246.

explained, though sometimes coarse and Western, always had an uplifting purpose. His melancholy presented a more difficult problem: often it was simply ignored. The clearest evidence of Clemens's final black and tormented nihilism was not yet available. *The Mysterious Stranger* was not published until 1916; *What Is Man* existed only in a limited edition. Occasional outbursts of bitterness were explained by Howells, and also by Clemens's 1912 biographer Albert Bigelow Paine, as uncharacteristic but understandable reactions to a host of personal calamities. Western crudity, and even a melancholy streak, were after all to be found in Lincoln himself; surely both could be forgiven in the man Howells called the Lincoln of our literature. Lincoln and Clemens, both extraordinarily mysterious and complex personalities, had both been made over into expressions of the basic goodness and simplicity of Western America. Whitman of course fitted this interpretation far more easily; it was his own conception of himself.

Immediately before and after 1912, a new school of critics challenged the conventional balance between East and West, refinement and strength, by an all out commitment to the virtues of Whitman and Twain. This school was really less of a departure than it has often been considered. John Macy, writing in 1908, took Whitman quite at the poet's own valuation, and stoutly attacked those who were trying to present Mark Twain as a kindly humorist who never hurt anybody. Yet Macy, like his predecessors, blinked the question of Clemens's pessimism. Mark Twain's philosophy was, he admitted,

> desolating to timidity, but very brave for those who can square their shoulders and look things straight in the eye. It teaches that we have an interior Master whom our conduct must satisfy and whom nothing but good conduct will leave in peace. . . .[8]

In any case, most readers "quite properly care nothing" for Mark Twain's philosophy.

[8] John Macy: *The Spirit of American Literature* (3rd ed., New York, 1913), p. 274.

Like Macy, Fred Lewis Pattee, another partisan of the West and its strong virtues, found little to admire in Henry James, whom he took to be "feminine rather than masculine, exquisite rather than strong." [9] Macy, Pattee, John C. Underwood and others were not really breaking with dominant convention but exalting one standard attribute of America, progress, at the expense of another, culture. This was not the path of real innovation; the real innovators already at work in 1912 were proceeding in quite different directions.

The conservative critics of 1912 deeply damaged the literary tradition they were trying to preserve. Poe and Hawthorne were underrated, Melville ignored, Emerson, Whitman, and Mark Twain grossly simplified. The young writers, growing up with an appetite for stronger meat than Lowell or Howells, found even the greatest Americans hidden behind a thick veil of platitude. Before they could rediscover the profound tragic resources of the American past, they had to go through a stage of flatly repudiating American literature and the culture it embodied.

It was not conventional in 1912 to deal with living writers at any length in textbooks of literature. As most readers learned, there had been at the end of the century a brief, unfortunate outcropping in America of European decadence and, a little less deplorably, a short-lived tendency to imitate the sordid naturalism of the Zola school. Actually, of course, neither of these currents had stopped short, but it was true that both had gone underground. Stephen Crane and Frank Norris were ten years dead; Jack London was becoming exhausted by his own contradictory emotions. Theodore Dreiser was silent from the suppression of *Sister Carrie* in 1900 until 1911.

Most of the fiction published in the years immediately before 1912 belonged in several related categories of the extremely popular. The problem novel, often though not always raising mild questions of progressive politics, was still common though declining

[9] Fred L. Pattee: *A History of American Literature Since 1870* (New York, 1915), p. 195.

slightly in popularity, and the same was true of the historical romance. The novel of sheer uplift and honest sentiment was perhaps dominant in the market. In 1912, for instance, Churchill's *The Inside of the Cup*, a story of a young and cultivated minister and his social conscience, was being serialized by the still muckraking Hearst press. O. Henry had died in 1910 but he had left so many of his adroit, sentimental stories that new volumes appeared in 1911 and 1912. Two of the best-sellers of 1913 were Eleanor Porter's *Pollyanna* and Gene Stratton-Porter's *Laddie*, a story narrated by a little girl, dealing principally with her admired elder brother. A few of the reviewers found *Laddie* a little too sweet.

It is not surprising that the dominant critics were sure that both naturalism and decadence, the two chief dangers of recent literature, had been stopped and turned back at the water's edge. Some intelligent conservatives sensed another danger, the sentimental vulgarization of conventional values. A hopeful and surprisingly common prediction was that the next years would see the rise in America of a new type of realism, wider and deeper than any that had yet appeared here, free from exaggeration of the unpleasant, but willing to deal with life's deeper and sadder realities. Arnold Bennett in England seemed to be pointing the way, and so did Romain Rolland in France with his gigantic *Jean Cristophe*.[1]

A sounder realism was the hope of some of the more serious reviews; the more innocent *Independent* added a still less accurate guess about the coming trend. The next years, it thought, would see literature liberated from one of the most persistent and hampering conventions, the excessive concentration of romantic love, "an experience that in real life is always transient and sometimes insignificant." [2]

The dominant critics, who in 1912 hardly looked toward Chicago when they thought of poetry, were sure that verse was as safe as fiction. The two exquisite but gloomy Harvard poets of the turn

[1] An American translation of *Jean Cristophe* was being published by Henry Holt & Company, the successive volumes appearing from 1910 to 1913.

[2] Editorial, "Breaking the Romantic Tradition," *Independent*, February 29, 1912, p. 474–5.

of the century, George Cabot Lodge and Trumbull Stickney, had died young like the naturalists. The moderately Bohemian vogue of Richard Hovey and Bliss Carman's *Songs from Vagabondia* was declining. Always easily satisfied, the *Independent* took comfort in the inspiring and uplifting work of three of the period's countless conventional, triple-named poetesses, Anna Hempstead Branch, Josephine Preston Peabody, and Edith Matilda Thomas. These were apparently not enough for the more fastidious *Nation*, which thought that the country's appetite for poetry was fast declining. George Edward Woodberry, one of the less cheerful custodians of culture, summed up the state of the national letters for the *Encyclopaedia Britannica* in remarkably languid terms, ending with the flat statement that "the imaginative life is feeble, and when felt is crude; the poetic pulse is imperceptible." [3]

American literature in 1912 had immense importance as a part of the vehicle of national tradition, a register of the national spirit. For their actual reading and rereading, however, most of the older Americans turned to the "Classics," the accepted novels and poems of the English nineteenth century. The works of Tennyson and Thackeray and Dickens meant more to a large number of people, in all probability, than any literature means to a similar number today. Progressive and conservative politicians alike continually quoted the standard poets, and people knew which were standard. Nineteen-twelve was Thackeray's centenary; the following year was Dickens's. This provided a pleasant debate, less upsetting than the presidential contest, for writers in both popular and select magazines. Naturally the *Dial* preferred Thackeray's superior culture, while *Collier's* chiefly admired Dickens's sounder and warmer sympathies.

[3] *Independent*, "Three Poets," November 21, 1912, pp. 1209–10; *Nation*, "Interest in Poetry," February 15, 1912, p. 154; G. E. Woodberry: "American Literature," *Encyclopaedia Britannica*, Eleventh edition (London, 1911), I, 842.

With a certain insistence that raises doubts about their real confidence, most of the custodians of culture prophesied that America would prove able to deal with the immigrant flood, the vulgar plutocracy, the rising materialism of the middle class, the attacks on sound education, and the many incomprehensible vagaries of the youngest generation. Within democracy but under the leadership of its proper guardians, idealism would be strengthened and culture spread through the land. Naturally such a victory would demand the strenuous effort which was a central ingredient—perhaps the most surely surviving ingredient—of the Puritan heritage.

When we encounter this bland vision in the year of beginning cultural upheaval, when we remember that every article of the standard creed was being sharply attacked, when we remember that young men had long been reading Marx and Nietzsche, that Veblen and Shaw and Mencken had loosed their arrows, we have a sense of double vision. To explain the complacency of the still dominant custodians of culture, we must look at their power in strategic terms. Obviously, their ideology was buttressed in places by conscious class interest. Exclusiveness was not really part of their purpose, and when it became rigid and narrow, it helped prepare the way for their overthrow. For the time, though, it seemed to make them stronger within their own constituency; some kinds of innovation coming from some kinds of people could be condemned without a hearing. In 1912, the champions of moralism, progress, and culture still retained a hold on nearly all the strategic centers of cultural war, on the universities, the publishing houses, the weightier magazines, and most of the other centers of serious opinion. This led to something like a Maginot psychology; those centers were to prove less solid than they looked. To understand their strengths and weaknesses, we must look closely at a few of them, with their garrisons intact and their flags still flying.

V

Fortresses

Most of the country, when it used the words *culture* or *tradition,* was likely to use another faintly comical word, *Boston.* The area that included Beacon Street, Cambridge, and Concord was the historic center not only of morality and culture but even, to some extent, of progress. Howells, who had moved to New York in 1888, paid the conventional tribute in 1902:

> Boston, the capital of that New England nation which is fast losing itself in the American nation, is no longer of its old literary primacy, and yet most of our right thinking, our high thinking, still begins there, and qualifies the thinking of the country at large. The good causes, the generous causes, are first befriended there. . . .[1]

Though the New England conscience was probably no longer the principal source of reform, it was still active. One well-known Eastern political type combined a kind of political progressivism with impeccable conservatism of taste and manners. Ever since the seventies young men of firm social position had ventured into politics to fight the machines. Progressives like Charles Evans Hughes and Henry L. Stimson had little in common with La Follette or Bryan. On the other hand they remained on friendly terms with old friends like Henry Cabot Lodge or Elihu Root who never put a toe in the progressive water. Even Roosevelt's fastidious friend Owen Wister made a venture into city politics:

> Up and down the seventh ward of Philadelphia, I made speeches in stinking halls amid rank tobacco smoke to dirty

[1] Howells: *Literature and Life* (New York, 1902), pp. 282–3.

niggers and dingy whites. . . . It was extraordinarily good fun, once you got going.[2]

Respectable young Harvard graduates from New York or New England, venturing into progressivism in this spirit of adventure, were a product in part of the complacency and security of the nineteenth-century Eastern upper class. Yet Emersonian idealism sometimes produced much stranger fruit among New Englanders with deeper roots. Oswald Garrison Villard symbolized almost too neatly the heritage of the New England reformer, being descended on one side from the most militant abolitionist and on the other from the Northern Pacific. A pacifist, an aristocrat, and by temperament a foe of compromise, Villard eventually moved all the way from nineteenth-century uplift to twentieth-century radicalism. With a few other descendants of the abolitionists, he continued to be interested in Negro equality at a time when most progressives ignored this cause. It took a special kind of courage to help found the N.A.A.C.P., another to stick to pacifism in 1917, and still another, perhaps even more characteristic of New England, to walk down Fifth Avenue in feminist parades.

The extreme fringe of moral absolutism and inner tension, never missing from any period of New England reform, was represented by John Jay Chapman, who is chiefly remembered as the man who burned his own hand until it had to be amputated to punish himself for a wrong action. An extreme Christian anarchist rather than a progressive, Chapman had something in common with Thoreau. In 1911, when a wounded Negro accused of shooting a white man was tied to his hospital cot and burned alive in Coatesville, Pennsylvania, Chapman held a meeting of repentance and prayer in Coatesville, despite local threats. It did not matter that only three people attended. This kind of violently antipractical idealism was later to appeal to some of the younger generation who were repelled by the blandness and complacency of 1912 majority pro-

[2] Owen Wister: *Roosevelt, The Story of a Friendship* (New York, 1930), p. 267.

gressivism. Traces of it can be found, for instance, in Randolph Bourne or E. E. Cummings.

At an opposite extreme, Boston had produced a special variety of the unhappy, even the despairing custodian of culture. Ellery Sedgwick, arriving in 1908 to take charge of the *Atlantic*, was startled to find the prevailing dinner-party conversation, from the oysters to the champagne, filled with cultivated pessimism.[3] Only a few of the fashionable pessimists were worried, like Henry Adams, about the prospective end of the planet. A great many were concerned instead with the decline of manners and good taste. Wit, seldom associated with uplift, was the forte of the Back Bay supper clubs; the presiding ghost was not Emerson or even Lowell but Dr. Holmes. Instead of reform, one section of Boston society had embraced Anglo-Catholicism, Jacobitism, and the cult of Dante.

Neither aristocratic wits and aesthetes nor old-fashioned, idealistic radicals were what most people thought of in connection with Boston, but rather a combination of settled habits, solid literary interests, and sedate good works. A writer in *Collier's*, for instance, told his readers in 1912 that the Brahmins were not, like other upper classes, snobbish aristocrats. They were frugal, hard-working, and the mainstay of the nation's best family life.[4] This stereotype, which really referred to the upper middle class of Boston rather than to the fashionable and brilliant top layer, had a good deal of truth in it. And one thing remained true of Boston society more than of any other: from the wealthy and sometimes bizarre top through the solid and hard-working middle, Bostonians read books and took them seriously.

In the next decade, when its customs and ideas were attacked by outside critics and internal rebels, Boston was to become distinguished in contemporary literary history mostly for its bans. In 1912 its surviving magazines and book publishers were actually a shade more liberal than those of New York. The *Atlantic Monthly*,

[3] Sedgwick: *The Happy Profession* (Boston, 1946), pp. 167–8. Many other autobiographies bear this out.

[4] Peter Clark MacFarlane: "Alexander Mann," *Collier's*, September 21, 1919, p. 15.

Boston's most distinguished survivor of the Golden Age, had become less parochial and less distinctive than it had once been. In 1898 its owners, worried about a declining circulation, had called in the bustling, aggressive North Carolinian Walter Hines Page as editor. He had cut the *Atlantic's* long critical articles, which he called "sinkers," and revived the magazine's interest in political controversy. After two years of Page, who moved on to greater reorganizations, the *Atlantic* had settled back a little with Bliss Perry, and then with Ellery Sedgwick, who had bought the magazine outright in 1909. The magazine was again under New England control though Barrett Wendell, for one, continued to lament that it had lost touch with its proper Harvard constituency. In 1912 it published the criticism of Henry James and William C. Brownell and the stories of Edith Wharton. With these it mixed some best-selling romances and also a taste of real innovation which none of the standard, heavy New York magazines would have touched. It was in the *Atlantic* that Randolph Bourne, the voice of the newest generation, and H. G. Wells, the period's radical prophet, each published one of his most striking manifestoes.

Somewhat the same sort of policy was followed by the Boston publishing houses, Houghton Mifflin and Little, Brown. Houghton Mifflin, divorced from the *Atlantic* since 1909, continued to publish standard, many-volumed editions of the New England worthies. It too had been through its Page house-cleaning and joined the competition for best-selling romances and historical novels. Bliss Perry describes how he learned, at editorial conferences, that Kate Douglas Wiggin cut more ice than Sarah Orne Jewett, whatever the critics said.[5]

Boston publishing stood in few last ditches and led no forlorn hopes. Yet occasionally, in the next years, the Boston firms were to venture just a little further into innovation than their conservative New York counterparts. Few noticed this; the important early battles were fought in New York.

The one area in which New England retained its historic primacy

[5] Bliss Perry: *And Gladly Teach* (Boston, 1935), p. 182.

was higher education. This was partly because the social stamp of the eastern colleges was at the peak of importance. Much of the American leadership in all fields continued to emerge from this strange tribal initiation, consisting as far as we can tell of a complex and esoteric social hierarchy, a mystical loyalty enshrined in customs and songs (most of the college songs date from this period), and four years of energetic though innocent dissipation qualified by athletics. The rebels against this pattern, the college writers and protesters, were still few, except at Harvard.

This exception, observed at the time and obvious later, needs serious examination. As a contemporary survey showed, Harvard was leading in the production of eminent lawyers, educators, government officials, researchers, and "distinguished men of letters." [6] All this might be explained by the head start many of Harvard's wealthy young men could count on. But Harvard had another boast, more relevant to our purpose: it led in the production of rebels. As William James said at a Commencement Dinner in 1903: "Our undisciplinables are our proudest product." [7]

In part, Harvard's production of rebels was probably a result of causes deep in her earliest history. In part, it was explained by the revolution through which she had passed in the last generation. Earlier than any other old American institution, Harvard had been changed from a New England college into a great university, and yet she still retained some vestige of the earlier type. There were, in fact, at least five Harvards in the prewar years: a national center of strenuous educational reform, a world center of research, the parochial pleasure-ground of the clubmen (through which passed both Roosevelts), the teaching institution, and, already, the mecca of the disaffected young men who wanted to write.

A considerable minority of the faculty had been uneasy under Eliot's long regime of liberal nineteenth-century reform. His elective system had seemed to some disintegrating; his "New Definition of a Cultivated Man" with its utilitarian and pragmatic over-

[6] E. E. Slosson: *Great American Universities* (New York, 1910), p. 475 ff.
[7] William James: *Memories and Studies*, p. 215.

tones, had made others profoundly uneasy. Abbott Lawrence Lowell, inaugurated in 1908, seemed to promise changes which were at once conservative and reforming. His inaugural address seemed to attack by implication the social and academic laissez-faire of Eliot's Harvard and also the low standards of the American university in general. As much as in any one sentence of the period, the whole heritage and function of New England culture was implied in Lowell's flat statement that "one object of a university is to counteract rather than copy the defects of the civilization of the day." [8] Autocratic, yet for his place and time libertarian, Lowell had for a while a magic touch. He managed to raise both the level of instruction and the endowment; he lost neither freedom and diversity nor the support of his own still-influential class.

One explanation of Harvard's production of rebels lies in the fact that the real sources of insurrection lay not within Cambridge but in the whole Western World, and Harvard, more than some other colleges, was in touch with that world. The tolerance and diversity of the University's academic life, the surviving heritage of Eliot, exposed some students to strange and foreign ideas. As Santayana put it, Harvard would have been willing to have any point of view whatever represented on the faculty—even atheism, even perhaps Catholicism—provided it was represented with distinction and good manners. For those who were tough, Harvard provided a diverse social life, ranging from extremely snobbish clubs to intellectual coteries and the Harvard Socialist Society. Autobiographies suggest that Harvard students were more often unhappy than students at rival institutions, and some of the unhappiest were later the best-known.

In part, however, rebellion came from Harvard *because* Harvard was so much a center of American nineteenth-century culture. At Harvard the stresses and strains of that culture were intensified. Throughout the nation, the guardians of culture were divided be-

[8] Reprinted in Samuel Eliot Morison: *The Development of Harvard University Since the Inauguration of President Eliot, 1869–1929* (Cambridge, 1930), xxxvi.

tween Yea-sayers like President Eliot and Nay-sayers like Professor Norton, but nowhere outside Harvard was the division so nearly even. On a faculty whose members were all, if Van Wyck Brooks remembers correctly, to some extent men of letters, the weight of eloquence lay a little on the side of gloom. Certainly not the weight of numbers; many Harvard men of letters reflected very accurately the outlook of the cheerful majority among the custodians. The famous readings aloud by Charles T. Copeland were not in the least in the style of Norton's Dante evenings; "Copey" stressed the sturdier virtues of Defoe and Kipling. He was admired far more by John Reed, a talented reporter, than by Van Wyck Brooks, who wanted and found at Harvard a different kind of literary training. Bliss Perry, called from the *Atlantic Monthly* and Princeton in 1910, had to exert himself to keep his survey class below six hundred. An optimist by temperament, Perry insisted in his 1913 lectures, *The American Mind,* that:

> From the very beginning, the American people have been characterized by idealism. It was the inner light of Pilgrim and Quaker colonists; it gleams no less in the faces of the children of Russian Jew immigrants today.

Admitting that America lacked a clear code, whether of speech or behavior, Perry faced this fact in a way that puts him clearly on one side of a great critical divide.

> And nevertheless, one's instinctive Americanism replies, may it not be better, after all, to have gone without a code for a while, to have lacked that orderly and methodized and socialized European intelligence, and to have had the glorious sense of bringing things to pass in spite of it? [9]

Less optimistic about America than Perry, but less gloomy and less dull than his later reputation made him was Barrett Wendell, for the next decade the favorite symbol of snobbery and Puritanism. A vigorous teacher long denied promotion, Wendell had become

[9] Perry: *The American Mind* (Boston, 1912), pp. 69, 73.

a good deal of a conscious eccentric and pessimist in the Johnsonian tradition; he was Harvard's chief representative of the genus Grand Old Man. His Anglophile pronouncements and exaggerated English manners can be set aside as part of the equipment for this role, and so can his cantankerous depreciations of American literature.

If one can take for granted the occasional snobbery and consistent provincialism of Wendell's *Literary History*, one can find there insights into the religious, political, and even economic basis of New England culture that were rare in the early twentieth century and almost forgotten in the two decades after the war. Wendell understood by direct contact the heritage of Puritanism, Unitarianism, and Transcendentalism that modern scholars have labored to recapture. He knew, as those who scorned him after the war did not, that the oldest New England tradition was religious and intellectual intensity and not literary gentility. In New England, Wendell found also a special variety of the English tradition of ordered political liberty, admired by outsiders like Santayana and already rejected by many contemporary Americans.

Fully recognizing the decline of this culture and relating it to the loss of New England's economic leadership, Wendell spent much of his time in mourning. Naturally he disapproved of President Eliot's optimistic experiments with an elective system and naturally he blamed them on Eliot's Unitarian optimism, which he correctly traced to William Ellery Channing. If one remembers only his laments, however, it is worth rereading the eloquent final paragraph of his *Literary History* which foresees a future of world democracy, and hopes as the best American conservatives have always hoped that democracy will not hate and destroy excellence. What he looks back to here in the literature of the New England harvest time is not aristocracy, but a point at which "the warring ideals of democracy and excellence were once reconciled." [1] This paragraph places Wendell among the more optimistic custodians, and if he had always expressed himself as moderately and clearly,

[1] Wendell: *Literary History of America* (New York, 1901), p. 530.

he might possibly not have been caricatured in the twenties as an extreme Tory.

Irving Babbitt represented at Harvard the extreme of pessimism about modern and democratic culture. It is doubtful whether he belongs at all to the group we have called custodians—certainly he did not wish to defend the culture of Howells and Roosevelt, or even that of Longfellow and Lowell. Babbitt placed his trust only in "Greek" balance, order, and restraint, finding inadequate even the neoclassicism of the French seventeenth century, and dating the final decline of culture from the French Revolution. Politely but definitely Babbitt made it clear in his first book, *Literature and the American College*, published in 1908, that President Eliot as a scientist and humanitarian was part of this decline.

In his prewar writings Babbitt, who later grew angrier as he saw the advance of the chaos he predicted, still tried to avoid the position of an extreme reactionary. There was a place, he repeatedly conceded, for spontaneity and self-expression in art as well as for form. But he devoted far the greater part of his space to his enemies, and these summed up with considerable accuracy the leading tendencies of modern culture. The root of the trouble was naturalism, the impious view of man as a part of nature indistinguishable from the rest. This root heresy led first to arrogant materialist trust in science, the error of Bacon, and then by reaction to sentimental gush about the goodness of natural man, the error of Rousseau. Of the two, sentimentality was Babbitt's favorite target and included most of the politics of the Enlightenment and all of the poetry of the Romantics. In his own day, the dominant tendencies of European art seemed to him to be toward the complete collapse of standards, toward impressionism, subjectivism, and monstrous, overweening Titanism. If we look at the art of Europe in 1912 or America in the next decade through his spectacles we will find much to bear him out.

It is difficult, however, to understand Babbitt's prescription for arresting this drift. As his French admirer L. J. A. Mercier said of him, he had only the Inner Check to take the place of Divine Grace; evil was to be overcome not by good but by will power.

At times, in his quarrelsome use of epithets, his zestful belaboring of his contemporaries, his dwelling on the extremes of contemporary foolishness, he resembles nobody so much as his arch-opponent H. L. Mencken.

Pointing to Baudelaire, Rimbaud, and Verlaine as final, disastrous consequences of the Romantic revolt, Babbitt undoubtedly introduced them to many students who would never otherwise have encountered them. To young men brought up in the majority sentiments of 1912 he must have seemed at least as much iconoclast as preserver. His first book carries a note of gratitude to Charles Eliot Norton; the most impressive article in the book of tributes to him published in 1941 is by Thomas Stearns Eliot. His Harvard career thus spans the entire distance from the old to the new pessimism, skipping only the cheerful position of the great contemporary majority.

Babbitt's loyalties were to Europe or Greece, yet his strenuous and argumentative manner was American. Santayana on the other hand was genuinely detached, not only from Harvard and America but from all times and places. To him Charles Eliot Norton, whom he liked, and President Eliot, whom he distrusted, were essentially part of the same Anglo-Saxon and Protestant tradition; Santayana was sure that even in Norton a moral conscience, and not his famous "fastidious retrospective nostalgia," was paramount.[2] In 1912 Santayana left Harvard, after twenty-three years, without regret though not quite without affection. He claims in his autobiography to have preferred Yale, which he saw as a visitor and a friend of William Lyon Phelps. His approval of Yale, however, like his friendship for Phelps, was that of the connoisseur of national types; Yale was better than Harvard precisely because it was narrower, more enthusiastic, more robustly American. As Phelps pointed out, Santayana could hardly have lasted at any American college but Harvard be-

[2] Santayana: *The Middle Span* (New York, 1945), p. 166.

yond that point in 1891 when he defined his position, elegantly and without emotion, as that of an atheist and pessimist. Even President Eliot had his qualms. William James, typically, made loyal and strenuous efforts to keep Santayana at Harvard, though he regarded his younger colleague's philosophy as a mass of "rottenness." Above all else Santayana disliked Protestant uplift and cheerful liberal eclecticism. The European culture, the pagan harmony and aesthetic naturalism he believed in could hardly have been understood by many of the students. Yet he made it possible for a good many of them to glimpse the fact, always difficult for Americans, that some people really don't like democratic progress, that there is a conservatism compared to which the most reactionary American is a revolutionary. Thinned and distorted, his strictures on modern society are recognizable in the writings of several of his students in the twenties.

No doubt the great majority of Harvard students in the prewar years imbibed from Eliot and Lowell and most of the faculty the standard mixture of morality and gentlemanly taste; Franklin Roosevelt, in his young and conservative days, was doubtless a better representative than Conrad Aiken or T. S. Eliot. Yet a few went beyond the optimistic doctrines of official Harvard, beyond the crusty Yankee conservatism of Wendell, beyond the fashionable and amusing Boston cult of Anglo-Catholic monarchism, into a more serious dislike of contemporary civilization. Even these young pessimists, however, were living in a time and place full of the spirit of reform; they were impelled by their doubts not toward passive contemplation but toward action. If progress and politics were dismissed, literature at Harvard was still taken seriously. Thus the basis was laid, here in the very center of nineteenth-century tradition, for a literature at once strenuous and unhappy.

❧

It is surprising how much of the literary culture of the newer capital had been, like William Dean Howells, transplanted from the old. Yet transplanting made a difference; Boston writers and editors in New York were not the same. As Wendell pointed out, intellectual life had sometimes seemed to be Boston's principal activity. This might be a delusion even in Boston, but in the gigantic financial and commercial metropolis it was a delusion impossible to entertain. Yet the New York representatives of established nineteenth-century culture retained considerable importance. Obtuseness and power combined made some of them ideal opponents for the coming rebellion.

Columbia University had never attained in New York anything like the position of Harvard in Boston. Yet the nation's largest university, partly because of its situation in the great formless city, had considerable importance. At Columbia students could encounter several kinds of radicalism, from the pragmatic innovations of Dewey and Beard to the elegant, antimoralist aestheticism of Joel Spingarn and others.

Columbia, like all colleges of the time, had its custodians of tradition. These were led by President Butler, a constant oratorical defender of optimism and morality. Yet Professor Brander Matthews, Columbia's specimen of the literary Grand Old Man, saw a difference between a professor and a professor who lived in New York.

> At Columbia the professor is not uncommon who is both urban and urbane, who is not only a gentleman and a scholar, in the good old phrase, but also more or less a man of the world and even on occasion a man of affairs.[3]

Matthews himself, and some of his colleagues, went far to live up to this prescription. As an essayist, he was an exact exponent of practical idealism. His specialty however was the drama, which he reviewed with passionate interest and remarkably tolerant taste. Famous for his clothes, his beard, his wit, and his snobbery, he brought to the campus a special New York flavor combining, as

[3] Matthews: *These Many Years* (New York, 1917), pp. 411–12.

one could now do with caution, the gentleman's club and the most respectable Bohemia.

An example of a New England species that flourished at Harvard but did not transplant successfully to Columbia was George Edward Woodberry. With deep roots in Beverly, Massachusetts, trained and formed under Henry Adams and Charles Eliot Norton at Harvard, Woodberry was much admired by distinguished contemporaries for his poetry and critical essays. Both seem to a modern taste to reflect an Emersonian mysticism too removed from its philosophical foundation, fleeting and delicate and personal.

Woodberry had resigned in 1904 after an unexplained disagreement with the president. From Beverly, he continued to influence a circle of younger colleagues and admirers. To John Erskine, in 1911, he wrote a letter which expressed exactly the older, idealistic discontent, opposite in some of its specific proposals to the coming manifestoes of the Young Intellectuals, but similar in its basic complaints:

> I have come to think of America as a backward nation, in all those things that are in a region above the material and mechanical parts of life and civilizations. . . . The democracy in which I was bred was of the souls of men; but the fruit here seems to be of their bodies—comfort and mechanical convenience—admirable but not what we most believed in.[4]

This was the voice of transplanted Harvard rather than of Columbia, and Columbia in any case was not New York. The city's claims to the leadership of American culture were solidly based on book and magazine publishing. This great industry was, in 1912, still a fortress of nineteenth-century culture, crumbling and damaged, but a victim rather of economic weather than of hostile assault. The Golden Age was a little more recent here than in Boston; one might locate it in the eighties, when publishing had been safely in the hands of the great houses, founded from the teens to the sixties. Each of these institutions had had its circle of authors

[4] G. E. Woodberry: *Selected Letters* (New York, 1933), pp. 97–8.

linked to the presiding family by friendship and contract. Houses had competed vigorously, but with mutual respect and no major differences of literary credo.

Surprisingly, this tradition had managed to keep alive in the rapacious business world of the last few generations. The old idea of publishing was perhaps best represented in 1912 by William Crary Brownell, chief literary adviser to the great house of Scribner. Brownell's brief opinions on manuscripts were by no means market advice but carefully written little essays, comparing the aspiring authors kindly but firmly with the authors of the past, and often stating his conclusion in a damning epigram. A man of wit, of elegant appearance, greatly respected and slightly feared by his younger colleagues, he clearly loved both the House and his work.

Brownell had learned the function of criticism from Matthew Arnold, whose views on religion and on culture had been part of his mental habit since his youth.[5] The function of criticism, he maintained, was to help more and more people to distinguish the good and the beautiful from the false and ugly. Like Arnold, and like Babbitt, Wendell, and Perry among his contemporaries, Brownell greatly admired the French literary tradition, and wished some of its urbanity, discipline, and measure could be imported. This allegiance made his judgments of standard American literature less enthusiastic than those prevalent in 1912—he thought Emerson shared some of Poe's excess and unbalance, found Lowell well below the first importance. Like Arnold, he prided himself on his modernity and liberality. Yet undisciplined impressionism, or unmoral aestheticism, or what seemed to him deliberate crudity violated all his ideas of what literature was for. In the next few years he was to be confronted with literature he simply could not accept, and he was temporarily to lose some of his ripe good temper. It may be, however, that the relative intelligence and liberality of his judgment, communicated to Maxwell Perkins and others, helped to explain why Scribners was in the twenties to open its doors wide.

[5] W. C. Brownell: "Matthew Arnold," *Victorian Prose Masters* (New York, 1901), pp. 149–202.

These doors and others like them were not open in 1912. The taboos of the older publishers reflected primarily their opinions rather than their fears. In a nineteenth-century sense they were not illiberal. Some of them would fight rural prejudice on behalf of established foreign literature. Others, like Henry Holt, himself something of an iconoclast, welcomed serious discussion of socialism or of the conflict between science and religion. It was not the social message but the "sordid" or "sensational" qualities of Dreiser or Upton Sinclair that caused them trouble, but by 1912 publishers could take an occasional chance on the "sordid" kind of realism. On the other hand, books that could be classified as either decadent or flippant had little chance. Here publishers and public agreed: morality must be taken seriously.

For the publisher of serious conservative tastes it was not yet the unusual, shocking Jennie Gerhardt or Susan Lenox that raised the most acute kind of problem but rather the ubiquitous, cheerful, and golden Barbara Worth or Pollyanna. For the best-selling popular author these were bonanza years; the new high-school-educated public was growing fast and the moving picture had barely begun its competition. The new public did not differ from the old in most of its allegiances; it was entirely in favor of morality and even—by its own definition—culture, but not the culture of W. C. Brownell. Profit and the best conservative taste often pointed different ways; a house might accept a late James novel, but it had to make up for it with an innocent costume novel or a tearful story of family trials and triumphs.

Twentieth-century business conditions pressed hard against the leisurely, traditional ways of the older publishers. Technical costs were rising. The problem of national wholesale distribution was completely unsolved, after a half-century of experimentation with different methods. Advertising budgets had been raised slowly and reluctantly; it was hard to measure their effects. Nobody was sure how seriously to take the pontifical judgments of the leading critics; breezy newcomers like Walter Hines Page scoffed at them, and yet their verdicts were still studied in most firms. The new literary agents threatened to alter traditional relations with authors.

Despite these and other pressing problems, most of the old houses had managed to survive. Traditional firms like Putnam, Scribner, and Dodd, Mead, together with the slightly lesser and newer Holt, Dutton, Crowell, Century, and Stokes were all still under the management of the founders or their families. These familiar American firms, with equally solid and traditional American branches of British firms like Macmillan and Longmans, Green, still far outnumbered the innovators.[6] Yet a few major changes had sent a chill through the comfortable air.

At the turn of the century the oldest and greatest house of all, Harper and Brothers, had fallen a victim of its easygoing family ways. To William Dean Howells the news of this event "was as if I had read the government of the United States had failed." Like the government in some of its hours of need, Harper's had turned to J. P. Morgan. After several experiments, the new owners had turned to George Brinton McClellan Harvey. (Gossip said Morgan had "appointed" him; the remaining Harpers insisted he had been their choice.) In any case, the atmosphere had changed for the brisker; Howells had said, when he ventured to visit the historic Franklin Square headquarters: "In the space without, where the kind Harper brotherhood and cousinhood had abounded at low desks or high, I did not see one familiar face." [7] But the firm, much to Howells's own immediate benefit, had got back on its feet and the old novelist had long been a firm friend of the new president. By the time of his lavish Howells dinner, the most ambitious of a series of tributes to Harper authors, Colonel Harvey might well have been considered the typical publisher of the day—conservative but

[6] Since 1896 Macmillan had been incorporated as a separate American firm. Most of the major American branches of British houses dated from the nineties. The International Copyright Act of 1891 had made sales of British books profitable in America, but had made American manufacture a prerequisite of legal protection.

[7] Howells, quoted in J. H. Harper: *The House of Harper* (New York, 1912), p. 324. Ellery Sedgwick describes similar emotions at seeing Mr. William Appleton sitting at a desk on the employees' side of the rail at Appleton's. Sedgwick: *Happy Profession*, pp. 152–3.

not highbrow, respectable but not idealistic, fond of the great names as long as they continued to sell books, more interested in national politics than in the national literature.

Only a few new firms had recently been established; of these the most important was that of Frank N. Doubleday, who in swift combination first with the dashing magazine tycoon S. S. McClure and then with the dynamic Walter Hines Page represented all that was up to date in turn-of-the-century publishing. All that was up to date and nothing that was ahead of time: it was Doubleday that had accepted and then suppressed *Sister Carrie* in 1900, and it was the rejuvenated Harper's that felt able to take a chance on *Jennie Gerhardt* in 1911.

Still loving the traditional ways of the realm of letters, yet conscious of changing business needs, the publishing houses were understandably cautious. The last thing that seemed to hold out any inducements, either of money or prestige, was assault on traditional definitions of culture. Yet a few small mavericks were already raising a new question in the worried minds of the large publishers: suppose some of the current vagaries turned out to be what the future public wanted?

❦

The magazine world changed faster than book publication, and in 1912 was a diverse and superb register of competing tendencies. Until about 1900, the scene had been dominated by the grand old magazines of the nineteenth century, magazines like the *Century*, *Harper's*, and *Scribner's*, the literary monthlies of the great publishing houses; or the *Nation* and *Harper's Weekly*, major organs of respectable reform; or the *North American Review*, since 1815 a competitor of the great British quarterlies. In the old days, the great monthlies had as a matter of course serialized the best authors of the day (*Harper's*, for instance, had published novels of Clemens, Howells, and Henry James). In this happy period of lower costs, these magazines had been illustrated lavishly with technically excellent engravings of Scottish scenery and Italian paintings and Civil War battles, pictures which, according to the later nostalgic memory of a member of the *Century* staff, "gave one a certain dignity merely by being the subscriber of the magazine that contained them." [8] Great reforming editors like E. L. Godkin of the *Nation* or G. L. Curtis of *Harper's* assailed corruption, vulgarity, and inflation wherever these evils dared raise their heads, confident that their courage would be applauded by the right kind of readers.

The old magazines had just managed to weather one revolution, and were about to confront another. The muckraking vogue was just beginning to die down. In the century's first decade, the heyday of muckraking, the movement's objectives had been a strange mixture of money-making, moral renovation, and democratization. Probably the motives of S. S. McClure, the principal entrepreneur of muckraking, were not very different from those of other technical innovators like Henry Ford. The motives of the muckraking writers were more complicated: most of them wanted to fight entrenched greed and many to write well in a new way.

A few muckrakers were socialists, and a few more were impatient with conventional culture, continually attacking the older colleges as well as the trusts. One, Lincoln Steffens, had broken sharply with the prevalent moral assumptions. Most of the muckrakers, however, were devoted to standard morality and respectful even to culture. *Collier's*, for instance, was staffed by such men as Norman Hapgood, an alumnus of Harvard and of Godkin's *Evening Post;* and Mark Sullivan, of Harvard and the *Boston Transcript*. Part of the magazine's furious attack against Uncle Joe Cannon was directed against his low, swearing, tobacco-chewing manners. When *Town Topics*, a mere scandal sheet, printed some false innuendoes about Alice Roosevelt in 1904, Robert J. Collier himself said in an editorial that the *Town Topics* editor was a man

[8] L. Frank Tooker: *The Joys and Tribulations of an Editor* (New York, 1923), p. 322.

no decent person would meet, the equivalent of a horse thief or forger—and Collier won the ensuing libel suit.

Those who believed in the whole of the current credo made a distinction between various kinds of muckraking. Some of it was dangerous, some not. The *Nation* contrasted Thomas W. Lawson's frenzied articles on "Frenzied Finance" with Charles Evans Hughes's sober, patient investigations of insurance companies. The *Century,* in an editorial note about the centenary of that great muckraker Charles Dickens, reminded its readers of the perennial need for "Lying Awake Nights" over injustice if they wanted "to keep civilization from being dragged down by the submerged tenth." [9]

The most sweeping and the most successful revolution carried out by the muckrakers had been in the two realms of business and style rather than in the realm of articulate ideas. They had caught the moment when a new public would buy a ten-cent magazine, and captured circulations that ran into millions. This made it possible for them to send special reporters and artists anywhere, and to offer almost irresistible pay to the authors they wanted. To understand the impact of their style we should turn from the *Nation,* say, in 1906, which might have an article about "Proposed Legislation Concerning Adulteration" to *Collier's,* which would report the same facts with lurid illustrations and a caption like HOW THE TRUSTS ARE POISONING OUR CHILDREN.

The height of the muckraking boom was over in 1912, partly because nearly everything had been exposed that fitted the formula, and partly because of financial pressure on a few magazines. Yet a glance at the popular press shows that the muckraker spirit and the muckraker style—warmhearted, indignant, sensational—were still alive. In 1912 *La Follette's Magazine* assessed the current muckraking potential.[1] *McClure's* and some others had applied the soft pedal, but there remained as dependable exposers of evil, in this

[9] *Nation,* March 22, 1906, p. 234; *Century,* "The Need of More Lying Awake Nights," LXXXVIII (1911–12), 949–50.

[1] William S. Kittle: "Is Your Magazine Progressive?" *La Follette's Magazine,* July 27, 1912, pp. 7–8, 12.

order of merit, *La Follette's* itself, *Collier's, The American, The Twentieth Century Magazine, Everybody's,* the *Outlook,* the *Saturday Evening Post,* and the *World's Work.* This list, including magazines of Hearst, Lyman Abbott, George Horace Lorimer, and Walter Hines Page, sufficiently demonstrates the continuance of the vogue and its variety. And it could have been extended to include Bryan's *Commoner,* the social-worker *Survey,* the single-taxer *Public,* and some of the socialist press. Even relatively conservative popular magazines muckraked in special fields; the *Outlook* constantly attacked political graft; the *Ladies' Home Journal,* which had led the fight against patent medicines, also crusaded in defense of herons against the wearers of aigrettes and showed up the evil of the common drinking cup.

The muckraking magazines and, more durably, the muckraking style had clearly captured the huge new public. Yet the old public was still sizable and important, and some of the older magazines still thoroughly alive. The least altered in 1912 were the monthly *Century* and the weekly *Nation.* The editor of the *Century,* Robert Underwood Johnson, sang a moving swan song in an article in the *Independent* in that year about the "Responsibilities of the Magazine." [2] Johnson had come to the *Century* at its start in 1870; he had been with it through the great days when Gilder's salon was the center of New York taste; he had played a part in such coups as securing for the *Century* Civil War memoirs by nearly all surviving generals: he had helped to lead crusades like those for international copyright and removal of customs duties on works of art. Since 1909, when he had taken over as editor, the magazine had faced constant crisis, caused, he was sure, by the new cheap competition and the vagaries of the new public. Johnson had tried various expedients, old and new—humorous sketches telling how to get into New York Clubs, cartoons about the Irish, violent attacks on slang and modern art, incessant Lincolniana, and commissioned articles by such solid figures as President Taft, Charles W. Eliot,

[2] Johnson, "The Responsibilities of the Magazine," *Independent,* December 19, 1912, pp. 1487–90.

and Washington Gladden. Yet he knew that crisis and drastic change were around the corner.

Drawing on his memories and justifying his practice, Johnson in 1912 summarized the duties of the magazine under three heads, accuracy, impartiality, and tone. Accuracy meant more than scrupulousness in checking facts, more even than unremitting warfare against sloppy and slangy language. It included realism in fiction, to a point:

> No one paints life as it is—thank heaven!—for we could not bear it. Somewhere he must compromise with the dulnesses, the secrecies, the indecencies, the horrors of life.

Impartiality was fairly simple; magazines must have no ax to grind except the public good, and must particularly eschew the concealed advertisement. Tone was the subtlest and most important responsibility; it included style, taste, and moral influence. The editor must preserve a standard based on the highest conduct and the highest literature of the past; he must fight the literary anarchists who consider good taste effeminate or constricting; he must above all refrain from praising the shady, the second-rate, and the meretricious. The ideal, like the magazine, was too negative and severe for survival, yet the *Century* refused as yet to surrender it and still claimed a hundred thousand loyal readers.

The *Nation*, the great weekly founded in 1865 by E. L. Godkin, was still alive partly through its link to the *Evening Post*, the only daily newspaper that could certainly be counted among the major guardians of traditional culture. The *Nation* still proclaimed itself "A Weekly Journal Devoted to Politics, Literature, Science, Drama, Music, Art, and Finance," and it very nearly lived up to this claim. Its breadth of coverage, and also its consistent intelligence had reached a peak in 1912 which astonishes the magazine reader of today. Events in Washington were commented on in detail from a consistent, uncompromising, moralist and Manchester Liberal point of view. A new book of philosophy, whatever its doctrine, was likely to get a six-column discussion by a philosopher, adequately technical and yet not impenetrable to the layman. Readers were assumed to know French, German, and Latin. Moreover, though the *Nation* ranged itself on the side of the moral and intellectual *status quo*, it shut its eyes to nothing. Freudian psychology, the dawning Einsteinian physics, new theories of sexual relations, naturalist literature in Europe and America all received careful and serious discussion. With its usual stark honesty, the *Nation* in 1912 claimed only 6,000 weekly readers; it had never wanted many, and it demanded the best.

Doubtless the great weekly's excellence was partly the result of tradition, but the man immediately responsible was Paul Elmer More, who had been associated with the *Evening Post* and *Nation* since 1903 and became editor-in-chief of the magazine in 1912. More was a curious figure to find in the magazine world, a spiritual aristocrat and troubled seeker after truth. Like his friend Professor Babbitt, More deplored the whole tendency of modern civilization, rejecting both naturalism and its obverse, sentimentality. More clearly even than Babbitt, More opposed the drift toward equalitarianism, insisting that natural aristocracy was essential to order and justice. The two men, always associated by their enemies, agreed in their central dualism, their separation of man and thing, and in their insistent praise of the inner check, the mysterious curb on man's natural propensities. But More differed greatly in temperament from the Cambridge critic; where Babbitt belabored, More reasoned; where Babbitt's taste was for teaching, More's recurrent need was for withdrawal and contemplation. Babbitt, at this period, insistently resisted supernaturalism; More throughout his life sought for the source of the inner check through Greek, Hindu, and Christian philosophy, ending in the recognition that moral certainty demanded a sanction beyond the realm of argument. Until 1914 More stamped the *Nation* with his own high standard of prose and thought (though not with his own opinions outside his own articles). After this he wrote for Henry Holt's crusty, short-lived, *Unpopular Review*, leaving the magazine world in 1918 for retirement and the more leisurely, thorough expression of his ideas in books. With Babbitt, he was to serve as a major whetstone for the knives of the coming generation and then enjoy at least one period of revival.

Stuart P. Sherman, a frequent contributor to More's *Nation,* was a minor critic soon to find himself caught in a major role, fighting off the onslaught of the younger—that is his own—generation. Born in Iowa and intellectually shaped by a classical course at Williams, Sherman as a Harvard graduate student had been an easy convert for Babbitt and a fervent, literal disciple. Since 1906 he had been a professor at Illinois and a constant reviewer for the *Nation* and the *Evening Post*. In comparison to his mentors, Babbitt and More, Sherman was less intelligent and more amiable, more democratic in intention and more snobbish in practice, more timid and sometimes more belligerent. At this period Sherman called himself a Puritan and his essays usually denounced, in a youthful, bookish style, whatever traces he could find in current literature of exoticism or decadence. He was beginning, in private letters, to test his latent liberalism by arguing with More, defending certain types of democracy or humanitarianism, putting in a good word for Jane Addams or even Rousseau.[3] His emotions, easily aroused, superficial, and a little contradictory, were soon to get him into serious trouble.

Less hidebound than the *Century* and less distinguished than the *Nation,* a handful of other magazines managed to maintain some of the standards of the earlier day. Colonel George Harvey had bought the *North American Review,* the grandfather of American magazines and a contemporary and equal of the great English and Scottish reviews, in 1899, and continued to edit it. Since Harvey had been head of *Harper's,* he had retained in office Henry Mills Alden, editor of *Harper's* magazine since 1869 and a conservative landmark. Yet *Harper's,* and still more the *North American,* showed the Harvey touch. Both magazines were less reformist and less learned than in their great days, though still serious in their interests and conservative in style. *Scribner's,* being younger,

[3] Jacob Zeitlin and Homer Woodbridge: *Life and Letters of Stuart P. Sherman* (2 Vols., New York, 1929), I, 221, 240, 241.

was somewhat livelier and more venturesome. All these magazines assumed the existence of a well-informed but unspecialized public; all mixed the same established political and literary bigwigs with the same respectable writers of popular fiction; all showed some consciousness, that is, both of tradition and circulation.

In terms of prestige, these formed the top layer; between this group and the muckraking magazines was a middle class of magazines, less exclusive and less conscious of tradition, but still intensely respectable. Two of these, the *Independent* and the *Outlook*, were weeklies that descended directly from the powerful religious newspapers of the nineteenth century. Both were now liberal in religion and reformist in politics (the *Outlook* of Abbott and Roosevelt more vigorously so); both stood for the family, clean politics, and pure literature; both supported culture vigorously and defined it loosely. The *World's Work*, a monthly founded at the turn of the century by Page, was as one would expect consciously brisk. It too believed in culture, but admired Kipling more than Howells and thought education needed to be made more practical. It prided itself on covering the South and West at least as fully as the Northeast. Verging on the most respectable kind of muckraking, it crusaded against such unquestioned evils as the hookworm. *Harper's Weekly*, once a major trumpet of moralistic reform, had been converted by Harvey into a conservative rival of these three, full of political fulminations and genteel literary claptrap, at once staid and sensational. Here the Harvey touch was not proving to be golden: the *Weekly* could not compete with the Sunday supplements. After the 1912 election Harvey sold it to the McClure syndicate. Differing from all these in function, but not in ideas, the *Bookman* was devoted to a chatty, catholic coverage of current literature. It praised most of the books it mentioned, and most of them raised no problems for readers of conservative tastes.

These two groups of magazines, ranging all the way from the austere *Century* to the bustling, Rooseveltian *Outlook*, formed a solid front in defense of American nineteenth-century culture. Nowhere in this varied range could a reader encounter either unorthodox moral doctrine or startling literary manners. The relatively conservative magazines claimed something close to a million subscribers.[4] Many of these were people of some weight, and many of them had never ceased deploring or started reading the McClures and the Hearsts. Soon they were to learn from their favorite journals that still more startling newcomers existed—absolutely insane and unbelievable magazines called *Poetry*, the *Masses*, or *The Little Review*.

❦

Manning all the defenses of tradition, ranging back and forth from campus to publishing house to magazine, were a few powerful critics and moralists who would, in the age of Luce, have been called pundits and who in 1912 still called themselves Men of Letters. The term connoted distinction, allegiance to traditional standards, and versatility; in 1908 Barrett Wendell had defined it with characteristic accuracy:

> It is the privilege of the man of letters that he may venture on occasion to discuss matters in which he makes no pretence to be expert.[5]

Heading the list of leading men of letters was of course Howells, still commenting authoritatively on current books in *Harper's* and the *North American Review*. In Boston, perhaps Bliss Perry was the most widely influential figure, with his threefold magazine, publishing, and university role. Wendell and Babbitt were restricted to a smaller public by their drastic opinions, yet both expressed themselves frequently in the *Nation* and *Atlantic* respectively as well as in their classrooms. In New York Brander Matthews as a professor, textbook author, drama critic, literary adviser to Scribner's and

[4] This figure is obtained by adding the figures given in N. W. Ayer and Sons's *American Newspaper Annual and Directory* for 1912. Ayer's statistics are of varying reliability. Estimating readers presents further difficulties; some families subscribed to several magazines, yet many magazines were passed around among a number of readers.

[5] Wendell: *The Privileged Classes* (New York, 1908), p. 3.

Longmans, Green was almost the perfect specimen of the man of letters. Woodberry, even after his retirement, remained an important critical authority for young writers and a much praised and published poet. More and Sherman of the *Nation* and Brownell of Scribner's complete the most exclusive list; these were the acknowledged champions of traditional and conservative taste.

On a somewhat different level, but still within the circle of Men of Letters, were three critics; Hamilton W. Mabie of the *Outlook*, Henry Van Dyke of Princeton, and William Lyon Phelps of Yale. These three, friends and associates, were qualified to defend culture before a larger public than the others. None was fastidious or precise, all had a genuine and uncritical love of literature, and all were incessantly optimistic. These three popular speakers and writers spoke the language of Roosevelt and not that of Norton or Babbitt; they dealt primarily in moral idealism and only secondarily in good taste.

Mabie in 1912 was actually what writers of a decade or two later believed Howells to have been: a dealer in the most saccharine morality and the most standard textbook opinions. His friend Van Dyke, whom Mabie considered one of the greatest American authors, was a popular minister turned popular lecturer (at Princeton) and a prolific author of comforting, semireligious poems and tales. Despite his saccharine writings, Van Dyke was a fighter by temperament, quite willing to do battle against social or literary innovation. He both earned and repaid the blows that later rained on him from pacifists and prize-winning literary iconoclasts.

William Lyon Phelps, on the other hand, was a man of sweetness as well as enthusiasm, a friend of Santayana, Henry James, and Joseph Conrad as well as, a little later, the supreme favorite of lecture audiences and Sunday supplements, a man, in short, almost impossible to dislike. Not yet arrived at his peak of popularity, he was already a prolific and admired writer in the better magazines. Phelps had studied with Wendell, but he had picked up none of the Harvard tendency to deplore the times. After a nervous crisis in 1891 (it is surprising how often such an episode figures in the lives of the period's distinguished optimists) Phelps had settled down to a long, happy, and valuable lifetime of teaching at Yale, where he had introduced in 1895, against the opposition of the defenders of classic tradition, the first college course anywhere in contemporary novelists. Phelps very likely conveyed a love of literature to more of his fellow citizens than any contemporary. He had a boundless store of enthusiasm to draw from, enthusiasm so determined that it could find uplift as well as beauty almost everywhere, so broad that it could praise Edith Wharton and Edna Ferber in alternate weeks in much the same terms.

The circle of custodians of culture defined itself best by function and prestige, but a promising effort was under way to give this circle official limits. Since 1904 America had had, like France, an Academy. Founded in conscious imitation of French precedent, this central donjon of the fortresses of culture had been formed by a complex process of election and co-optation out of the larger National Institute of Arts and Letters. Robert Underwood Johnson of the *Century*, the Academy's permanent secretary, described its purpose as a battle against utilitarianism, sensationalism, and his old bête noire, colloquial language. In the statements of more than one leading academician of this period one recognizes an objective something like that of an A.F. of L. trade union, the protection of traditional acquired skills against pretentious novices.

The members of both bodies, the fifty-man Academy and the larger Institute, were well chosen for this purpose. Of the leading Boston and New York men of letters discussed in this chapter all but Wendell, Babbitt, More, Sherman, and Phelps were Academicians in 1912, and these five were to be selected for the Academy before their deaths. University presidents like Lowell and Butler and Woodrow Wilson, literary statesmen like Roosevelt and Lodge, conservative novelists like Thomas Nelson Page and Owen Wister completed the short list. Of all the names, only Theodore Roosevelt's could in 1912 have been associated with active innovation, and he had been chosen before his last distressing vagaries.

In the papers read before the Academy's public meetings and

published in its proceedings, the artists, musicians, and architects were much more broad-minded than the writers. Academy speakers praised and explained such still controversial figures as Manet, Rodin, and Richard Strauss. (A year later they were to react in horror against Picasso and Cézanne.) But the men of letters, who greatly outnumbered the rest, seemed to be always on the defensive. Henry Van Dyke, presiding in Howells's temporary absence in December 1912 listed a series of purposes, all negative:

> Not to encourage the trampling of our noble English language with the hooves of buffaloes, not to confuse advertisement with criticism, not to acquiesce in the vulgarizing of the arts or to mistake hysteria for originality, not to admit that the only way to be American is to be provincial . . .[6]

Even these negative purposes, let alone the Academy's positive aims of encouraging and recognizing achievement, could have been important in America in 1912; vulgarity and provincialism were real and formidable opponents. But the task of conserving tradition demands a solid understanding both of the nature of tradition and the reasons for preserving it. This was hard to acquire in America in 1912. American nineteenth-century culture badly needed redefinition; the version current was incomplete. The more acute of the custodians knew this and were uneasy about it; it was left to the Mabies, Johnsons, and Van Dykes to man the really indefensible ramparts.

Like many lesser custodians of culture, the Academicians lacked flexibility and humility as well as a clear and consistent set of values. Like all academies, this one often seemed to turn into a mutual admiration society. Many years later Ellen Glasgow recalled her encounter with the Academy of this period:

> . . . The more I saw of these agreeable authors, the more I liked them. The trouble was that I thought of them as old gentlemen, and they thought of themselves as old masters.[7]

[6] Academy of Arts and Letters, *Proceedings*, Vol. I, 1910–13 (New York, 1913), p. 6.

[7] Ellen Glasgow: *The Woman Within* (New York, 1954), p. 141.

VI

Culture and the Continent

The cultural revolution, just ahead in 1912, has often been thought of as an uprising of the West, or even of the West and South, against the effete and worn-out East. This interpretation had already been foreshadowed by the more rugged, pro-Western, Whitman-loving school of critics. It had been foreshadowed also by the custodians of culture themselves, who talked a lot about protecting Eastern civilization against Western barbarism. During the coming literary upheaval, Western and later Southern writers were to state their purposes partly in geographical terms. The uprising against the East continues to be the theme of much literary history, as it is of much political history.

This geographical interpretation of culture is not even altogether false. There actually were new sources of vitality in the West and South waiting to be tapped. But they remained hidden until revolution was under way in the established centers of culture. This revolution spread from the metropolitan centers to the far more conservative provinces. To oversimplify history only a little, the West and South were liberated by, not from, the East.

Ever since the eighties, the banner of regional culture had been flung to the breezes repeatedly. In the heyday of local-color literature, exotic landscapes and quaint dialects had been almost the main requirements for publication in the best Eastern magazines. Local-color stories were still being ground out in 1912, but the formula had lost whatever vitality it had once had. The much-heralded provincial magazines and publishing houses had nearly all withered and died. The trouble had been partly one of basic intention: the believers in local culture had never been able to decide whether what they wanted was to be different from the East or just like it and a little better.

Once, of course, the frontier had clearly needed civilization even more than local independence, and obviously civilization had had to mean Eastern civilization. The Western presses turned out the Anglo-American classics first; Western audiences flocked to hear Emerson or Dickens. Provincial colleges and churches had been largely adapted from Eastern patterns.

In 1912 the most acute, direct need of nineteenth-century frontier America for culture of any kind at any price was over. The country was tame and united, and regions could concern themselves about local identity. Yet the magic of the word *Eastern*, applied to family or way of life, remained, and so did the jealousy of the East that went with it. In every new town of any pretension from Oklahoma to Washington the people who could be depended on most to back local cultural enterprises were those who were proud of the standard New England poets behind the glass-fronted bookcases, conscious of the weight of the *Century* or *Atlantic* on the mahogany table, and aware of the importance of minor formalities in social intercourse. These sanctities might be a little out of date in Boston or New York; if so they were all the more dangerous to tamper with. Until cultural revolution broke out in the capitals, provincial conservatives were everywhere too strong for serious provincial rebels.

❦

The South, of course, denied that it was a province. It was a producer, not a consumer, of tradition, and past its own historic capitals it looked to its own England. Yet in 1912 the South was really a reluctant tributary, a destroyed rival whose cultural counterrevolution had not really succeeded.

The cultural leaders of the South, like those of New England, looked constantly back to the nineteenth century, but not to the nineteenth century of moral and material progress. The childhood of Walter Hines Page and his friends had been spent under the immediate shadow of defeat and in the palpable presence of the poverty, the despair, and the hatred of Reconstruction. As young men, this generation of Southerners had been faced in the eighties and nineties by the dilemma of the Southern literary revival and the New South, one devoted to enshrining the separate, Confederate past and the other to making the South over in imitation of the progressive, commercial North. In the South of 1912, despite fifty years of heroic efforts to find a new road for Southern culture, these two ways, nostalgia and imitation, were the only ones open.

The romantic and defeated Old South of Thomas Nelson Page and his many rivals, the picturesque regional South of the local-colorists were still magazine staples. With Southern folklore and flavor, the Southern versions of slavery and Reconstruction had swept the North. The Radicals were villains, the Negroes either barbarous or pathetically inadequate, and the white South heroic and misunderstood. This picture, laboriously constructed, was now taken for granted and therefore, to some people, beginning to be a bore.

Ever since the eighties some Southerners had been trying to break, or at least to supplement, this pattern. The South had strained its resources to get cotton mills, railroads, and Yankee capital, and with them had sometimes seemed to welcome the Yankee creed of progress, with its components of science, popular education, and reform. Southern progressives had accomplished a lot, not only against the boll weevil and the hookworm but against ignorance and prejudice. If they made tactical concessions, one must remember the obstacles they confronted, the devastating poverty, the ever tightening and narrowing religious orthodoxy, the sensitivity to criticism, and underlying all, the racial dogmas that had grown more and more rigid since the tensions of Populist times.

It took courage for Walter Hines Page in 1897 to tell a North Carolina audience that the state's way of life was antiquated and unproductive and it is not surprising that this gentleman and promoter, a perfect specimen in most of his tastes and opinions of the more optimistic section of the Yankee custodians of culture, should have moved out of the South all the way to the *Atlantic Monthly*.

Some patriotic Southerners had devoted themselves to bringing Southern culture, rather than the Southern economy, back to life. With the help of Northern philanthropy, they had made a considerable beginning on popular high-school education and had brought back several colleges and universities from collapse to respectability. On the South's upper border and without a very cordial welcome in Baltimore itself, the largely Northern venture of Johns Hopkins University had played a big part in developing Southern academic standards as well as American graduate education. Fortified by Hopkins training, a new generation of professors at the best Southern institutions was challenging religious fundamentalism and occasionally, cautiously, questioning the most rigid forms of sectional tradition. They sponsored an active corps of historians, mostly of course devoted to the Lost Cause, and had made a beginning with William Peterfield Trent and others on the restudy of Southern literature. As an integral part of this deliberate revival of Southern culture, forward-looking Southern intellectuals had started and managed to keep alive two general literary magazines, the *South Atlantic Quarterly* and the *Sewanee Review*.

Here again, as often in Southern history, irony overtakes us; what devotion had produced in these two magazines was an imitation of the *Century* and *Atlantic* so literal that the originals seemed to be parodied. At its beginning in 1902 the *South Atlantic Quarterly* lamented abjectly the backwardness of Southern letters and blamed it on the lack not only of a wealthy leisure class but even of a class of "well-paid and lightly worked professional men" like "the English rectors or the college teachers of the North." In 1912 the *Sewanee Review* carried a South Carolina Founder's Day address by a Virginian dealing with "Our Heritage of Idealism" and quoting at length on the nature of this heritage "Ex-President Eliot" (not otherwise identified). This tradition had been given its best lyric expression, said this article in very slight correction of the Northern canon, by Longfellow, Emerson, Poe, Lowell, Holmes, Whittier, and Lanier. All this is so familiar to the reader of Northern magazines of the same date that one is startled to come across a quotation from *Hayne's* reply to *Webster*.[1]

In 1912 nobody would have expected, least of all a Southerner, that there was a Southern literary renaissance around the historical corner that would make that of the eighties a minor and local affair. Literary rebellion, though more profoundly successful when it came, did not occur as soon as in either the Northeast or the Middle West, and Mencken was still almost right when he talked, a little later than 1912, about the Sahara of the Bozart. From the times of William Gilmore Simms to those of Allen Tate, devoted Southerners have tried to explain why the South failed for so long to produce creative literature.

Clearly poverty was part of the reason, as was the premium placed on the manly, or, as Veblen would say, the barbarian, virtues. Montrose J. Moses, a Southern historian of literature, complained that in the South letters were still regarded as a "dainty pursuit." [2] Another explanation is that the South, unable to look clearly at slavery in the midst of a Christian and democratic tradition, had developed an inveterate taste for shallow fantasy. For this unpalatable suggestion one does not have to rely on recent historians who make use of the forbidden tools of Freud. Long before 1912, George W. Cable had clearly stated this explanation of Southern romanticism. More recently, it had been suggested by such varied commentators as William Peterfield Trent, W. E. B. DuBois, and Henry James.

It is most tellingly presented by the two Southern writers, neighbors, intimate friends, and opposites, who were as yet the only signs of the life at work in this barren ground. James Branch Cabell had tried to escape the Southern dilemma by treating both Southern romanticism and Northern progress in a light, satirical manner. Yet

[1] Editorial, "Problems of the Author in the South," *South Atlantic Quarterly*, I (1902), 202–8; C. Alphonso Smith: "Our Heritage of Idealism," *Sewanee Review*, XX (1912), 235–51.

[2] Moses: *The Literature of the South* (New York, 1910), p. 471.

his affectionate play with Southern tradition amounted, he found, to blasphemy and he deliberately retreated into allegory. His road, that of withdrawal from moral controversy into aestheticism, ran from the nineties straight into one phase of the twenties. It had little to do with the later Southern literary revival which, whether its method was naturalist or symbolist, almost always dealt with moral issues in tragic terms.

Ellen Glasgow was a more recognizable ancestress of the later Southern literature. Since the turn of the century her novels had attacked Southern hypocrisy and sentimentality from the inside. Handicapped triply as a Southerner, a woman, and a lady, she had survived the scoldings of Confederate Daughters for her skeptical attitude toward the Lost Cause. Winning a considerable national success, she had already discovered in the North a further ring of convention surrounding thc Southern boundaries she had broken. As she later described the most constricting necessity of the period:

> Until American idealism had been safely buried in Flanders fields, a belief in the happy end was as imperative in philosophy as it was essential in fiction. The universe, as well as a love story, must lead to romantic fulfillment. But only the older novelist, who has suffered under the artificial glow of the past American idealism, can appreciate the blessing of the liberty not to believe, and of the even more hardly won liberty not to be glad.[3]

Howells and even his descendents could manage in the North in 1912 to carry out this duty without hypocrisy or undue strain. But it was hard to be cheerful, and impossible to be both cheerful and honest, if one lived in the South in 1912, the South where progress was associated with tubercular mill children and tradition invoked to justify grandfather clauses and even, every year, the burning alive of Negroes, the South which genuinely valued generosity and honor and had turned in fear and frustation both mean and tricky.

As Miss Glasgow says, only when the whole of intellectual Amer-

[3] Ellen Glasgow: *A Certan Measure* (New York, 1938), p. 118.

ica had experienced tragedy and the failure of hope could Southern writers begin to look at the South with both affection and profundity.

Negroes, like white Southerners, had to break into the dominant respectable culture of the day before they could break out of it. In 1912 ninety percent of the Negroes still lived in the South, where most of them were small tenant farmers or servants. The very worst period of racial fear and violence in the section's postwar history was just over, and it had left the Southern Negro more systematically excluded from politics than he had been since emancipation and far more thoroughly cut off from ordinary social contact with whites in parks and streetcars than he had ever been. The yearly rate of lynching had declined from the frightful 155 of 1893, but in 1912 sixty-one Negroes were killed, often with torture, by mobs. In addition to violence and oppression, the Negro had to face constant defamation, North and South. Perhaps more damaging than the abuse of the current generation of professional nigger-hating politicians, the Bleases and Vardamans, was the constant, gentle regret by polite historians and essayists in the North that the Negro had failed to justify the efforts made in his behalf by Northern reformers. Science, as yet, usually seemed to confirm the doctrine of Negro inferiority. On the stage, in vaudeville, in popular story one could hardly escape the most damaging stereotype of all, the happy shiftless illiterate Negro that everybody loved. It is not surprising that conscious leaders of Negro culture in 1912 looked with longing at respectability.

Still the greatest leader, the intimate of philanthropists and pundits, was Booker T. Washington who had been preaching since 1895 the Atlanta gospel of work, patience, and acceptance of Southern mores. In his confidence in the solution of all problems through industry and progress, his belief in practical good manners, his sturdy reiteration of the clichés of laissez-faire, he resembled nobody so much as the other great educator, Charles William Eliot. His whole career was, as nearly as it could be, a replica of that of one of the other custodians of culture of the more practical, optimistic variety. Washington's usual anecdotal, didactic style is not very different from that of his white contemporaries. Occasionally, out of his own tough education in reality and through his desire to communicate with a nonliterary audience he produced an earthy, telling figure of speech that reminds one more of Poor Richard than of the Academy. Few have forgotten, whether or not they accepted, his advice to cast down your bucket where you are.

The Northern Negro poets and writers who in this period courageously claimed their full human and civic rights were, ironically, far more imitative. Of two Ohioans, Paul Lawrence Dunbar wrote elegant poetry in the manner of the Stedman circle and dialect verse like Riley's, and Charles Chesnutt dealt bravely with the "Problem" in the local-color manner. Both culture and courage were symbolized most clearly by W. E. B. DuBois of Harvard and Atlanta, the founder of the Niagara movement and, with a devoted group of white reformers, of the new organization for self-defense, the National Association for the Advancement of Colored People. Yet the culture to which DuBois demanded admission, that in which he found solace, was the culture of the most conservative custodians, and the way he talked about it was the way that was soon to be rejected:

> I sit with Shakespeare and he winces not. Across the color line I move arm in arm with Balzac and Dumas, where smiling men and welcoming women glide in gilded halls. From out the caves of evening that swing between the strong-limbed earth and the tracery of the stars, I summon Aristotle and Aurelius and what soul I will, and they come all graciously with no scorn nor condescension. So, wed with Truth, I dwell above the Veil. Is this the life you grudge us, O knightly America? [4]

Neither Washington nor DuBois could possibly have guessed what bucket to cast down or where to cast it. Jazz, despised by serious Negroes, was already blooming in New Orleans dives and, in

[4] DuBois: *The Souls of Black Folk* (Chicago, 5th ed., 1906), p. 109.

St. Louis, W. C. Handy was publishing his great blues. The Negro was to have a bigger part in the coming change in American culture than he had ever had in any American cultural movement before. Not through admission to the realm of polite letters but through its overthrow Negroes were to win money, world-wide fame, enthusiastic white imitation, and even, in the long run, some solid steps toward real equality.

Of all the provincial rebellions, the first and most exciting had taken place in California. None was so decisively over. Looking back to the sixties and seventies, the days when the San Francisco press had published Clemens, Bret Harte, Henry George, and Ambrose Bierce, Californian patriots since the nineties had been talking about reviving past splendors, without much to show for it. In the nineties San Francisco had, like Chicago and New York, produced its mildly shocking little magazines. Finally, in the stirring days of Norris and London, California naturalism had seemed a major turn-of-the-century phenomenon.

All the major figures of all these brief booms had departed. A scattering of conventional authors remained in San Francisco, trying to revive the past, and another group had founded a "colony" among the pines of Carmel. Poets like Edward Rowland Sill, Charles Warren Stoddard, and George Sterling described California scenery with rhetoric that conservative Eastern critics considered old-fashioned. They were soon to be labeled by the Imagist rebels "the cosmic California school."

So far, what had lasted here as elsewhere was what was least native. Visitors agreed that San Francisco had achieved a relaxed, pleasant, "Continental" way of life. Across the bay the University of California, product like the other California colleges of a New England enterprise as well as a land grant, was regarded as humanist and conservative among state universities. Stanford, hailed on its foundation by William James for its unique, untrammeled opportunities, continued to amaze visitors by its architecture, "Mediterranean" rather than Gothic or Greek. Its president, David Starr Jordan, closely resembled Charles W. Eliot in his devotion to nineteenth-century liberal Christianity, Spencerian progress, and morality. He carried his racism further than most of the Eastern custodians and departed from their pattern later by sticking to pacifism, but these deviations had nothing regional about them. Like Eliot, he wrote for the national press on all subjects from eugenics to trade unions. Life in California, he had prophesied in 1898, would eventually be richer and freer than life anywhere else in the country, but yet it would make no dangerous departures:

> Under all its deviations and variations lies the old Puritan conscience, which is still the backbone of the civilization of the republic.[5]

Southern California, still the hygienic and Protestant "American Mediterranean" of the pre-Hollywood Era, looked askance at corrupt, Bohemian San Francisco. For a long time it had been making strenuous efforts to create a unique culture. The result was perhaps the country's most eloquent lesson in the dilemmas of regionalism. So far, Southern California higher culture was a bizarre and unbelievably innocent mixture of Mission Days and Chautauquas, fiestas and Ebell Clubs, false exoticism and genuine uplift.

From the Coast Range to the Great Plains, culture was frankly an import rather than an export. Mary Austin had begun to write about the Southwestern "Land of Little Rain," first, not surprisingly, in the *Atlantic Monthly*. She had not yet turned to the region of Santa Fe, which had been explored by devoted archeologists and described by a few professional writers, among them Hamlin Garland, but was still awaiting Mabel Dodge Luhan and a new kind of nature cult to put it on the map.

Looking westward from the other side of this whole vast region of plains and mountains, only Willa Cather was beginning

[5] Jordan: *California and the Californians* (San Francisco, 1907), p. 46.

to treat the Nebraska prairie as a place where actual people lived. The great plains were still almost entirely the domain of the cowboy romancers, of whom Owen Wister, a Harvard man, was the most admired and Zane Grey, an Ohioan, was beginning to be the most successful. Wister at least sounded to Eastern ears like an accurate reporter of exotic customs; most people who tried to write about this startling region sounded like travel promoters.

In politics, as in literature and social tradition, the Far West, from the plains and mountains to the coast, was trying to live down a reputation for extremism and violence. Easterners remembered Populism; many besides President Taft were jolted by Arizona's and New Mexico's proposals for popular review of judicial decisions. Far Western progressives often had to fight their way between tough proletarian radicalism and ruthless, often absentee-owned mining and ranching and railroad corporations. It is not surprising that some Far Western politicians, like some Far Western writers, did their best to be as soundly progressive, as solidly cultured, as the best citizens of the older states.

❧

In 1912 the only region that shared with the Northeast a claim to cultural leadership, and consequently the only province that was able to contribute to the first phases of the Rebellion, was the nearest, least rugged, superficially least colorful area, the Northern Mississippi Valley. Whether this old settled area was a province, the real center, or an equal partner with the East was a question debated at the time by its citizens and ever since by its historians. The East over several generations had fought a long campaign to "save" this decisive section, with colleges and churches, and this had meant to assimilate it. The college towns scattered over the vast area from Ohio to Kansas were likely to have elms, an abolitionist past, and a considerable flavor of archaic New England culture and religion. The Civil War, of which this section was particularly conscious, had established the political unity of East and Midwest and left a Midwesterner as the undisputed common hero. Yet it had left its resentments also. In culture and politics, the Midwest regarded itself as an equal of New England, an ally and even a relative, part of normal, dominant America in contrast to the defeated South and the violent, exotic Far West. But like most allies or relatives, it had its suspicions and did not mean to be put upon.

In 1912 Edward Albion Ross of the University of Wisconsin contrasted the two leading sections in the *Century*.[6] Clearly the Midwest was both more moral and more progressive than the worn-out, alien-infested East. As one could see by the stature of its men and the status of its women, it had received only the desirable kinds of immigration. Eastern progressives, Ross conceded, had contributed more to some of the less immediate causes like Indian rights, Negro rights, and international peace. These appealed to what he called "investors' idealism." But the hard fight against privilege centered in the West; it was the West that was going to save free government and private property. Ross granted also that the East was probably still ahead, because of its long head start, in some kinds of culture. It had more nearly got rid of the common American faults, barely faults at all, of emphasis on quantity and action as against quality and reflection. But this was changing; in the only ways in which the Midwest was not already ahead, it was fast catching up.

This was the Midwest's conception of itself; a rival of the East in culture, and superior in morality and progress. Western and particularly agrarian superiority went far back of political speeches; it lay deep in the whole inheritance of this generation. In college some Midwesterners had read those urban lovers of the country, Horace and Vergil; educated people knew that the loss of the rural virtues had caused the fall of Rome; everybody was familiar with the agrarian parables of the Bible; Populist orators had quoted Burns and Shelley and Goldsmith. Practically no American statesman, whatever his origin, failed in public to express his devotion to the farm way of life.

[6] Ross: *Changing America* (New York, 1912), pp. 163–86.

In the Midwest, morality was linked to progress even more closely than elsewhere. For many Southern and Western progressives, a part of the current generation's job was to end the curse of liquor. This would be a defeat for all the evils of the city, including big business, the immigrants and their bosses, and the Catholic Church. Thanks to the relentless work of the Methodist Church and the Anti-Saloon League, drying up one state or local district after another, it began to seem probable that the saloon would soon be a big-city phenomenon.

Once, mixed with the West's sense of superiority, there had been a good deal of resentment at the growth of urban and Eastern power. Some kinds of Western protest had been not progressive, but at once radical and reactionary. Farmers had banded together both to save the old ways and secure redress. Now, Ross assured his readers, the Populist fury was gone; revenge had turned into uplift. Frederick Jackson Turner, who thought that progress, like idealism, had always come mainly from the West, agreed. The agrarian past was being, and must be, fused with a constructive future:

> Let us see to it that the ideals of the pioneer in his log cabin shall enlarge into the spiritual life of a democracy where civic power shall dominate and utilize individual achievement for the common good.[7]

Beneath the surface, as we will see, there was still a strong current of rural resentment and reaction, but it was easy to miss. The most conspicuous farm organizations seemed to have abandoned crusades for skilled pressure tactics. For the urban public, farm opinion in the period was mostly represented by a group of farm editors, farm experts, and other professional spokesmen. This group, agitating for scientific advance, good roads, rural education, and in general a share of the period's amenities, was within the dominant pattern. Occasionally they might be skeptical about culture, but not to any very damaging length. *Wallace's Farmer*, a typical farm journal

[7] Turner: "Contributions of the West to American Democracy," *Atlantic Monthly*, XCI (1903), 96.

of this group, occasionally made jokes about the relative value of a Greek root and a corn root. Yet it urged its readers not to desert to the cheap rivals of the standard magazine, but to stick to the man

> who stands for truth and justice and righteousness, who aims to elevate, inspire and sweeten those who pay him the compliment of purchasing his periodical.[8]

One major Western variant of the national progressive and moralist pattern continued to be represented by William Jennings Bryan. Once feared as a Robespierre, Bryan had of course never been a radical either in culture or politics; he was the best instance of the truism that a provincial culture is conservative. He had been educated not in his adopted Nebraska but at Illinois College, a typical transmitter of archaic New England culture; while there he had not only distinguished himself as a debater but won a prize for Latin prose.[9] Neither traditional culture nor traditional moralism had anything to fear from Bryan, except that his overliteral and old-fashioned version of both invited parody. His graduation speech had been on "Character" and one of his endlessly repeated Chautauqua favorites was "The Value of an Ideal." This was far from lip service; already in his actions Bryan had shown his devotion to the ideas of his youth. More courage was yet to be demanded of him as these ideas became more rigid and more obsolete, and he was part way on the road to becoming the arch-conservative of the Scopes trial. Yet Bryan had not shaken off the onus of 1896. For much of the country he was not quite respectable; for others in the West or South, including many readers of the Hearst Press, he was still a radical hero.

In the Midwest east of the Mississippi, which Bryan had not carried in 1896, the rising progressives did their best to shake off all traces of the Populist stigma. The leaders who had won control of

[8] *Wallace's Farmer*, February 14, 1913, p. 259; November 21, 1913, p. 1572.
[9] George R. Poage: "The College Career of William Jennings Bryan," *Mississippi Valley Historical Review*, XV (1928–9), 165–82.

one Western Capitol after another in the last decade sounded the old war cries against corporations. However, they avoided inflation, did their fighting within the Republican Party, and insisted that they were trying to help business too. Henry Wallace of Iowa explained in the *World's Work* in 1912 "What the Middle West Wants" and insisted that railroad regulation, direct legislation, and the rest hurt practically nobody:

> I call special attention to the fact that every enactment of the statesmen of the Middle West to protect the man that God made from the oppression of the artificial man (the corporation) has been beneficial to both.[1]

The toughest, the most combative—his enemies said the most arrogant—of Western progressives was Robert M. La Follette. Yet even he took pains to explain that he was against exploitation, not profit-making. On its front cover on April 6, 1912, his magazine insisted that "The Wisconsin Way Brings Business Security," and claimed that under careful regulation "The old feeling of class antagonism and distrust is fast giving place to peace, confidence, and prosperity."

This probably exaggerated the prevailing harmony in Wisconsin; La Follette's enemies found him no lamb. These enemies did not include traditional culture or morality; La Follette like Bryan was steeped in both. He had first distinguished himself by winning an oratorical contest on "Hamlet," which he alternated with "Representative Government" on his Chautauqua tours. Justice and principle, he constantly insisted, were the real political issues. In his autobiography in 1913 he proudly told how his old teacher, President Bascom, had told him before his first inauguration, "Never mind the political mistakes so long as you make no ethical mistakes."

In literature, as in politics, the West seemed to have turned from angry protest to constructive progress. Howells himself, twenty or

[1] Wallace: "What the Middle West Wants," *World's Work*, XX (1910), pp. 12894–5.

thirty years earlier, had pointed out and fostered what looked like a Midwestern school of pessimistic realism. Edward Eggleston, Joseph Kirkland, and E. W. Howe had painted a depressing, though not unrelieved picture of Midwestern-village drabness, violence, and hardship. Now this movement seemed to be over, and the new revolt against the village had barely begun.

That all-important place, the Midwestern village, hallowed home of log cabins and barefoot boys, hateful source of provincial bigotry, was in rapid transition. Its pattern was strong enough to cause revolt, and not strong enough to prevent it. The schools until recently had still exposed their students to the McGuffey readers, bibles of conventional literature and morality alike. The village was still partly united, and suspicious of outside criticism.

In the villages, and among people who had been brought up in the villages, the emotionalism and mysticism of the old-time religion still challenged the blandness of up-to-date 1912 culture. Liberalism and the Social Gospel dominated middle-class Protestantism in the Midwestern cities. Yet many a boy growing up in the village in this period or a little earlier remembered the ecstasy and terror of evangelical preaching and revival hymns all his life. Some who left the doctrines behind, like Sherwood Anderson, and some who did not, like Vachel Lindsay, were to draw on their old-fashioned religious emotions for new kinds of expression.

In 1912, as everybody knew, village traditions were breaking down as village isolation decreased. Village storekeepers were complaining that the mail-order house, rural free delivery, and interurban trolleys were taking business to the towns. The automobile was beginning to appear on the village streets (in 1912 the country had 860,000 cars and was demanding a better highway system). Even the Chautauqua was in danger. Its jubilee singers and lectures on Bible lands continued to draw crowds. The young people, however, were more attracted to another kind of entertainment, the flickering, fascinating Saturday-night movie, the bank-robbery and the custard-pie comedy, centrally produced for rural and urban taste alike.

An occasional young man, his curiosity aroused by disturbing rumors, looked further than the movies for new ideas. Usually he found at least one person who could tell him about some heresies of the recent past, a socialist, a freethinking admirer of Colonel Ingersoll, a sympathetic librarian who lent him the *Rubaiyat*. Restless, but with many of his village standards still intact, the young man sometimes went straight from the rural nineteenth century to twentieth-century New York.

❦

The center of the Midwest's own literary culture in 1912 was not in the country but in the middle-sized city, and, more than anywhere else, in Indianapolis. Some Midwesterners liked to say this city had displaced Boston as the nation's literary capital. Yet in the older capital, for some reason not only the claims but the name of Indianapolis was considered funny. In 1912 Meredith Nicholson, an Indianapolis novelist, told Easterners he wished they would stop accenting the "Injun" in such a way as to suggest that the war-whoop still sounded. Actually it had not been heard for some time. Indiana prided itself on its century of settlement, its New England colleges and southern hospitality, its high literacy rate, its Republican and pulpit eloquence, and above all its authors. Nobody could deny that Bobbs-Merrill was the only literary publishing house that managed to stay alive outside the East. Even more eagerly than other Westerners, Indianians had always flocked to hear visiting authors, from Matthew Arnold to Arnold Bennett. When Howells visited Indianapolis in 1899, he was welcomed by a half-dozen literary clubs and only the social elite could get tickets to his lecture.

Yet things were changing, here as elsewhere. Indianapolis, Terre Haute, and other cities had their immigrant slums as well as elm-shaded avenues of solid frame houses, and Indiana coal was blackening the capital. Nicholson, like other Indiana writers, was sure that:

> . . . the changes are, after all, chiefly such as address the eye rather than the spirit. There are more people, but there are more good people! [2]

His own latest novel, *A Hoosier Chronicle,* reached the same conclusion. It dealt in part with corrupt politics, but at the end the boss's heart was changed by his discovery that the heroine was his long-lost daughter, and finally, on page 606, the inevitable wise old lady summed up the message of most Indiana literature:

> It's all pretty comfortable and cheerful and busy in Indiana, with lots of old-fashioned human kindness flowing round: and it's getting better all the time. And I guess it's always got to be that way, out here in God's country.

Apparently this message was well received outside Indiana, since the state's authors had an extraordinary selling record. Some Indiana successes were costume romancers, like Lew Wallace in the previous generation and among contemporaries Charles Major (*When Knighthood Was in Flower*), George Barr McCutcheon (*Graustark*), and Maurice Thompson (*Alice of Old Vincennes*). The most popular of all was Mrs. Gene Stratton-Porter, author of *Freckles, A Girl of the Limberlost,* and the 1913 sentimental success, *Laddie.*

The prose-writers that Indiana was most proud of were, however, realists, not of the old depressing kind, but of the neo-Howells school. Indiana realists were led by Booth Tarkington, whom Howells had called a "master." Tarkington had experimented with the costume romance, and in the recent past he had spent a good deal of his time in Paris and New York supervising production of his plays. In 1911, he had had the kind of nervous crisis which seems routine for the period's cheerful authors, and to get over it had come home. Home now in every sense, he was just settling into the most serious and ambitious phase of his work. Just ahead were not only *Penrod* but also the tetralogy starting with the *Turmoil* (1915) in which Tarkington dealt with the current changes in In-

[2] Nicholson: *The Provincial American* (Boston, 1912), pp. 86–7.

diana society—the replacement of old families by ruthless upstarts, the smoke and noise, the commercial corruption and underlying soundness. In 1912 Tarkington was not only a skillful and polished writer but also exactly in line with current moral and political taste. To many he looked like the most promising aspirant for the mantle of Howells. Unfortunately that mantle, worn quite a while, was to fall apart before Tarkington could quite get it on.

Indiana's other current favorite was often referred to as "the poet Riley." James Whitcomb Riley had indeed written a good deal of serious verse, perfectly conventional in diction and meter. He swore whenever he even thought of Whitman. A fastidious and dapper city-dweller, he disliked the familiarity that people on trains sometimes thought appropriate. His whole role must have grated on him a little; we know that he carried on a long and brave struggle against compulsive drinking. The public of 1912 suspected no cracks: Riley was the incarnation of home on the farm.

Riley's greatest successes had come through those two favorite nineteenth-century art forms, the dialect poem and the humorous public reading. Naturally, his first success on the platform outside the Midwest had been in Boston, and in 1888 he had been formally inducted into polite literature with an invitation from Robert Underwood Johnson to participate in an International Copyright League benefit-reading with James Russell Lowell in the chair. Nobody admired Riley's work more than Johnson, the archfoe of slang—it was customary to compare Riley to, of all people, the Rabelaisian Burns. In 1912, we are not surprised to find, Riley received from his fellow academicians the organization's first gold medal for poetry. He was extravagantly admired not only by Phelps and Van Dyke but also by Kipling, who wrote him an affectionate poem. Howells called him flatly one of our greatest poets.

In his own country Riley was by no means without honor. Since a stroke in 1912 he had been frequently serenaded by school children, and the Indianapolis schools had begun to celebrate his birthday officially. His poems, skillful in versification and painstakingly correct in dialect, were becoming part of the national stock along with those of Whittier. The dominant sentiment was extreme optimism mixed with gentle nostalgic tears:

> O, the Raggedy Man! He works for Pa;
> An' he's the goodest man ever you saw!

or again,

> I cannot say, and I will not say
> That he is dead.—He is just away!

Not only the reputation of Indiana literature, but the literature itself, was soon to pass out of existence. Theodore Dreiser, the only Indiana author whose reputation long survived, had left the state at sixteen and lived, while there, on the uncheerful, immigrant side of the tracks. Yet Dreiser, always charitable and always baffling, frequently praised the state for its innocence and "faith in the ideals of the Republic," and stated his wholehearted reverence for James Whitcomb Riley.

❧

A very different capital of Midwestern civilization was what some admirers described as the German state of Wisconsin, with its German university. In Madison, more than anywhere else, culture and progress seemed to have come together in a characteristic Western combination. President C. R. Van Hise, a classmate of La Follette's and a progressive of some standing, had announced at his inauguration in 1903 that the university must be the servant of the state.[3] Lowell, we may remember, had said at his inauguration that the university must counteract the defects of the civilization of the day. In these two statements lie much of the difference between two academic traditions, and even between the Midwestern and Eastern variants of the dominant credo. In the Wisconsin variety,

[3] The speech, an illuminating one, is reprinted in Merle Curti and Vernon Carstensen: *The University of Wisconsin* (2 Vols., Madison, 1949), II, 611–24.

the idealism was a little more practical, and the version of culture more thoroughly compatible with progress.

It was at Wisconsin that Richard T. Ely and John R. Commons were insisting that economics was the study of institutions, not theory. And the university, perhaps more than any university in the world, was in the thick of politics. Its critics said it served not just the people but the La Follette machine. La Follette enemies, and also some well-meaning progressive writers, were continually pointing to the professors on state commissions, the work of university experts in preparing regulatory legislation, and the expanding work of the Legislative Reference Service. In 1913 the *World's Work* started it all up again with an admiring article injudiciously entitled "A University that Runs a State." [4]

Part of the distinctive history of the University of Wisconsin arose from its continuing struggle for existence. Unlike some neighboring states, Wisconsin had squandered its land grants. Once embarked on a progressive course, Van Hise had to depend for the University's life on the support of the people, half of them not brought up in English-speaking culture at all. One of the current surveys of colleges naturally called a chapter "Wisconsin, an Utilitarian University," [5] but Van Hise was constantly having to prove to his constituents that the University did not waste too much time on the humanities.

Nobody can say that idealism was lacking in the Van Hise or La Follette conception of a university. As Van Hise put it, he was determined to demonstrate that a republic could support a university as handsomely as any monarchy. The University proudly announced that it stood ready to teach anything whatever, through extension if not otherwise, to any citizen of the state. Admitting that standards suffered a little under this kind of program, E. E. Slosson, a sympathetic critic, said that a state university was not worth its name "if it is not willing to risk its reputa-

[4] *World's Work*, XXV (1912–13), 699–708.
[5] John Corbin: *Which College for the Boy?* (Boston, 1908).

tion to save some young man or woman in a backwoods county from an illiterate life." [6]

One cannot have one's cultural cake and eat it too, and certainly this is a far cry from Irving Babbitt's conception of the role of a university. John R. Commons, defending agricultural education against classical snobbery, gave an enduring statement of the Wisconsin variety of practical idealism:

> Of course a cow is just a cow, and can never become a Winged Victory, but within her limits she is capable of approaching an ideal. And, more than that, she is an ideal that every farmer and farmer's boy—the despised slaves and helots of Greece—can aspire to.[7]

In 1910 the graduating class gave the University a plaque containing a statement made by the Regents in a crisis over academic freedom in 1894. The same statement, calling for a "continual and fearless sifting and winnowing" in the search for truth, was incorporated by La Follette in the state Republican platform of 1910. Wisconsin Republicanism has been through some changes since this point, yet La Follette's University has survived, a major monument to the progressivism of his day. In many of its products one recognizes the heritage: courageous, democratic, a little hostile to modern complexity and pessimism. Many products of this progressive institution continue to believe not only that one can find the truth by winnowing and searching (a standard, fairly conservative academic belief) but that one can tell it to the people.

Chicago was hardly a part of Midwestern culture. Young Midwesterners flocked to it because it was different from all that they had experienced. It was a meeting-point for Midwestern and East-

[6] Slosson: *Great American Universities*, p. 295.
[7] Quoted in ibid., pp. 515–6.

ern and European ideas and customs. Almost everybody who talked about this huge and terrible city was conscious of paradox. The most obvious impression was of chaos; visitors talked about the smell of blood, the mile after mile of unrelieved slum, the lavish and pretentious palaces of the rich. They did not talk about, but people knew of the weird combination of prudery and vice, the concern in the recent past about whether one *had* to wear low-necked dresses at the opera as people did in the East, and the wide-open and elegant brothels. The city's name brought to mind a history of ruthless violence, from the Haymarket riot and the Pullman strike to the newsboy war of 1910 and the recurrent killings in the tributary mine regions.

Yet there was another Chicago. To H. G. Wells the city was principally a horrible example of capitalist disorder, but Arnold Bennett penetrated more deeply. Unlike New York, said Bennett, "Chicago is openly anxious about its soul." [8] A special combination of shame and pride, reform and grandiose prophecy characterized prewar Chicago and explained some of its paradoxes. Well before 1912, Hull House, a great pioneering center for many kinds of reform, had won its way to acceptance and the city was proud of it. The traction ring had been destroyed by the efforts of the moral and civic-minded men of wealth, and like other cities Chicago had elected, off and on, a reform administration.

Culture and reform were even more closely linked than elsewhere in Chicago, where both required heroism. The same civic-minded millionaires who fought the boodlers provided the city, between the fire of 1871 and the panic of 1893, with a first-rate complete set of the standard furnishings of a cultural capital: a symphony orchestra, a magnificent hall for it to play in, a magnificent Art Institute, two splendid libraries, and a number of literary magazines. To crown Chicago's culture, John D. Rockefeller had added a great university. The whole achievement was symbolized in 1893 by the colossal Roman grandeur of the World's Fair.

[8] Wells: *The Future in America* (London, 1906), pp. 82–6; Bennett: *Your United States* (New York, 1912), pp. 41–6.

Chicago gentility had to fight so hard it sometimes turned into caricature. The literary magazine *America*, published for a few years at the end of the eighties, had linked uplift with Anglo-Saxon dictatorship and the war against literary realism. But the *Dial*, founded by a New Englander with local backing, was a well-edited counterpart of the Eastern magazines of the day, only a little more conservative than the best of them. In the poetry of William Vaughn Moody, or in the reforming novels of Robert Herrick, who blended moralism and progress as successfully as anybody, Chicago's relatively conservative literary output attained real excellence.

Alone among provincial cities, Chicago by the nineties was so secure in its cultural attainment that it could play a part in the decade's movements of revolt. As we will see, long before the apparently peaceful and complacent period at which we start our story, important kinds of dissent had been at work beneath the surface of American civilization. Chicago had contributed to all these. John Dewey and Thorstein Veblen, among others, had made the University from its beginning a center of innovation in the social sciences. Louis Sullivan, who had designed the Auditorium for polite Chicago's symphony concerts, had played a major part in an architectural revolution of eventually worldwide significance. And Chicago literature, born in uplift, had ventured away from its origins into both the major literary heresies of the late nineteenth century, decadence and naturalism.

In 1893, before they were out of college, two Harvard students from Chicago, both admireres of Charles Eliot Norton, started the publishing house of Stone & Kimball. When they came home the two young men startled Chicago not only with afternoon tea and dandified dress but also with the *Chap-Book*, the most widely imitated and influential of the *fin-de-siècle* crop of little magazines. Before it went out of existence in 1898 the *Chap-Book* had published Mallarmé and Verlaine, commissioned a poster by Toulouse-Lautrec, and been attacked by the *Bookman* as immoral. The publishing firm and its successor, which lasted until 1905, published elegant editions of Poe and Stevenson and also, for the first time in America, George Bernard Shaw. Anna Morgan directed members of the Stone & Kimball set in some of the first Shaw performances in America, twenty years before the Little Theater movement. Until 1909, members of this coterie met members of the uplifting *Dial* set and also Potter Palmers and Armours in the Little Room after the symphony performances.

Chicago realism derived in part from the city's newspaper writers, who for some time had gone in for the earthy rather than the precious type of Bohemianism. Eugene Field became mannered and sentimental and attended the Little Room, but Finley Peter Dunne did not. His Mr. Dooley, the sharpest of the dialect commentators, used dialect for very different purposes than Riley's. Howells and Brander Matthews both admired George Ade, the author of *Fables in Slang,* though Mencken later called him an original author neglected by the polite critics. Theodore Dreiser went on from newspaper iconoclasm to a new kind of Chicago naturalism in *Sister Carrie.* By 1912, however, both *Carrie* and Norris's *The Pit* seemed to most people to have been part of a temporary flurry. One Chicago author, admired in his time and revived sporadically since, Henry Blake Fuller, had tried both modes. His fanciful Italian novels had been admired by Norton and Lowell, his stories of Chicago brutality by Howells.

Hamlin Garland, having conquered literary Boston with his Midwestern realism, moved to Chicago at the height of its first flowering, the Fair and panic year 1893. In *Crumbling Idols,* published elegantly by Stone & Kimball, he had called for a fresh, truly Western Chicago literature, at once realistic and full of idealism. Alone among prophets of regional literary revolution, Garland had been right about the place but wrong about the time. The Chicago movement of the nineties petered out before the "Chicago Renaissance" began. Chicago critics, Garland found to his chagrin, did not like his Middle Border stories of sweat and misery. His trips to New York got longer, and he admitted that he missed not only Gilder and Howells, but appreciation. Getting ready to move East himself, Garland moved his literary world West, out of the homely Dakotas to the colorful Rockies and deserts:

> My later themes were, happily, quite outside the controversial belt. Concerned less with hopeless drudgery, and more with the epic side of western life, I found myself almost popular.[9]

Garland's great triumph, and the culmination of twenty years of Chicago effort for uplift, came in 1913, when he persuaded the Academy and Institute to hold their annual meeting in Chicago. This momentous decision was thoroughly debated: most of the Academicians were getting along in years and had never ventured so far West. However the Chicago press and the patrons of the arts got behind the invitation, the Academy made the journey in a special train, and the first meeting, in the shadow of the heroic equestrian statues in the Art Institute, delighted everybody. To Garland, this left nothing to hope for in Chicago and when his father died in 1914 he back-trailed for New York.

Exactly when Garland gave up, his prophecy for Chicago literature was, in its way, coming true. A new group of writers already living in the city were to make it, for a short period, the national literary capital. Direct connections between the literary movements of the nineties and the movement that began in 1912 are few. Yet Harriet Monroe, who presided over Chicago poetry in the later movement, had composed and recited the official ode at the opening of the 1893 fair, and Theodore Dreiser, the storm center of 1915, had been working the same naturalist vein since 1901.

It was not the rawness and crudity celebrated by Carl Sandburg that made Chicago the only provincial center of the new movement; neither was it as others suggested her proximity to the life-giving, untrammeled villages and prairies. Omaha could have provided both these qualifications for literary creation. The new Chicago writers often came *from* the villages, but they came *to* a rich city, well endowed with nineteenth-century culture and also familiar with nineteenth-century dissent. Neither the sleepy back-

[9] Garland: *A Daughter of the Middle Border* (New York, 1921), p. 35.

waters nor the great metropolis alone provided the crucial experience, but the shock of moving from one to the other.

The Chicago writers of the rising generation no longer had to strive to bring conventional culture to the West. It was present, it had already been both established and questioned; they could learn from it and then, quite naturally, smash it.

Everywhere in the country in 1912 young people were getting restless. This was happening in small towns like Davenport, Iowa; in pleasure-loving and corrupt St. Louis; even in sleepy, complacent Philadelphia. The restlessness usually arose from a contact between new ideas and traditional, even obsolete environment. Usually the new ideas came in the form of books, such strange books sometimes that they could only be half-understood. At a certain stage in their restlessness, not only for expression but for education, the young people had to go to the few places, Chicago among them, where traditional culture was taken for granted and subjected to criticism. Most of the country still needed tradition too much to tamper with it.

VII

The New Augustan Age

Barrett Wendell, watching the classic three-cornered presidential race of 1912, was comforted by the thought that all three candidates, Taft, Roosevelt, and Wilson, were gentlemen and even acquaintances of his.[1] Lacking this kind of reassurance, most Americans found the turbulent campaign immensely exciting. Exciting, rather than deeply disturbing; the fundamental principles were not at stake. Progress was hardly the issue between Roosevelt and Wilson, and even Taft could lay some solid claims to progressive achievement. Neither, for those who cared about it, was culture in question; the three candidates neatly represented the three major ivy-league colleges. For many voters, the issues of personal morality loomed large; they could form their judgment with all the intense partisan excitement of people who are arguing inside a secure common set of standards.

As it had for more than a decade, popular interest at first centered on Theodore Roosevelt. Many sensed that his formidable bid for a comeback was a mistake. If so, and if it was to result in a humiliating failure, it was a tragic mistake. Ever since his Rough Rider days, Roosevelt had been more than a successful politician, he had been a compelling symbol of the country's regeneration. After thirty years of frock-coated pomposity and backstairs shabbiness, the presidency itself had furnished the model for right-thinking American youth. Roosevelt the rough-rider or bear-hunter, Roosevelt the civic reformer or trust-buster, Roosevelt the indulgent father, fond of a pillow fight but serious about essentials,

[1] M. A. de W. Howe: *Barrett Wendell and His Letters* (Boston, 1924), p. 252.

reflected exactly the country's image of itself, combining the old virtues with the new, breezy, twentieth-century methods.

Even when we try to go back of this picture, Roosevelt at first seems simple, his message the old moralities with pepper added. Labor and capital, the coal Barons and the Los Angeles *Times* bombers, Russia and Japan, Panama and Santo Domingo, Dickens and Henry James were all to be judged on the basis of simple rules of conduct. Conduct and not class; Roosevelt, an aristocrat through and through, repudiated any hint that people were to be judged as capitalists or workers rather than as moral individuals. With Lincoln Steffens he argued in long letters that good and evil, not the system, determined the existence of corruption and reform. In his famous warning about the muckrakers he expressed his concern that people might, by concentrating on evil, forgot about good, and it was a warning he often repeated.

Because Roosevelt stood so confidently outside class, because he insisted on being a friend of cowboys and bankers—and also because it was 1912—he could speak about class leadership in a way that would be regarded as political suicide by any politician today. About his new party of radical reform he said in 1912:

> I mostly earnestly hope that in this movement for social and industrial justice and betterment the lead may be taken by those among us to whom fate has been kind, who have themselves nothing material to gain from the movement, and not by those who are sullen with a sense of personal wrong.[2]

So far, Roosevelt can be defined, in the terms we have been using, as a member of the majority, optimistic wing of the custodians of culture. Actually he was this but more. There was much that was unpredictable, intuitive, in Roosevelt's own term "feminine" in his actions. His morality could be colored not only by ambition and bad temper, but by a kind of ruthless realism that was rare in

[2] Roosevelt: "Two Phases of the Chicago Convention," *Outlook*, July 20, 1912, p. 630.

the Progressive Era. This shows most clearly in his foreign policy, a mixture of bluster, overconfidence, and shrewd realization that the United States lived in a world of wolves. His decision to moralize about the trusts rather than destroy them arose partly from defeat, partly from his realization that the productive power of big industry had become indispensable. This kind of "realism" was the element in Roosevelt's thought that delighted the younger, tougher progressive intellectuals who were beginning to be impatient with moralism.

Sometimes Roosevelt seemed to be a little ahead of the Progressive Era, at other times he seemed to recall an earlier day. When he talked about the things that meant most to him, his children and the perils they must meet, he seemed occasionally to draw on a set of assumptions that went back of the optimism of the Progressive Era, perhaps remotely to the Calvinism of his Dutch origins. Unlike nearly all his political contemporaries, Roosevelt reveals more depth as one knows him better: he would almost have to, the first impression makes him seem at times so shallow.

In his literary doctrines, Roosevelt, an Academician and full-fledged Man of Letters, again mixed the conventional standards with originality. One of the most confident literary critics of his period, he was by no means the least tolerant or the least shrewd. Like many of the more "Western," red-blooded critics, he condemned the expatriate James. He also deplored the immoral side of Tolstoi, and overvalued many of the simpler novelists of reform. Yet he ranged much further than most Men of Letters, into foreign literature, philosophy, and history for instance. Edith Wharton, no progressive optimist, was his warm friend. When he read Edwin Arlington Robinson's pessimistic poems, he found them excellent and trusted his own judgment. Since the United States had no pensions specifically for poets, Roosevelt could not act exactly like an enlightened king, but he did give the unknown poet a customs-house job. He explained to Robinson, with characteristic charm, that he did not really expect him to be a good customs-house worker. Then he reviewed the poems for *The Outlook:*

> I am not sure that I understand "Luke Havergal," but I am entirely sure that I like it.[3]

In reading, as in everything, Roosevelt told the people always to remember their moral principles; his own were so secure that he could sometimes forget them and enjoy himself. Still more important, he was no literary snob. We should be proud, he pointed out in his autobiography, not of the narrowness of our taste but of its diversity. Yet we need not try to like everything, and should not worry too much about being called Philistine:

> I still read a number of Scott's novels over and over again, whereas if I finish anything by Miss Austen I have a feeling that duty performed is a rainbow to the soul. But other book-lovers who are very close kin to me, and whose taste I know to be better than mine, read Miss Austen all the time. . . .[4]

In 1910–12 Roosevelt, out of power and bored, fascinated with his own latest version of the progressive vision, started enunciating a sweeping program, including a barrage of the usual progressive reforms: direct legislation, a child-labor law, an eight-hour-day law. Beyond these familiar though controversial proposals, some thought they found more original implications in the new Roosevelt program. There was to be "far more active governmental interference with social and economic conditions," and yet big industry was to be mastered and used, rather than broken up. Some of the dissenting young intellectuals of the day thought they had found in the Bull Moose Party an escape from standard moralistic progressivism rather than a continuation of it. Some historians looking back at the movement have seen it as a beginning rather than an end, a beginning of something like the alliance of nationalism and welfare capitalism that emerged in the twenties. What Roosevelt really meant we will never know. Most Roosevelt voters probably voted for a familiar leader and a largely familiar set of planks.

[3] Roosevelt: "The Children of the Night," *Outlook*, August 12, 1905, p. 913. The fullest account of Roosevelt's discovery of Robinson is in Hermann Hagedorn: Edwin Arlington Robinson (New York, 1938), pp. 209–23.
[4] Theodore Roosevelt: *Autobiography* (New York, 1913), p. 364.

They voted also against theft; specifically, Taft's theft of Republican delegates.

To most of the custodians of culture, the issue was equally clear. Roosevelt was one of them, and he had violated his duty as such. The recall of judicial decisions (a slightly misleading phrase for what Roosevelt supported) was dangerous demagogy. At times Roosevelt had sounded as if he was doubtful about the sanctity of private property. Above all, he had attacked an old friend, perhaps forgotten promises, and used violent language. George Harvey's magazines, still supporting Wilson despite Harvey and Wilson's falling-out, were calling Roosevelt a criminal madman. President Eliot, regretfully, found him headstrong and impulsive, and thought the times called for a man who could preside over the necessary social changes with wisdom and prudence. Old friends of Roosevelt's, according to Owen Wister, regretfully decided they could never again have him in their houses. The *Dial* found the emotionalism of the Bull Moose convention, the fist fights and singing and vituperation, part of a general decline of Anglo-Saxon sanity and law, and remarked prophetically that "Whoever seeks to weaken that restraining shell has small appreciation of the forces that may be unloosed if it once breaks." The *Nation* went further, suggesting that the campaign's political extremism might be related to current mysterious outbreaks of irrationalism in philosophy and art. To "multitudes," the *Nation* believed, Roosevelt's infringements of the standard code of personal honor would "seem a fall like Lucifer's, that other son of the morning." [5]

Most people evidently did not consider either the sin or the punishment quite as final as this analogy suggested. In 1913, with Wilson president, Roosevelt was voted the greatest American in a contest sponsored by the *American Magazine*, doubling the vote of the nearest contender.[6] Yet the downfall did have its tragic ele-

[5] For comment on Eliot's choice, see *Independent*, October 3, 1912, pp. 801–2. For other attitudes toward Roosevelt: Wister: *Roosevelt, the Story of a Friendship*, p. 304; *Dial*, July 1, 1912, pp. 5–7; *Nation*, June 13, 1912, p. 580; February 29, 1912, p. 202.

[6] *American Magazine*, LXXVIII (1914), 63.

ment. It destroyed some of Roosevelt's symbolic power, and it destroyed whatever chance he may have had of modernizing progressivism. To some extent Roosevelt had destroyed his own personality; after his mistake of 1912 his egotism and bitterness increased; his realism and humor grew less. With Roosevelt's influence waning, the leadership of progressivism and of the whole nation, to an unusual extent its cultural as well as its political leadership, was turned over to Woodrow Wilson. For Wilson, and probably for any one man, the burden was too great.

❧

Woodrow Wilson, who for the next few years personified for many Americans their whole civilization, like that civilization drew his ideas from the nineteenth century. A man who did not change easily, he had adapted these ideas to twentieth-century conditions less than some of his contemporaries, and less than it seemed. To many who heard him in the summer of 1912, however, he seemed a perfect symbol of the twentieth-century future they expected, a blend, that is, of sound morals, faith in democratic progress, and traditional culture.

Brought up a Southerner and a Presbyterian, Wilson was not narrowly limited by either of these elements in his heritage. His father had come from the North. His clerical ancestors on both sides were men of firm piety, but not rigid dogma. His uncle had been dismissed from a seminary for his efforts to reconcile Darwinism and Christianity. Wilson was able to combine the fairly easy doctrines of nineteenth-century Christianity and the inner certainty of the old religion. This had its advantages and its drawbacks. In a crisis he could find, within, the sustaining certainty that he was a humble instrument of God's will. Since this was the source of his confidence, to doubt a decision once taken was to doubt all that made life possible.

At Princeton as an undergraduate in the seventies, Wilson had found the nineteenth-, almost the eighteenth-century verities untouched. The college lay under the shadow of James McCosh, who had been a principal exponent in America of the Scottish common-sense philosophy. In college Wilson learned the maxims of the old political economy, which he never entirely abandoned.

At Johns Hopkins in the eighties and nineties, Wilson encountered a series of new ideas, all of them exciting but none of them incompatible with his early training. As a believer in Gladstonian reform, he assimilated easily enough the mildly reformist economics of Richard T. Ely, his former fellow student. As a Southerner he was quite willing to cut New England down to size, and welcomed the frontier theory of his near-contemporary at Hopkins, Frederick Jackson Turner. In the famous historical seminar of H. B. Adams, Wilson encountered the current Germanic zeal for tracing the ancient origins of existing forms. This fitted in with a conservative, realistic bent in his own thought. An admirer of Burke, Wilson in this period seemed to be developing a realistic rather than a speculative or contemplative attitude toward political institutions. Of all the Victorian innovators he most admired Walter Bagehot, who seemed to describe British government as it had actually evolved, and not in terms of legal abstractions.

Princeton and Hopkins furnished his basic intellectual equipment, and it is doubtful whether he ever found it seriously unsatisfactory. In the eighties he applied it with zeal and success. Later it became easy to forget that Wilson had once been an innovator. In 1885 he pointed out that the country was really governed by congressional committees rather than by the system outlined in the *Federalist Papers*. In his early articles he urged, much as certain young men were to urge thirty years later, that the United States needed to give some attention to administration and method as well as to political principle. This was not, of course, because political principle was unimportant, but because our political principles were so firmly established.

These were the limits of Wilson's unorthodoxy, and this was enough to make him, in the eighties, part of a large movement for realistic reconsideration of political thought. From this point on the innovating note in his writings declined. One can see the change most clearly in his style: the crisp and witty manner of his earliest writings has little in common with the lofty idealism, sometimes prophetic, sometimes thin, of his later speeches.

In his literary essays, of which he was particularly proud, there is no shade of departure from the conventional tone. Literature to Wilson was a refuge and an inspiration, a repository of the ancient verities rather than a subject for serious and critical study like politics. Wilson took and read the *Nation* and the *Edinburgh Review*, thought *Lorna Doone* a major classic, and liked Matthew Arnold's poems better than his criticism. In his own narrow terms, he loved literature intensely; his companion for an ocean voyage was the *Oxford Book of English Verse*; suffering from a breakdown, he made for Wordsworth's lake country to restore his soul. As an educator, he became a fervent, sincere champion of conventional literary culture against scientific innovation and popular impatience.

> If this free people to which we belong is to keep its fine spirit, . . . it must continue to drink deep and often from the old wells of English undefiled. . . . The great spirits of the past must command us in the tasks of the future.[7]

The young Wilson, ambitious and intelligent, innovating but sound, serious but not oversubtle, was made for success. In his thirties he was the perfect young professor, a fervent football rooter, a fairly prolific writer, a ready and innocent after-dinner wit, and always a gifted evangelist. In his forties he was president of one of the great and old universities, a member of the Academy of Arts and Letters, one of the custodians of culture barely below the most distinguished circle.

In Wilson's Princeton career we can hardly help seeing patterns relevant to what we know happened later: first universal, fervent enthusiasm and sweeping success, then bloody deadlock. It

[7] Wilson: *Mere Literature* (Boston, 1896), p. 26.

is impossible, and no part of our purpose, to probe his mysterious personality very deeply. Even he knew and said of himself that the well-known cold and controlled exterior was deceptive. Somewhere inside was a contradiction, on the one hand the Calvinist's humble, ruthless determination and on the other an inordinate need to be loved. Wilson knew that he was "deeply covetous of friendship and close affection" and that he had continually to guard against a painful overflow of emotion.[8] By 1910, some of his Princeton friends had turned against him, though others still gave him their devoted allegiance. As often later, he felt betrayed.

It is not surprising that Wilson attracted the attention, beyond Princeton, of leading liberal conservatives, people who wanted to bring a fine, cultivated man into politics and at the same time spike the guns of Bryanism. Everybody knew that Wilson had vigorously opposed Populism and upheld the open shop. At the same time he had fought for innovation and against special privilege at Princeton.

When Wilson in politics turned out to be much more of a progressive than his promoters had expected, no betrayal of principles was involved. He found, on reflection, that the initiative and referendum really restored, instead of destroying, representative institutions. To achieve free competition, trusts would have to be disciplined more, labor unions somewhat less, than he had once believed. When one understood the politics better, it became clear that Bryan had always been a brave—Wilson never said a completely sound—toiler in the progressive vineyard. All these were minor changes: on his 1911 western tour Wilson was still insisting that we must never judge progress by material standards, that her ideals had made America great.

By 1912 Wilson had become a major champion of progress who could not possibly be feared by any believer in ideals or culture. In the presidential campaign, while Roosevelt was violent, Wilson was impeccably polite to both his opponents. While Roosevelt

[8] Ray Stannard Baker: *Woodrow Wilson, Life and Letters,* III (Garden City, New York, 1931), pp. 157, 160.

called for recognition and regulation of big business, Wilson stuck to the much more traditional objective of restoring competition. The fundamental objective of government was not efficiency, as the younger Bull Moosers were implying, but liberty, the traditional liberty of the small man, "the man on the make." Measures like a lower tariff, publicity for corporate actions, and the right kind of regulation would usher in a "peaceful revolution," a mighty liberation of creative energies. Yet, Wilson had recently assured his friends in Virginia, "No man that I know of and trust, no man that I will consent to consort with, is trying to change anything fundamental in America." [9]

Wilson's victory, a mere plurality in the three-cornered race, was a more significant personal triumph than it seemed. Even during the campaign, many who voted against him made it clear that they were suspicious of the Democratic Party rather than of Wilson personally. When he won, most people found some reason to be glad. The friends of Taft, and Taft himself, were delighted that Rooseveltian demagogy had been repudiated. The reformers who had followed the Bull Moose banner, except for the passionate Roosevelt partisans, could accept Wilson as a promising second best.

Except for a few of the least optimistic variety, the custodians of culture were overjoyed. The *Dial* had been reassured even by the Wilson nomination: a short time ago, it pointed out, nobody would have thought it possible that a scholar could get that far in our short-sighted democracy. Walter Page wrote Wilson that his leadership would bring a new impetus not only to "sound economics" and "right social ideals," but even to "sincerity and human sympathy in literature." It was left to William Randolph Hearst to announce that the election meant a new Augustan age of democracy.[1]

[9] Speech of February 2, 1912 at Richmond, reprinted in *Congressional Record*, 62nd Congress, 2nd session, Vol. XLVIII, 3921.

[1] *Dial*, "The Scholar in Politics," July 16, 1912, pp. 35–7; Page to Wilson, July 3, 1913, facsimile in James Kerney: *The Political Education of Woodrow Wilson* (New York, 1926), facing p. 244; *San Francisco Examiner*, November 1, 1912, p. 28.

In 1912, and for a few years afterward, Wilson's victory seemed to many the final vindication of all the major components of the national faith. We can see now that this confidence was a mistake. The basic nineteenth-century coupling of moralism and progress had been a difficult engineering feat; traditional culture had never been properly welded to either. The early twentieth century accepted its triple credo too easily from the past; it did not undertake fundamentally necessary adaptations.

Already some rebels were pushing progress far beyond its conventional bounds, some were repudiating culture, a few were directly attacking the moral interpretation of the universe. Wilson and his generation, still in charge of the country, reassured by the progressive sunshine, were not really listening to the most difficult questions. Soon history was to repeat them in universal and devastating form.

PART TWO

Older Insurgents and Invaders (1890–1917)

I

Outsiders

This set of simple certainties, inherited from the nineteenth century and still strong in 1912, fell to pieces when it was seriously attacked. Obviously, its individual items survive in different form, and some Americans still hold to it all. Yet the unity, simplicity, and sureness with which Americans held to it in 1912 are long gone. This decline or partial disintegration of belief is usually associated with the postwar twenties. Actually, however, it was a long process, well under way before 1917, and then sharply accelerated by war. The rest of this book will examine the process of disintegration.

The process was not a simple one. The dominant ideas finally fell before direct attacks by foreign invaders and domestic rebels. But the direct attacks would never have succeeded if the dominant doctrines had been as strong as they looked. Actually they had never been a complete success. Put together in defense against the scientific materialism of the nineteenth century, the semiofficial American credo had never altogether lost its defensive tone. It had failed to solve some pressing intellectual problems. It did not command the support of all sections of the people. It had never managed to extirpate the major heresies of the late nineteenth century. Thus, when a new group of enemies appeared, they could take advantage of old cracks in the defenses. This section of the book will look back at the kinds of disaffection and heresy that originated in the nineteenth century and were still alive in 1912. The next section will describe the new and successful assault.

Some Americans, in 1912, were neither convinced defenders of the dominant ideas nor articulate insurgents against them. Some were uneasy doubters, who ordinarily gave lip service to the official credo, but had reservations about it, or about one of its three parts. This group of doubters is the hardest of all groups for the historian to deal with; its members were largely inarticulate, and when their ideas were expressed they formed no consistent pattern. Yet the existence of this partial or potential disaffection was important. We must try to penetrate the cheerful surface, and get what glimpses we can of underlying doubts.

To begin with, a number of Americans, citizens of the nation, were excluded from full citizenship in the civilization. They were, of course, expected to render allegiance to the ideals of morality, progress, and culture, but on a sort of probationary basis. Sooner or later, this emotional taxation without representation was likely to produce revolt. Some of the most vociferous champions of the dominant code were, in the years right before the war, doing it great disservice by narrowing its base.

As we have seen, many of the custodians of culture, including some of the best intentioned, continually identified the heritage of tradition with the Anglo-Saxon Protestant stock. Similarly, some champions of progress constantly sounded the trumpet to battle with the unprogressive immigrant: he must either be excluded, or driven from his political strongholds, or at the least drastically re-educated. The constant, often well-meaning discussion by both these groups of the question, can our civilization be spread to the less fortunate? must have sounded very different from outside the fold.

Still far more rigidly than the most recent immigrants, one of the oldest American stocks was largely excluded from active participation in progress, as it was from a major role in culture. Only a very few social workers, socialists, and New England mavericks were working to make the Negro a full citizen. Most believers in idealism and progress had concluded, with varying degrees of regret, that Negro equality was an impossible dream. It was to be a long time before the Negro himself was to be in a position for revolt, but his exclusion impaired the whole cheerful picture. Soon some young rebels were to notice this dangerous exception.

American universality had always had some tacit limits: its defenders had often had to close their eyes to some flaws. Many well-meaning believers in Anglo-Saxon leadership answered the question of exclusion in much the same way they answered all questions; by introducing an evolutionary dimension. In time the lesser breeds could be brought within the law. It might happen, though few realized it, that these lesser breeds might decide they did not want to be helped and led.

In the long run, either all had to become active, not passive participants in American civilization, or that civilization would have to abate its democratic claims. Democracy under partly hereditary guidance was a halfway house, apparently satisfactory for a while but untenable in the long run. Already some were demanding full equality for immigrant cultures; others were urging sharper exclusion. Just before the war, tension among races and nationalities sharply increased; no fact held more menace for the compromises underlying the dominant credo.

Aside from those who were wholly or partly excluded, a number of completely Anglo-Saxon and Protestant Americans withheld their full assent from the dominant ideology without repudiating it altogether. It will be simplest to discuss this partial dissent in terms of the three main tenets already outlined. Some Americans, mainly articulate intellectuals, rejected moralism. A larger group had its doubts about progress, and a still larger number was suspicious of culture.

Ever since the eighteenth century, one kind of American objection to progress had come from farmers. From Jefferson through Jackson to Bryan, the farmer had always played an ambiguous role, half democratic and progressive, half deeply conservative. His favorite spokesmen had demanded radical change and at the same time restoration of the ancient rural virtues.

In the early twentieth century, spokesmen of progressivism almost forced the farmer into a similarly ambiguous position. In political rhetoric he was a part of the progressive movement, marching beside the other good citizens to triumph over his old enemies, monopoly and usury. Often, at the same time, he was a representative of a kind of moral superiority, nearly destroyed by city bosses and tyrannical industrialists, badly needing restoration. Then again the farmer was sometimes portrayed as a hick—an ignorant, provincial objector to progress. None of these roles was entirely a fictitious creation.

In the late nineteenth century, the farmers' movements culminating in Populism had been a particularly explosive combination of radicalism and reaction. The early twentieth century was a period of comparative farm prosperity, and the Populist fury had abated; many farmers prided themselves on being up-to-date. Many, but not all; possibly not even most. The nonprogressive farmer is an elusive figure, but he is an important one.

Even in the prosperous, up-to-date states of the old Northwest, some farmers were skeptical about improvements in the farm way of life. The Country Life movement was, for much of the rural press, highfalutin foolishness. Scientific agriculture came from people who were not dirt farmers; good roads and school reform might end the dominance of the village and the traditional one-room school.

In the South and on the Northern great plains, the old centers of Populism, the old kind of mixed radicalism and reaction was more obviously alive. The *Non-Partisan Leader*, organ of the latest and angriest Northwestern movement of farm discontent, always cartooned Good in suspenders, carrying a pitchfork, Evil as a city slicker and sometimes a Jew. In the South, the teens were the heyday of the professional gallus-snapper, the nigger-hating, corporation-baiting friend of the plain people, who knew that too much education led straight to free love and racial equality.

The most important kind of objection to progress that came from rural sources in the years before the war had little to do with direct economic or social controversy. It was religious. Later, in the mid-twenties, when a well-financed Fundamentalist movement became a public sensation, many urban Americans wondered where it had come from. They did not realize that the old-time religion had never really surrendered. While evolution, liberalism, and the Social Gospel had been winning the seminaries and the city pulpits, millions had clung doggedly to old-fashioned evangelical Protestantism.

This faith, the dominant form of nineteenth-century American Christianity, was not necessarily inimical to all kinds of secular progress. Indeed, many nineteenth-century reform movements owed a great deal to evangelical beginnings. The majority faith was not Calvinism, it did not heavily emphasize human depravity and inability. It did, however, teach that human beings needed Divine Grace for salvation. Grace was freely offered to all who earnestly sought it. A true Christian, a saved man, was expected by many kinds of nineteenth-century Protestant thought to show his altered nature in his deeds. The work of Grace even pointed the way, for some, to a world free of drink and war and some other forms of evil. Thus it had long been possible to believe in the improvement of society without accepting either relativism or up-to-date liberal Christianity.

Since the late nineteenth century, however, the combination of old-fashioned Christianity and progressivism had been becoming increasingly uneasy. The main reason for this was the rise of Darwinism and the many kinds of thought, relativist and materialist, related to it. Urban, articulate Protestant leaders had met this challenge by developing a radically evolutionized and socialized form of Christianity. This was the Social Gospel, which seemed to many in our period both triumphant and durable.

A great many, perhaps most, Americans, however, were neither wholehearted converts to this new kind of religion nor passionate defenders of the old. Probably most combined, somehow, a belief in the supreme importance of the individual's relation to God and a belief in the gradual, universal improvement of society by human effort. In the prewar period, it was thus possible for William Jennings Bryan, always a conservative Christian, to agree on many concrete and immediate matters with Clarence Darrow. A progressivism which included both Bryan and Darrow and also John Dewey and Woodrow Wilson was obviously a somewhat volatile compound.

Two kinds of religious conservatives were already voicing their doubts about the tendencies of modern progressive society. The first and milder of these expressed itself in a series of spectacular revivals. Since about 1905, a number of gifted preachers had been attacking the devil where he obviously lived, in the great cities. These revivalists were not much concerned, either as friends or enemies, with most contemporary movements for social betterment, though they supported attacks on liquor and prostitution. Their message, however, consistently stressed the importance of sticking to old ways and old beliefs.

Though several of these revivalists achieved notoriety, none was a complete success until Billy Sunday arrived on the urban scene in 1912, bringing a new combination of old doctrine and up-to-date methods. Sunday was not then, as he later became, a rigid reactionary in social and economic matters. He could throw into his sermons a denunciation of child labor or slum profiteering. Yet his main purpose, like that of his immediate predecessors, was to rebuke those who were departing from traditional ways. Radicals already instinctively disliked him and had noticed that he turned up in strike-torn towns. Sunday made it quite clear that God preferred those who stuck to the old customs:

> Mary was one of those sort of uneeda-biscuit, peanut-butter, gelatin, and pimento sort of women. Martha was a beefsteak, baked-potato, applesauce with lemon and nutmeg, coffee and whipped cream, apple pie and cheese sort of woman.[1]

[1] *Literary Digest*, April 24, 1914, pp. 959–60.

God was angry, one could gather from Sunday's sermons, not with man in general but with the minority of boozers, backsliders, and innovators. Hope for triumph against these and all other forms of evil lay only in the Word. Whatever departed from the Book or underminded its authority weakened this hope. Sunday tolerated no traffic with the compromises of nineteenth-century liberalism. If a minister taught and believed evolution, he was a stinking skunk, a hypocrite, and a liar.

In doctrine basically a conservative, Sunday was in language a conscious and effective revolutionary. Carl Sandburg, who as a socialist and freethinker attacked Sunday in the *Masses*, did not realize that in terms of style Sunday was on his own road and far ahead. Mencken, who agreed with Sunday at least in his attitude toward the polite "uplift," admitted that Sunday impressed him.

Since the days of D. L. Moody, most city evangelists had used conventional literary language. In the concrete terms of mourner's-bench statistics, this had not paid off. Sunday, as he put it, had once himself used "sentences so long they'd make a Greek professor's jaw squeak for a week after he said one of them." Now he had learned: "I loaded my Gospel gun with rough-on-rats, ipecac, dynamite, and barbed wire." Common speech, slang, earthy figures were Sunday's stock-in-trade, and at times he threw in a liberal dose of conscious virility:

> I want to see the color of some buck's hair that can dance with my wife! I'm going to monopolize that hugging myself.[2]

Theodore Roosevelt and Woodrow Wilson both approved Sunday's labors and so, gingerly, did most of the city churches that profited from his campaign. But the *Nation*, Harvard, and Princeton knew an enemy of culture when they saw one. The devil, Sunday complacently observed, didn't like his methods either.

A second large minority of American Christians considered Sunday, most other recent revivalists, and the official leaders of evangelical Protestantism all pussyfooters and renegades. They did not

[2] Ibid.

preach pervasive and uneradicable Original Sin in clear enough terms; they laid too little stress on commitment to such central doctrines as the Virgin Birth. Fundamentalists, in the Progressive Era, felt themselves to be surrounded by enemies of a bewildering variety: diabolically clever professors, proud scientists, dissolute society people. Worst of all were the churches of their fathers, now dominated by compromisers, pharisees, and efficiency experts.

Fundamentalists, like Populists, looked back to a better and always an agrarian day. Sometimes they found hope in the submerged people; as William Bell Riley, the Minneapolis preacher, put it, "The plain farmer is not so superficial in his thinking that you can palm off on him a spurious gospel by calling it novelty." [3] Most of the time, however, Fundamentalists in the Progressive Era were pessimistic about the chances of saving their contemporaries. Discouraged, they were turning from one of their old methods, revivalism, to another, watching the signs of the times and seeing in them the swift approach of doom.

The great error of recent Protestantism, some of them were convinced, had long preceded the rise of extreme modernism and Social Christianity. This fundamental mistake was the post-millennial interpretation of Bible prophecy. This doctrine, predicting that Christ would come again only after a thousand-year reign of peace and justice, lay at the root of all false hopes for worldly progress. The true doctrine was the opposite one: pre-millennialism. Christ would come at any moment, and he would come in blood to the judgment, which would precede the thousand years of peace. The righteous minority would then be given the chance, from Heaven, to watch the revilers and backsliders suffer. This was the only prospect that put Fundamentalists, in the Progressive Era, in a relatively cheerful frame of mind.

Unnoticed by their progressive fellow citizens, Fundamentalists were actively consoling each other. They commanded a number of

[3] William Bell Riley: *The Crisis of the Church* (New York, 1914), p. 165. This quotation, and much of my interpretation of Fundamentalism, I owe to Carroll E. Harrington (see Bibliographical Note).

centers of power, some in small towns and small colleges, some, like the Moody Bible Institute of Chicago, located in cities swollen with rural migrants. In Los Angeles, Amzi R. Dixon was editing *The Fundamentals*, a ponderous compilation of orthodox testimony for which a circulation of three million was claimed by 1912. The Fundamentalist presses were turning out a flood of literature, read only by the faithful. Able leaders, from 1914 on, were summoning Prophetic Conferences. All that was lacking for a great counteroffensive, another major struggle for the nation's soul, was a little more money and organization and a lot more confidence in the chances of success. Confidence was soon to be revived by the coming of world war. To Fundamentalists, there could be no clearer demonstration of the weakness and vanity of progressive civilization.[4]

Fundamentalists and other agrarian conservatives objected to progress, and also to the current definition of culture. An opposite group of partial dissenters fully accepted progress, but found both culture and moralism a little musty and obsolete. This group believed that what was measurable, immediate, and concrete was what was important. To distinguish these from pragmatists, since they did not make their opinion into philosophical argument, we will call them practicalists.

Practicalists, with roots deep in the hard-working American past, were of many kinds. Some of them differed only in emphasis from believers in the dominant form of moralism: practical idealism. Major leaders like Theodore Roosevelt continually insisted that we

[4] Curiously enough, some of the Fundamentalist complaints against the dominant progressive civilization were echoed by an extreme opposite group, the rebellious Young Intellectuals. The latter, as we will see in Part III, similarly objected to the emotionally unsatisfying smoothness and uniformity of the dominant kind of progressivism. In the period before 1917, many of the new writers were mystics. Some of them derived their mysticism from fashionable philosophic sources but others, like Vachel Lindsay and Sherwood Anderson, were strongly influenced by traditional and rural religion.

must approach our ideals by practical steps. For practicalists, the steps were all that mattered. The goals hardly existed, and talk about them was a waste of time.

Practicalists could be found in all sections of American life. One of the most rigid, for instance, was Samuel Gompers, entrenched in the leadership of organized labor. For a generation he had been telling labor to concentrate on immediate aims and forget schemes to change society. The enemies of labor, to Gompers, were less dangerous than its friends: untrustworthy reformers, patronizing social workers, well-meaning ministers, doctrinaire socialists, and particularly "intellectuals," a word Gompers used before it became generally current.

Gompers often called his kind of program "business unionism," and businessmen took it for granted that they themselves were supremely practical. Yet in this period, business practicalism was not really opposed to the dominant idealistic beliefs. We are used to the recent image of the businessman, the disgruntled and defensive protester against the New Deal and its successors. In 1912, businessmen seldom thought of themselves as an oppressed group, and in fact for many purposes were not a group at all. Individual businessmen thought of themselves as good citizens, Americans, and of course progressives. By far the majority of the reforms of the period were easy for them to approve. Only a small group was really frightened even of socialism. On November 30, 1912, right after the Socialists' most successful election campaign, the *Commercial and Financial Chronicle*, most conservative of bussinessmen's organs, calmly discussed "The Contributions of Socialism";

> Socialism is no longer to be feared, and may be calmly reviewed, as we ask what permanent contribution it has made, or is making, to the economic and social world. . . .[5]

Determined believers in progress, businessmen in this period talked continually about idealism, and sounded less specious than

[5] "The Contributions of Socialism," *Commercial and Financial Chronicle*, November 30, 1912, p. 1443.

they were sometimes to sound in the postwar Babbitt heyday. Altruism, they honestly thought, was their special province. The Rotary Club, founded in 1905 and burgeoning after 1912, was especially the choice of small and small-town business, and no group talked the language of uplift more fervently:

> Out of the mire and decay of centuries upon centuries of human experience there is growing a better understanding of the law of the survival of the fittest. We now recognize divinity working through this law. . . .
>
> There may be those who think these sentiments too lofty for the age in which we live, as suggesting the millennium in business or as bordering on transcendentalism. If there are any such, I take issue with them. These sentiments are coming to be 20th century business.[6]

A little further up the ladder of size and profit was the movement referred to as the New Business. This movement, already widespread and destined to achieve great power in the twenties, was in part an effort to cut down destructive competition, in part an answer to radical and trust-buster criticism, in part (before 1917) an extension to business of the period's optimistic mood. Adherents of the New Business preached trade associations, humane personnel policies, and sometimes scientific management. By 1914 Ida M. Tarbell, once the exposer of Standard Oil, was convinced that American business had discovered the Golden Rule.[7]

Since the end of the business crisis of 1907–8, businessmen were in an increasingly cheerful mood. Some of them worried at times about the closed shop and the new possibilities of heavier taxation. Ordinarily, however, progress meant something they could accept: movement of the world toward republican government and efficient, moderately regulated industry. In a few years, war, regi-

[6] Stewart C. McFarland, "Rotarianism, A Flower of the New Consciousness," *Rotarian*, III (1913), 59–60.

[7] Tarbell: "The Golden Rule in Business," *American Magazine*, LXXVIII (1914), series starting 26–9.

mentation, and revolution abroad were to put businessmen seriously on the defensive, and their spokesmen were to call for an end of some kinds of idealism, a turn toward a more sharply defined kind of practicality.

❦

The purest variety of practicalism extant in the prewar period came partly from business circles, but spread through wide and diverse parts of society. This was the efficiency movement, centering in Scientific Management. Impatience with lofty sentiment, belief in methods rather than defined goals sometimes led to outright rejection of traditional leaders and values. The efficiency movement may be defined as an unsuccessful effort to add the word "efficiency" to the national watchwords, to make room for it by throwing out "culture," and to put a little less emphasis on "morality."

The Scientific Management movement proper, which dated from the eighties but reached its peak under the leadership of Frederick W. Taylor after 1911, prided itself on being a movement of engineers, not theorists. Nevertheless, it rested on several sweeping theoretical assumptions. These were first, that in both physical science and human affairs there is one right answer to everything; second, that right means efficient and efficient means, in human as in mechanical affairs, whatever reaches a maximum of production with a minimum of energy. Taylor himself, in the years when he was still able to dominate the movement, brought to it an emotional slant which seemed to be related to the Protestant past. He really hated laziness and waste, was quite sure that work was good for people, and had a deeply ingrained belief in the authority of the superior man.

Efficiency, which became a shorthand word for the sum of all good things, could be achieved only by strong central planning, and strong central planning must not be thwarted. A Taylorite psychologist put it frankly in a section of a textbook headed "Punishment Can Never Be Entirely Abolished." In the long run, the workers would realize that punishment, since it was entirely disinterested and scientific, was in their interests.[8]

Efficiency could, before its spokesmen became cautious, speak very frankly about its conception of human raw material:

> . . . One of the very first requirements for a man who is fit to handle pig iron as a regular occupation is that he shall be so stupid and phlegmatic that he more nearly resembles the ox than any other type.[9]

The central planner, studying such a man's movements with a stop watch (the tool and hallmark of the early movement), could find exactly the best way for him to do a simple repetitive task. Then he must never be allowed to do anything else.

Between 1880 and 1910 the Scientific Management movement had won converts among engineers, and Taylor, his disciples, and his numerous rivals had been hired to put the system into effect in a number of plants. How far the actual operation of these plants resembled the paper principles it is hard to say. In part Scientific Management embodied principles that were already highly developed in America such as the standardization of parts or the careful improvement of simple processes.

In 1910 Louis D. Brandeis, the People's Lawyer, used the methods of Scientific Management to prove that the railroads could pay higher wages without an increase in freight rates. This brought the movement's principles before the public, and particularly the progressive public, in a new context. Before this, Scientific Management, generally opposed by trade unions, had seemed to many progressives a combination of speed-up and snooping. Now it began to look like a possible road to Utopia, a means of combining higher production, higher wages, and universal harmony. Scientific Management became a fad; its methods were advocated for

[8] L. M. Gilbreth: *The Psychology of Management* (New York, 1914), p. 308.

[9] Frederick W. Taylor: *Scientific Management* (A collection of his basic writing, New York, 1947), p. 59.

homes, schools, churches, and colleges. Psychologists studied and spread them. More than one university created a Department of Efficiency.

Like every other widespread doctrine of the period, Scientific Management was often stated in moral terms. A writer in the *Outlook* in 1912 called the movement a modern expression of Divine Law, a new combination of the Golden Rule and evolution. It "gives us a definite standard—that of a money reward—for testing the degree of obedience to this law." An article in *100%, the Practical Magazine of Efficient Management* went a step further in 1917, arguing that "The Perfect Man of Nazareth" embodied in life and character "One Hundred Per Cent Efficiency." Yet moralism and efficiency did not lie altogether easily in the same bed. When efficiency, regardless of aim, became itself a standard for all action, traditional ideas of morality disappeared. Harrington Emerson, an early rival of Taylor, came right out with it:

> Efficiency is not to be judged from preconceived standards of honesty, or morality, but honesty, morality, are perhaps to be reconsidered and revised by the help of the fundamentals of efficiency.[1]

This kind of statement, fairly common in the period and often sandwiched between perfectly conventional moralisms, was thoroughly revolutionary in terms of the whole Western tradition.

Only occasionally challenging moralism, the efficiency movement combined easily with progress, the second most important article of the dominant creed. Progressive leaders often made efficiency one of their major demands: the nation's cities and its natural resources, for instance, needed better management.

Yet the standard progressivism of 1912, so full of moral idealism, was not really compatible with any strict version of the efficiency movement. The progressives who were most impressed with Scien-

[1] *Outlook*, "Scientific Management and the Moral Law," November 18, 1911, pp. 659–63; 100%, January 17, 1917, p. 128; Harrington Emerson: *Efficiency as a Basis for Operation and Wages* (New York, 1909), p. 157.

tific Management were those young men who were in revolt against the dominant kind of moralistic and individualistic progressivism. To some of the young intellectuals of the *New Republic* group, for instance, H. G. Wells, Thorstein Veblen, the more radical of the social scientists, and the Taylorites all seemed to point in much the same direction. All these seemed to say that the thing to do was to abandon obsolete moral scruples, to give free scope to the engineers, and thus to move forward to a society dominated by dashing, unsentimental young experts.

Scientific Management had little patience with traditional culture, the weakest element in the ruling trinity. Though Taylorism greatly influenced a number of colleges, it seemed continually to clash with academic tradition. The Harvard School of Business Administration had at first taken Taylorism as one of its guiding sets of principles, and in 1907 Taylor was a member of the visiting committee for engineering at Harvard. He was appalled to find "that an institution of such national importance as Harvard should be managed on lines which are almost a century old. . . ." [2]

In 1910 Morris L. Cooke published a Taylorite study of eight colleges and universities. He found many conditions that appalled him: professors worked too long without enough intensity, performed some functions that subordinates could do better and (even this early) served on too many committees. The output of teaching was not efficiently measured and research was done with only a minimum of central control. At a famous Dartmouth conference in 1912 academic efficiency was argued back and forth by management experts and professors and then in the press. In 1915 the University of Wisconsin, damned by some critics as utilitarian, was investigated and found old-fashioned and inefficient by William Harvey Allen, the most dogmatic and philistine of all the efficiency-mongers.[3]

Naturally by this time the custodians of culture were up in arms.

[2] F. B. Copley: *Frederick W. Taylor* (2 Vols., New York, 1923), II, 267.

[3] *Addresses and Discussions at the Conference on Scientific Management* (Hanover, 1912); William H. Allen: *Efficient Democracy* (Chicago, 1907); Curti and Carstensen: *University of Wisconsin,* pp. 272–3.

To the *Atlantic* the Dartmouth conference meant "the setting of the dollar-mark over against things of the intellect, or of the spirit." The *Nation* was indignant that Harvard professors had been asked for time studies of their private research and predicted, entirely accurately, that what was now voluntary might some day, in some places, become compulsory. It had already commented on Scientific Management in religion by means of a sample time sheet for a young minister:

> 9:30 to 10:27, visited the widow and the fatherless.
> 10:27 to 11:03, bound up three brokenhearted.[4]

The Scientific Management movement is the supreme embodiment in the period of the practicalist spirit. Its actual achievements in areas from bricklaying to steel production, its hate of waste and laziness, and its astringent scoffing at the period's polite verities gave it great power. Practical means to humane ends had been central in the country's tradition since Franklin. The gospel of efficiency in its most blatant form abolished the ends and became both dangerous and self-contradictory. Exciting to many in the Progressive Era, it was yet held at bay by the powerful forces of moralism and culture.

❦

Practicalism of a less doctrinaire kind spread far beyond the limits of any class or movement. Its favorite target was traditional education. The *Saturday Evening Post,* the most popular general periodical, led the pack, closely followed by Page's bustling *World's Work.* The *Post,* under the direct and detailed supervision of George Horace Lorimer already insisted that it spoke for the plain, hardheaded citizen and particularly the businessman. As yet it spoke also for a kind of progressivism. The trusts were regressive and the

[4] Henry Davis Bushell: "Educational Efficiency," *Atlantic Monthly,* CVII (1911), 501; *Nation,* January 16, 1913, pp. 49–50; October 31, 1912, pp. 402–3.

lawyers were stuffy; fuddy-duddy constitutional interpretation was holding up the people's will; questions of railroad rates or even of local public ownership should be decided on the basis of dollars and cents, not ideas. Turning to a really congenial subject, the *Post* insistently asked how long "Our Medieval High Schools" would be dominated by the believers in that snobbish, useless, indefinable conception, culture. When would they start teaching men how to get jobs and women how to keep house? The fault in the long run lay with the colleges, especially some of them:

> We are much pleased to hear that out of a Harvard class in comparative literature, containing about a hundred students, not one could tell when Aristotle lived, though half a dozen guessed that the period was subsequent to 1840! Knowing when Aristotle lived—or anything else about him—is one of the least profitable uses to which lay human brains can be put. . . .

David Graham Phillips, a favorite *Post* writer, a best-selling member of the Indiana School of authors, and the author of the famous Hearst muckraking series on "The Treason of the Senate" complained that the colleges were encouraging "that most un-American thing called class and culture. . . ."

> There should be no such thing as a superior mind in a mighty country where the destiny of conquest has been planted in every heart, in every brain.[5]

A new kind of popular hero was beginning to symbolize the rejection of traditional culture and traditional idealism. In the *American Magazine*'s 1913 Great Americans poll, Theodore Roosevelt came in first, but the second place went to Thomas A. Edison, the simple, practical benefactor of humanity, who had recently denounced not only standard education but belief in the soul. Fourth place went to "Mr. Ordinary Citizen," and fifth to Henry Ford.

[5] *Saturday Evening Post*, March 9, 1912, p. 26; Phillips, quoted in Isaac F. Marcossen: *David Graham Phillips and His Times* (New York, 1932), pp. 288–9.

In the last name two kinds of disaffection from the dominant beliefs began to come togther. Ford represented at once agrarian nostalgia and up-to-date practicality. He was a farm youth who understood machines. Scoffed at by big business, hindered by city slickers and financiers, he had accomplished miracles by mother wit. Ford was admired by some of the Taylorizers, but had accomplished his miracles of efficiency on his own. Through large-scale production and mechanical ingenuity, he had brought the automobile within reach of the ordinary citizen. He had combined unprecedented high wages and rising profits. His famous 1914 announcement of the five-dollar minimum wage was hailed as a superb example of the kind of altruism that pays, a really practical kind of practical idealism.

Whatever its truth, this picture of Ford, the homespun and kindly genius, was already widespread. The press reported Ford's salty sayings, quoted him on peace and Prohibition, described his experiments in rehabilitating convicts. Ford, delighted readers already knew, would not give five cents for all the art and all the history in the world. He had once said he "would like to get all the college professors in the world, bar none, and put them out in that factory and see what they would do with it." [6] This bizarre suggestion could hardly have been intended in the interest of efficiency; it must have reflected some kind of resentment.

At this point it is necessary to remember that the alienations we are suggesting were potential, not actual. If all the foreign-born and all the Negroes had been entirely shut out of the dominant civilization; if large numbers of farmers, fundamentalists, businessmen, efficiency experts, and readers of the *Saturday Evening Post* had been seriously disaffected, the dominant credo would have been supported mainly by the membership of the National Academy.

[6] *Harpers*, LX (1914), 518.

Actually, few of these kinds of people repudiated directly even one of the three major items of belief, let alone all three. Not culture, but outworn, effete culture was denounced, not moralism, but rigid, reactionary preaching was opposed. One strength, as well as weakness, of the dominant credo was its vagueness. Henry Ford and Billy Sunday and Josiah Royce all considered themselves not only moralists, but idealists.

Yet disaffection and even resentment were not far below the surface. Recent studies have shown that the articulate leadership of business and politics was small; the circle of makers of moral opinion was smaller. Most people, cheerfully and willingly enough, followed the lead of the national spokesmen with only a few reservations.

Two kinds of reservations were made most often by people who had little access to brand-new ideas. First, nostalgic agrarians, and Fundamentalists in particular, were hostile to progress. Second, practicalists were skeptical about culture and sometimes moralism. These two complaints seemed to be opposite, yet sometimes they were applied together in criticism of the bland, cheerful civilization typified by the Howells dinner. The American credo of 1912 was not close enough to actuality, and it also failed to satisfy the darker, fiercer, more violent human emotions. Both these complaints had deep sources in the American past and both were continually reinforced by exciting, superbly stated ideas from abroad.

II

Questioners

Well before 1912 the dominant American credo had been partly rejected by some people on simple, instinctive, emotional grounds. It had also been subjected to criticism by a whole school of American philosophers and social scientists, all relativists of one kind or another who denied the validity and necessity of fixed moral standards. Most of these thinkers were less radical than they seemed. Few of them broke completely with the dominant assumptions of their period. Their questions, however, paved the way for the more devastating questions originating in Europe.

Though partly original, American relativism was related to the main movement of Western thought in its day. This movement was, in America and in Europe, a rejection on one ground or another of the mid-nineteenth-century cosmos, the familiar combination of adapted Christianity, science, industrialism, and middle-class mores. In England and America, the revolt was directed particularly against the world of Herbert Spencer, a world of progress *toward* moral perfection.

Three gigantic questions, familiar in one form or another for centuries, disturbed this nineteenth-century world. First, scientists asked whether the physical and biological laws on which Spencer's theories rested were true, and few practicing scientists ever thought all of them were. Second, philosophers continued to ask how limited human beings could know whether any world picture was true or not, and failed to find any permanently satisfying answer. Third, moralists, poets, and preachers asked whether human beings really wanted or liked to believe in an automatic, progressive, developing universe and concluded, to their own surprise and dismay, that the answer was no.

In Europe, all these questions were being asked with devastating effect. Before 1912, however, many kinds of recent European thought and literature were too alien to penetrate the American mind very deeply. Their day was shortly to come, and American criticism was preparing their way.

In the last decades of the nineteenth century, American thinkers, like others, had become impatient with the Victorian universe of regular, predictable evolution in the direction of rational order and freedom. Keeping the evolution, many of them had discarded the regularity. Instead of a single universal movement, particular adaptations to circumstances might be enough of an explanation of evolution. Similarly, it might be possible to judge human institutions and ideas in terms of the particular needs of a given environment, rather than in terms of universal processes or goals. The world, in short, might be fluid and plural, rather than orderly and single.

It remained a pretty cheerful place. Morality was no longer a fixed unchanging code, but something remarkably like the old code turned up in the particular findings of almost all these transitional thinkers. Progress was no longer a universal single movement, but wherever one looked things were getting better. People no longer needed the old fixities; they could do better without them (and few doubted, at bottom, that they knew what better meant). Repudiate, commanded a generation of relativist thinkers, the outworn notions of universal moral absolutes. When this is done, we will be able to advance toward truth, freedom, and justice.

Thus the relativists of the period were half in revolt against the assumptions of ordinary people, half engaged in restatement of these assumptions. Most people thought, with Roosevelt or Abbott, that the eternal moral principles were proved and demonstrated in the events of daily American life. Most of the relativist thinkers put it another way around: the events of daily life in modern times were a sufficient source of moral value.

Obviously the relativist path led further than this, and some young disciples of the older relativists were moving in dangerous directions. The dangerous directions, in terms of prevailing American assumptions and mores, were two: the direction of sweeping irrationalism and the direction of thoroughgoing and unmoral materialism. The older relativists were prevented from moving far in these directions not so much by their theories as by the world in which they lived.

❦

The greatest of the American relativists, and perhaps the central figure of American intellectual history in the early twentieth century, was William James, who had died in 1910. More than any relativist colleague, James was at home in Europe and a part of European thought, and we will have to look at him again from a European angle. Yet nobody could possibly be more uniquely American. Few surviving Americans were as deeply rooted in American thought of the early nineteenth century and much earlier as James, who remembered Emerson as a family friend and was himself the son of a major transcendentalist and post-Calvinist thinker. Yet few were more insistently modern, or welcomed more eagerly, even indiscriminately, the latest developments in philosophy and science. James moved in both the main directions we have indicated, toward skeptical practicality and even materialism, and also toward an acceptance of the promptings of intuition and faith. All these contradictions were held together by an optimism only possible in this place and time—a rare and genuine enthusiasm for variety, change, and freedom, a faith that this was the proper and healthy condition of man. Yet James's faith was not the easy and robust one which he slightly caricatured as the "religion of the healthy-minded"; like so many of his leading contemporaries he had known the terrors and anxieties of an early mental crisis, never quite forgotten.

With the approaching general denigration of James's whole generation he was sometimes to be consigned to the special hell of gentility. He was indeed enough a man of his time to dislike sexual looseness more than most kinds of rebellion, and he could make statements about culture and education that had a snobbish ring in ultrademocratic ears. Yet the general impression one gets from a reading of James today is one of charm and freshness, mixed perhaps with a slight nostalgia. This was the man who came nearest bringing together the old and the new; this was the man who best embodied all that men of good will expected from the twentieth century.

James, who grew up in a society of seekers after truth and was hit hard in his youth by the Darwinian bombshell, was never at heart either a natural scientist or an aesthete. Capable of intense intellectual and aesthetic delight, he yet retained heavy traces of the inherited moral responsibility. This combination of quick, various tastes and inescapable purpose shaped his conclusions.

The challenges which James met and overcame included most varieties of nineteenth-century thought. He rejected Spencer's impressive but ponderous system as early as the seventies, and with it all varieties of simple nineteenth-century materialism. James was both unwilling and unable to believe, as he put it, that the movements of the molecules of the nebula out of which the earth developed had predetermined his own intense and contradictory emotions. These emotions in fact were and remained the most certain data he possessed.

Even more certainly than materialism, the Absolute Idealism of his friend Royce failed to convince James; he could not be at home in any system that reduced all existence to *any* unity. Of existing schools of philosophy, he felt closest to British empiricism, but was far too active a Yankee to make the mind an empty or passive receiver of sensation in the manner of Locke. Unlike some of the other radical young thinkers who met together in Cambridge in the 1870's, he was not able to rest as a skeptic, though until nearly the end of his life he continued to be troubled by a doubt of the existence of external reality.

Thus James, earlier than many, rejected, with alternate moods of fearful doubt and gay defiance, all the familiar ways of looking at the universe. Since he had to have one, he constructed his own, in several distinct stages, out of the single material of experience.

In his first major work, his enormous and stimulating *Principles of Psychology*, James was closest to accepting nineteenth-century materialism, and did a great deal to move later American psychology in the direction of physiological determinism. Yet he refused to reduce thought to biology and chemistry. All our mental impulses, he agreed, probably originate with external stimuli. Yet thoughts themselves may come to have a determining effect. No amount of knowledge of Shakespeare's physiology and environment could explain his plays; the problem of free will can never be solved by psychology.

To contemporary psychologists, eager to give their work the status of a laboratory science, James was an irritating impressionist. It was possible, and it remains possible, for extreme mechanistic behaviorists, pragmatists, and mystics to find encouragement in the *Principles*.

From general psychology, James moved to the study of religion. Like many heirs of New England puritanism he was at once a man of deeply religious temperament and a persistent doubter. In his doctrine of the Will to Believe and in his classic description of *religious experience* he came near to setting American religious liberalism on a sounder path than that of the rather tired and unexciting compromises of evolutionary theology. James's novel suggestion here, typical of all his thought, was that the philosophy of experience, considered usually the enemy of religion, should be its ally. Not in doctrine, but in human emotion and feeling, lay the real testimony to religious reality. For radical Protestantism, this had perhaps always been so and certainly James's infinitely adaptable, intense, charitable, and exciting religion had a better chance of lasting through the twentieth century than Lyman Abbott's. Except for its optimism—a big exception—it was not very far from the existential variety that became fashionable a generation later. The trouble was, James's readers could never be certain whether this was religion at all. It was one thing to say, with mystics of all periods, that intuition takes us closest to religious truth, another to suggest, as James certainly seemed to, that religion was true only in that we experienced it.

Taking the word *pragmatism* from Charles Peirce, a much more careful, less exuberant thinker, a man who valued consistency as James did not and was sometimes alarmed at what happened to his creation, James defined this word, like many others, in his own way. Pragmatism was a habit of mind that looked away from principles and categories and toward consequences and facts. It was also a method of judging the truth of an idea by the difference made when it was acted upon. In these definitions James was closest to the other pragmatists, like John Dewey, and to the underlying practicalist temper which, as we have seen, was deeply imbedded in American society. Yet he really was no closer to this temper than to its opposites. He meant far more by consequences than most pragmatists—that which could be measured was no more real to James than that which could only be felt. It was never quite clear whether the consequences which determined the truth of an idea were consequences known and felt by you, by me, or necessarily by everybody.

What James had been doing all his life can perhaps be summarized by two very general statements. First, he had been rejecting all theories that held the universe to be constituted in any one way or of any one substance, whether molecules, Idea, or anything else. Relations, purposes, facts, things, consciousness, were all equally real, all to be summed up only in the word which James came back to at the end, *experience*, and this was not any one substance but a word for everything. Second, James had made the human will and emotions a more important part of the universe than most philosophers.

It may be that these two directions explain why he seems at some times to sum up the whole of modern thought and at others to be rooted forever in the Progressive Era. As the philosopher of experience—at times a mystic, at times a practicalist, always a skeptic, he is modern, and Alfred North Whitehead, for one, dates modern thought from his announcement that consciousness was a function, not a separate entity. As the philosopher of purpose, hope, and will, he sometimes seems confined to the Progressive Era. When he pointed out—a fact experience tells us all—that we are more likely to be able to jump over a ditch if we think we can, Santayana answered not altogether irrelevantly that it made some difference whether the ditch were six feet wide or twenty.

The ambiguity remains: did James finally think that our thoughts and emotions are important to the universe, or only important in themselves, to us? Perhaps ambiguity is for an American thinker the major key to influence; only Emerson had been so baffling and only Emerson had had as wide an influence. In his last phase particularly, when James seemed to be part of a movement of all Western thought in the direction of cheerful irrationalism, he was the special favorite of the prewar Young Intellectuals. His student Gertrude Stein went on from his theory of the stream of consciousness into literary revolution. A generation of Harvard rebels found him the great liberator, and so did impatient young men as far from Harvard as Davenport, Iowa, where Floyd Dell encountered him. Yet the *Commercial and Financial Chronicle*, organ of both practicality and conservatism, in 1912 praised "the late Professor William James." Pragmatism, it said, was especially useful to businessmen who had to make decisions, and the editorial's definition of James's method of thought was by no means a caricature.[1]

Moral to the core, with deep idealist tendencies, devoted to standard culture though impatient of its stuffier tendencies, progressive above all, James was clearly a part of the surviving nineteenth-century American civilization we have described, and he died just before the crucial phase of its disintegration. Yet nobody

[1] *Commercial and Financial Chronicle*, "Pragmatism in Business and Politics," October 19, 1912, p. 1009.

opened more doors; one wonders what James would have said of some of the bizarre and disturbing company that came streaming in.

Like James, John Dewey was an enemy of final goals and eternal categories; like James he insisted that reality lay in the concrete, the immediate, the developing. He was not, however, the same kind of a pluralist; Dewey did not share James's Emersonian liking for the unresolved contradiction. Experience was diverse, but for all that continuous. The principal error of philosophers had been to separate the knower from the known, mind from action, morals from science. The root of the confusion lay in the original radical separation between man and nature.

Unlike James, Dewey went the whole distance with nineteenth-century naturalism. Man, he specifically said, was continuous with the rest of the animal world. Animals were continuous with "the physico-chemical processes which, in living things, are so organized as really to constitute the activities of life with all their defining traits." [2] With compromises of this position Dewey had little patience.

Dewey had not, like James, come to philosophy through art and medicine, nor had he been brought up in a society where metaphysical argument was taken for granted as part of life. He had been trained in academic idealist philosophy, but before this he had been shaped by small-town American life. His thought, he always insisted, was inseparable from the tendencies of democratic society, and democratic society needed his general kind of philosophy to survive. The purposes of philosophy must not depart too far from the purposes of ordinary people trying to deal with the problems that arose in daily life.

Dewey's belief in practicality should not be, as it often has been, simplified and exaggerated. To Dewey, art, science, and religion

[2] Dewey: *Creative Intelligence* (New York, 1917), p. 36.

were all important insofar as each could be controlled and refined by intelligence; to James, and to many in the coming decades, what was most important in each was exactly that which eluded such control. History was of use in charting our course, even fantasy could be a means of generating progress. Dewey's purposes were humane and various. They were always in sight, on this side of the hill; he insisted that a conception of the other side was impossible and unnecessary. Yet we must keep walking; for thought without a purpose Dewey had no use. Like most of his countrymen, and unlike most philosophers, Dewey was an activist through and through. For contemplation, for mystery, for delight in those things we cannot make use of, he had little taste. He had no taste at all for unresolved paradox; contradictions were calls to action.

In a sense, therefore, Dewey was more completely a relativist than James; he was even less tolerant of fixities. In a sense, too, he was less relativist; the one thing that seemed absolute was movement and purpose. This has given rise to much criticism. A world in which there are no built-in purposes and goals, is yet a world in which everything can be grasped and used. Tradition, metaphysics, natural laws fail, but intelligence faileth not.

Dewey's work, vast and various, extends far beyond the scope of this book. Its value and consistency are being debated by authorities more competent than the present historian. Yet one opinion is relevant and necessary. Dewey's thought, like that of the other leading relativists, was inescapably rooted in the Progressive Era. A powerful critic of some aspects of the prevailing intellectual and moral order, he remained also a part of it.

Progress was, of course, the center, and to Dewey as to most of his countrymen, we were just entering the period in which progress would be possible. Fixed, arbitrary, codified morality was almost his chief enemy, yet he was absolutely confident that the destruction of moral codes would make moral choices sounder.

> . . . The abandonment by intelligence of a fixed and static moral end was the necessary precondition of a free and progressive science of both things and morals. . . .

> . . . The abolition of *the* final goal and *the* single motive power and *the* separate and infallible faculty in morals, will quicken inquiry into the diversity of specific goods of experience, fix attention upon their conditions, and bring to light values now dim and obscure.[3]

Dewey was conscious that a belief in the efficacy of the intelligence demanded faith, and he used the word *faith* about his commitments. As far as a nonexpert can follow him, his faith was placed exactly where that of his simpler contemporaries was, in human nature:

> The substitution, for *a priori* truth and deduction, of fluent doubt and inquiry meant trust in human nature in the concrete; in individual honesty, curiosity, and sympathy.[4]

Dewey usually stated this faith in temperate and tolerant terms. Yet he sometimes had words of condemnation for those whose trust lay elsewhere, and once, as we will see, he sharply condemned those who interpreted differently a single catastrophic event. To him, and much more obviously to some of his less tolerant and benign interpreters, his solution of the problems of life and thought is *the* solution, his method the ultimate compromise among conflicting methods.

It is in this sense only that Dewey, with other American thinkers of his day, failed, and it is in this sense too that he is less modern than James. James, whose conclusions remain fleeting and ambiguous, has been able to speak to many kinds of people, to Randolph Bourne, to Gertrude Stein, even (his admirers must remember) to Mussolini. He is, the historian dares guess, going to be revived from time to time in the future.

Dewey, who came closer to building a system, was immensely influential on people who basically agreed with him. In 1912 his career was still beginning, though he was fifty-three. It was after

[3] John Dewey: *The Influence of Darwin on Philosophy* (New York, 1910), pp. 56, 70.
[4] Ibid., p. 60.

the approaching breakup of unity that he achieved his greatest power, and that power was huge. Yet it was confined to those who shared his assumptions about human intelligence and his faith that values could be constructed out of social achievement. In the twentieth century, which has departed so drastically from the expectations of 1912, such people have grown fewer. In the future it seems highly possible that Dewey will be a big figure in the area in which he would least like to be: in the history of thought.

A firm believer in progress, a believer in the moral possibilities, if not the essential morality, of the universe, Dewey was at least half in touch with two of the three fundamental orthodoxies of 1912. Of culture, in the sense of the conservation of tradition for its own sake, he was the most powerful extant enemy. Like American reformist thought for a century, Dewey's ideas led up the path to the schoolhouse.

Dewey's program for education was from the beginning an integral part of his philosophy, and also of his psychology. The Chicago school of functional psychology, established by Dewey and James W. Angell in the nineties, was, like the rest of Dewey's work, part of an attack on traditional methods and rigid classification. The mind-body problem, one of the main preoccupations of traditional psychology, could be abandoned along with metaphysics. Not one faculty or instinct or any set of them, but the whole individual functioning in his environment, was the proper object of study. This also was the proper object of education.

Dewey's criticisms of traditional educational theory and practice were part of a great and various movement of revolt. Other kinds of psychologists were finding current methods inadequate; businessmen and farmers were calling classical education useless; worried citizens were demanding that the schools take on more boldly the job of assimilating the immigrants; efficiency experts and social scientists were bringing forward precise proposals. Like all great pamphlets, Dewey's early works on education seized the exact hour, and survived long after that hour had passed.

As early as 1899 in *School and Society*, a simple pamphlet related to his immediate experience at his Chicago experimental school, Dewey pleaded eloquently for an education fit for a changing environment. The purpose should be neither to conserve a received tradition, as the custodians assumed, nor to produce a new society according to blueprint. Rather education, like thought itself, must be a means of selecting from the existing situation its best impulses, of helping society to move along the most promising of the directions already taken. The book glows with the excitement of the new century and its possibilities.

To Dewey and his followers it seemed obvious that in a democratic, industrial, changing society, it was essential to get rid of the distinction, inherited from the Greeks, between cultured people and workers, and therefore of the false separations between science and humanities, or liberal and mechanical pursuits. The basis was to be history and geography, taught as a widening-out of the actual environment, and supplemented by collective experience in such pursuits as carpentry, cooking, and making textiles. The cover of the 1916 edition of *School and Society* (it was reprinted almost every year) has an attractive picture of a little girl at the spinning wheel, with a boy sitting beside her looking at a book. (It was inevitable that some carping critic would ask why a spinning wheel was any more relevant to industrial society than a Latin Grammar.)

The center of Dewey's demands was a change in method, though method was not to be separated from content. School was not to be carried on according to the age-old assumption, flatly rejected by Dewey like so many of his contemporaries, that the human being is naturally egotistical and needs "artificial" discipline. Social traits were as natural as individualistic ones and the two kinds were complementary. The school must be a society, selecting and developing naturally and freely the best traits generated by the greater society in which it lived.

The resemblance between this program and the suggestions of the practicalists was superficial. Dewey and the advocates of vocationalism agreed only in what they were against. His purpose was not to increase production or improve the labor supply: his aim was freedom. This was what made him attractive to some rebellious intellectuals like Randolph Bourne, though in Dewey spontaneity and responsibility go together.

The democracy and apparent practicality of Dewey's proposals were making converts in different quarters. Though progressives were still a minority among educators in 1912, they were gaining fast. A number of private schools had adopted Dewey's program, and a few city systems such as that of Gary, Indiana were experimenting with it. More important in the long run, it was making big inroads on professional discussion.

Dewey's influence can be seen clearly, for instance, in the 1913 report of the National Education Association's Committee on the Reorganization of Secondary Education. Instead of being concerned, like previous committees, with transmission of culture or even with mental training, this group called for education that would develop every good trait in everybody. High schools must admit by age, not attainment, and colleges must admit all graduates. The common purpose must be to

> develop in each individual the knowledge, interests, ideals, habits, and powers whereby he will find his place and use that place to shape both himself and his society toward ever nobler aims.[5]

Obviously this genuinely noble commitment is at once rooted in the dominant ideas of its time and deeply revolutionary. Nothing could be more permeated by moral idealism, or more optimistic about both the nature of man and the future of America. Yet the program left no place whatever for a conserved or transmitted culture, and none for fixed and given moral norms. Naturally the custodians of culture expressed alarm and dismay over what they rightly saw as a powerful attack on their central fortifications. Every time they did so, they made converts for the attackers.

[5] Quoted in Lawrence A. Cremin: "The Revolution in American Secondary Education, 1893–1913," *Teachers' College Record* (1955), p. 306.

Many arguments which came to the fore in the much later widespread reaction against progressive education could not possibly have occurred to conservatives in 1912. It was not yet apparent that progressive principles could themselves sometimes be inculcated in a rigid and authoritarian manner. Teaching the principles and methods of freedom in a large, uniform system, breaking authoritarian habits from above leads to paradoxes that were apparent to very few. Perhaps part of the difficulty lay in the theory of social control which Dewey shared with the social scientists of his day. In the school as elsewhere, Dewey believed overt authority should be replaced, and actually was being replaced, by subtler means of inducing co-operation:

> The very existence of the social medium in which an individual lives, moves, and has his being is the standing effective agency of directing his activity.[6]

This sentence has an altogether different ring today than it had in 1916. Only by painful experience have we learned to fear, even more than the old-fashioned visible tyrant, the pressures against which it is unthinkable to rebel.

❦

Social science, the other chief path of American relativism, started from the same sources as pragmatism and crossed its course at many points. Like the pragmatists, the older social scientists, still dominant in 1912, were halfway innovators. They liked to sound more iconoclastic than they were.

Most of the founders of American social science, the grand old men of the late nineteenth century, started with two principles drawn from Auguste Comte and Herbert Spencer: the development of society through regular stages, and its progressive adaptation to a changing environment. These principles had once seemed

[6] Dewey: *Democracy and Education* (New York, 1923, *c.* 1916), p. 33.

novel and disturbing; they seemed to imply that moral choices depended on changing circumstances. Two very different American social scientists of the first generation, Lewis Henry Morgan and William Graham Sumner, had indeed implied that social values and mores altered with such things as technology and population pressure.

Most of the older social scientists, however, found a place in the course of evolutionary development for the exertion of human will and choice. Their work consisted in combining social Darwinism with belief in some kind of deliberate, scientific, more or less collective social progress. To construct their systems they drew on many sources. Many of them had studied in Germany, and learned there to believe in some sort of mysterious, emerging ethical purpose for the state and society. Others drew on the social gospel, on pragmatism, even on Marx. Most of them emerged with a new set of laws or stages through which society moved. Nearly always it moved out of extreme anarchic competition into a new stage, the present, of emerging social science, a stage in which men could gradually take control of their own destinies.

This essentially reassuring picture was painted by two kinds of nineteenth-century American professors of social science: the liberal Christians and the Victorian positivists. Most belonged to the former category, finding a place for a liberal God in the movement from chaos to control. Such were John Bascom, from whom at Wisconsin La Follette drew much of his inspiration, or in the next generation Albion F. Small, of Chicago, as much as anybody the official leader of American sociology in the first decade of the century.

The smaller positivist group descended from Lester F. Ward, who claimed a place in evolution for human knowledge and will, independent of Divine Aid. In the progressive generation Ward's chief heir was Edward A. Ross of Wisconsin. Crusty and contentious, Ross prided himself on being a hard-boiled skeptic as well as outspoken foe of big business. With a loud uproar, he had been dismissed from Stanford and had drawn conservative fire even in progressive Madison. He may well serve as a sample of the outer edge of unorthodoxy among established academic social scientists.

Ross, like his contemporaries, exploded some certainties and cherished others. One of the remaining pillars was of course science itself, and for Ross psychology was a part of it. Human desires operated almost as predictably as physical laws, which still looked predictable indeed. Science furnished plenty of basis for moral judgments: among the things Ross denounces in his autobiography are subjectivism, morbidity, and, coupled with these, any pussy-footed refusal in the name of academic purity to make value judgments. Ross certainly never fell into this particular error; all his books speak out strongly for such causes as sexual purity, the moral function of art, decency in literature, and preservation of the superior Germanic race.

In *Social Control* (1901), Ross's masterpiece, he presented a cheering prospect. Mystical, customary, authoritarian agencies of control would be increasingly replaced by such forces as enlightenment, self-respect, and even a strictly nontheological social religion. Ross's books went through large editions; he was extravagantly admired by Ray Stannard Baker, Mark Sullivan, William Jennings Bryan, and others. Theodore Roosevelt, explaining exactly why he liked *Social Control*, translated it into his own terms:

> You do not confine yourself to mere destructive criticism. Your plea is for courage, for uprightness, for far-seeing sanity, for active constructive work. . . . Your book is emphatically an appeal to the general sense of right as opposed to mere class interest. . . . You insist, as all healthy-minded patriots should insist, that public opinion, if only sufficiently enlightened and aroused, is equal to the necessary regenerative tasks and can yet dominate the future.[7]

We can, that is, destroy determinist dogma but retain moral certainty; we can be skeptical about the *status quo* but confident about the future. This is the message which American progressivism

[7] Reprinted in Edward A. Ross: *Sin and Society* (Boston, 1907), pp. ix–xi.

learned from the older social science, whether it was stated in terms of nineteenth-century liberal Christianity or nineteenth-century positivism. In either case, it was almost entirely a part of the prevailing ethos, a rivet for progress and morality.

❦

In the prewar years, most but not all of the younger social scientists remained within this halfway relativist camp. E. C. Hayes, in a textbook of 1916, put the prevailing view neatly: sociology wanted to make ethics an objective science. Science was the study of what is, but what is included good and evil.[8] A glance at the *American Journal of Sociology* in the prewar years is a rather startling experience for anybody in touch with mid-twentieth century social science: it is a mixture of social service, ethics, and liberal Christianity. Only occasionally can one gather that any other sort of social science exists: an article by C. A. Ellwood in November, 1915 takes disapproving note of a new school of "external behaviorists," who have no place in their theories for feelings, ideas, and standards.[9]

The youngest generation was moving, sometimes gradually and sometimes violently, out of general evolutionary uplift, and out of the dominant American assumptions, in two familiar directions: irrationalism and extreme practicalism. Both these tendencies were associated with developments in recent psychology. Psychology in the early twentieth century was becoming increasingly social in its interests, and social psychology was merging with social science. The old effort to anatomize the individual mind was out of favor. Not only Dewey, but many different kinds of psychologists were saying that one must investigate the whole man in a social context.

Yet psychological theory was in a state of extreme conflict, and psychology seemed to bring with it into social science a number of

[8] E. C. Hayes: *Introduction to the Study of Society* (New York, 1916), pp. 4–5.

[9] C. A. Ellwood: "Objectivism in Sociology," *American Journal of Sociology*, XXII (1915–16), 289–305.

conflicting precepts. Many psychologists had long been trying to reduce all mental phenomena to functions of the brain and nervous system. Some were talking already in terms of stimulus and response, and this kind of simplification was beginning to have a big effect on social scientists. Yet many influential psychologists seemed to be going in an opposite direction, toward an increased emphasis on inherent, unlearned instincts. Instinct theories were many, and differed about how many basic unlearned tendencies existed, and how they had originated. Some psychologists, James for one, gave the instinct of sex a specially powerful place. Crowd psychology sometimes suggested the existence of separate collective instincts. All these movements had one common direction: they led away from the old assumption, common to the majority credo and the early social scientists, that human beings were coming into control of human destiny.

Some of the younger social scientists, like some psychologists, were avoiding the problem of reason and its limits by demanding more facts, especially more statistical facts. The heyday of the social survey was beginning; already thousands of Americans had filled out questionnaires on rural life, labor relations, and urban vice. Commenting on this tendency, a summary of current trends said in 1914 that "*a priori* generalization survives today only as an intellectual atavism." [1]

Sometimes an insistence on moral neutrality was being coupled with a frank demand for authority. L. L. Bernard, in a Ph.D. thesis published in 1911, condemned almost all the older social scientists for sentimentality. Ward, for instance, believed in the power of education; actually activity came not from knowledge but from the set of the whole nervous system. Now, said Bernard at some length, we could throw out the whole inheritance of subjectivistic, idealistic, solipsistic ideas of personal liberty and individual wants. For all these we could substitute objective standards of social control, to be enforced, eventually, in the whole world:

[1] Herbert N. Shenton: "Sociology," *American Year Book*, 1914 (New York, 1915), p. 671.

> . . . Social control cannot be individually determined, but must proceed from a controlled environment which provides the individual with a uniform and constant source of stimuli. . . .
>
> The counter plea of "interference with individual liberty" should have no weight in court, for individuals have no liberties in opposition to a scientifically controlled society but find all their legitimate freedom in conformity to and furtherance of such social functioning. . . .[2]

This thoroughly revolutionary program, with its slogans of All Power to the Scientists, was perhaps stated more frankly in its early enthusiastic days than later. It was a startling but perfectly direct and clear result of a tendency which started with relativism and liberty.

Economics, an older discipline, was moving more slowly than sociology along the same relativist path. It had inherited from the nineteenth century a particularly rigid kind of theory. The idea of the guiding hand, presumably Divine and clearly indifferent, had been gradually displaced by the idea of the built-in, all-sufficient natural force controlling economic behavior. This force was unalterable human nature, seeking pleasure and avoiding pain in a predictable, almost automatic manner. Much qualified and refined, the classical assumptions still held the field. One started with a perfect pattern of production and distribution and then explained the exceptions and departures.

In economics, as in sociology, determinism had been challenged by American optimism. As early as the 1850's a few American economists had insisted that the harsh laws of Victorian economics did not apply here. In the eighties Richard T. Ely and others had

[2] L. L. Bernard, *The Transition to an Objective Standard of Social Control* (Chicago, 1911), pp. 90, 95.

learned in Germany new arguments for departing from English orthodoxy. Ely, John R. Commons, and in his early works John Bates Clark found room in economics for social progress and even liberal Christian ethics; for this school, economics became, like everything else in America, purposeful.

In the early twentieth century psychology furnished still another set of arguments for relativism and optimism in economics. Simon Patten, in 1905, predicted the coming of a new civilization in which poverty would be eliminated and all men raised above the highest present moral and cultural level. Part of the basis for Patten's prediction lay in American resources, part in the new understanding of the malleable, undetermined nature of man. Selfish tendencies were not inherent; once clear away bad conditions and latent virtues would emerge.[3]

The most important of the rising generation of economists was Wesley Mitchell. At Chicago in the nineties, Mitchell had encountered both Dewey and Thorstein Veblen. Mitchell found listening to Veblen something like "vivisection without an anaesthetic,"[4] but learned from him to distrust traditional economics, with its rationalist assumptions about human motives for action.

Reading deeply in psychology and anthropology, Mitchell insisted that the proper field of the economist was nothing less than human behavior, irrational as well as rational, never detached from a context of history and institutions. A modest, patient man, with a love of statistical information, Mitchell never followed the path from relativism toward its opposite, a new kind of dogmatism.

Relativist history burst on the public with all the drama that institutional economics lacked. History after all, was more than an academic matter; it was a conserver of tradition, a source of reassurance. Its special role in the dominant American culture was to demonstrate the compatibility of progress and idealism, the perpetuation, especially in America, of old truth in new forms.

[3] Simon Patten: *The New Basis of Civilization* (New York, 1912), *passim.* These Lectures were first given in 1905.

[4] Lucy Sprague Mitchell: *Two Lives* (New York, 1953), p. 86.

Dewey, in *School and Society* and later, had announced flatly that history, conceived as a study of the past, was of no use whatever. Antiquarianism, myth, and "merely literary renderings" were to be avoided. The true purpose of history was to show the growth of human co-operation.[5] Dewey was not primarily interested in history and not very much at home in discussing it, and his lack of interest shows in an unusual simplicity. What he seems to be saying is that the past would not be interesting unless we could fully understand its direction and unless that direction were cheerful. He comes close to suggesting also that whatever does not demonstrate this direction had better, at least in the schools, be left out. It seems questionable whether these dicta are properly called either relativist or pragmatic.

The same principles, in all their attractive simplicity, form the assumptions of James Harvey Robinson's immensely influential *The New History*, published in 1912. Robinson, in a hymn of praise for the present, drew his most exciting figure from evolution. If we consider the whole of man's history on earth as twelve hours, the period of progress started only at one minute to twelve, and that of conscious, deliberate progress much more recently still. The figure was not intended to imply any imminent end, or any cyclical movement. The purpose of history was to help us to understand and speed up the progress now under way.

The main source of progress was science, and Robinson's ideas of science and the scientific method were those of the nineteenth century.[6] Science progressed through the rejection of all supernaturalism, concentration on the commonplace detail, and the formulation of laws. To become more like it, history must give much less space to periods of confusion and turmoil and emphasize instead the moral, simple, slightly dull periods during which progress had been made. (Here Robinson sounded a good deal like Howells, who had long before urged American writers to dwell on

[5] Dewey: *School and Society* (Chicago, rev. ed., 1915), pp. 155–60.

[6] See James Harvey Robinson and Charles A. Beard: *The Development of Modern Europe* (2 Vols., Boston, 1908), II, 405–21.

the cheerful aspects of American life because they were the most typical.)

History must draw on the more developed sciences for a number of specific insights. From evolution she must learn to look at slow processes of change rather than catastrophe (this was actually already difficult to learn from evolution). From social psychology, though Robinson admitted that this science was "in an inchoate state," history could learn, for instance, that all progress proceeded by imitation. Animal psychology and comparative religion could help us to get rid of anthropocentric and superstitious views.

In Robinson's exuberant pages there is little hint of skepticism, except about long-dead traditions, and no whisper of doubt about our ability to understand what was happening. So important was it to co-operate with change that Robinson was willing to borrow a term from religion:

> At last, perhaps, the long-disputed sin against the Holy Ghost has been found; it may be the refusal to cooperate with the vital principle of betterment.[7]

For most of Robinson's readers, this was stimulating rather than startling doctrine. It was not really much of a novelty to make European history chiefly a dark contrasting background for the recent emergence of science and liberty. Robinson's precepts were officially echoed by committees of the American Historical Association, by state teachers' organizations, and by the powerful National Education Association. To decrease the emphasis on earlier periods, to make history point up the lessons of progress, to free the child from undue memorizing of dates seemed to all these bodies to make a great deal of sense. Eventually, though this was hardly Robinson's purpose, some school systems in the country were to take the logical final step and free the child from history altogether.

When it touched on American institutions, historical criticism was getting onto more dangerous ground. Although moral idealism still held sway in the textbooks, monograph writers were chipping

[7] Robinson: *The New History* (New York, 1912), p. 265.

away at the traditional story and the values it implied. Already, for instance, the American Revolution was being interpreted as something quite different from a simple uprising against oppression. Already resentment against this kind of iconoclasm had been expressed, though the violent patriotic reaction did not occur until after the war.

From all sides, relativists converged inevitably on the greatest symbol of American fixity, the Constitution. Political scientists turned on it the full battery of new theories of the state. Neither eighteenth-century natural law, checks and balances, nor any of the classical conceptions of political theory were the main interest of modern students of politics. Government must be studied as a competition of pressure groups, an expression of social instincts, a basis for expert administration. One of the most familiar, and one of the most important paths of relativism had run through the study of law itself. American sociological jurisprudence and legal realism did not necessarily involve repudiation of the Constitution, but they inevitably led to a reconsideration of its nature. Law was a means to carry out the purposes of society, and society had changed a lot since 1787.

Approaching the Constitution by all these paths, relativist thought merged with popular progressive demands. To many progressives, the Constitution was the most obvious road block in the way of the new democracy. The Supreme Court, bastion of American conservatism, had drawn the fire not only of Robert M. La Follette but of Theodore Roosevelt. J. Allen Smith, a Western democratic progressive, argued that the eighteenth-century checks and balances were no longer necessary since "the accepted standard of morality has itself been raised." Algie M. Simons, the socialist historian, went much further, exposing the Constitution in 1911 as a conspiratorial trick of the upper class.[8]

Charles A. Beard, political scientist, historian, and progressive,

[8] J. Allen Smith: *The Spirit of American Government* (New York, 1912), p. 362; A. M. Simons: *Social Forces in American History* (2nd ed., New York, 1926), p. 92.

drew on all these sources and many more. His own early statements about history combined two familiar and somewhat contradictory principles of advanced progressive thought. First, he had said, we must learn to approach history in the spirit of pure science which means without preconceptions in favor of such principles as laissez-faire or property rights. We must, that is, get away from the assumptions of our own age. Second, we must recognize the importance, not to say the primacy, of economic interests. Beard was less relativist in this period than he later became; it still seemed to be implied in his work that economic motives were more real and powerful than any others.

With immense ingenuity of research, persuasiveness, and (compared to his muckraking contemporaries) moderation, Beard repeated and buttressed the fairly familiar progressive argument that the Federal Constitution was framed by and for a class. This seemed, though it was not, an easy deduction from the innumerable statements in favor of limiting democracy made by the Founding Fathers themselves. It is not surprising that this doctrine, shocking even to Justice Holmes in 1913, swept the younger and progressive historians off their feet and became, in the next decades, accepted academic doctrine.

In recent years Beard, like other progressive thinkers, has been subject to intensive re-examination. The pendulum-swing of opinion has very likely gone too far, and yet one of the recent criticisms of Beard says a lot about his whole period. By incomplete quotation, doubtless unintentional, as well as by the whole drift of his argument, Beard makes of some of his eighteenth-century statesmen, particularly Madison, less profound and sophisticated thinkers than they were. Their theories of government did not start, like those of Beard's generation, with questions about property rights and majority rule. They started with the nature of man. The moderate conservative theory of the eighteenth century, at its best, did not say that the educated majority was always right, but that all men were likely to be partly wrong. This was a point of view hard for the Progressive Era to grasp, and Beard's failure fully to appreciate it has helped to deprive America of a rich ingredient in her national tradition. We still tend to see American history through the eyes of the Progressive Era, as we tend to see American literature through the eyes of the twenties. Despite his insight and acumen, Beard failed to get outside the assumptions of his own time. Like many of his relativist contemporaries, he was not relativist enough.

The greatest figures of American relativism, starting with James and Dewey, had their roots firmly in the nineteenth century. The evolution that reigned in the intellectual world of their youth had been an evolution upward, into the present and toward the future. The upward direction remained inescapably part of their assumptions. Still more deeply rooted was the habit of moral judgment, in whatever new terms it might be disguised, and however complex its basis had become. Great innovators, they were also conservative forces; they were, that is, a part of the prewar world.

This duality helps to explain a paradox about the Progressive Era that has troubled some historians and, regrettably, has not troubled others. It was at once the period of Wilsonian moral idealism and of Deweyite relativism. This is only a paradox if one takes a rigidly rationalist view of history. Logically or not, Wilsonian moralism included progress, and Dewey's pragmatism included a large measure of traditional morality. In one combination or another, morality and progress together ruled the American scene.

It was inevitable, however, that the progress would begin to edge out morality. Some younger political progressives, drawing on the pragmatists and taking them literally, influenced also by more radical currents of thought from America and Europe, pushed their relativism clear out of the moral universe of 1912. A few of them realized, as their elders could not, that words like "upward" and "better" had little meaning in a really relativist world, unless they meant "useful for my specific purpose" or "attractive to me right now."

We will deal at length with some of the young intellectuals who were revolutionizing progressive thought from within. Their chief organ was the *New Republic*, founded in 1914. Many of the older relativists found its pages congenial, and in May 1915 James Harvey Robinson contributed an editorial. Despite our belief in being open-minded, despite our brand-new scientific knowledge of the nature of man, said Robinson, we persist in setting up "a conflicting set of ideals—sound doctrine, consistency, fidelity to principle, the teachings of the ages, God's will, the dictates of conscience, eternal verities, immutable human nature, the imprescriptible rights of man." It may be, he suggested, as vain for us to hold onto these things

> . . . as for Galileo to have attempted to reconcile his discoveries in mechanics with Aristotle's theory of light and heavy, or for a modern chemist to think in terms of earth, air, fire and water. Why *should* we respect the conclusions of past centuries? [9]

In this editorial Robinson carried the relativist position to its ultimate prewar position. There is no question that in terms of existing American beliefs this position was revolutionary.

[9] James Harvey Robinson: "A Journal of Opinion," *New Republic*, May 8, 1915, p. 10.

III

Scoffers

American literature, said George Edward Woodberry in 1911, was increasingly out of touch with European tendencies.

> With Tolstoi, Ibsen, d'Annunzio, Zola, Nietzsche, Maeterlinck the American people can have no effectual touch; their social tradition and culture make them impenetrable to the present ideas of Europe as they are current in literary forms.

This made the outlook gloomy, since Woodberry was sure also that nothing "has been developed from within that is fertile in literature." [1] Woodberry turned out to be wrong in both parts of his assessment. A lot was going on at home, and each of the foreign writers he named, except perhaps d'Annunzio, had or was about to have a powerful effect.

The role of Europe had always been twofold. On the one hand the old continent was the conservative center against which America had rebelled, and on the other she was the source of subversive ideas, dangerous to American stability. In 1912 and after, the old schoolbook Europe was still real to many Americans, the haughty Europe of Philip II, Bloody Mary, and George III. Still powerful, this Europe was also increasingly effete; sooner or later she would have to surrender her power to the young, progressive Western giant. Yet somehow or other this ancient, overcivilized continent was still the source of radicalism. Since the eighteenth century a long stream of violent and dangerous ideas had crossed the Atlantic westward. These had included Jacobinism, romanticism, posi-

[1] Woodberry: "American Literature," *Encyclopaedia Britannica*, Eleventh edition (New York, 1911), I, 841.

tivism, evolution, anarchism, socialism, and naturalism. Much of the meaning of American intellectual history lay in the struggle to exclude or adapt these disturbing ideas. In periods of creative vigor, America managed to adapt the new tendencies from Europe to her own uses; in periods of comparative stagnation, she tended to ignore or resist them.

In the late nineteenth and early twentieth century, many Americans tended to reject current European ideas. What these ideas had in common seemed to be their violence. American pictures of Europe differed greatly, but all were painted in lurid colors—red revolution, black reaction, yellow decadence. The idea of Europe as a continent of extremes, to be contrasted to the bland American mean, was not without validity.

The Victorian compromise had been harder to arrive at in England than in America, and in continental Europe it had never really worked. In the terms we have been using, European civilization had never really managed to mix together moralism, culture, and progress. Progress seemed to turn into revolution; moralism and culture into last-ditch defense of archaic codes.

Many of the reasons for European extremism are very familiar. In Europe the industrial revolution, superimposed on a layer of other revolutions, all resting on the remains of feudal society, had inevitably produced deep divisions. The busy, adaptable middle class had been less powerful. European ideas had been formulated partly by groups that did not exist in America, including a bewildered, resentful aristocracy and an angry, oppressed proletariat. Two smaller groups, each only beginning to exist in America, had been particularly articulate: a detached, secure, prestige-conscious professoriat and a detached, drifting, irresponsible intelligentsia.

Ideas and events which in America were taken for granted as part of the whole nation's development were associated in Europe with militant minorities, each with its roots in past conflict. Both the Reformation and the Age of Reason, for instance, were disasters from the point of view of important European groups. The cheerful utilitarianism of the nineteenth century had been rejected by a number of important thinkers even in England; in continental Europe still more had hated and despised it.

Separate experience had separated America and Europe, the two branches of a common civilization. Generations of travelers have tried to define the differences. These remain elusive, and yet we all sense their existence. For our purpose it is almost enough to ask: why is it impossible to imagine either William Dean Howells or John Dewey coming from Europe?

In the recent past, Europe and America had differed somewhat in the way each had handled the common task: the adjustment of traditional civilization to the new technological and scientific universe. All the major American ways of doing this had been ways of compromise: Spencerian social science, practical idealism, and pragmatism. Variants of all these had existed in continental Europe, but none had achieved central importance. Europe, reacting to the world of science and industry, had produced three separate movements of thought, all spectacular and extreme.

First, Europe had given birth to an all-out kind of naturalism, an uncompromising doctrine of a world uniformly indifferent to human values. This picture was sometimes painted in the colors of scientific progress, but often, and more consistently, it took on the dark aspect of mechanistic determinism. Second, Europe gave birth to a determined and passionate aestheticism, an uncompromising refusal to accept the apparent message of the nineteenth century; a repudiation of science, progress, and the utilitarian standard. Often this meant also a flat rejection of traditional moral and social values; often it led to a belief in salvation by art alone.

Both naturalism and aestheticism were tendencies of the late nineteenth century, though in the prewar years each still had important European spokesmen and American converts. The third wave of ideas, especially important for our cultural upheaval, began in about 1890 and reached its crest in both Europe and America in the first fifteen years of the new century. This wave consisted of a special kind of mysticism, a rejection of both utilitarian progress and aesthetic despair in favor of a rather vague, cheerful, wide-open universe, a doctrine of flux and chaos, a suggestion that since nothing was certain everything was possible. To distinguish all three of these movements more clearly in advance, and to show the immense range of each, it may be helpful to cite some familiar names. Marx, Zola, and Thomas Hardy all belong in different divisions of the naturalist camp; Baudelaire, Nietzsche, and Oscar Wilde in the aesthetic one. The most convincing spokesman of the third movement, vitalism or cheerful neomysticism, was Henri Bergson, and its most popular prophet H. G. Wells.

Naturalism has been defined in so many ways, especially by students of literature, that we will have to start with the word's most obvious meaning. This is simply the denial of the supernatural, the refusal, that is, to grant the reality of anything separate, transcendent, or mysterious. Much of the American relativist movement skirted the edge of naturalism in this sense of the term.

Often, but not always, the word naturalism carries a further connotation. This consists not merely of a denial, but an angry and hostile denunciation of mystery and transcendence. Naturalists in this sense are likely to detest, not merely to reject, idealism or religion; they tend to dwell and insist on the sordid and brutal aspects of experience. More than deniers, they are also scoffers. In this sense naturalism, by no means unknown in America, usually had some direct European sources.

The simple mechanistic picture of the world, with no specific social or literary implications, had reached its fullest development in the second third of the nineteenth century. At about that time the physical doctrines of the conservation of matter and energy seemed to be combining with the biological theory of automatic evolution to make a complete picture of the universe. From the origin of the world to yesterday's newspaper all events seemed to form one chain of cause and effect, meaningless and yet unbroken. Life was a chance product of the right climatic conditions and the right extremely complicated chemical combinations. Once life had occurred, evolution proceeded by interaction of the organism and its environment. In humans, that adaptation took the form of thought, a specialized activity of the brain and nervous system.

Particularly for the scientific philosophers of the German universities, fighting a battle against old and new kinds of idealism, any compromise of the naturalist position, any careless mention of the soul or of human destiny was a cowardly surrender to reaction. This view of things had recently lost some ground in Germany, but a good many American students had brought it home with them. In medical or psychological circles, militant naturalism of this kind was sometimes a matter of loyalty to science itself.

Outside scientific circles, Marxism was probably the most living variety of nineteenth-century German materialism. This was partly because its vision of the future was a cheerful one. To the Marxist, history was based on the interaction of material forces, but not chaotic or random forces. Thus Marxism, in Europe or America, attracted many who hated to relinquish their humanist hopes, and yet longed to be detached and scientific. Its tone of hard-boiled derision served admirably to conceal a paradox that ranged through nineteenth-century social thought: Human history and thought itself are shaped by a vast impersonal process. Yet you and I, standing here in this point of history, with the aid of science can understand and influence this process of which we are a part.

Not all varieties of naturalism shared this paradoxical confidence in the human future. Some natural scientists were less optimistic and less certain about the future than either the bourgeois Spencerians or the radical Marxists. Darwin and Huxley themselves, and many biologists since, had been troubled by the evidence that evolution was bloody, expensive, and—still worse—lacking in clear direction. To many physicists, the universe was indeed a great machine, but not one that worked as we might wish. Eventually, it would destroy us: the sun must burn out and the accident of life might never be repeated.

Naturalism in literature reflected all kinds of scientific naturalist thought. It usually implied militant hostility to religion, and it was often pessimistic. In France, where social and religious conflict had long compelled literary men to take sides, thorough skepticism was a part of the tradition of resistance to clerical tyranny, and cosmic pessimism was likely to be the answer to bourgeois complacency. To men of free minds, the universe was perhaps an open book, but not a book with a happy ending. The story, as literary men of all ages had often suggested, was a pointless joke.

Despite this conclusion, much of naturalist literature continued to preach. Novelists and playwrights can hardly put man anywhere but in the center of the stage, even when they do not think he belongs there. Emile Zola, the official dean of naturalists, preached but did not practice the neutral, scientific examination of the terrible human condition. He and other naturalists presented the most sordid poverty, the most inept and meaningless fornication, the most revolting disease. Zola himself believed human misery inevitable; yet he was obviously trying to stir men to action against it.

The Zola school was perhaps the best-defined kind of literary naturalism, but there were many others. Within the naturalist rank room had to be found for the moral paradoxes of Ibsen, the defiant irony of Hardy, and even for Flaubert's cool, nearly detached, devotion to exactitude for art's sake. Naturalism often threatened to turn into its opposite, pantheism; the relentless natural forces of Hardy or Conrad seem sometimes more cruel than indifferent. If one must force the naturalist message into a formula, it is one that is hardly new in literature: that the world is not as we would like it to be. It is the way this was said, and the time it was said in, that gave nineteenth-century literary naturalism its importance.

❦

One might have expected America, whose national credo was centered on universal morality, to have repudiated naturalism wholeheartedly. Actually, the American reaction was by no means uniform. Some kinds of naturalism were much more acceptable than others. Religious skepticism itself was not very startling. Though most Americans were believers, and the overwhelming majority moralists, a minority had always been skeptics. One enemy of conventional religion, Colonel Robert Ingersoll, had become a popular orator and an influential Republican. Conventional in everything but religion, Ingersoll had been a large-scale reproduction of that familiar figure, the small-town scoffer.

This familiar type was not so much materialist as Deist. He usually read Paine and Voltaire. Though he delighted in raising the hackles of the orthodox, he was seldom really antireligious, and never unmoral. His enemies were censorship, prudery, and the lies of the churches, particularly the cruel and unfair doctrine of Original Sin. He delighted, in the name of real morality, to expose hypocrisy and to smoke out the sins of the godly. He usually espoused some kind of mild social radicalism, often a type of monetary inflation. His style was violent and deliberately picturesque.

The defenders of culture and morality looked askance at such people, but more for their coarseness than their irreligion. Educated, urban Americans could tolerate those naturalists who expressed themselves politely, believed in the improvement of society, and left some place in their systems for moral judgment of conduct. The only kind of naturalism that was really intolerable was that which hinted at a world without secure moral values.

Naturalism coming directly from scientists was usually treated with respect. Scientists were benefactors and progressives by definition. Even if their philosophies were wrong, their purposes were good, and American practical idealists were much more concerned about goals than starting-points. The Progressive Era could tolerate, though it did not approve, blasphemy against God; it was only blasphemy against man that really shocked it.

Most of the naturalism that reached the American public through the press and the scientific popularizers was thoroughly optimistic.[2]

[2] An exception to optimism among scientists was widely reported in November 1912. Alfred Russel Wallace, the co-discoverer of evolution, said to the press on his ninetieth birthday that he had concluded that man had not progressed in intellect or morals since the days of the Egyptians. American press

The favorite European scientist of the American press, which treated European scientists with almost superstitious reverence, was Ernst Haeckel, the white-bearded sage of Jena, with Alfred Wallace the chief survivor of the great Darwinian age. Haeckel was as uncompromising as any iconoclast could wish; he delighted to repudiate purpose, freedom, personal immortality, and especially that "gaseous vertebrate" God. In 1913 it was reported that thousands of people were leaving German churches to support Haeckel's doctrines in Monist societies.

Yet Haeckel failed to shock. In 1914 Edwin E. Slosson, a remarkably accurate specimen and an effective shaper of American taste, published a collection of six reports of visits to great contemporaries. He had no difficulty in including Haeckel in his uplifting series, originally published in the semireligious *Independent*.[3] It could be pointed out that Haeckel was not only thoroughly and conventionally moral, but patriotic. In early 1914 it still counted in his favor that he got along well with German authorities. Moreover, as Slosson did not need to point out, his atheism, for all its forthrightness, was a little ambiguous. His best-selling *Riddle of the Universe*, much reprinted in translation since its publication in 1899, drew together energy and matter, life and nonlife, man and animals into a great, mysterious unity. Man, the earth, and the sun were surely mortal, but to Haeckel the great sum of things was not; worlds would go on indefinitely dying and being born. Haeckel realized that his view was not far, really, from pantheism; he ended the *Riddle* with a quotation from Goethe; readers of Emerson could swallow Haeckel's conclusions without much trouble.

The nonreligious religion of Monism was spread in the United States partly by the devoted efforts of Paul Carus. Carus, a German immigrant, believed that the spiritual and material realms were one, and that both could be understood by scientific exploration of

---

comment makes it plain that this was a shocking statement. *Literary Digest*, November 22, 1912, pp. 1008–9.

[3] Slosson: *Major Prophets of Today* (Boston, 1914), pp. 242–99.

natural law. His Open Court Publishing Company printed some of the classics of European science and also works of iconoclastic philosophy. His own views and those of many more militant naturalists were spread before the public in his magazines, the *Open Court* and the more technically philosophical *Monist*. All these enterprises were subsidized by a Chicago manufacturer who admired Carus and hoped to contribute to the establishment of religion and ethics on a clear, modern, scientific basis.

A number of other books and magazines brought the materialist case to American attention. Beginning in 1872, Edward L. Yeomans's *Popular Science Monthly* had been championing the views of Spencer, Tyndall, and Huxley. Occasionally the muckraking magazines liked to expose the universe in much the same way they exposed the trusts. Books like Carl Snyder's *The World Machine* (1911) described the cosmic mechanism in popular terms. George W. Crile's *Man, an Adaptive Mechanism* (1916) anticipated some of the postwar vogue of explaining all human action by glands.

Jacques Loeb of the Rockefeller Institute for Medical Research spoke for uncompromising naturalism with the authority of German training and scientific achievement. His clear, authoritative essays, printed in *Popular Science* or condensed in *McClure's*, his speeches at Monist Congresses moved convincingly from descriptions of his own experiments to materialist theory. In his own laboratory Loeb in 1900 had fertilized the eggs of the sea-urchin without the assistance of a male sea-urchin. Soon, he was quite sure, physical-chemical explanations would be extended from birth and death to cover all life, emphatically including mental activity. The path of understanding led, he suggested, through the study of instincts. The maternal instinct, the sexual instinct, "the instinct of workmanship" were little different from the tropisms that cause some forms of life to react in a predictable way to light or electric energy.

Despite his uncompromising and combative materialism, Loeb was read and widely respected. He was, like his materialist predecessors of the eighteenth century, emphatically an optimist. Beneath the harsh formulas of stimulus and response lurked natural goodness. Our hereditary physical natures forced us to be social beings.

> We struggle for justice and truth since we are instinctively compelled to see our fellow beings happy. Economic, social, and political conditions of ignorance and superstition may warp and inhibit the inherited instincts and thus create a civilization with a faulty or low development of ethics.[4]

The Progressive Era could tolerate almost any view that made moral responsibility natural and selfishness artificial.

Loeb pointed clearly toward the crucial area for naturalist research, the study of the human mind. Some kinds of American psychology already took an uncompromising naturalist, even a mechanist view of the mind, for granted. Making psychology into a science was the great object, and the first step was to overcome idealist prejudice. Another tendency was toward extreme practicality: psychology should produce objective data, useful to educators, businessmen, and social scientists.

Both these tendencies were carried to a new stage by John Broadus Watson, who in 1913 announced to the American Philosophical and Psychological Association a new movement and a new word: Behaviorism. "Psychology as the behaviorist views it," Watson's opening sentence firmly stated, "is a purely objective experimental branch of natural science." Most of his audience, the paper implied, wanted psychology to become such a science, but their hopes so far had been thwarted. They were bogged down in disputes whose terms had no common definition. They could not even agree on the limits of their field; some of them were snobbish, for instance, about animal psychology because it did not deal with consciousness, the psychologist's traditional field.

The trouble, said Watson, was age-old. Despite their naturalist objectives, psychologists thought in terms of the ancient, meaningless argument of philosophers about the relation of the mind to

[4] Jacques Loeb: *The Mechanistic Conception of Life* (Chicago, 1912), p. 31.

external objects. His solution to this dualism was as radical as Solomon's way of dealing with babies. Consciousness, which could not be defined and therefore made all the trouble, should be eliminated. The psychologist henceforth must stick to behavior, studying the nervous and muscular adjustment of organisms, animal and human, to their environment. It was not necessary to assume any separate mental activity. In a long footnote Watson suggested a corollary which later became central: thought was to be dealt with as latent speech. In the long run, all psychological study could be carried on in behaviorist terms; the difference between experimenting with rats, with savages, and with cultivated Europeans was only one of degree of complexity. The method Watson advocated would finally, after so many failures, make psychology usable by "the educator, the physician, the jurist and the businessman." [5]

This exciting doctrine, in a sense the culmination of many trends of the Progressive Era, was actually a little ahead of its precise historical moment. A few elements needed to be added; Watson was very shortly to seize on the Russian experiments with conditioned response. These, combined with the dicta of some of the boldest young social scientists, were to produce in the next decade a vision of Utopia. Sunday supplements and women's magazines were to announce, and millions were to believe, that the way had been found to produce new and better human beings at will. Behaviorism, turned into a simple panacea, was apparently to take the place for some people of progressive hopes that had failed.

This was still well in the future; in 1913 the response to Watson's program was widespread but academic. Some psychologists protested; others approved. John Dewey for one thought the new program might help bring psychology closer to life, though he thought Watson's definition of behavior excluded a good deal of commonsense reality.

Behaviorism, with its arbitrary and narrow definition of human

[5] Watson: "Psychology as the Behaviorist Views It," *Psychological Review*, XX (1913), 158–77.

experience, obviously ran counter to every major tendency of articulate American thought, religious or secular, Protestant or humanist. Yet it was very American; it was an emergence into dogmatic statement of the old, latent practicalism of American life. It was the extreme form of a widespread, still unsuccessful tendency to separate progress from traditional moral criteria. Many of the tendencies we have examined were working toward this momentous separation.

Militant naturalist dogma preached from left-wing soapboxes attracted more public attention than did the same doctrine announced from the laboratory. Watson, who was a conservative in politics, and other naturalist scientists who were neutral, were useful to radicals. They proved what the latter had long suspected, that talk about the soul was a fraud intended to cover up oppression.

Some Americans inherited this hard-bitten suspicion from generations of radical doctrine; others arrived at it largely through experience. To large groups of immigrant workers, the liberal Protestant language in which the dominant doctrines were phrased was a completely foreign tongue. The Social Gospel and the political reform movement were meaningless; generations of experience had demonstrated that neither church nor state could be the worker's friend. To the garment-workers on the East Side of New York, as idealistic a group as any in the country, it was impossible to take seriously the forms of idealism prevalent in the bourgeois, Anglo-Saxon world. The only question worth debating on the hot tenement roofs on summer nights was what kind of socialism should prevail in the whole world. One largely native group was far more deeply alienated: nobody took a harsher view of conventional moralism than the Industrial Workers of the World.

This much-loved and hated organization, produced by a series of fusions and fissions, grouped together a good sampling of the American disinherited, especially in the Far West. Some of the I.W.W. old-timers remembered the dramatic radical episodes of the past, the Pullman strike, the anarchist propaganda of the deed, the uncompromising socialist offensives of Daniel De Leon. A few of the younger Wobblies were in touch with French syndicalist theory, which repudiated political reform in favor of the eventual general strike. Both theory and experience, their loyalties of the past and their hard migratory existence in the present confirmed the Wobblies in their proud and sweeping rejections. Not only the political institutions of the possessing class, but their ideas as well were to be thrown on the ash heap, from patriotism and pussy-footing legalism to religion. The harsh, tough, skeptical songs of Joe Hill convey most clearly the nature of the I.W.W.'s appeal to well-brought-up intellectuals of radical sympathies. Here, if anywhere, was a clear breach with timidity, moralism, and the whole manner and content of the standard American culture. "Long-haired preachers" try to tell us what's right and wrong, but turn out to offer only "pie in the sky." Only Joe Block, "born by mistake," swallows the pious promise that he "may Be President some day" and is therefore willing to "go jump in the lake For Liberty's sake."

Outwardly the most promising radical movement of twentieth century America, the Socialist Party, reached its high point in 1912. The myth has persisted that it was on the road to achieving its goals, and that only the coming of the war derailed it. Recent sympathetic students, sometimes, one suspects, to their own surprise, have damaged this attractive radical myth. In 1912–13 the American socialist movement was seriously set back by internal splits. Socialists could not agree whether they wanted to reject, like the Wobblies, the whole of the dominant civilization or only its political forms.

One of the main issues was religion. Socialists were in theory Marxists and therefore materialists. Many of them included the anticlericals of the past on the long roll of radical heroes. Sets of Socialist pamphlets included works by Darwin and even Spencer; some of the socialist press liked to quote such naturalist social scientists as E. A. Ross. In Kansas or Oklahoma, the party sometimes spoke with the familiar accents of the village atheist. Young urban socialists took it for granted that agnosticism, sexual freedom, Ibsen, and Shaw were parts of the cause.

Such assumptions shocked some other kinds of socialists, Social Gospel ministers, and former progressives, who expected the triumph of the workers to end temptations to vice and show the way to a pure moral order. Arguments about religion and morality, in socialist circles, were sometimes blended with other arguments that transcended politics: arguments over revolutionary purity as opposed to gradual gains, the brotherhood of man against deep-seated suspicions of immigrants and Negroes, comradeship with other groups on the right and left, even such symbolic matters as whether it was a revolutionary gesture or a lapse in good taste for a party speaker to wear overalls.

Even among socialists, the pull of respectability was very strong. In 1912–13 the right wing won. Big Bill Haywood, hero of the overall brigade and also of Greenwich Village intellectuals, was recalled from the National Committee. A resolution excluded from the party those who condoned violence. This seemed to many to mean even more than it said: those who wanted to repudiate American culture and society as well as capitalism had to carry on outside the main socialist camp.

One can easily sympathize with the irritation felt by hard-working socialist politicians, who saw their chances of success imperiled by the loudmouths of the far left. Yet these chances of success proved illusory. It may well be the excluded radicals who played the more important role. Social Revolution in America has so far proved a dream; cultural revolution has been an important reality. Indirectly and directly, the cultural changes of the twentieth century owe a large debt to the bold iconoclasts of the left, the Wobblies and anarchists and others, hard-boiled and yet romantic, outspoken, and unwilling to compromise. Many important young Americans of impeccable middle-class upbringing first heard from the radicals of this period a ringing challenge to all their complacent assumptions.

For some, Thorstein Veblen brought together the historical materialism of the Marxists, the detachment of the scientists, and the relativism of the American pragmatist movement. Veblen had learned from all these and many other sources. Perhaps more important still, he was the first major American social thinker to come from the wrong side of the tracks.

Veblen's own emotions cannot be separated from his doctrine. His biographers have suggested that his harshness and sourness came partly from even deeper sources than his upbringing in a frostbitten Norwegian village in Minnesota. In Veblen's description of society, and also in his curious career with its spoiled jobs and broken marriages, there seems to be a tendency to equate whatever is pleasant, luxurious, or conventional with evil. As a relativist, an objective social scientist, Veblen coined for evil a number of marvelously polysyllabic synonyms, such as pecuniary emulation, conspicuous waste. It is easy to see, however, that to him capitalism and its culture were not only obsolete; they were repulsive. It is easy to see what he hated, and only a little harder to guess what he loved.

Certainly the official credo of the day, as we have described it, was part of what repelled him. Moral idealism, as the official spokesmen conceived it, was obsolete; industrial society must learn to be matter-of-fact in a scientific age. Culture was worse, the deliberate conservation of whatever was useless exactly because it was useless. Progress, at first glance, seemed meaningless in a system in which human instincts survived long after they had become useless and destructive.

Yet even in Veblen, as in Marx, there was a core of nineteenth-century optimism. The ugly traits of our society were survivals of the period of aristocratic barbarism. In time, he hinted they would be stripped away. Beneath them lay a more promising layer, the instincts, imbedded most deeply in the working class, inherited from the earliest, savage stage. These were the instincts Veblen obviously admired, the parental bent, the instinct of workmanship, the instinct of idle curiosity, or in ordinary terms disinterested love and disinterested science. In the long run, he hinted, these traits would be revived by industrial experience, and they would displace competitive chaos by sensible organization, perhaps in a society run by engineers.

The earliest human traits, and those which the future would revive, sometimes sound very much like fundamental human goodness. In an article in *Ethics* in 1910 Veblen declared that, according to his analysis, "the ancient racial bias embodied in the Christian principle of brotherhood should logically continue to gain ground at the expense of the pecuniary morals of competitive business." [6] Though the suggestion would have dismayed him, this prophecy puts Veblen into the same universe as the Social Gospel.

In the prewar period Veblen's thought, adapted and expurgated, was chiefly influential on the respectable academic economists. In wartime and afterwards, he was to become the hero of a quite different group, the young radicals. At the beginning of an age of disillusion he exactly suited their needs. At the heart was social idealism and hope for the future, but it was thoroughly concealed by his mask, a mask which seldom slipped: the mask of a hard-boiled, scientific, savagely ironical dissector of a moribund society.

Well outside theoretical argument, the radical kind of naturalism cropped out too in a special kind of doctrine about crime and punishment. Clarence Darrow, for instance, read in his early youth the radical classics Voltaire and Paine. His father was known in a little Ohio town as the village infidel. Experience of the seamy side of Chicago life impressed Darrow with the truth of some charges in the radical indictment of society but not with the validity of radical premises. Darrow was unable to swallow the Single-Taxer or anarchist talk of natural rights. These did not exist, any more than other moral absolutes.

Following these premises, Darrow became deeply skeptical of prevalent social standards of right and wrong. Criminals, he

[6] Veblen: "Christian Morals and the Competitive System," *Ethics*, XX (1910), 185; quoted by David W. Noble: *The Paradox of Progressive Thought* (Minneapolis, 1958), p. 227.

thought, were victims of society. He came very close indeed to justifying the *Los Angeles Times* dynamiters, who never meant to kill eleven people. Crime and terror would disappear, he was able to believe even after a long career in criminal law, if social injustice were abated. Meantime sympathy and understanding, not obsolete moralistic punishment, were most needed.

Darrow was not the only man of his day who questioned the dominant legal standards of right and wrong. Ben Lindsey, the Denver friend of delinquent children, was still a hero of the muckraking magazines, all the more because he was so bitterly attacked by Colorado conservatives. Lindsey had not yet turned to the dangerous cause of marriage reform. People of good will were delighted with accounts of delinquent boys, long regarded as hopeless, parading unguarded through Denver and returning to the reformatory.

Darrow and Lindsey and others, understandably revolted by the stupid and vengeful idea of punishment, looking for a rationale for compassion, found it in the theory that crime is caused by the environment. Sometimes this generous doctrine carried them far toward moral revolution. They could often demonstrate that vice and crime were linked to corporate profits. This suggested that all vice and crime were caused by faulty social arrangements. It was not hard to take the final step, and conclude that vice and crime, and also virtue, were words without meaning.

Sometimes the same kind of skeptical sentimentality emerged from the muckraking movement. For the most part, muckrakers were anything but skeptical. Their work, like that of much of progressivism, rested on the assumption that if one points out what is evil, people will choose the good. Yet some muckrakers made this purpose silly by showing good and evil to be product alike of hidden, irresistible forces. The most influential of all muckrakers, Lincoln Steffens, was the most effective moral revolutionary of the day.

Steffens's brand of skepticism was his own. Fresh from the idealistic doctrines of Howison at Berkeley, he had gone to Europe for the Wanderjahr fairly common in the early nineties. In rather priggish letters home he had announced to his best college friend his conversion to materialism. As a New York reporter he had encountered corruption and learned some of the obvious paradoxes of reform. These became, quite early, his stock in trade, a golden stock for the period, titillating and at the same time essentially sentimental. Steffens reversed exactly the progressive clichés: the bosses and the businessmen behind them always turned out to have hearts of gold; the earnest reformers were likely to be wicked at bottom. The best way to work for progress was to appeal to the good bad people for a change of heart and thus short-cut and embarrass the bad good reformers.

Steffens's few efforts to apply this formula himself, culminating in his disastrous intervention in the trial of the *Los Angeles Times* bombers in 1911, often failed; the bad people proved to be not quite good enough in practice. There is no doubt, however, that he successfully confused a number of good people, especially good young people, with his exciting reversals of morality. Mercurial, charming, at home everywhere, the friend of anarchists and big businessmen and Theodore Roosevelt, always full of ironic wisdom and seldom really involved, Steffens was a far more powerful figure than the outsider radicals of the far left. Before the war and after, he served as an effective bridge between their ideas and the literary enthusiasms of the young intellectuals.

❦

Loeb, Watson, Darrow, even at bottom Veblen were, on naturalist grounds, optimistic about the future promised by advancing science. A vastly different kind of naturalism, elegant rather than strident, despairingly conservative rather than crusading, and above all sad, came from an opposite quarter. The less hopeful minority among the custodians of culture, often more directly in touch with Europe and especially England than their countrymen, had seen through the Victorian complacency to the omnipresent Victorian doubt. Some had listened with Arnold to the roar of the receding sea of faith, others had shared Tennyson's struggle to stem it. Still others had formed their own conclusions, listening to the prophecies of scientific progress and finding them probably true, but abhorrent.

The extreme of polite naturalistic pessimism was represented by brothers Henry and Brooks Adams. Brooks, an eccentric yet influential figure, mixed too much romantic conservatism, militarism, geopolitics, and twisted radicalism with his prophecies to be taken altogether seriously. Less violent and therefore probably more important, Henry shared his naturalism and his hopelessness about the future.

According to his autobiography, before 1918 available only to friends in privately printed form, Adams had suspected the honesty of the cheerful kind of Darwinism at its first appearance; uniform upward development was contradicted by the evidence. One cannot be sure that Adams suspected this quite as soon as he suggests; much of his autobiography is clearly poetic metaphor rather than literal account. By 1912, however, he had certainly been constructing for a long time his own brand of regretful, pessimistic naturalism. In 1910 he set it forth in a *Letter to Teachers of American History*, privately printed and mailed to a few hundred scholars.

Evolutionary historians, Adams argued, were on the wrong track. They were following obsolete and false deductions from Darwinism; not biology, but physics, held the key to past and future. The meaning of history lay not in progressive natural selection, but in the steady, irreversible dissipation of energy. What historians should be explaining to their classes, that is, was not the development of liberty and democracy, but the approach of death.

Even if Adams's argument had been more compelling, historians in 1910 would hardly have been much interested. Some of them were still insisting that the job of history was to preserve moral values; others were attracted by Robinson's daring proposal for using history to abolish the past. The frontier theory was as near to a scientific determinism as most of them wanted to go. Many historians, like other prewar Americans, apparently found sufficient satisfaction and meaning in their daily work, sticking to particular problems and leaving larger problems alone. Adams, increasingly obsessed by his hunger for ultimate answers, remained a distinguished but not very influential historian until 1918, when his *Education* was first made available to the general public. In 1918, for the first time since the nineties, alienated Victorians were to be really welcome.

❦

When they talked about foreign literature, the more tolerant of the arbiters of American taste drew about the same lines as they did in discussing scientific or social thought. Naturalists who, like Zola, dealt with coarse and sordid subjects were forgiven when they seemed to be fighting for social progress. Pessimistic naturalists, though less acceptable, could be tolerated when they expressed themselves in elegant and conventional terms.

Howells had won the battle for most kinds of French and Russian naturalism a long time ago. At the time of Zola's death in 1902, Howells had said in a fiery essay that the defender of Dreyfus "was an artist, and one of the very greatest, but even before and beyond that he was intensely a moralist, as only the moralists of our true and noble time have been." [7] Henry James defended Zola in somewhat different terms. When he stuck to outward and especially collective action, James said flatly, Zola was great, and his grossness was necessary to this kind of greatness.

Turgenev, a superb and delicate technician, a pessimist without grossness, was James's idol. Flaubert and Maupassant, artists from whom James had learned much, seemed to him unduly cold and aloof. Maupassant's view of sex, James said quite calmly, was one that Anglo-Saxons simply could not share. Aside from this special and rather unimportant matter, James's main objections to some of the naturalists were on intellectual rather than moral grounds.

[7] Howells: "Emile Zcla," *North American Review,* CLXXV (1902), 592.

Their view of man was too narrow. James had found, listening to the talk in Flaubert's salon, that European writers assumed that morality and art belonged in different universes; one had nothing to do with the other. James found this doctrine not so much horrifying, as unforgivably simple.[8]

Lesser critics, aside from those who were shocked by all kinds of naturalism, tended to follow the Howells line. Naturalism was acceptable when it could be associated with reform. Major works of most of the great naturalists—Zola, Flaubert, Turgenev, Ibsen among them—had been translated and published in America. So had those of Maupassant, sometimes in a limited edition advertised as frank and unexpurgated. Stendhal, whose cold dissection of human motives could not be made into moral allegory, remained almost unknown. Gorky, associated with the popular cause of democratic revolution in Russia, was lionized on a visit of 1905 by radicals and pundits alike, entertained by a committee led by Mark Twain, showered with praise by everybody from Howells to Edwin Markham. Then suddenly the *World* disclosed that the woman he was traveling with was not, technically, Madame Gorky, and the limits of the period's tolerance were quickly and brutally demonstrated by sudden ostracism.

On the stage, in this period of opulent and gay entertainment, naturalism had had harder sledding. Ibsen's plays, first seen in the 1880's and performed a good deal since the 1890's, were old hat in advanced circles, where his attacks on conventional bourgeois morality seemed themselves rather heavy and old-fashioned. Yet some Americans still found Ibsen challenging. Professor Otto Heller of Washington University thought that American optimism had prevented Americans from appreciating the great Scandinavian. Only now, Heller thought, was the country ready for Ibsen's critical message. A writer in the *New England Magazine* disagreed sharply.

[8] James: *The Art of Fiction and other Essays* (Morris Roberts, ed., New York, 1948), pp. 103–4. Other opinions mentioned are found in his *French Poets and Novelists* (New York, 1878).

The only people ready to welcome Ibsen were "the set of dirty-collared Socialists and artist garret-dwellers" who "have not the price of a haircut." [9]

This was surely exaggerated. James Gibbons Huneker, from a very different point of view, agreed that Ibsen was being ruined by the Ibsenite cult. But a man with a very clean collar and no connection either with socialism or little theaters, Professor Brander Matthews, had been defending Ibsen for decades. Determined theatergoers were also acquainted with, and perhaps a little bored by, didactic naturalists like Eugene Brieux, whose *Damaged Goods,* a play about prostitution and venereal disease, was staged in New York in 1913 under the auspices of the Sociological Fund of the *Medical Review of Reviews.* Galsworthy's early problem plays were easily accepted. Naturalism on the stage, in fact, no longer shocked urban audiences unless it was either heavily sexual or unusually depressing. August Strindberg, grimly determinist and given to "morbid" treatment of sexual obsessions, was still a storm center. A series of Strindberg translations and a few performances in 1912 produced thrills and alarms.

On the whole, when we remember the standard prescribed by the older critics for American literature, we are surprised by the broad tolerance of their view of foreign naturalism, and not by their occasional taboos. Part of the reason lies in their confident assumption that American society was, and would remain, different from that of Europe. Not life, but the Second Empire, was being terribly described by Zola. There was little danger that a young American, reading Flaubert's *Sentimental Education,* would start looking for a fashionable married woman willing to become his recognized mistress. If even Turgenev was a pessimist, it must be because things were sad in Russia. Howells's famous statement that the smiling aspects of life were the more American, which seemed to a later generation willfully blind, still seemed to most people in

[9] Heller: *Henrik Ibsen, Plays and Problems* (Boston, 1912); Ethel Syford: "Ibsen in America," *New England Magazine,* XLVIII (1912), 330.

1912 unescapable, obvious truth. This being so, properly escorted excursions into the European murk were instructive, and even, in a shuddery manner, pleasant.

❦

Native naturalism obviously raised a harder problem. Here too a reforming intent could make up for a lot. When muckraking novelists dealt with subjects like prostitution, objections were raised by professional censors, not by the literary pundits. New sights, even new smells, in literature could be tolerated; new points of view were much more alarming.

The story of the darker kind of naturalism in American literature should start with Mark Twain, but the savage irony present in much of his work was, as we have seen, something that the period managed to ignore. In 1916 *The Mysterious Stranger* was published posthumously. This is the story of a supernatural visitor to the earth, who demonstrates that even with miraculous power, the only favor one can do human beings is to let them die. They are doomed to misery and hate, primarily by their moral sense, which is the source of most cruelty. This fable was published by Harper's for the Christmas trade, with delightful pictures by N. C. Wyeth, a much admired illustrator of books for the young. The *Nation*'s reviewer said that "he had proved by experiment that a boy of nine can read this brightly pictured magical romance of the sixteenth century with delight and without undesirable stimulation." [1] He may even have been right.

Edwin Arlington Robinson was not so much a naturalist as a New England seeker, forever struggling to resist the naturalist vision. Beset by the common Victorian doubts and fears, he had at Harvard in the nineties encountered the whole range of pessimistic Europeans. He had intensely admired Hardy and Ibsen among others. He actually wrote a sonnet to Zola, characteristically not so

[1] *Nation*, December 21, 1916, p. 588.

much about Zola as about his own difficulty in accepting Zola. Robinson's early poems were bleak and comfortless, but elegant and reasonably conventional in diction. This made him acceptable even to Roosevelt. Yet Robinson did not score his first public success until 1916 with *The Man Against the Sky*. Then this nineteenth-century pessimist was swept into popularity by a poetic movement with which he had nothing to do, a movement of exuberant youth.

For a short space in the nineties, that decade when doubts and fears almost cracked the cheerful surface, an American naturalist movement fully analogous to the European one had issued its challenge. All the members of this school, Frank Norris, Jack London, Stephen Crane, and Theodore Dreiser had been stimulated at a critical point either by European science or European naturalist literature or both. In every case also they read their foreign books with eyes opened by native experience. Sometimes this came from early poverty, sometimes from exposure to radical politics, most often of all from newspaper work. Reporters seldom took moral uplift or literary convention very seriously, except in their published writing. As Dreiser found:

> One can always talk to a newspaper man, I think, with the full confidence that one is talking to a man who is at least free of moralistic mush. Nearly everything in connection with those trashy romances of justice, truth, mercy, patriotism, public profession of all sorts, is already and forever gone if they have been in the business for any length of time.[2]

Turn-of-the-century naturalism, a startling but brief episode, disappeared with the death of its authors. It seemed to have no meaning to the hopeful new century. So successfully was this movement buried that some of the youngest rebels learned about naturalism first from Europe and discovered only later this recent American naturalist school.[3]

[2] Dreiser: *A Book About Myself* (New York, 1922), p. 396.

[3] Van Wyck Brooks, for instance, says that when he lived in New York in

Of the turn-of-the-century naturalists, only Theodore Dreiser refused either to die young, disappear, or reform. Changing little, learning little, he hung on through several stages of cultural revolution until pessimism got another hearing. In the prewar years, although he was quite outside the main currents of literary rebellion, he inevitably became a major storm center. From beginning to end of his career, he embodied all the elements of naturalism that dominant opinion feared most.

Dreiser was almost the ultimate underdog; his family was not only poor and foreign, but shiftless, sporadically unmoral, and nearly always unhappy. His career fits neither the conventional pattern of the struggle out of the depths nor the radical stereotype of the oppressed but battling proletarian. Clearly Dreiser needed no education beyond that afforded by Terre Haute and Chicago slums to make him a pessimist.

Yet this is obviously too simple; one can point to many children from the late nineteenth-century jungle who rose to respectability and optimism. Dreiser himself thought abstract philosophical ideas had a lot to do with literature; few recent novelists drag them in as baldly. His ideas did not come mainly from foreign literature, though he describes an important encounter with Balzac. It was science and scientific philosophy, first Spencer and Huxley and Darwin, then Jacques Loeb, that gave him a new way of seeing the universe. Spencer, who had convinced Andrew Carnegie in a flash that all was well, since all grew better, had a different effect on Dreiser:

> . . . When I read Spencer I could only sigh. All I could think of was that since nature would not or could not do anything for man, he must, if he could, do something for himself; and of

---

1907 he hardly knew the names of Robinson, Crane, Norris, or Dreiser. Brooks: *Scenes and Portraits* (New York, 1954), p. 152. F. Scott Fitzgerald, stimulated by foreign writers before the war, encountered Norris, Dreiser, and Clemens only after 1918. Henry Dan Piper: "Fitzgerald's Cult of Disillusion," *American Quarterly*, II (1951), 69–80; "Frank Norris and Scott Fitzgerald," *Huntington Library Quarterly*, XIX (1955–56), 393–400.

this I saw no prospect, he being a product of these self-same accidental, indifferent, and bitterly cruel forces.[4]

Dreiser, because he was very far from being a doctrinaire naturalist of the Zola school, was in a sense the only real naturalist in our literature. His universe comes the closest to being really indifferent; the catastrophes in his novels fall on his characters not as the blows of tragic destiny but with an appalling random thud. Yet there is a layer of ideas in Dreiser deeper than that forced on him by sordid experience and scientific materialism.

Despite the struggles of the Dreisers, he was brought up so full of Christian assumptions that he could never forgive the God who, he early concluded, did not exist. No writer had less of the clinical coldness Henry James found unacceptable in Flaubert or Maupassant. Dreiser could not suppress his wonder and pity. "Why did He do it?" he asked in commenting on his earliest experience of Chicago misery, and then dropping the capitalized pronoun went on in the next sentence. "Why did nature, when left to itself, devise such astounding slums and human muck-heaps?" [5]

Because Dreiser was neither hopeful nor clinically objective, he was intolerable to official prewar America. Rejecting idealism of the conventional sort in every word, denying progress, he affronted culture more than any other writer had managed to. He was not only crude, which could be forgiven, but vulgar and slick in the manner of the cheap magazine fiction he edited for a living. Moreover he didn't care; when his errors were pointed out he went on in the same way. He was not even deliberately shocking; the most devastating thing about Dreiser was not what he *said* about prewar American society, but what he almost unintentionally *showed.* It is not surprising that a public which could stand London and Norris, Loeb and Watson, Zola and Ibsen, even at times Debs and Haywood, could not stand Dreiser.

[4] Dreiser: *A Book About Myself*, p. 459.
[5] Ibid., p. 66.

PART TWO: *Older Insurgents and Invaders* (1890–1917)

At the beginning of the teens the conservative and optimistic defenders of American civilization took for granted, as a familiar feature of the scene, cheerful atheism and purposeful exposure. They congratulated themselves, from time to time, that the brutal and sordid naturalism of the turn of the century, the worst enemy of all they represented, had disappeared. They were mistaken on two counts in this judgment: naturalism had not disappeared, nor was it, immediately, their most dangerous enemy. Naturalism had gone underground. The most successful kind of prewar rebellion, the one that did most to shake the old order, had little directly to do with it. Yet its long-run effect was very great. The questions posed by naturalism had never been satisfactorily answered, and they would be presented again and again.

IV
Amoralists

To those Americans who knew about it, another kind of late nineteenth-century thought was even more shocking than naturalism. It was bad enough to insist on the harshest implications of materialist science. It was still worse, however, to repudiate science altogether, and with it progress, social morality, democracy, and the whole accomplishment of the nineteenth century. When this kind of repudiation extended further still and included reason itself, when words hardly had any definite and predictable meanings, insanity seemed to be at hand.

This was the direction taken by the European neo-romantics of the late nineteenth century, a tremendously gifted and diverse group of writers who had in common mainly their alienation. Like some of the naturalists, the neo-romantics rejected the optimistic Victorian version of recent history: the triumph of science and progress. They rejected also the simple materialist picture of a universe of matter in motion. What fascinated the neo-romantics was whatever remained mysterious: bizarre reversals of conventional moral values, dreams more real than reality, new ways to manipulate words and symbols so as to approach the unexpressible.

This was not the fervent romanticism of an earlier period, though it drew on the romanticism of all times. The new believers in art did not expect, as Coleridge had for instance, that intuition would transfigure and illuminate the universe. They did not hope, like Ruskin, that beauty would ennoble society. Art did not necessarily lead to any truth but its own; there might not be any other kind of truth for it to lead to. Aesthetic values, down to the last delicate nuance, must be cultivated for their own sakes, desperately, without regard to ordinary morality, if necessary at the cost of madness and despair.

In 1857, the same year that Flaubert published *Madame Bovary*, caricaturing the old romanticism, Charles Baudelaire inaugurated the new with *Flowers of Evil*, the bible of the antimoralists. Unlike many of his followers, Baudelaire meant what he said and was superbly able to say it. In his famous invocation he recognized as the worst of mental monsters, the most likely source of horror and destruction, an apparition fully familiar to Europeans in the nineteenth century but hardly glimpsed in busy America: Ennui.

Baudelaire and his followers made a cult of Edgar Allan Poe, admiring in him exactly the qualities which American critics continually deplored: his febrile intensity, his love of exotic and bizarre subjects, his rejection of modern civilization, and his insistence that "Poetry" was independent of moral judgment. For three quarters of a century after Baudelaire, a series of schools of poets moved further into many kinds of moral and technical experiment. French verse, fertile, various, and brilliant, experimental in both form and point of view, became the single most important influence on Western Literature. Its great figures, particularly Mallarmé, Verlaine, and Rimbaud, became the heroes and martyrs of the aesthetic cause in all countries except America. These poets, different as they were, had in common at least a new kind of devotion to art, a dedication so proud, so intense, and so exclusive, that it seemed simply insane to the surviving believers in material progress.

Toward the end of the century European aestheticism, or part of it, branched off the main road into decadence. The distinction is not precise; perhaps it is only one of seriousness and intensity. Defying conventional morality became, instead of a desperate necessity for a few, a fashion. Conscious artificiality, deliberate cultivation of the perverse and excessive were the hallmarks of decadence. Perhaps the epitome was the over-rated, languid, black-mass foolishness of Joris-Karl Huysmans. Even matter-of-fact England had her amoral aesthetes; from Victorian preachers of beauty the path led through Swinburne to the brief vogue of Oscar Wilde and Aubrey Beardsley. Witty and courageous, the London decadents were fundamentally trivial and imitative. When the public learned that

Wilde had defied its standards in action as well as words, the movement collapsed. On the continent, however, aestheticism, experiment, even the extremes of decadence continued in vogue. Everywhere in Europe the picture of the artist, drawn by himself, was familiar to the bourgeoisie.

The revolt against nineteenth-century progress and morality took a more vigorous form in Germany with Friedrich Nietzsche. Nietzsche, who continually prophesied that he would be misunderstood, has been made into many things, including an old-fashioned idealist in disguise and a modern naturalist. If he was an idealist, the disguise was a good one; if he was a naturalist, his kind of naturalism was new in Western culture. God, he announced, was dead, which was not at all the same as saying that He had never existed. Science was dying, too, and intelligent men, having realized that it could never get very close to reality, were abandoning it.

Nietzsche, in contrast to his predecessor Schopenhauer, and in contrast also to the antimoralist aesthetes, was called an optimist, the great yea-sayer. Again, if he was an optimist, it was in his own terms only. Progress, utility, reason, democracy—the things on which modern civilization prided itself, were to Nietzsche symptoms of sickness and approaching death: joy and health lay only in the self-fulfilling and self-transcending individual. For him there was hope, but only if he boldly threw aside the restraints of Christian morality. The abandonment of outward cruelty and selfishness had been a dreadful error, a source of inward sickness, the result of a plot by the feeble and cunning against the strong and beautiful. Only by moral revolution, by a reversal of values, could man recover tragedy, his only real kind of happiness.

In his long and tortured search for a new god to replace the old one, Nietzsche considered and rejected art as well as science. The true principle of reality was the will to power, present in all things and reaching its highest form in the noble, overcoming, superman. Thus Nietzsche cannot be classified with aesthetes except in a very broad sense. What he had in common with them was their enemy: modern culture. In this sense Nietzsche's "joyful wisdom" was a part of the same great turn in the history of European thought.

In the period of its apparent triumph, the modern world and its values—humanitarian progress, comfort, and conventional morality, values often identified with America—were violently rejected by scattered groups of intellectuals. The true morality, these sad protesters agreed, lay in experience and its expression for their own sake, not in success but in tragedy and transcendence.

❦

This uncheerful code, in part new and startling, in part as old as literature itself, was eventually to dominate much of the most admired American literature. Before the war, however, its recent exponents were not only unknown to most Americans but nearly incomprehensible to those who did know them.

Few knew, for instance, that *Flowers of Evil* had bloomed in 1857, only two years after *Leaves of Grass* had pushed their way through an unfriendly soil. European neo-romanticism, that is, had already begun when American romanticism was still having its first vigorous heyday. Yet the contrast was not this simple: American romanticism itself had been less cheerful and robust than the critics of 1912 realized. The affirmative mysticism of Emerson and Whitman had survived; the tragic mysticism of Melville had been forgotten. Nobody had yet suggested that symbolism was one of the major tendencies of American literature, yet from Jonathan Edwards on, important Americans had held unconventional views on the nature of symbol and reality. Just as young Americans in search of naturalism had to discover Flaubert before they could admire Mark Twain, so young Americans in search of symbolism had to encounter Baudelaire or Rimbaud before they could rediscover Poe and Hawthorne.

Even the least optimistic of the older critics had been unable to enter the neo-romantic path. It was a long way from Arnoldian doubts about science and progress to outright hatred of both.

Charles Eliot Norton, or even Henry Adams, had faced their doubts and their duties with what courage they could summon. When European romanticism pushed beyond mere unhappiness into a strange world of despair and perverse delight, even the most perceptive and tolerant nineteenth-century Americans were left behind.

The custodians of culture has been somewhat divided in their attitude to naturalism. There was no division on the subject of decadence. Howells, of course, had thrown all his weight on the side of art that dealt with external reality. Brownell and Babbitt, the chief admirers of French literature, were devoted to the classic tradition against which the symbolists were rebelling. Even Henry James, himself dedicated to a life of the most intense aesthetic effort, refused to follow these poets when they separated art from life. Art provided meaning to experience, and for James the meaning was ultimately moral. The morality might be immensely complex, but it was not insane or upside-down. Baudelaire, to James, was merely "a gentleman in a painful-looking posture, staring very hard at a mass of things from which, more intelligently, we avert our heads." [1] Here the James brothers agreed: William James, when he spoke of Baudelaire, used the tone of the "healthy-mindedness" he deplored in *Varieties of Religious Experience*. Benjamin Wells in his 1896 survey of *Modern French Literature* summarized the verdict of the older generation. Baudelaire's influence in Europe simply proved that "unfortunately disease is more contagious than health." [2]

Aside from the small group of critics who read French fluently, Americans were denied access to the major sources of neo-romanticism. Although some of the most startling naturalists were published in America, decadents like Huysmans or moral revolutionaries like Stendhal were not. Only an occasional minor critic even mentioned the symbolists; only an occasional little magazine pub-

[1] James: *French Poets*, p. 65. Ralph Barton Perry: *The Thought and Character of William James* (2 Vols., Boston, 1936), I, 364.

[2] Wells: *Modern French Literature* (Boston, 2nd ed., 1909), p. 340.

lished two or three of their poems in French. Translating them was almost impossible; this was demonstrated in 1912 when Jethro Bithell published an anthology with a few samples of symbolism in English.[3] Even Bithell omitted Baudelaire. In 1912 a writer in the *Dial* commented with much surprise on the European influence of this poet whose name, he said, was unknown to American readers.[4]

By 1913, in the midst of an American poetic renaissance, a few Americans were finally discovering the symbolists. The lateness of this discovery was to give it a special importance. The poetic innovators of the last fifty years were usually encountered very suddenly, as complete unknowns, by isolated Americans who had long been looking for new literary leaders. John Gould Fletcher, for one, has described the unforgettable thrill of running into the symbolists at Harvard, where he encountered them not in the classroom but in his own desultory reading.[5] At that university at roughly the same time, half a dozen other poets were making the same discovery. One of these was T. S. Eliot. This marked an important instant in the fragmentation of American taste. For the next generation, leading critics were to proclaim these great and disturbing French poets the very models of literary achievement. Yet to most literate Americans they were to remain as unknown and unapproachable as they had been in 1912.

The English decadence, impossible for American readers to ignore altogether, left more obvious traces. The English *Yellow Book*, itself edited by an expatriate American, was imitated in America by a series of *fin-de-siècle* little magazines: the elegant Chicago *Chap-Book*, the Bohemian and cheerful San Francisco *Lark*, the insistently naughty *M'lle New York*. These magazines perished quickly, and so did the American decadence of the nineties, at best an imitation of an imitation. Some of the writers who had taken part in it moved abroad; others fulfilled tradition by dying young. Richard

[3] Bithell, ed., and tr.: *Contemporary French Poetry* (London, 1909). Stone & Kimball had published an edition of Verlaine in translation in 1895.

[4] Lewis Piaget Shanks: "The Problem of Baudelaire," *Dial*, LIV (1913), 285–7.

[5] Fletcher: *Life Is My Song* (New York, 1937), p. 22.

Hovey and Bliss Carman remained to experiement with what they thought was an American symbolism, free and experimental, but clean.

Right up to the war, however, there were a few poets and novelists who made no such compromise, but continued to do their best to be as languid as Wilde and as experimental as Huysman's Marquis des Esseintes. The most famous of what Percival Pollard called the "school of tiger-skins and clinging garments" was Edgar Saltus. His specialty was Imperial Rome, a civilized country where the delicate beauties of sadism, unappreciated in a vulgar democracy, could be understood. The young George Sylvester Viereck worked as hard before 1914 in the cause of sex as he did later in the cause of Germany. Some Americans had known both, but few were willing to be as undiscriminating about either. Yet Viereck, who annotated his own works to make up for the fact that Goethe and Shakespeare had left theirs unexplained, was taken almost as seriously by the press as he took himself. A good deal of regretful admiration, as well as a good deal of headshaking, greeted his *Nineveh*, published in 1907. Donald Evans, whose *Sonnets from the Patagonian*, published in 1910, included one in praise of flagellation, predicted with Viereck a few years later that America would be punished for her narrow hostility to beauty.

These writers had so little connection with American thought or taste that they were at most titillating. Yet the European decadence which they were trying to imitate was not entirely forgotten. The reality was assumed to have vanished; the legend remained. In its mildest form, this legend of devotion to art and Bohemian freedom survived in Puccini's opera or in Du Maurier's *Trilby*, much read in the United States. Beyond this lay the shadowy figure of Wilde, who had lectured in America and then been put in jail for something one's parents would not explain.

To young men in the teens, the nineties had some of the glamor that the misrepresented twenties have acquired for today. More young Americans dreamed of Beardsley's London or, from a third-hand acquaintance, of Huysmans's Paris than had ever been interested in Saltus's New York. There were guides available to these past delights. Perhaps the most serious was Arthur Symons's *The Symbolist Movement,* itself a monument of turn-of-the-century aestheticism. Symons led Eliot, for one, to Rimbaud and Verlaine. Max Nordau's *Degeneration,* published in America in 1895, furnished a convenient summary of all the kinds of recent literature Nordau disapproved. Holbrook Jackson's *The Nineties,* new in 1913, recalled the brilliance, lavishness, and wit of aristocratic London in the years when no party was complete without Wilde. Frank Harris continually boasted in American magazines about his friendships with the English and French authors of the nineties. From all these sources young Americans could get an impression of a brilliant episode, scandalous, altogether interesting, and regrettably just over.

The heritage of the nineties was wider than this enticing legend. The dogma of the moral interpretation of art had been flatly challenged, and Americans who wanted to question it had foreign authority, for many the unquestioned authority in artistic matters, to back them up. At least two groups of Americans, not themselves decadents or antimoralists, not necessarily followers of any particular European fashions, began by the turn of the century to call for separate standards for art. These two groups were utterly different; one consisted of respectable academics and the other, more influential and more variously rebellious, of raffish newspapermen.

The small group of professorial aesthetes was all the more important because its doctrine was not very shocking at first glance. They said simply that the function of the critic was not to judge but rather to appreciate, with the most delicate and experienced sensitivity he could bring to bear. Lewis E. Gates at Harvard had said as early as 1900 that the critic's sole concern was with the "sincere and significant mood." His should be neither to explain nor to judge, but to enjoy the "manifold charm" of a work of art and to interpret this charm with all its nuances to his own generation.[6] These rather tenuous principles influenced such different students

[6] Gates: *Studies and Appreciations* (New York, 1900), p. 211.

as Frank Norris and Edwin Arlington Robinson. Gates was not far from the Norton tradition; his views could fit the far deeper skepticism of Santayana.

This kind of academic impressionism was strongest at Columbia, whose professors sometimes prided themselves on a harmless urbanity. A considerable group of Columbia professors interested themselves in moderately unorthodox Continental writers, Brander Matthews for instance in the realist theater, Hjalmar Hjorth Boyesen in Scandinavian and German writers. Harry Thurston Peck, professor of Greek and Latin, was editor of *The Bookman* and a prolific and sprightly essayist until 1908, when involvement in private scandal suddenly ended his career. None of these men can be called anything like a radical: Peck for instance, comparing Poe and Conan Doyle, found the latter perhaps less original but more pleasing because his moral standards agreed more with those of his readers. The French writer on Symbolism in America disposes of Peck cruelly: his *Bookman* was "*un magazine très américain au pire sens du mot,*" and yet Peck's own treatment of Mallarmé in 1898 was "*remarquable pour l'époque.*" [7]

The manifesto of this movement, if movement it was, was delivered in 1910 by Joel E. Spingarn, professor of comparative literature.[8] The task of the critic, and his sole task, Spingarn announced, following Benedetto Croce's new kind of idealism, was to enter imaginatively into the viewpoint of the author, whatever this might be. Everything else must be discarded, the rigid categories of the classic critics, the naturalist effort to be scientific, and also all effort to impose moral standards. This doctrine, coming from a respectable quarter like Columbia, seemed to some conservatives, in 1911 and later, more dangerous than the noisier blasts from outside the walls.

The noisiest came from newspapermen. An unbroken line of

[7] Peck: *Studies in Several Literatures* (New York, 1909), pp. 110, 112; René Taupin: *L'Influence du symbolisme français sur la poésie américaine* (Paris, 1929), p. 31.

[8] His essay, "The New Criticism" is printed in his *Creative Criticism* (New York, 1917).

newspaper iconoclasts stretches all the way from the pale aesthetes of the nineties to a surprising, improbable conclusion in H. L. Mencken. Mencken's early writings are one of the few places, in fact, where the minor newspaper skeptics, men like Vance Thompson and Percival Pollard, are commemorated at all. Thompson, originally of *M'lle New York*, published a precious and gushy collection of *French Portraits* in 1900. Pollard, a far more discriminating writer, saw through the standard pretensions of the decadence, but inherited from it its contempt of the Philistine mob. Like Mencken later, Pollard denounced literary commercialism, took potshots at Hamilton Wright Mabie, and praised cynics like Bierce. But Pollard, like the rest of these writers, was handicapped by preciosity and aloofness; he remained partly *fin-de-siècle*.

Mencken himself, looking back nostalgically at this handful of early iconoclasts, makes a serious case only for James Gibbons Huneker:

> . . . He gave some semblance of reality in the United States, after other men had tried and failed, to that great but ill-starred revolt against Victorian pedantry, formalism and sentimentality which began in the early 90's.[9]

Reality is exactly the quality that the modern reader misses in Huneker—catholicity, learning, and good temper are easy to find. Huneker was no languid aesthete; he seems from this distance a highly developed specimen, unusually articulate, of a type that was not rare in America even one generation ago: the enthusiastic, bubbling-over connoisseur, so eager to introduce one to Europe, so full of anecdotes about Whistler's epigrams or the suppressed poems of Baudelaire that one cannot bear to break in with heavy-handed questions such as what all this is doing in an essay on Stendhal.

Starting as a music critic in Philadelphia in the seventies, from the nineties until the twenties Huneker wrote, in little magazines, big magazines, daily papers, and volumes of essays, about nearly

[9] Mencken: *A Book of Prefaces* (New York, 1917), p. 163.

every major figure and many minor ones in recent literature, art, or music. He was at his best discussing music; his work on Chopin is still admired. So is his daring; far ahead of critical fashion Huneker praised Stendhal, Baudelaire, Cézanne, Matisse, James Joyce. It is only fair to add that he also delighted in Max Stirner, Maeterlinck, and Huysmans.

It is hard to make this lover of Pilsener, of café life and first nights, into any kind of a radical. There is little evidence in Huneker's writings of late-romantic self-torment, none of any wish to smash his delightful connoisseur's world. Huneker corresponded in a respectful, almost timid manner with William Crary Brownell and valued the praise of the ultraconservative dean of art critics, Royal Cortissoz. He disliked the gloomier naturalists, and by the mid-teens, like other venturers of the nineties, complained a little peevishly that the latest artists were going too far for him.[1]

Huneker was admired not only by Mencken but also by G. K. Chesterton, the *North American Review*, and the chief pundit of European criticism in his time, Georg Brandes, who paid him the compliment of finding his work hardly American at all. Huneker had one consistent message for his contemporaries. This message was not complex, but in his time it was important. There was much more variety in the world, Huneker announced, than most Americans had suspected. They should forget their prejudices and enjoy the feast spread out for them.

William Marion Reedy, a friend of Pollard and Huneker and Mencken, cannot be classified as a member of their circle or any other. Certainly he was not a languid aesthete of the nineties. The son of an Irish policeman, he did not have to secede angrily from Anglo-Saxon culture. Like St. Louis, a relaxed and corrupt city, proud of its theaters, restaurants, and saloons, Reedy was anti-Puritan by inheritance rather than conversion. He was well-known as an eater and drinker, and did not deny stories about an unconventional sex life. Yet there were limits to his unconventionality; he

[1] Huneker to Mencken, April 11, 1916, in Josephine Huneker, ed.: *Letters of James Gibbons Huneker* (New York, 1922), p. 210.

urged that Oscar Wilde be excluded from the country. While most Americans wouldn't catch the drift of Wilde's tastes, some would, and Reedy argued that America's "healthy vices" should not be endangered. One of Reedy's close friends was Elbert Hubbard, the sage of East Aurora, that weird combination of William Morris arts and crafts, 1890 aestheticism, progressive uplift, rags-to-riches inspiration, and village eccentricity.

Reedy's *Mirror*, which was to play one of the biggest parts in the prewar literary outburst, came to life in 1893, by mutation from a Sunday Supplement. For the most part it was and remained a magazine of politics, liberal in a nondoctrinaire, individualistic way; opposed to socialism, trade unions, and New England reformers, favorably inclined toward the Single Tax, really militant about free speech.

Reedy himself was a cheerful, salty libertarian and a moderate skeptic of a fairly familiar American kind. The *Mirror* gave St. Louis a chance to sample all varieties of recent literature. Anything but a decadent, Reedy had published Frank Harris and Ernest Dowson in the nineties. He now accepted poems from Viereck and praised Saltus as an American Baudelaire. He did not care much for the gloomier European naturalists or for Nietzsche, but admired, like his contemporaries, the earthy, well-intentioned realism of Mark Twain. Crane and Dreiser were praised and defended in the *Mirror*. As a matter of course, when a new group of writers turned up just before the war, Reedy was glad to publish them. In 1914, as we will see, one of these newcomers suddenly made the *Mirror* a national sensation.

The older newspaper iconoclasts, Vance, Pollard, Huneker, and others, moved back and forth in the first decade of the twentieth century among the surviving little magazines, the *Bohemian*, the *Criterion*, Reedy's *Mirror*. They wrote for the daily press, sometimes for large magazines like the *Bookman*, and also for the *Smart Set*, a magazine with a somewhat different future.

The *Smart Set* had been founded by Colonel William D'Alton

Mann, the publisher of the scandalmongering *Town Topics*. In part it was another elegant literary magazine in the manner of *M'lle New York*; in part it remained a chitchat sheet for and about the "fast" section of high society (its advertising specialized in European liners, expensive automobiles, and cures for alcoholism). Its slogan subtitle in the teens was sometimes "A Magazine of Cleverness," sometimes "A Magazine for Minds That Are Not Primitive." An advertisement of 1915 defined its clientele, by implication, still more carefully:

> Between Tea Gown and Dinner Gown—between office coat and dinner jacket, there is often an hour or two when entertainment is welcome.[2]

Yet the *Smart Set*, between its incredibly lush stories of high society and Parisian artists, printed authors ranging from Sara Teasdale to Lord Dunsany and even James Joyce; writers of the earlier decadence like Saltus and Thompson mixed with names not yet known like Carl Van Vechten, Floyd Dell, or D. H. Lawrence. Most of whatever excellence the magazine attained was due to one fact; in 1908 it added to its staff a young, inexperienced drama critic, George Jean Nathan, and a little-known newspaperman and free-lance writer, Henry L. Mencken.

Mencken helped bring to the magazine from the *Los Angeles Times* a young acquaintance named Willard Huntington Wright. In the hygienic and uncongenial sunshine of prewar Southern California, Wright for some years had been denouncing the stupidity of the American masses and pleading for art, erudition, and an end of bourgeois moral restraints. In 1913, with Mencken's approval, Wright became editor. As his admirers point out, he attracted an impressive list of authors. Yet the contributions by Joyce, Lawrence, or Max Beerbohm were short and few; much of the content of Wright's *Smart Set* was insistently exotic and boringly naughty. Not only the publishers but Mencken thought Wright was pushing the

[2] *Smart Set*, XLI (1913), 163.

erotic tendency too far, and in 1914 Mencken and Nathan took over the magazine.[3] Wright devoted himself for a few years primarily to well-informed art criticism. After the war he turned to detective fiction under the name of S. S. Van Dine. In the languid erudition of his famous detective, Philo Vance, one can catch an echo of the *Smart Set* tone.

For the next ten years the *Smart Set* became increasingly the organ of Mencken and Nathan, battling the censors, baiting the bourgeoisie, and booming the new writers. Yet between the robust Mencken blasts, the magazine remained inescapably arty. Mencken never seemed entirely at home there.

❦

The *Smart Set*, like its predecessors of the nineties, referred often and with admiration to the doctrines of Friedrich Nietzsche. Of all the Europeans who repudiated the nineteenth-century world of scientific progress and moral advance, Nietzsche enjoyed the greatest popularity in prewar America. The Nietzsche vogue, running from the *fin-de-siècle* through various byways to Mencken and beyond, is a prewar phenomenon of the middle magnitude, clearly more important than the aestheticism of the imitation *Yellow Book* variety.

Nietzsche began to be talked about by advanced thinkers with the appearance of the first English translations. These started in 1896, and continued sporadically through the century's first decade. In 1909–13 came the authorized translation of the complete works, edited by Oscar Levy, and at the same time a burst of Nietzsche interpretation, praise and denunciation which continued until the war.

[3] This explanation of the change is that given by William Manchester: *Disturber of the Peace* (New York, 1950). It differs from that of Burton Rascoe in his introduction to the *Smart Set Anthology* (Rascoe and Groff Conklin, eds., New York, 1934). The Manchester explanation seems to me to be borne out by the magazine's content.

Superficially, as some of the commentary pointed out, Nietzsche had something in common with American predilections. Emersonian self-confidence, captain-of-industry ruthlessness, and even Rooseveltian robustiousness, seemed to some Americans to be suggested by the doctrine of the Superman. Nietzsche, however, had hated what he saw as the land of dollar-chasing democracy. Most Americans who wrote about him, expressing one or another variety of latent discontent, used Nietzsche's doctrines to belabor their own enemies.

Often Nietzsche, who had accepted the findings of nineteenth-century science as far as they went, was co-opted into the materialist army, and even into its Marxist regiment. The Chicago socialist publishing house of C. H. Kerr published one of Nietzsche's works as part of its "Library of Science for the Workers."

Yet Nietzsche, who had moved through and beyond naturalism, was sometimes placed with the revivers of religion. George Burman Foster, a liberal Chicago theologian, insisted in several prewar books that Nietzsche was essentially religious, at least a fellow fighter against soulless mechanism. From an opposite point of view, Paul Carus agreed with this analysis: Nietzsche, betraying science and progress and reverting to mysticism, was a shocking reactionary. Paul Elmer More saw the problem less simply: he approved Nietzsche's rejection of sentimental humanitarianism, but insisted that it was impossible and insane to make this rejection, as Nietzsche tried to do, without drawing on the resources of Christian tradition.[4]

The earliest and most consistent American version of Nietzsche, however, was not the naturalist or the religious one, but the aesthetic. Ever since they had learned about him in the London little magazines of the nineties, Huneker and the lesser newspaper aesthetes had continued to praise him. They were fascinated with his relation to Wagner, they saw his doctrines reflected in Ibsen and

[4] Foster: *Friedrich Nietzsche* (New York, 1931, but drawn from prewar lectures); Carus: *Nietzsche and Other Exponents of Individualism* (Chicago, 1914); Paul Elmer More: *Nietzsche* (Boston, 1912). There were many other summaries.

the early Shaw. His greatness was confirmed by his friend Georg Brandes, the Danish critic. Brandes, who visited America in 1914, confounded the philistines and delighted the rebels by proclaiming American culture a materialistic failure in familiar, European, and somewhat Nietzschian terms.

To Huneker, to Benjamin de Casseres, to Willard Huntington Wright and others of the *Smart Set* circle, Nietzsche had three uses. First, he was an opponent of the dreary democratic mob, an aristocrat. Second, he was an apostle of art and joy: this tortured ascetic was made into an anti-Puritan. Third, he was European, and only those could appreciate him who really understood Europe.

Since Nietzsche wrote in aphorism and, like other seers, frequently contradicted himself, it was not hard to make him into an aesthete, a materialist, or even a transcendental Christian. H. L. Mencken made him, as he made some other writers he liked, into Mencken. This was apparently the most interesting version; Mencken's 1908 summary went through several editions and was widely discussed.

To start with, Mencken's Nietzsche was "an utter and unquestioning materialist," who "knows nothing of mind except as a function of the body." Jubilantly quoting Nietzsche against various kinds of idealism, Mencken used him, somewhat incongruously, to bolster his own version of history. The priest-ridden middle ages were "unspeakably foul," while the nineteenth century (which Nietzsche abominated) "witnessed greater human progress than all the centuries before it saw or even imagined." [5]

Here Mencken agreed with the majority, but he soon made up for it. In a manner electrifying in 1908, Mencken used Nietzsche to bombard women, democracy, and sentiment. Nietzsche's doctrine of superiority was given a special American application in "the futile and fatuous effort to improve the Negroes of the southern United States by education. . . . Even though they were everywhere in a great majority numerically" in the South (a common

[5] Mencken: *The Philosophy of Friedrich Nietzsche* (2nd ed., Boston, 1913), p. 159.

though wild mistake) the Negroes were kept down with ease by the educated Southern whites, a class which "there represents, though in a melancholy fashion, the Nietzschian first class." [6]

This particular instance would have found fairly ready acceptance among many of Mencken's readers in 1908, but Mencken, never a coward, went on to challenge, through Nietzsche, the strongest and most central American belief of all:

> And what is this king of all axioms and emperor of all fallacies? Simply the idea that there are rules of "natural morality" engraven indelibly upon the hearts of man—that all men, at all times and everywhere, have ever agreed, do now agree and will agree forevermore . . . that certain things are right and certain other things are wrong. . . .[7]

With this statement and others like it, a lonely glove was thrown down and a whole period of revolution foreshadowed.

In the most sensible and scholarly of this rash of Nietzsche books, William E. Salter in 1917 denied that the brief Nietzsche vogue, obviously ending by then, had made any great impact on the American public beyond popularizing a few phrases like "superman" and "blond beast." For the America of this day this doctrine was obviously too alien to penetrate. For one thing Nietzsche was aristocratic. Second, he was irrevocably imbued with the outlook of German idealism, never very successfully naturalized in America. And finally, his view of the world was thoroughly and sweepingly tragic: his philosophy was a search for a way to deal with the intolerable. This was not what Americans, including the rebels, needed in the teens. More cheerful iconoclasts made a deeper impression.

He did serve, though, to help many young people who encountered him in these years break with the whole set of ideas in which they had been brought up. He was a most effective shocker: that was the deliberate purpose of his paradoxical and aphoristic style.

[6] Ibid., pp. 167, 195.
[7] Ibid., p. 282.

And Nietzsche put H. L. Mencken, as Mencken put Nietzsche, on the American map.

In Mencken, one of the most challenging and paradoxical figures in the history of American culture, all the European influences of the late nineteenth century came together with much that was intensely native and much that was irreducibly personal. Though by no means the doughty champion of the intelligentsia that he became after the war, he was already in the early teens a well-known and disturbing voice of rebellion. In the *Baltimore Sun*, in the *Smart Set*, and in a series of books culminating in *A Book of Prefaces* (1917), he was already giving voice to the whole set of ideas that later became familiar. More important, his invective style, always startling, sometimes embarrassing, at its best superb, sounded already, from time to time, its full trombone and tuba blast.

Obviously one cannot treat Mencken solely in terms of intellectual influences. He was, on two counts, an outsider in terms of the older America. A militant German-American, he fought the Anglo-Saxon monopoly of American culture from the start. And, like so many of the naturalist writers, he had learned as a newspaperman to be skeptical of the standard cheerful picture of life. Yet Mencken did not, like Dreiser, draw from his early knowledge of the seamy side a shocked and brooding sadness; some native toughness enabled him to enjoy the whole spectacle; a mixture of indignation and affection marked from the beginning his interest in the underside of American life. Writing about hypocrisy and vulgarity, he was more the gloating, delighted collector than the muckraker.

From his earliest writings Mencken was committed to an uncompromising naturalism. To him the mild, watered-down Protestantism of the Social Gospel was as abhorrent as hell-fire revivalism, and less amusing. His first requirement of any writer was that he accept frankly the meaninglessness of life and the animality of humans. He battled for Crane, admired Joseph Conrad's uncompromising pessimism, and came before the public in one of his major roles as the defender of Dreiser. Before anybody else, he saw the depth of the pessimism in Mark Twain, rejecting both conventional pictures: the humorist and the benevolent battler for the good and true. As early as 1913 in the *Smart Set* he said flatly, as few then would have, that Clemens had been "one of the great artists of all time," "the full equal of Cervantes and Molière, Swift and Defoe." [8] Praising also Crane and the best of Norris, he served as a bridge from the naturalist outburst of the turn of the century to the time when Dreiser was joined by a new group of naturalists.

Yet naturalism was not the whole story; the literal realism of Howells and even the crudity of Dreiser bored Mencken. To outward appearance, in style and personality, nobody could be less an aesthete of the nineties than Mencken, yet his links to that movement were many. Though he demanded that art be taken seriously, he hated the idea that it should convey any overt message. This position led him, as it had led others, into occasional statements that were as shallow as the aesthetics of Oscar Wilde. Even Clemens, said Mencken, shared with the rest of the country "the Puritan incapacity for seeing beauty as a thing in itself, and the full peer of the true and the good." [9]

Mencken retained throughout his life some of the affectations characteristic of the newspaper aesthetes of his salad days, the turn of the century. Like Huneker, whom he greatly admired, he dropped too many European names and foreign phrases. He seemed of two minds about the prospects for American art. As early as 1913 in the *Smart Set* he was campaigning for the American language against standard literary English; he admired tremendously the magnificent vulgate of *Huckleberry Finn.* Yet he was continually berating America for not being Europe, and even for not being the imaginary, universally cultivated Europe of the American aesthetes:

> One might throw a thousand bricks in any American city without striking a single man who could give an intelligible account of either Hauptmann or Cézanne, or of the reasons for

[8] Mencken: "The Burden of Humor," *Smart Set,* XXXIX (1913), 151–8.
[9] *Prefaces,* pp. 204–5.

holding Schumann to have been a better composer than Mendelssohn.[1]

Europe to Mencken meant primarily Central Europe, and this was not entirely a matter of his ancestral loyalties. Many of his friends of the older generation, including Pollard, Huneker, and Reedy, were Germanophiles. Some of Mencken's most lyrical writing was about his 1912 visit to Munich; Paris left him cold. Germany was the land of naturalism and Rhine wine, music and beer and love of life; it was also the land of Nietzsche.

In Nietzsche Mencken found, for one thing, a way of combining his naturalism and his aestheticism. Despite his misunderstandings, Mencken really could draw from his early master much that he needed: nobody else was so deeply versed in European tradition and yet, without being at all an uplifter, so revolutionary. Nobody else could be quoted so aptly against women, Christianity, progress, and Anglo-Saxondom. Mencken's own idea of the Nietzschean superman, lordly and masculine, disillusioned but cheerful, a chastiser and yet a yea-sayer, may have furnished some of the model for his own role.

More completely than anybody else so far, Mencken had by the early and middle teens raised the standard of battle against all three of the main elements of the dominant American culture. His dislike of the assumptions of practical idealism was central and pervasive. Any kind of absolute morality was to him a farce, and the cheerfulness that found morality in everyday life the height of vulgarity:

> Search where you will, near or far, in ancient or modern times, and you will never find a first-rate race or an enlightened age, in its moments of highest reflection, that ever gave more than a passing bow to optimism.[2]

Culture, in the sense in which it was understood by its 1912 custodians, was a peculiarly American substitute for any real art or

[1] Ibid., p. 191.
[2] Ibid., p. 14.

understanding of life. In his essay on Huneker, Mencken defined the main enemy:

> Not so much the vacant and harmless fellow who belongs to the Odd Fellows and recreates himself with *Life* and *Leslie's Weekly* in the barber shop, as that more belligerent and pretentious donkey who presumes to do battle for "honest" thought and a "sound" ethic—the "forward-looking" man, the university ignoramus, the conservator of orthodoxy, the rattler of ancient phrases—what Nietzsche called "the Philistine of culture." [3]

Finally, Mencken, more completely than any other intellectual of the prewar period except Irving Babbitt, repudiated progress, root and branch. Anywhere in a *Smart Set* essay on any subject he might strike a sharp sideways blow at Roosevelt, La Follette, Wilson, the muckraking novelists, or best of all Bryan, already his favorite enemy. In 1915, after the New Freedom had been in power two years, Mencken considered it and its works systematically:

The Uplift, "the business of saving the dear people from their wrongs and woes unspeakable," had finally, said Mencken, come to power in the land, no longer under the patronage of pious old women and clergymen but under the direction of smart, ruthless, professional reformers. Georgia had gone dry. Oregon had adopted the initiative, referendum, and recall; Colorado, woman suffrage. Most striking of all, the United States Senate was no longer filled with corrupt but intelligent servants of the trusts, but with recognized uplifters, products of the rule of the people, reflecting the people's "immemorial hatred of the superior man." Was this a net gain, asked Mencken, and answered with little hesitation:

> I doubt it, Messieurs. And doubting it, I arrive at a low, sniffish opinion of the whole rumble-bumble of the Uplift. It has failed in all directions. . . . And thus we shall be quack-ridden and folly-ridden until mobocracy comes to its unescapable *débâcle*, and the common people are relieved of their present

[3] Ibid., p. 193.

> oppressive duty of deciding what is wrong with their tummies, and what doctor is safest for them to consult, and which of his pills is most apt to cure them.[4]

This was strong stuff for 1915, or for any time. Remembering his consistent geniality and personal kindness, his occasional generosity toward opponents, above all remembering the delight with which they heard his first liberating shouts of battle, Mencken's friends have often denied that he meant all he said in this vein. The historian's business is not with what Mencken was, an impenetrable mystery, but with what he said, which constitutes his historical importance. What he said amounts to a complete repudiation of all the most fundamental tenets of the dominant American credo of his time. Yet this very violence of repudiation gives rise, like everything about Mencken, to another paradox. The role Mencken chose for himself, the one he enjoyed dramatizing, was that of the aloof, amused observer, the superior man who took for granted and genially enjoyed the follies of democracy while he devoted himself to more important matters. Yet Mencken's best writing is not about Nietzsche or music or art, but about Bryan and the American language and the whole culture of the American small town. However he might deny it, his affection for these things was more than that of a connoisseur: he cared. This is the difference between him and his merely bourgeois-baiting, alienated contemporaries.

The Mencken doctrine was too new and startling to make its deepest impression in the cheerful prewar years. His roots lay deep in the European and American thought of the late nineteenth century, a darker and in many ways more profound period. Before the war he looked back to the nineties and foreshadowed his period of glory, the twenties. In such an essay as "Puritanism as a Literary Force," published in *A Book of Prefaces* in 1917, he states the whole case of the mid-twenties intelligentsia against American culture, and states it far better than his imitators. The origin of the

[4] *Smart Set*, XLV (1915), 153.

trouble is Puritanism compounded by evangelism and political moralism, soured and coarsened by money-grabbing. In wartime, Mencken continued to say this and was attacked by just the right people: a whole generation of intellectuals concluded that he was correct.

Meantime, Mencken was already, in the years before 1917, a somewhat older and quite separate voice in the rising chorus of the liberated. The typical young rebels of 1912–17 were above all cheerful, and Mencken did not like many of them. Most of the novelists between Dreiser and Sinclair Lewis left him cold. He had little use for the new poetry, the main literary production of the prewar years; his rather surprising tastes in poetry ran to a few quite sentimental and conventional contemporaries like Robert Loveman and Lizette Woodworth Reese, and back of them to William Watson, Kipling, Henley, Kingsley, and Christina Rosetti. He abominated the new, mystical wave of Europeans of the immediately prewar years and objected, as a nineteenth-century gentleman, to the manners of Greenwich Village. His day had passed, and was still to come.

This was true also of naturalism and aestheticism, the two movements of moral, social, and literary criticism which flowed from Europe to America from the late nineteenth century on. Both remained essentially alien; even so American a writer as Mencken could not yet naturalize them. Yet both had, and continued to have, a major effect on important American minorities. In two writers already much praised by Mencken, Dreiser and James Branch Cabell, both movements had effective representatives in the prewar years. Yet neither Dreiser nor Cabell yet enjoyed his full recognition. Both were to enjoy it in the twenties, when naturalism and aestheticism finally were able to flower, here as in Europe.

The dominant rebellious movement of the prewar years was quite different. Like these older movements, it drew its authority from Europe but found thoroughly American expression. For a short day, it seemed about to sweep all before it. This movement, often called the Liberation, was mystical rather than naturalist, passionate about art but not amoral, iconoclastic but full of hope and even, in its own terms, of reform. Though it vigorously attacked the cheerful, moralistic doctrines of the dominant majority, this Innocent Rebellion had a lot in common with them at bottom. For precisely this reason, because it was shocking and exciting but not repulsive or frightening, the Innocent Rebellion succeeded in breaking down the barriers. Then it quickly disappeared, leaving the road open for older and deeper kinds of dissent.

PART THREE

The Innocent Rebellion

(1912–17)

1
Liberators

The Liberation, the movement of thought which reached America in the prewar years, is easy to taste and observe, but hard to define. Pervasive and vigorous, it was over very quickly. Iridescent and shifting, insistently gay (its critics would say irresponsible), it was based not so much on a theory as on a way of getting along without theories. One understands it most easily through characteristic episodes recalled in memoirs or described in the press—the explosion of popular poetry in new modes, the excitement of the Armory Show, the dramatic succession of intellectual fashions, the way Bergson and Wells and Freud became crazes like the Turkey Trot or the Tango. To see the Liberation in its dazzling colors—the colors of the Russian Ballet and Matisse, one must place it for contrast against the solid true-blue background of the Progressive Era.

If the Liberation had a characteristic doctrine, it was a simple and old one, very close to the central assertion of earlier romantic periods, the assertion that life transcends thought. The dogmas of the nineteenth century, idealist and still more scientific naturalist, were dead; the twentieth century was to have no place for any dogmas at all. Nothing, especially nothing depressing, had been proven; science had suddenly become wide-open at the ends, and the arguments of philosophers had cancelled each other out. Therefore the road was clear for the creative intuition: one could believe almost whatever one wanted. Traditional values, like traditional means of establishing them, were highly doubtful; it was permissible to prefer violence to peace, creative destruction to building, primitivism to civilization. The only thing that was not permissible was fear, especially fear of change or of the future.

The Liberation reached America some time not long before 1910 and it was clearly over by 1917. It directly affected only certain small groups of young people, and yet its influence was pervasive during these years. Because it was so brief, historians of thought and literature have often failed to describe it clearly. Sometimes they have confused it with earlier tendencies; more often its fugitive note has been drowned out by the brass bands of the twenties. A distinct movement in itself, the Liberation was related to what went before, and it opened the way to all that came after.

The Liberation, partly a mood or a manner, could make use of almost any of the doctrines from the recent past, as long as they were emotional, combative, and joyful. Pragmatism was part of it, but the freewheeling, radically pluralist pragmatism of the late James, not the practical problem-solving of the social scientists. European naturalism was acceptable, but usually it was turned upside down and made into pantheism: nature was all, but nature had come alive. Aestheticism was fully a part of the new credo, but not the tired aestheticism of the nineties; rather the dawn of a new art that would transform life. On the whole the Liberation was not a movement of outsiders; its headquarters were the centers of the older culture, Chicago and New York, its American leaders mostly members of the dominant minority. If they were social radicals, vaguely socialist or (more characteristically) anarchist, it was out of generous emotion rather than disaffection.

Though it was a movement of challenge and revolt, the Liberation was connected at its roots with the dominant American culture it condemned. It was thoroughly moral in its own sense; indeed it believed so deeply in the morality of the universe that it was sure men could get along without moral rules. The spirit of Transcendentalism pervaded it, though it did not call on Emerson. The Liberation loved culture, though it found it everywhere *except* in the Anglo-American nineteenth century. (Of the older Americans, only Whitman, who had escaped becoming a standard author, remained acceptable.) Progress ran in its veins; progress not to be measured primarily in labor legislation or direct elections, but in terms of a free and joyous life for all. Above all, the Liberation was cheerful, still more cheerful than the doctrine of the conservative majority, and equally vulnerable to approaching disaster.

Blurred by historians (with a few brilliant exceptions), the Liberation was fully and very often described by participants, who were not confused either by the future, which they did not foresee, or the past, which they had abolished. The most famous and often quoted phrase is that of the Irish painter John Butler Yeats, who said that the fiddles were tuning up all over America. Van Wyck Brooks, a major spokesman, compared America to "a vast Sargasso Sea—a prodigious welter of unconscious life, swept by ground swells of half-conscious emotion." [1]

Its opponents described the Liberation even more clearly than its own heralds. To Irving Babbitt, of course, it was the final conclusive proof of the folly of romanticism and the need of classic rules and inner restraint. At an opposite pole, John Dewey was disturbed by something that went beyond systematic, rational relativism:

> Unstable equilibrium, rapid fermentation, and a succession of explosive reports are thus the chief notes of modern ethics.[2]

Professional philosophers in America were not ordinarily attracted by the doctrines of the Liberation. They took more seriously an opposite movement, the New Realism. This was an effort to defend the actuality and certainty of our knowledge of the external world against all opponents. Many American philosophers were impressed by the spare and disciplined thought of Bertrand Russell, who was battling sentimentality and striving for exactitude of statement. But neither the New Realism nor Russell captured the imagination of the prewar public. Both the young literary people and the followers of popular summaries preferred the mysterious, iridescent glitter of the modern mystics.[3]

[1] *America's Coming-of-Age* (New York, 1915), p. 164.

[2] Dewey: "Ethics," in Columbia University, *Lectures on Science, Philosophy, and Art* (New York, 1908), p. 19.

[3] The New Realism and its sources are covered in the standard histories of American philosophy, and in Perry: *Present Philosophical Tendencies*. Among

H. L. Mencken rejected the Liberation, sticking cheerfully to his own kind of pessimism. To him Wells and Shaw were less than first-rate, and Bergson and Maeterlinck, the principal prophets of the creative intuition, were swamis and spiritualists, disguised allies of the uplift, half-brothers of Mary Baker Eddy.

Neither its friends nor its active enemies described the Liberation best, however, but the one genuinely detached, though disapproving, observer, George Santayana. In 1912, after twenty-three years of uncomfortable ambivalence, Santayana managed to say his polite, final good-by to Harvard and America. In 1913, in an essay on "The Intellectual Temper of the Age," he paid his respects to the Liberation.

The age, in Santayana's balanced judgment, was one of transition. Traditional Christian civilization was dying, and the nineteenth-century forces of atheism, democracy, and progress still gaining. These would lead, in the long run, to complete subjection of the individual to the majority, "the most cruel and unprogressive of masters." Instead of defending reason and tradition, the current age was reacting to the materialist and progressive threat with various kinds of irrationalism. Everywhere, in art, literature, religion, and philosophy, anarchy had broken out. This upsurge of instinct, barbarism, archaism, and sheer whim was not altogether to be despised; it was what made the age interesting. But it could not make it great.

Santayana's description, given his austere assumptions, was cor-

---

the most powerful arguments against the Liberation were a number of essays by Morris Cohen, reprinted in his *Reason and Nature*.

Russell was warmly received in philosophical journals, but his books received mixed reviews in nontechnical sources. (The *Nation*, for instance, found his Lowell Lectures of 1914 arrogant and one-sided.) His visit to America in 1914 attracted less attention, according to his admirer Morris Cohen, than the visits either of Bergson or of Rudolf Eucken, the German idealist. It was after the war that Russell started to become a major figure for most American intellectuals. This was partly because of his accomplishments in mathematical logic, but also because with the postwar collapse of the Liberation, many admired Russell's consistent courageous naturalism. *Nation*, January 21, 1915, pp. 33–4; Morris Cohen: "The New Philosopher's Stone," *New Republic*, July 31, 1915, p. 338.

rect, and so was his account of the movement's origins. The new philosophy and the new art and literature were consciously reacting to nineteenth-century materialism and contemporary progressive democracy. In the eyes of the Liberators, however, they were not destroying science and progress but carrying them further.

Much of the authority for the new irrationalism, often called antiscientific, seemed to come from science itself. To many people science seemed, as Santayana suggested in his 1913 summary, to be:

> . . . eating its own words, through the mouths of some of its accredited spokesmen, and reducing itself to something utterly conventional and insecure.[4]

Actually science was by no means committing suicide, but moving into another profound and unsettling period of transformation, like that which had culminated in Darwin. In the long run, the scientific revolution of the early twentieth century was to be greater than that of the mid-nineteenth, probably more nearly comparable to that which produced Newton.

How much this revolution, still in its fairly early stages, affected the thought of nonscientists, is an extremely difficult, perhaps an impossible question to answer. Nobody, not even the greatest theoretical scientist alive in 1917, understood its full direction in all its parts. Yet many people, nonscientists, philosophers, and writers and even readers of the magazines, knew that something was happening to the nineteenth-century world.

Nearly all important varieties of nineteenth-century thought, both rebel and respectable, started by accepting the validity and permanence, as far as they went, of Newtonian physics and Darwinian evolution. The dogmatic materialists said that these scientific theories were sufficient to explain the universe. Followers

[4] Santayana: *Winds of Doctrine* (New York, 1913), p. 4.

of the Victorian compromise, still dominant in America in 1912, alleged that scientific truth, properly interpreted, led to moral and idealistic conclusions. The aesthetes and decadents turned their backs on science, but ordinarily because they found its teachings ugly or boring rather than untrue.

Now, suddenly, the nineteenth-century scientific fabric was being re-examined, and it seemed to be fraying at the seams. So far, what was newly proved did not seem as important as what had been disproved. Part of what was disproved was the method of Darwinian evolution. Most literate Americans had learned to think in terms of a self-contained, very gradual evolutionary progress, in which tiny changes accumulated in large ones, principally through the mechanisms of natural and sexual selection. Beginning exactly with the century and the rediscovery of the work of Gregor Mendel, the new science of genetics cast doubt on this conception of gradual change. New species were not developed through any nineteenth-century compromise: the units of heredity, the genes and chromosomes about which more and more was known, remained constant and recurred in certain patterns. Like Darwinian evolution before it, the new genetics was used to prove all sorts of social theories. For the moment it seemed to give color to all kinds of racialist nonsense; in the long run it was to make students of heredity extremely cautious.

Still more unsettling was the conclusion, emerging from the work of August Weismann, that evolutionary change could not reflect the life experience of the individual; heritable changes had to occur only in the germ plasm. While most laymen had not thought very hard about the matter, many of them were unconscious Lamarckians; they assumed that what one did affected one's heirs. The new doctrine wiped out at one stroke the whole race of Lamarckian giraffes, lengthening their necks by munching the leaves of trees. More important, it made nonsense of a half-century of sermons about avoiding sin in order to improve the race. Equally devastating to nineteenth-century scientific assumptions and also their social corollaries, was the related assertion of Hugo deVries and others: evolutionary change occurred not in tiny gradual steps, but in leaps.

Life, that is, was more mysterious than the nineteenth century had thought. To some scientists, this meant only that men must work harder to find out more, but to a few quotable scientists and many laymen, it meant that the science of life would never be reduced to physics and chemistry, because life was unique and by definition mysterious. Here was born the "Life Force," a power which was up-to-date and defensible in the latest scientific language, but yet indefinable and sacred. The Life Force was the early twentieth century's substitute for the nineteenth century's natural law. It often sounded like a new name for God.

In physics, the Newtonian world machine had been the common assumption of Christians and atheists for a century and a half: the disagreement had been whether or not it needed the constant services of a Great Mechanic. Now the layman who tried to keep up with science, the reader of the summaries in the *Nation* for instance, was beginning to find the whole conception of a world machine inadequate. If this immensely convenient metaphor had to go, nothing would be left but the Life Force, in physics a still vaguer conception than it was in biology.

In physics as in biology, the great leaps had been made shortly before and after the turn of the century. The first vague and disturbing rumor to reach the layman concerned radioactivity. It appeared that one element could change into another by atomic disintegration; either matter was not indestructible or it was quite different from anybody's previous picture of it. Little remained of the familiar universe in which indestructible particles of matter circulated in predictable motion. Atoms might be units of energy; matter and energy might have no separate meaning.

The name of Albert Einstein, already well known in European scientific circles, was beginning to be heard in America. About all that was known by the conscientious layman was that Einstein had suggested that time itself was a relative term, that it had no absolute meaning independent of the motion and position of the observer. This was a notion that could hardly have been more shocking to the minority that received it. It had long been suggested by mathematicians, who had demonstrated that classical space and time were not inescapable assumptions, necessary for human thought. Hardly anybody could imagine that still worse was in store: that Einstein in the teens was developing a set of theories which would alter and expand past recognition the entire Newtonian cosmos, and indicate the nature of a new synthesis.

European philosophers of science were still more disturbing, and more approachable, than the scientists themselves. Ever since Hume, the debate had centered around the nature of scientific generalization. Were scientific theories mere summaries of what sometimes seemed to happen, were they approximate statistical results, or were they predictions of the future? Of many major figures associated with this argument, the one most often discussed in America in 1912 was the French mathematician, Henri Poincaré. Poincaré, considered by the *Nation* the greatest mind of the age, said that the laws of science and the axioms of mathematics were conventions of human thought. Geometry, for instance, was useful: that was all one could say about it; the question of its truth or untruth to external nature was either unanswerable or meaningless.

What was destroyed once and for all in these years was the central idea of the Enlightenment, an idea deep in the basic assumptions of most Americans still, the idea of the unified, coherent universe, understandable as a whole by man through the use of his reason. One could still believe in a unified and real world as a matter of faith, and many, including some scientists, did; one could not prove its existence by argument. Only a few people in prewar America realized how completely the eighteenth- and nineteenth-century confidence in scientific deduction had been destroyed. Yet a number were beginning to perceive some of the dimensions of this change.

Perhaps the most indignant reaction to the suggestions of the new science came from the simpler nineteenth-century mechanists. Religious leaders, delighted at the demise of old-fashioned materialism, were usually pleased by what they heard. They probably exaggerated the relevance of the new scientific doctrines to their purposes. Santayana saw this with characteristic clarity: faith that depended on a recent and perhaps transitory turn in scientific thought was hardly faith. To a few isolated individuals, like Henry Adams, the only consequence of the new science or the new philosophy was despair and confusion.

The most common American answer was the pragmatist one, or the simpler one based on popular practicalism. For some temperaments it was enough to say that theories about the nature of the universe were and always had been a waste of time; what we needed was to solve pressing human problems.

But brighter and more colorful roads beckoned the young people of the Liberation, and some of their unsettled elders. These were the various new kinds of mysticism or idealism dawning in Europe, offering at once liberation and confidence. Some continued to turn to Nietzsche (often in versions more cheerful than Mencken's). Some followed the Italian idealist Benedetto Croce; a number were interested in Rudolph Eucken, who at Jena was using the new vitalism to rescue religion. Edwin E. Slosson, a first-rate American popularizer of current thought and a good barometer of public opinion, interviewed twelve "Major Prophets of Today" for the *Independent* in 1913 and 1914.[5] Most of Slosson's great men were presented as part of a new and inspiring turn in modern thought toward something halfway between pragmatism and idealism. The exceptions were Dewey and Haeckel; the representative vitalists included writers like Shaw and Maeterlinck, scientists like Wilhelm Ostwald and Poincaré, and philosophers like Eucken and Bergson. Slosson, like others, found the new tendency somewhat hard to define; it was optimistic, scientific, yet wide open to the

[5] These interviews were published in book form as *Major Prophets of To-day* (Boston, 1914) and *Six Major Prophets* (Boston, 1917).

claims of the spirit. It led toward a belief in the Life Force or, as Slosson put it, "the reanimation of the universe."

In the early teens the most authoritative spokesman of the new vitalism, and for a brief spell the most influential thinker in the world as well as the rage in intellectual America, was Henri Bergson. People on all intellectual levels seemed to respond to the eloquence of the French philosopher. It was to Bergson that William James turned in his last phase for the courage formally and finally to abandon logic as incompatible with experience, though many other European thinkers of the period helped James on the way toward this goal. Theodore Roosevelt, Lyman Abbott, and John Burroughs praised Bergson as a restorer of spirituality, the chief spokesman of what seemed to them a modernized, more exciting version of practical idealism. He was digested and soberly discussed in the serious magazines, interviewed about America in the popular ones and, most surprisingly, admired by the new organs of the rebellious younger generation, from the *New Republic* to the *Little Review*. Walter Lippmann, the chief pundit of the most fashionable kind of political liberalism, wrote an enthusiastic article in *Everybody's* about Bergson as "The Most Dangerous Man in the World." [6] Through his syndicalist disciple Georges Sorel, Bergson was even associated with the I.W.W.

When Bergson finally came to America to lecture at Columbia in February 1913, a line of automobiles (still the vehicles of the well-to-do) clogged Broadway, one lady fainted in the crush at the lecture-room door, and regular students were crowded out of their seats by well-dressed auditors. According to Slosson, Bergson's American publisher sold in two years half as many copies of *Creative Evolution* as had been sold in France in fifteen years,[7] and the presses poured out a flood of semipopular explanations.

Bergson's philosophy, presented in poetic prose that is hard to summarize, dealt principally with two subjects, evolution and thought. Life could not have developed, he argued with much

[6] *Everybody's*, XXVIII (July, 1912), 100–1.
[7] Slosson: *Major Prophets of To-day*, p. 14.

biological learning, through a series of small changes produced by random circumstances. In the long development of the eye, for instance, nature obviously kept on in the same direction before results were apparent. Evolution to Bergson was both creative and unpredictable. The organism itself played a major role. The whole story could never be told by science, which, with all its great accomplishments, was limited to the typical and repetitive.

Like science, the human intellect itself distorted whatever was alive and developing. In order to look at any phenomenon, the mind had to stop the flow of time; like the camera, it had to break actual duration into separate instants. Only through his intuition could man deal with the living, flowing universe.

This doctrine was neither gloomy like Nietzsche's, Christian like Eucken's, difficult and apparently contradictory like James's in his later years, nor overly antiscientific like Croce's. It was stated with the authority of a vigorous student of science. It was new, and yet not destructive. A writer in the *Dial* in 1912 explained the attraction very well:

> He invites us to leave the too stony, dusty roads of intellectualism and naturalism and follow him across country. The grass is springy beneath us, flowers bloom around, the air is fresh and sweet. . . . It is a delightful adventure. Perhaps our shortcut will not lead us to the City of Truth, but certainly neither of the two great highways which mankind has tramped for so many centuries seems to have done that.[8]

The metaphor was a little dangerous: this third road sounded a good deal like the Primrose Path. Quite a few eminent Americans from Dewey to H. L. Mencken managed to resist the attraction. At the other end of the spectrum, some of the crustiest custodians of culture related the Bergson craze to other growing symptoms of unreason, from political violence to the new dances and postimpressionist art. These attacks, of course, increased Bergson's popularity

[8] Charles Leonard Moore: "The Return of the Gods," *Dial*, November 16, 1912, p. 372.

among the liberated; all he had needed was to be made just a little less respectable.

For those who did not worry about respectability, popular spokesmen of the new mysticism went much further. Francis Grierson seemed to many one of the prophets of the age. It was not hard to see in Grierson's own career one of the more mysterious whims of the Life Force. He was born in England and brought up in America. Suddenly in 1869, at the age of 21, with very little musical training (some accounts say none at all) he had astounded and delighted critical audiences in Paris with his piano improvisations. Later audiences had continued to respond enthusiastically. In 1889, equally suddenly, he had started a second career as a writer in both French and English. Most of Grierson's work consisted of mystical and aphoristic essays, at worst a mixture of Carlyle and Elbert Hubbard.

The most surprising episode of all had occurred in 1908: Grierson had produced one highly effective book. In *The Valley of Shadows* he turned back to the Middle West for his subject, and presented Illinois of the fifties in a series of sketches, half reminiscence and half romantic impression. The Midwest Grierson depicted was a region full of foreboding and mystery. He seemed to relish revival hymns and sermons, strange and gifted old men who remembered the earliest frontier days, sudden waves of popular emotion, intuitions of coming disaster. Certainly Grierson's Midwest was a long way from that of Tarkington or Riley: it was a good deal closer to the section of Sherwood Anderson or Edgar Lee Masters. Perhaps the book's effectiveness derived from a combination of fashionable European and latent American mysticism. Grierson was admired greatly by Stephane Mallarmé and also, a little later, by Francis Hackett, Floyd Dell, Mary Austin, and many others.[9]

For some the Life Force seemed to make possible a literal tri-

[9] A representative and rhapsodic account is in Edwin Bjorkman: *Voices of Tomorrow* (New York, 1913), 154–85. Bjorkman places Grierson with Bergson and Maeterlinck as representatives of the period's main tendency.

umph over death. Sir Oliver Lodge; the president of the British Association; the British pragmatist F. C. S. Schiller; and Bergson himself were active in "psychical research." William James's spirit of open-mindedness and catholicity carried him into séances. Jack London in his last years wrote about astral bodies. Still further extremes occurred in the shadowy land where popular American cult religion merged with new doctrine. As in previous periods, mysticism could attract the profound and the shallow, the disciplined and the undisciplined. In America it had always attracted more than its share of the literal-minded.

Even the social sciences, with their nineteenth-century relativist origins and their common materialist implications, sometimes played with the doctrines of the Liberation. From Europe via England, the Young Intellectuals drew a cheerful, progressive, and also destructive irrationalist political theory. Already the winds of social science had blown away most of the ghosts of classical political thought: natural law, natural rights, and the social contract. To the younger English political theorists, the state, like these, was a discredited fiction, and probably a German fiction at that. Harold Laski, immensely exuberant and brilliant, was spreading at Harvard and in the *New Republic* the doctrines of pluralism. Like G. D. H. Cole, the guild socialist, and many others, he was sure that the creative energies of man could best be liberated by a spontaneous network of free associations. Among historians, in general a soberly rationalist group, Carl Becker was expounding the doctrines of Eucken, Bergson, and Maeterlinck, and announcing the demise of historical materialism.[1]

Nineteenth-century socialism, either in the harsh materialist form of Marx or the painstaking Fabian version, was regarded by some of the influential young men as admirable, but incomplete and a little out of date. The socialism of H. G. Wells, with its respect for differences in human capabilities, its insistence on sexual and

[1] Carl Becker: "Some Aspects of the Influence of Social Problems and Ideas upon the Study and Writing of History," *American Journal of Sociology,* XVIII (1913), 641–75.

artistic as well as economic freedom, its very large place for a managerial and intellectual elite was far more compelling. Some American rebels merged the new English radicalism with still more stirring doctrines from the continent: the egoistic, more or less Nietzschean anarchism of Max Stirner, or the proletarian syndicalism of Bergson's fiery disciple Georges Sorel. One doctrine was common to all the European political theorists most influential on the Liberation: the new society must be not only just and free but also varied and spontaneous, above all, interesting.

Graham Wallas, the Fabian scholar who memorably visited Harvard in 1910 and impressed such different kinds of Americans as Wesley Mitchell and Walter Lippmann, made an ambitious attempt to bring together the new politics and the new psychology. It was not altogether clear which new psychology Wallas meant. Politicians must discard, he insisted, the nineteenth-century fiction of the individual making rational decisions on the basis of interest. They must learn to deal with such things as habit, instinct, and response. They must realize that political decisions are made partly on the basis of unconscious associations, buried out of sight in the mass of mental experience. Wallas, like many Americans, badly needed a new explanation of the irrational sources of behavior. He found it; in his 1914 book one encounters almost with relief a name evidently unknown to him earlier: Sigmund Freud.[2]

The history of Freud's arrival in America is marked by two major ironies. First, this Central European scientist, who hated false optimism and above all mysticism, who had deep loyalties to nineteenth-century materialism, who started as a neurologist and only with agony left the clear road of physiological psychology, was in this period welcomed chiefly as a liberator of the soul, or at least the creative psyche. Second, the theorist of sex, who dealt with matters that still could not be mentioned in many American circles, was, as he well knew, welcomed earlier, more widely, and more warmly in prudish America than in Europe.

Freud's early writings had been known in American medical and

[2] Wallas: *The Great Society* (New York, 1914), p. 66.

psychological circles since the nineties, but the American Freudian movement really dated from the famous Clark University conference of 1909, when it had been inaugurated, as Freud himself said, "under particularly glorious circumstances." [3] Freud, together with his disciples Sandor Ferenczi, A. A. Brill, and Ernest Jones, had been invited to take part in a great psychological congress to celebrate the University's twentieth anniversary. Two years later Brill and Jones founded the two official American psychoanalytic associations. By 1915 the movement itself was militant and articulate, though small; Freudian developments were very fully reported in professional journals; Freud's major works had been translated and widely reviewed; and the outlines of his theories were discussed in the popular press.

This sudden rush of interest can be explained partly by the chaotic state of American psychological theory at the time, partly by the deep splits and strains beginning to be apparent in American thought as a whole.

One major tendency of American psychology was militant materialism. Many of the older teachers had learned a strict physiological psychology in Germany; some of the younger theorists, the behaviorists, were banishing consciousness itself as the last relic of the soul. Another peculiarly American development was applied psychology; many Americans were less interested in theory than in statistical information useful for education or industry. Finally, one edge of psychology, at the opposite extreme from behaviorism, trailed off into the vague region between psychotherapy and religion. The idea that spiritual insight and exercise could tap hidden sources of energy was deeply rooted in American evangelical and transcendental thought. According to William James at least, it was borne out by universal human experience. It seemed to gain support from the French psychotherapeutic school of Jean Martin Charcot and others, with their liberal use of hypnotism and suggestion. Superficially at least, this kind of psychology was closely re-

[3] Sigmund Freud: "History of the Psychoanalytic Movement," in A. A. Brill, ed.: *Basic Writings of Sigmund Freud* (New York, 1938), p. 950.

lated to a host of protoreligious cults like the Boston Emanuel movement, which taught its believers how to draw on the mysterious "subliminal self."

All these movements and others, directly and indirectly, aided the early Freudian cause. One of the earliest and most devoted groups of early defenders of Freud was a handful of elder Americans with deep roots in nineteenth-century idealism. Freud, like Bergson, was drafted into the defense of the spirit. At least his theories, unlike those of the behaviorists, traced mental phenomena not to immediate environmental stimuli but to inner history.

One of Freud's first American champions was Professor James J. Putnam of the Harvard Medical School, an all-out Emersonian idealist. With genuine courage, Putnam tried to wrestle Freud's theories into congruity with his philosophical scheme. The psychoanalytic movement, he argued in 1915, was really a method of building character, a way to displace lower by higher motives. Childhood was a period of creative possibilities as well as one of temptations to be understood and overcome; in the midst of his discussion of childhood sexuality Putnam twice quoted Wordsworth. Putnam was undoubtedly baffling and annoying to some European Freudians but he remained loyal; Freud himself deals gently and understandingly with him in his history of the movement.

G. Stanley Hall, the president of Clark who invited Freud to America, was a typical Victorian seeker, troubled about the loss of faith and also, as he tells us in a very frank autobiography, about personal sexual matters. His first dependence was on evolutionary religion, his second on German science. Finally Freud came as a sympathizer and bringer of light, who restored to psychology an emphasis on "feeling" and fitted with no apparent difficulty into Hall's vast, complicated, and optimistic scheme.

Militant naturalists, as opposed to these elder idealists or strugglers with idealism, were in general hostile to Freud in this period. Yet even here there were exceptions. Freud himself, after all, was well known to be antireligious and deterministic. Edwin B. Holt managed to combine Freudianism with behaviorism and an emphasis on practical utility. This last combination had a big future. Freud clearly intended to help the suffering as well as to discover scientific truth. This was to produce the major drift of American popular Freudianism toward an emphasis on therapy. Already Freud was being presented in the popular press as a wizard, a surgeon of the soul who had a secret formula for ending mental disease and restoring social efficiency overnight, that is, for casting out devils.

Freudianism, like other doctrines of the Liberation, was publicized partly by its shocked opponents. To many Americans, such ideas as infant sexuality were not only wicked, but insane. More's *Nation* carried on an intermittent polemic, but yet reviewed the translations fully and seriously. Amy Lowell was one of many Americans who suggested that Freud's theories were applicable at best only to certain undesirable types of Austrians. Almost angrier than outraged moral conservatives were outraged believers in nineteenth-century science; Freud seemed to these to be part of an inexplicable new wave of reactionary occultism; the unconscious mind was purely imaginary—moreover, it was a contradiction in terms.

Freud's most receptive American audience in the prewar years consisted, as we will see, of the Young Intellectuals. Not all the uses which American intellectuals were later to make of his doctrines had yet been discovered. The Freudian vogue in social science had barely begun, and only a few poets and novelists had discovered the immense literary uses of this theory which puts poetic symbolism at the very center of thought. So far, Freud was mainly useful as a spearhead in the onslaught against Puritanism. Despite his own deep tragic sense, his recognition of inescapable conflicts, he was adopted by the Liberation as a patron of a new cult of happiness, a new freedom very different from Woodrow Wilson's. In certain Chicago and New York circles before the war Freudian jargon was compulsory, everybody's friends were being "done," and already references to dreams or slips of the tongue gave rise to knowing winks.

There were many versions of Freud, and this does not prove that any of them—the version of the older idealists or that of the popular press or that of the Young Intellectuals—was altogether wrong. Freud's brilliant insights, although they are a part of our casual conversation, are not even yet a part of our thought, not quite assimilated by either science or philosophy. The discussion still goes on whether Freudianism is or is not optimistic, whether it is sympathetic or hostile to art, whether its discoveries have universal or limited meaning. The ambiguities in Freud are probably deeper and more profound than those in the other favorite thinkers of the Liberation: the point at present is that ambiguity in these years was a source of strength. Like the others, Freud seemed to the Liberation to offer a way to experience traditional emotions in a brand-new, above all, scientific way.

Whatever the sources of the Liberation in philosophy and science, it flowed to America mainly in the form of imaginative literature. For a number of reasons the literary influence of Europe, immense for half a century, reached a peak in the immediate prewar years. One reason is of course the richness and variety of European literature itself at the end of the Long Peace. Another lies in its new and more palatable "message." The naturalist and the unmoral aesthetic schools were still vigorous, but the newest fashion was for cheerful, modern "scientific" mysticism. For a short time this drew together the younger intellectuals and some of the more tolerant of the older idealists. Starved by a long diet of Howells's realism, cut off from the deep symbolist and religious strain in their own literature by critical blindness, many rediscovered in the new literature a vast realm of emotion the period called "poetry."

European literature was influential as never before partly because it was increasingly available. The translators, busy since the eighties, were working faster and faster. A handful of venturesome new publishers were supplementing, and beginning to affect, the older ones. Libraries were sometimes timid, sometimes fairly daring. Miss Zora I. Schields of the Omaha Public Library rejoiced that at last some literature was coming in which was both modern and beautiful. Some of the Europeans, she told an audience in October 1912, had to be read if one wanted to keep up with modern thought, as she clearly did, at all costs. Others, one could actually enjoy.[4]

Finally there was the new drama, at first mostly imported. In the little theaters springing up all over the country, and even in an occasional Broadway venture, one encountered all varieties of the new European spirit. Naturalism, particularly in its most recent forms, played a part in the attack on drawing-room comedy, but to the boldest spirits much of the naturalist message, and still more clearly most of the naturalist technique, seemed a little passé. What was new was symbolism, suggestion, atmosphere. *Theater Arts Monthly*, begun in 1916, illustrated for its readers the work of European nonrealist producers like Gordon Craig and Max Reinhardt. Little-theater audiences were already familiar with Maeterlinck's symbolism, and with the misty Irish magic of Lord Dunsany, Synge, and the early Yeats.

England, still as a matter of course the literary capital for the conservative critics, evoked complicated emotions in the rebels. In part the Liberation was, as Ezra Pound and others wanted it to be, a Liberation from the Anglo-American tradition, from Thackeray and Tennyson, and from the recent adolescent favorites Stevenson and Kipling. Yet for Pound himself, London, with its new reviews and bookshops, was the literary center of the world in these years. Britain had her new literature, too. A few shared the taste of Huneker and Mencken for Conrad's tragic gifts. D. H. Lawrence was beginning to interest the extreme avant-garde. Shaw, by now, with his socialism and his paradoxes, had a little the flavor of the nineties: only a few realized with Floyd Dell that what he was making fun of was not really bourgeois respectability, but easy and shallow

[4] Zora I. Schields: "Foreign Literature in Translation" (Pamphlet, Omaha, 1912).

rebellion itself. John Galsworthy, a couple of decades later a symbol of respectability, was admired by the young rebels for his problem plays and his essays, full of the new mystique of art. Chesterton and Belloc were acceptably romantic and antibourgeois, though few accepted their medievalism.

The major English prophet H.G. Wells sounded in the *Atlantic Monthly* in 1912 the battle cry for the whole generation:

> We are going to write about it all. We are going to write about business and finance and politics, and precedence and pretentiousness and decorum and indecorum, until a thousand pretences and ten thousand impostures shrivel in the cold clear air of our elucidations. We are going to write of wasted opportunities and latent beauties, until a thousand new ways of living open to men and women. We are going to appeal to the young and the hopeful and the curious, against the established, the dignified, and defensive. Before we have done, we shall have all life within the scope of the novel.[5]

Brought up in one of the shabbiest subclasses of the still intact English social system, Wells could not be associated with the stuffier aspects of English culture. He had been freed by science and then, like the other figures of the Liberation, freed *from* science.

Wells's outspoken credo in his current middle phase (he was forty-six in 1912) was very close to that of the late William James, whom he greatly admired. As some saw at the time, Wells's philosophy was not unlike that of Bergson, whom he did not admire. Like James, Wells rejected logic, was highly skeptical of all categories and classes, and had come to believe that all movements were more important than their goals. His "scepticism of the (mental) instrument," as he called it, brought all "ethical, social and religious teaching into the province of poetry." [6] Belief, necessary to man,

[5] Wells: "The Contemporary Novel," *Atlantic Monthly*, CIX (1912), 11.

[6] Wells: "Scepticism of the Instrument" (Address of 1903, reprinted in *A Modern Utopia*, London, 1905), p. 392.

must be constructed, by living, not by taking thought. And in living, one was part of a mysterious whole:

> I see myself in life as part of a great physical being that strains and I believe grows toward Beauty, and of a great mental being that strains and I believe grows toward knowledge and power.[7]

Wells's peculiar literary device, ever since his early scientific romance, had been the smashup. Recently, Wells's catastrophes had been creative, not merely damnation for bourgeois society but also redemption; a constructive liberation of new growth. Mr. Polly burned his little shop and moved forth into life. In his more recent science tales the catastrophes, the brush by the comet, the interplanetary war, had shown the way to social reconstruction. In 1914, a few months before Europe's actual and uncheerful smashup, Wells published *The World Set Free.* The Wellsian miracle in this fantasy is the discovery of an atomic bomb, depending on human control of the disintegration of matter. This utterly incredible weapon, falling into the hands of several nations at once, results in the swift destruction of millions of people and most of the world's great cities. At the end of the story, in 1950, the Parliament of the World creates the new universal society, at once efficient and free.

Wells's political thought of the same period was as electrifying and novel as his fiction. In his *An Englishman Looks at the World* (1914), he flatly repudiated the key doctrine of much of his earlier social thought, and denied that any method drawn from the physical sciences could have any validity whatever for human affairs. Science dealt with number and ignored individuality; the true sociology, Wells said, must be literature.

Consulting his experience like a good Jamesian, Wells had long since decided that the last thing he wanted was for the existing lower classes of England to take over control. Like Matthew Ar-

[7] Quoted in Van Wyck Brooks: "The World of H. G. Wells," *Forum,* LII (1914), 28.

nold (Van Wyck Brooks in 1914 made this startling but shrewd comparison), Wells saw in America something like a warning of what would happen in such a plebeian upheaval. His Modern Utopia was disciplined, efficient, and above all elitist: like Plato, and still more like Frederick J. Taylor, whom he admired, Wells believed in giving superior people opportunities. Dedication, a pragmatic state religion, planning: all these were a part of his vision of the future; equality most emphatically was not.

Part of the method was to be frankness, liberating and hygienic. Sex, like religion, was to become sensible and realistic, yet at the same time creative, and not without a touch of cleansing humor. Wells's Ann Veronica, having passed clear through feminism as Wells had passed through socialism and naturalism, emerges in a delightful and modern relation to her scientist. And all is achieved with very little cost: even the Victorian parents finally see the light, and the author has at no time been compelled to refer to any specific part of the human body.

Paris, in these last years of its "*Belle Époque*," was the anticapital, as it had been for a long time. Though very few Americans understood French culture, a number admired it. They knew that it was strikingly different from their own. It was said to be more sympathetic to art, more tolerant of eccentric genius, and above all less puritanical about sex.

Among recent French books, the most discussed in America were Rolland's affirmative and realistic *Jean-Cristophe*, or the satires, witty but not to Americans seriously disquieting, of Anatole France. A very few students of poetry had caught up with the French rebels of the past generation, that of Mallarmé and Verlaine. Only a tiny group of Americans had heard more than rumors about the French avant-garde, which was already combining the nineteenth-century decadence and the twentieth-century Liberation, already experimenting more and more wildly with mixtures of the childlike and the obscene, the fantastic and the grotesque.[8]

[8] Roger Shattuck, in his interesting summary *The Banquet Years* (New York, 1958), dates the peak of avant-garde experiment 1885–1918. It is interesting

Gertrude Stein, after studying with William James, the common source of so many kinds of rebellion, had settled in Paris in 1903. Her friendships and her own experiments with language, though not her way of life, made her fully a part of the French avant-garde, and she transmitted some of its tastes and insights to her own still tiny circle of American admirers: Hutchins Hapgood, Mabel Dodge, Carl Van Vechten.

Although contemporary French art had its most startling impact on America before the war, contemporary French literature was still nearly unknown. After the war, when Paris had lost much of its exuberance, it was to become the literary capital of the United States for a few years; so far it was intriguing precisely because it was little known. Amy Lowell, a far more popular prophet of French culture than Gertrude Stein, gave her lecture audiences an impression as definite and reassuring as it was mistaken. France, like the rest of the world, was entering a period of sturdy affirmation. Mallarmé, Verlaine, and Baudelaire, great innovators as they had been, belonged to the gloomy nineteenth-century past. The rising generation was much less inward and complicated, and this was what made it modern:

> Paul Fort is the modern man. Exteriorizing, full of vitality and vigor, and 'la joie de vivre.' . . . He positively bounces with delight through poem after poem.[9]

Brand-new centers of literature seemed, like America, to be declaring their independence of the old literary capitals. Ibsen had started the Scandinavian vogue; Björnson, Lagerlof, Strindberg, and others were carrying it on. The Irish poets and playwrights were well known; in 1916 a new Irish name was heard. Joyce's *Portrait of the Artist* was not yet seen as part of a major new departure in method, but it was obviously a new, superb version of the novel of rebellion. Even the *Nation*, nearly always judicious,

---

in relation to our present subject that he finds the prewar experimental spirit, no matter how bizarre, gay rather than despairing or nihilist.

[9] Amy Lowell: *Six French Poets* (New York, 1916), p. 215.

though shocked by Joyce's "privy-language," found in both *Dubliners* and the *Portrait* a welcome quality of inwardness, something contrasting with the author's "naturalism" which it could describe only as "an ingrowing and indeterminate idealism." [1]

In Italy, the same antinaturalist rebellion was seen by some in d'Annunzio; even India, the only Asian country noticed by literary critics, produced the mystic poet Rabindranath Tagore, published in America in ten volumes and treated to the full ceremonial lecture tour.

The greatest new discovery was Belgium. Amy Lowell, like many others, specifically pointed out that Emile Verhaeren, though he had been through both his decadent and his naturalist phases, was really a "modern," meaning a cheerful poet. He had, she said, made poetry realize the beauty and romance of the modern world; he had in fact "made us understand that science and art are never at variance." [2] His name, associated with Belgian robustness and contrasted with French oversubtlety, was very frequently invoked after 1914.

A great many Americans of very different kinds were sure that the greatest living author was "the Belgian Shakespeare," Maurice Maeterlinck. Maeterlinck was the best link between the Liberation and the older idealism. More simply and reassuringly than even Bergson, he heralded a new mysticism, based on the latest science. Even though he was acceptable to some of their elders, the younger generation could not quite disown him. He had, after all, been a symbolist poet in Paris in the nineties. Better, his *Monna Vanna,* an allegory of pure and impure love, had recently been banned from the English stage. In the more moderate organs of the Liberation, and far more regularly in the conservative magazines, glad to approve at least one modern, Maeterlinck was regularly praised and quoted. Far beyond the circles of those who followed modern literature closely, Maeterlinck was admired as the author of *The Life of the Bee* and *The Blue Bird.* Henry Ford, who on principle read few

[1] *Nation,* April 5, 1917, p. 403.
[2] *Six French Poets,* pp. 3–4, 47.

books, ran across Maeterlinck's *Immortality*, a painstaking, nonreligious argument in favor of personal survival after death. "Well, you ought to read it," he assured Garet Garett in 1914.[3]

At the other extreme of the current fashion was the special cult of Russia. This was quite outside ordinary literary vogues. It was partly political and partly semireligious. The Russian Revolution of 1905 had thrilled Americans, and some of them had felt passionately about Russian revolutionary heroes ever since. William English Walling, the well-to-do and gifted American socialist, tried to explain "Russia's Message" in 1908. This great, religious, peasant people, said Walling (and many saw the same vision), would take the materialism out of socialism. This was the country where the intelligentsia were not bourgeois, where pseudoscientific sociology had long been discredited. Walling ended his description fittingly with a long quotation from "the great Belgian" Maurice Maeterlinck.[4]

Wherever one looked in these years Slavic genius seemed to be flowering. Some of it was new, some newly popular. American literary and artistic discussion was filled with names like Diaghileff, Nijinsky, Stravinsky, as well as Chekov and Dostoevsky. The *Literary Digest* conceded that the artistic leadership once enjoyed by the Greeks had clearly passed, via the French, to the Russians.[5]

John Dos Passos, an utterly unknown young writer, said in 1916 that Americans were turning to Russian literature because American literature starved them. Van Wyck Brooks gave this standard dictum the fullest expression:

> America is simply Russia turned inside out. Russia is the richest of nations in spiritual energy, we are the poorest; Russia is the poorest of nations in social machinery, we are the richest.[6]

[3] Garett: "Henry Ford's Experiment in Good-Will," *Everybody's*, XXX (1914), 472–3. E. E. Slosson put Maeterlinck at the head of his list of *Major Prophets of To-day*.

[4] W. E. Walling: *Russia's Message* (New York, 1908), p. 450.

[5] *Literary Digest*, August 23, 1913, p. 378.

[6] Dos Passos: "Against American Literature," *New Republic*, October 14, 1916, p. 270–1; Brooks, "An American Oblomov," *Dial*, LXII (1917), 244–5.

Since the time of Henry James, admiration had passed from the urbane Turgenev to Tolstoy, the sage and saint. With the Constance Garnett translations of Dostoevsky, beginning with *The Brothers Karamazov* in 1912, the young people found a new Russian master.

Dostoevsky, more than any other writer, brought into literature what the most acute of the younger generation had been missing, mystery and profound emotion. Unlike Wells or Maeterlinck or the other incongruously assembled heroes of the Rebellion, he was no optimist. To repudiate science and progress, he knew, would cost a lot. This part of his message the young people could not read. Randolph Bourne praised Dostoevsky for "his superb modern healthiness. He is healthy because he has no sense of any dividing line between the normal and the abnormal, or even between the sane and the insane." [7]

❦

Not literature but the graphic arts gave American taste its sharpest jolt during the prewar years. The story of the Armory Show of 1913 has been told so often and so well that one can easily miss, in the excitement, some of its significance for our story.

In literature Americans had been more or less aware of European innovation for almost a century. In the graphic arts, for which few of them cared greatly, they were far less sophisticated. The rich still dealt in the secure futures of the old masters. A few American artists had experimented in impressionism; gallery-goers had learned to appreciate Manet; liberals indignantly told the story of Ruskin's attack on Whistler. The most vigorous insurgent movement seemed to be the entirely native, realistic, and socially responsible Ash Can School. Sometimes associated with naturalist literature, this school was deliberately linked by its leaders to Whit-

[7] Randolph Bourne: "The Immanence of Dostoevsky," *Dial*, LXII (1917), 24–5.

man's artistic and political credo. Real innovation was to take an opposite form and it was to come not from the American past but from France. Only a handful of Americans, Alfred Stieglitz in his gallery, Gertrude and Leo Stein in Paris, had seen this new storm on the horizon.

Then suddenly the American public, first in New York and then in Chicago, Philadelphia, and Boston, and at second hand in the press everywhere, was dazzled by a masterpiece of carefully planned showmanship. What they saw was a catholic and excellent collection of every variety of contemporary nonrepresentational, nonmoralizing, untraditional experiment: the postimpressionists, the Fauves, the expressionists, the primitives, the cubists, and the abstract sculptors, mixed judiciously with first-rate French transitional and even classic figures.

The violence of the reaction, the charges of insanity, degeneracy, and anarchism might well have been taken for granted. They could hardly match the expressions of anger that had greeted the Salon des Fauves in 1905 in Paris, where painting was a more central matter. Quite as vehement as the outraged conservatives were the show's evangelical defenders, from Willard Huntington Wright in the *Forum* to the undergraduate E. E. Cummings in the *Harvard Advocate*. Both sides knew it was more than an art show. The excitable Mabel Dodge exaggerated the feelings aroused in her circle only a little when she called it the most important event in America since 1776.[8]

More surprising than the excitement was the show's sweeping success, financial and critical. A hundred thousand people went to the Sixty-Ninth Regiment Armory in the first month. Nearly all pictures by cubists, the most roundly denounced group, were sold. Within two years a group of leading modernists, including Wright and Stieglitz, found it necessary to hold another show, this time of American modernists, because they were afraid that new native tendencies would be forgotten in the rush to follow the new Euro-

[8] Mabel Dodge to Gertrude Stein, January 24, 1913, Donald Gallup, ed.: *Flowers of Friendship* (New York, 1953), p. 71.

pean styles. In 1917 Lee Simonson expressed the same concern in the rebel *Seven Arts*.[9]

The conservatives, here as in other areas of opinion, found it hard to hold their ranks firm. A number of by no means avant-garde critics, including Theodore Roosevelt in the *Outlook*, were good-humored and eager to be tolerant. Roosevelt, with his usual self-confidence and lack of pretense, scolded some of the artists and made fun of others, but thoroughly enjoyed the show, was delighted that everybody had his say, predicted a good effect on American art, and found the whole thing a healthy reaction to dullness. With humorous intent, but an underlying acuteness and freshness of vision, he compared a nonrepresentational picture to a fine Navajo rug hanging in his bathroom.[1]

A number of conservative journals whose critics did not like the show nearly as well as Roosevelt did, from the *Nation* to the *Commercial and Financial Chronicle*, fully agreed with its admirers that it was an important event, symbolizing and affecting the whole complex of modern movements in philosophy, politics, and literature. Correctly or not, the kaleidoscopic impression made by the new painting was linked to the Bergsonian idea that reality lies in movement rather than in rest. Inevitably, the revolt against the imitation of nature was linked with the repudiation of philosophic naturalism, and therefore with the defense of idealism. This link brought modern art, as it brought Freud, some strange defenders.

Arthur Jerome Eddy, a businessman, prophet of the trade association movement and the new industrialism, made a hobby of modern art. In 1914 Eddy said that "the key-note of the modern movement in art" was "the expression of the *inner self* as distinguished from the representation of the outer world." [2] This showed that the art of the future, like the civilization of the future, would

[9] Lee Simonson: "The Painter's Ark," *Seven Arts*, June 1917, p. 207.

[1] Roosevelt: "A Layman's View of an Art Exhibition," *Outlook*, March 29, 1913, pp. 718–20.

[2] Arthur Jerome Eddy: *Cubists and Post-Impressionists* (Chicago, 1914), p. 112.

become more and more spiritual. With this sentiment, though they put it in different terms, some of the young rebels heartily agreed.

The same story of conservative outrage and rebellious exuberance could be told in terms of music. In America music, which did not make direct statements about moral principles, did not command the same spotlight as literature or even painting. Yet for those who could follow them, musical battles also were under way. The previous century's controversies over Wagner and Debussy were not completely over. Richard Strauss, partly because of the moral controversy over *Salomé*, was perhaps the most discussed contemporary. For the avant-garde, Stravinsky, Scriabin, even Schoenberg were the equivalent of the postimpressionists.

Huneker, the great defender of musical innovation since the nineties, had already some heirs in a new generation. Paul Rosenfeld, an habitué of the Stieglitz gallery, a friend of Sherwood Anderson and Van Wyck Brooks, a frequent contributor to the *Seven Arts*, was the chief music critic of the Young Intellectuals. Like his fellows, he wrote about all the arts, praising the European moderns and looking for American equivalents. His style, like Huneker's, was romantic and a little flowery; his outlook, like that of his contemporaries, exuberant.

Finally, in January 1916 America got its first taste of a new art which seemed to link all the others. The Russian Ballet of Serge Diaghileff had left St. Petersburg for Monte Carlo in 1911. By 1916 it combined the traditional rigorous discipline of the Imperial Ballet with a bizarre amalgam of Russian folk art and Russian turn-of-the-century music and painting. It had also, in the days of Nijinsky, a flavor of scandal. Some Americans had reported first-hand the uproars in London and Paris, the moral outrage in 1912 over *Afternoon of a Faun* and the music riot of 1913 over the *Rites of Spring*. In New York the show was a little toned down and there was not much trouble. On its American tours of 1916 and 1917 the ballet seemed the last triumphant development of European art, and at the same time a unique creation of "barbarous," embattled Russia. Both the Hearst Sunday Supplements and the suddenly revolutionized *Century* presented their readers with Bakst costume plates.

❦

Aside from sheer innovation itself, the common intellectual content found by the American Liberation in the new European imports was joyful mystery, a repudiation of harsh and simple materialism. Conscious as we are that this cheerful and sometimes too easy doctrine was being expounded right before, or even right after, the dawn of a tragic period of history, we are likely to regard it as more foolish than it was. Its central dictum, that life transcends thought, has after all been the conclusion of many wise men in all periods, including our own. Its only obvious error was its extreme optimism, and that was the one most powerful and pervasive element in prewar American culture. This almost inescapable habit of mind was what led the prewar rebels to misinterpret the profound insights of Dostoevsky, to simplify the perplexing insights of Freud, to mix these with the up-to-the-minute attractive superficialities of Wells or Bergson. It was optimism, also, that enabled the Liberation to succeed where gloomy nineteenth-century insurrections had faileld.

The Liberation was, in its own way, pragmatic: it believed with James that ideas should be judged not by their conformity to any preconceived truth but by the quality of life they contained. Certainly these new doctrines, imported with older and more devastating European ideas into the superficially united American culture of the prewar years, released great quantities of stored-up energy. The effect in the long run was a little like the continuing atomic explosions imagined by Wells, and as hard to control.

II
Poets

In about 1912 some young men and women from the villages, small towns, and colleges of the United States began to move to two great cities. There they read, talked, and wrote. A little of what they wrote was good, much was interesting, much atrociously bad. We will not be primarily concerned with their success or failure, though literary judgment is not altogether irrelevant. What interests us is that, all of a sudden, young writers were trying to say new things in a new way. The *Rebellion,* a term we will use for the domestic upheaval as opposed to the *Liberation* from abroad, was the beginning of a major change in American civilization. It was also part of one of the creative and innovating periods of Western thought and culture.

A curious and inescapable duality runs through the Rebellion: its ideas, sources, and even its physical locations seem to come in sets of two opposites. Its most common article of faith was the importance of spontaneous, individual free expression in brand-new terms. The past, according to Carl Sandburg, was a bucket of ashes. A belief in spontaneity and self-expression, often approaching anarchism, was the characteristic doctrine of the Rebellion in all its branches. Yet very early, within the rebel ranks, a few proclaimed an exactly opposite creed. Against democratic spontaneity, this minority raised the standard of art, of discipline, even of tradition.

In the cheerful, somewhat mystical mood of the prewar years, these two opposites could sometimes come together. They were fighting the same enemy; believers in democratic self-expression and in aesthetic tradition could unite against the official credo of 1912. Both opposed the obvious and conventional kind of moralism, and both were bored with much of Anglo-American, nineteenth-century culture. Young writers for a while could find inspiration at once in Whitman and Flaubert. Sandburg and Pound could and did regard each other as allies. The two priestesses of the new poetry, Harriet Monroe and Amy Lowell, made use of two arguments at once: first, that new verse forms were appropriate to a new land and age; second, that free verse had a respectable ancestry in France and even Asia.

The clearly dominant doctrine of the early rebellion seemed to some of the rebels to need only statement, not argument. "If we are a crude and child-like people," asked Sherwood Anderson, "how can our literature hope to escape the influence of that fact? Why indeed should we want it to escape?" [1] What we needed to do, he went on, was to plunge "with greater daring" into American life, which was much more interesting than American literature. We should not worry yet about form: that might come later. Even more than his fellows, Anderson sometimes counted on it to come all by itself: he not only wrote spontaneous poems, but painted spontaneous pictures, and even threatened to sit down at the piano, which he had never studied, and play his ideas. Amy Lowell, in her most popular poem, asked the typical question: "Christ, what are patterns for?"

Actually the idea of spontaneity did not really come out of the virgin cornfields, as Sandburg and others thought it did. It came also from Europe and from older American sources. The completely spontaneous literary movement is always a myth; it takes some knowledge of tradition to defy tradition. However much some of the new poets tried to repudiate all ancestors, a glance at their early lives shows—if we need to be shown—that literary ancestors existed.

The Rebellion was in part a product of all the movements, articulate and inarticulate, European and American, that had been

[1] Sherwood Anderson: "An Apology for Crudity," *Dial*, November 8, 1917, reprinted in Alfred Kazin and Charles Shapiro: *Stature of Theodore Dreiser* (Bloomington, Ind., 1955), p. 81.

attacking nineteenth-century shibboleths for two generations. Often the rebels knew and respected, though they seldom followed, older naturalists like Dreiser. They were fascinated by the decadents and aesthetes when they encountered them, and they had been prepared by earlier acquaintance with the aesthetic revolt of Ruskin's generation. Above all the American Rebellion drew on the recent European Liberation, with its new, somewhat mystical promises of a wide-open future, free from nineteenth-century gloom, doubt, and materialism. Self-expression, creative freedom, and spontaneity were often suggested by a sudden encounter with Nietzsche or Wells and confirmed by a chance acquaintance, often secondhand, with Bergson. The European Liberation provided new methods and new forms for old discontents: the Rebellion put in words many of the long latent resentments against Eastern, upper-class, Anglo-Saxon cultural monopoly.

Finally, this Rebellion, like most rebellions, was deeply affected by the old order against which it was rebelling. For one thing, the polite culture of the day, with its Mabies and Van Dykes, provided the rebels with an unparalleled collection of sitting ducks. But this was not all it gave them. The doctrine of spontaneity had, after all, been stated in its most extreme form by Emerson, one of the most sacred figures in the official canon. Among the custodians of culture themselves the more cheerful and democratic camp had long been relatively cordial toward "Western" and democratic self-expression. The "strong" critics who admired Whitman more than Henry James had much in common with the new Chicago poets. Though the Rebellion shocked the defenders of the dominant credo, it offended them more by its form than its essential content. It was milder than it looked; this was why it was able to succeed, and this was why it soon succumbed to its own internal opponents.

❧

When we ask why, specifically, particular young men moved from actual small town to real cities just when they did we will find ourselves looking several ways at once. We must look hard at the cities themselves which had suddenly become so attractive. We must look back at the villages to see why they had been forsaken. And we must remember that these young men had read about other young men who had moved from the provinces to Paris and London during the past fifty years.

Felix Fay, the hero of Floyd Dell's autobiographical novel, found a picture recurring in his restless mind. It was of a map that hung in the small-town railroad station,

> the map with a picture of iron roads from all over the Middle West centering in a dark blotch in the corner . . . 'Chicago!' He said to himself.[2]

He, and Dell himself, had good reason. In the first place Chicago had culture. The culture of the Little Room, the Art Institute, and the *Dial*, however despised by the young rebels, gave them a lot that they needed. Its organs opposed the Rebellion, but not very consistently. At least the rebels were helping in the old effort to put Chicago on the literary map. The *Dial*, which fiercely condemned the first issues of *Poetry* in 1912, published two years later a summary article by *Poetry's* assistant editor. Two issues later still it carried a lead article praising Vachel Lindsay for trying, at least, to express the Middle West. Once more, Dell's fictional characters convey a verifiable insight:

> "And what does Chicago think of—of us?" he asked.
> "Oh, that's all right. Chicago is beginning to realize that it needs us. Chicago wants to be a metropolis. And all the stock-yards in the world won't make a metropolis. Enough of us, given a free-hand, can. [*sic*] And Chicago knows it. Just now we are at a premium here. We can be as crazy as we like." [3]

The older literary culture provided the right mixture of opposition and tolerance; it also provided education. Kroch's excellent

[2] Floyd Dell: *Moon-Calf* (New York, 1920), p. 2.
[3] Dell: *The Briary Bush* (New York, 1921), p. 34.

bookstore specialized in the new editions of continental authors being published in New York, and even made available foreign literary journals. In the Little Theater movement the line from the uplift movement to the Rebellion was particularly clear. At the turn of the century Anna Morgan had been producing Maeterlinck, Ibsen, and Shaw, for Chicago's enlightened high society. From 1912 to 1917, partly for the same audience, Maurice Brown's very influential Chicago Little Theater produced in the little theater in the Fine Arts building (seating capacity ninety-seven) Euripides, Yeats, Strindberg, and even the works of young Chicagoans.

The Chicago naturalist tradition was still alive. One could not live in Chicago and ignore the images of the city presented in *The Pit* and *The Jungle*. In 1913 Floyd Dell wrote for the decorous *Bookman* a pair of illustrated articles about Chicago's literary shrines, such as the site of the Haymarket bombing, commemorated in several novels, and even the apartment where Sister Carrie might have lived with Drouet.[4]

One stream of Chicago naturalism ran straight through the newspaper offices where many of the young rebels found employment. The latest important newspaper writer, heir to Finley Peter Dunne, George Ade, and others, was Ring Lardner. Lardner had been a Chicago newspaperman before his baseball stories were first published in the *Saturday Evening Post* in 1914. These stories, collected under the title, *You Know Me, Al*, in 1916, were only a little less biting than Lardner's later tales of greed and cruelty; they seem to have little in common with the work of such Chicago rebels as Sandburg or Dell. Yet disillusion, itself a valuable gift to some writers at some times, was not the only gift offered by Chicago newspaper circles to young newcomers. City room conversation, according to the memories of the rebels, was free, brilliant, and seriously concerned with literature. Dell's hero, once in Chicago, gets a job on a newspaper because a frustrated intellectual already on the staff learns that he has read H. G. Wells.

[4] Dell: "Chicago in Fiction," *Bookman*, XXXVIII (1913–14), 270–7, 375–9.

Finally the newcomers found the city itself, which offered them its own much-celebrated combination of rawness and wealth, provincialism and cosmopolitanism. On its own scale and in its own manner, Chicago possessed some of the attractions which had drawn other young writers to Paris: anonymity, learning, picturesque slums to live in, and also an entrenched old guard to fight.

Fairly easily, the newcomers established a Bohemian quarter in the run-down stores near the 1893 Fair Grounds. Rents were low, transportation downtown good, and the sand dunes to walk on and frolic in were near by. The memoirs abound in charming pictures: Eunice Tietjens dancing Nō dances, Arthur Davison Ficke reading the Song of Songs by candlelight. Sinclair Lewis, who spent a little time in prewar Chicago, inserted one of the few hostile sketches of Chicago Bohemia in *Main Street*. The year before her marriage, dated 1912, his Carol encountered the Rebellion:

> She almost gave up library work to become one of the young women who dance in cheese-cloth in the moonlight. She was taken to a certified studio party, with beer, cigarettes, bobbed hair, and a Russian Jewess who sang the Internationale. It cannot be remembered that Carol had anything significant to say to the Bohemians. She was awkward with them, and felt ignorant, and she was shocked by the free manners which she had for years desired. But she heard and remembered discussions of Freud, Romain Rolland, syndicalism, and the Confédération Générale du Travail, feminism versus haremism, Chinese lyrics, nationalization of mines, Christian Science, and fishing in Ontario. She went home and that was the end of her Bohemian life.[5]

The Rebellion could not have lasted long without organs of self-expression. The first outpost to surrender was the *Literary Review* of the *Chicago Evening Post*. From 1908 to 1911 this was edited

[5] Lewis: *Main Street* (New York, 1920), pp. 23–4.

by Francis Hackett, an able Irishman who praised Shaw and Wells, the Russian and Irish writers, and attacked current sentimentality without being particularly radical. In 1911 Hackett was succeeded by Floyd Dell, who had been his assistant since 1909.

Poetry, the most important Chicago organ, needs separate and detailed discussion. The *Little Review*, a rebellion against rebellion, started its hectic career in 1914 partly in protest against *Poetry's* staidness. Margaret Anderson, the *Little Review's* editor, was the perfect Bohemian, owning only one suit and one blouse and always looking her best, sometimes dining on bread and pickles, and, at one point, living in a tent on the shores of Lake Michigan and making it something of a salon. All the typical causes of the Rebellion were carried to their extremes in the *Little Review:* Liberty became anarchism, feminism became complete freedom for sexual experiment, free verse became rhapsodic monologue. Yet the Rebellion's innocence and cheerfulness remained intact: with Miss Anderson's exciting editorials in favor of "the splendor of life" it mixed quotations from Maeterlinck and even Emerson, articles on Nietzsche by his mystical and optimistic interpreter, George Burman Foster, paeans to Emma Goldman. The *Little Review* handled problems of money and circulation, like ideas, with charming gaiety. It thought nothing of skipping an issue or two, or moving its headquarters to San Francisco for a couple of months. Once, when material submitted was below par, it published most of an issue blank.

The *Little Review* moved to New York at the beginning of 1917, and achieved its most lasting fame shortly afterwards when it published part of *Ulysses* in installments, four of which were burned by the postal authorities. Joyce's massive and erudite experiment, however, has nothing in common with the magazine's spirit, either in its New York or its Chicago phase. It approached Joyce just as it approached everything new and stimulating. Its catholicity and its limits are both conveyed by Miss Anderson's famous exchange with Upton Sinclair:

> "Please cease sending me the *Little Review*," he wrote.
> "I no longer understand anything in it, so it no longer interests me."
>
> I replied, "Please cease sending me your socialist paper. I understand everything in it, therefore it no longer interests me." [6]

In 1914 when the *Friday Literary Review*, a year after Dell's departure, veered back toward conservatism, its place began to be taken by the *Chicago Daily News*, which employed a whole galaxy of aspiring authors, and this in turn was supplemented in 1917 by Burton Rascoe's fighting book page in the *Tribune*. The leading figure in this later phase of the Chicago movement was Chicago's minor Mencken, Ben Hecht. Hecht, an amusing and sentimental writer, took the Rebellion a long way from its early loyalties. Hackett and Dell had hailed Wells and Shaw; Hecht in his *Daily News* period titillated his readers with the praises of Verlaine, Nietzsche, and particularly Huysmans. Yet it was in Dostoevsky, says Harry Hansen, that Hecht first found a really kindred spirit.[7]

It is this second phase of the Chicago Rebellion that has been most affectionately chronicled, with its literary round table at Schlogl's Restaurant, its Dill Pickle Club, and its constant losses to New York. By about 1915 or 1916 the "Chicago Renaissance" was thoroughly self-conscious and therefore, by a law of regional rebellions, beginning to wane.

For a while St. Louis was both a contributor and a rival to the Chicago Renaissance. The old river city, according to Mencken the liveliest town in prewar America, developed enough of a literary movement to hold some of its own young people and attract others. The center of the St. Louis movement was William Marion Reedy, who had kept the flag of literary unorthodoxy flying so long. The circle of Young Intellectuals in St. Louis, including Orrick Johns, Sara Teasdale, Zoe Akins, and others, discussed the

[6] Margaret Anderson: *My Thirty Years War* (New York, 1930), p. 128.
[7] Harry Hansen: *Midwest Portraits* (New York, 1923), pp. 316–19.

new books and plays only a little later than New York and was stirred by nearly all the same influences. The writers who came from St. Louis, either to Chicago or later to the East, differed from the major Chicago pattern: they had no village in them. Perhaps for this reason, they included no major figure. (T. S. Eliot, who left St. Louis in 1905 at seventeen, was not associated with the St. Louis literary movement.)

❦

Chicago itself, with its old and new attractions, was part of the reason for the Midwestern literary rebellion. Another part lay hidden in the small towns the young men left behind them, and their attitude toward these towns. For the most part the prewar rebels left home in a mood of excitement and hope, not necessarily in a spirit of rejection, like small-town rebels somewhat later. Home was not necessarily ugly or sordid, but somewhere, perhaps in the city, new kinds of joy and beauty were waiting to be found.

The Midwestern writers often brought with them to the city two legacies of the region's past. One was the emotional inheritance of mystical, evangelical small-town religion. The other, apparently opposite, was the region's widespread, untheoretical radicalism: Debs and Altgeld were important figures to some of the young writers. The young Westerners were poorer than their Eastern counterparts, both in money and education; their hunger for ideas was greater, their feelings of awe toward Europe more frankly expressed. According to Sherwood Anderson, in the Ohio of his youth a man might get married or even go to war without writing a book about it, but a trip to Europe was important.[8]

The rebels who gathered in Chicago were divided into two groups, the young and the not quite so young. Chicago writers who were in their twenties or younger in 1912 were usually eager and a little brash; Chicago for a while was paradise to them but they

[8] Anderson: *A Story Teller's Story* (New York, 1924), p. 391.

achieved their literary distinction, if any, later and elsewhere. On the other hand, men like Anderson, Sandburg, and Lindsay, who came to Chicago in their thirties, had behind them some years of adult experience of nonliterary American life, and often a period of literary frustration. This shows in their work, which is unlike anything produced by the Eastern wing of the Rebellion.

Two figures will serve to represent the pre-Chicago influences on the two wings of the Rebellion. Floyd Dell was the unquestioned leader of the young; Sherwood Anderson the most interesting specimen of the slightly older. Because Dell's best-known novel, *Moon-Calf*, was published in 1920, the year of *Main Street*, he is often associated with the attack on the drab, puritanical Midwestern small town that became conventional in the twenties. Actually, both *Moon-Calf*, his fictional autobiography, and *Homecoming*, his much later and very similar nonfiction account, give a friendly, nostalgic picture of the prewar home town.

Dell knew severe poverty, was forced to quit school early, hated his brief spells of manual labor, and had occasional brushes with village religiosity. His adolescence, however, had mostly been spent in Davenport, Iowa, an old river town which prided itself on its intellectual culture. The chief, though not the only center of Davenport culture was its well-entrenched socialist circle, of the German, freethinking, beer-drinking kind rather than the puritanical or fiercely militant varieties. From socialists Dell heard talk about anarchism, Nietzsche, and Greek art as well as the cooperative commonwealth. A friendly librarian, a stock figure in Midwestern autobiography, befriended the lively and attractive youngster. Like other young men, he read Omar Khayyám, Ibsen, and Wells. Like other young men and women of Davenport, he experimented in writing. (To the Rebellion, Davenport contributed along with Dell, George Cram Cook, Susan Glaspell, and Arthur Davison Ficke.) He got a job on the paper, and had the entree to a series of self-consciously intellectual little groups. Davenport was proud of a bright young man, relaxed and tolerant about his radical opinions. When he left, it was because of trouble with a girl and an employer, and also because Davenport had prepared him for Chicago.

In Chicago, with letters of introduction from Davenport intellectuals, Dell arrived almost immediately in theatrical and literary criticism and in Bohemia. In his mid-twenties he became an important figure, in a position to fight effectively for every new writer, French, Russian, or Chicagoan. Everything went well for this talented young man, except his naïve experiments with the New Marriage. Dell left Chicago for New York in 1914 in much the same mood of gratitude and nostalgia with which he had left Davenport, and for similar reasons.

Anderson was by no means such a fortunate youth. Instead of a flourishing town like Davenport, his background was the bypassed, confused, inarticulate rural America of the late nineteenth century. Anderson's Midwest (Clyde, Ohio), was neither Garland's poverty-stricken Middle Border nor Riley's smiling village. It was a region in transition, looking both ways. The Civil War was still an important part of its emotional life, only beginning to grow tiresome to the young. An inward-looking, mystical Protestantism, far older and deeper than the Social Gospel, was still alive. Yet progress and the city constantly beckoned the young. Anderson himself shared the divided emotions of his characters; the self-contained, religious, old-fashioned village alternately contented and repelled him; the greedy, bustling city alternately excited and frightened him.

After short intervals in the army and in a small Lutheran college, Anderson chose the city, but not for art. He came for business, and did well at it. By 1912 he had moved to another small town, where he was a prominent citizen, well married, reasonably prosperous, and a popular "kidder." Then in 1912, according to his own account, which has become part of the legend of revolt, he stopped dictating in the middle of a letter, and walked out of his town, his marriage, and his whole life in an effort to find himself.

This story, like all Anderson's stories, must be taken as a symbol of reality. It did not happen exactly like this, but its essence remains true: Anderson was unhappy in a business civilization—too little at home and too much.

Arriving in Chicago in 1913 to take up a new life at least part time, Anderson was welcomed by the articulate younger generation. He calls Dell, eleven years younger, his literary father. From Dell and his wife, from Hecht, Sandburg, and the other writers, Anderson drew his first real intellectual sustenance. Literary conversation and the excitement of belonging to a movement complemented his yearnings and discontents.

It is hard to be sure just what Anderson read, since he alternately exaggerates and understates his ignorance. Like his juniors, he was steeped in Wells. He recalls an interest in Nietzsche. One of the members of his circle, Alexander Kaun, talked a lot about the Russians. A year or two before the war, one of his own accounts says, his brother Karl brought home a wonderful little yellow book called *Tender Buttons* by Gertrude Stein. Freud, the thinker who seems to pervade even his early work, may have been encountered first-hand only in the twenties, but Anderson himself says that in Dell's circle everybody was constantly being "psyched."

Anderson's first novel, *Windy McPherson's Son,* was published in 1916 by John Lane through Dell's influence. A very imperfect but underrated book, it reflects accurately the complicated and divided emotions of its author. The first part of the novel, which deals with Sam McPherson's boyhood in a small town, is written with a combination of nostalgic affection and horror. The second part tells the story of the hero's rise to colossal business success in Chicago. Like Wells, Anderson seems in this section to preach the virtues of the bold and efficient man as against the sentimental reformer. Yet success turns to ashes, and in the third part of the book Sam, like Anderson himself, walks out. On the road, he tries the various solutions of low-life, religion, and socialism. Inevitably, he runs across a virtuous prostitute, and in the end finds a dubious salvation in adopting three children.

Throughout the story, Anderson expresses his nearly religious feeling about a mysterious, resistless force, the power of sex. His hero continually wishes that sex could be clean and frank, that the dirty snickers of the small town hotel could be done away with. So far Anderson sounds a good deal like his contemporaries of Dell's generation. At the height of Sam McPherson's success he contracts a marriage that is pure Wells: equal, and dedicated to the noble, unsentimental, eugenic purpose of producing a finer generation. Yet this marriage is not a triumph like Ann Veronica's; it ends, like Sam McPherson's business career, in irony and failure. Anderson's handling of sex has little in common with Dell's confident naïveté, and nothing at all in common with the gaiety or cynicism of the postwar generation.

The style, like the plot of *Windy McPherson's Son* is full of evidence of inner divisions. At times direct and compelling, at times it is rhapsodic in the Rebellion's worst manner. Yet in about the same period, probably in 1915, Anderson was writing and rewriting his only completely successful stories, those published later as *Winesburg, Ohio*. Seven of them were published before the war, in *The Little Review*, the *Masses*, and the *Seven Arts*. (Since Anderson never published the same thing the same way twice, these stories differ in detail from the later, more familiar versions, but the style and plots are basically the same.)

Though they were not published as a book until 1919, the *Winesburg* stories are a product not only of the prewar period, but in many ways of the period before the Rebellion. For his subject matter Anderson said good-by to Chicago, business, and social movements. These stories are about his Ohio village in the nineties, before the coming of the factories. Yet the style, which was the beginning of contemporary American prose, deceptively simple, laconic, sharp, was brand-new. So was the way Anderson saw his subject.

No American writer for a very long time, perhaps none ever, had been able to face and use his own experience in the same spirit. Nearly all the people in the village except the adolescent protagonist George Willard are "grotesques." All are treated with compassion; the girls who are persuaded to go into the meadow with boys and those who are not and never forgive themselves, the fiercely religious patriarch and his cowed, bitter daughter, the women who turn thwarted affection into sourness, the men who shut themselves in their rooms and talk to imaginary people. These grotesques are not, however, a collection of freaks as Anderson's early critics charged; we are conscious that only the reader and the author know most of their troubles; they are carrying on life, as Anderson did, with fair success. They are suffering not from persecution but from loneliness and perplexity; Anderson was talking not only about the Midwestern village and America but also about humanity. All the stories say what the fearful and defeated doctor wants to convey when he expects to die:

> "The idea is very simple; so simple that if you are not careful you will forget it. It is this—that everyone in the world is Christ and they are all crucified." [9]

This was something few had said in America since Hawthorne and Melville; it was not surprising that the 1919 critics talked about Dostoevsky. For a moment, the vague unspoken, but profound discontents of the older America had been brought to the surface. Strangely enough, they had been brought to the surface partly by the sudden impact of the Chicago Renaissance, characteristically so cheerful. The *Winesburg* stories rested on a lucky coming together, an unstable compound. In his later work, straining either for naïveté or sophistication, Anderson could not recapture the formula.

❦

Dell and Anderson, like nearly all the new Chicago writers, considered themselves poets. Dell's poetry is slight, Anderson's memorably bad to the point of self-parody: "I come creeping, creeping,

[9] Anderson: *Winesburg, Ohio* (New York, 1919), p. 48. This story was first published in the *Little Review*, June–July, 1916, though these exact words do not appear in the earlier version.

out of the corn." Most of the Chicago writers were full-time poets; verse, like meat and steel, became a Chicago specialty and for a while Chicago was the poetic capital of the Anglo-Saxon world. The poetic movement which started in Chicago seemed at first to mark the triumph of spontaneity, formlessness, "democratic" and Whitmanesque looseness. From the beginning, however, the movement included a few fervent believers in rigorous technical precision. Before the war, even before the shift of the poetic capital from Chicago, the future of American poetry had been lost by the Whitman school. This fact had implications which extended far beyond the world of practicing poets.

The new poetry burst on the country in 1912 in great volume and variety. Not all of it was really new. Some of the poets were vigorous challengers of tradition; others were shy ladies who habitually referred to their work as "song," occasionally even "poesy." Still others were languid imitators of Swinburne or robust patriots in the Kipling tradition. If there was one common purpose deducible from the mass of 1912 poetry it was to save America from crudity and materialism: to uphold, that is, the standard of idealism. One result of the 1912 poetic revolution was the liberation of talent; another was the publication of reams of verses of the kind usually buried in bureau drawers.

Suddenly, recognition and publication were both available in many quarters. In 1910 Jessie Rittenhouse, a Boston lady who moved in the best New York society, founded the Poetry Society of America. This group met in the National Arts Club in Gramercy Park, and was as respectable as its location. It was there that Ezra Pound, just before he left for Europe, heard William Butler Yeats taken to task because of the negative character of Irish verse, its lack of the modern, positive "time spirit." [1] Mitchell Kennerley, in 1912, published *The Lyric Year*, a collection which spanned a considerable range, and is remembered partly because in its prize competition Edna Millay's "Renascence" came in second to Orrick Johns's conventional and socially progressive "Second Avenue."

[1] Jessie B. Rittenhouse: *My House of Life* (New York, 1934), p. 231.

This was the best known of the year's several anthologies, just as *Poetry* was one of several new verse magazines. Harriet Monroe, in fact, moved her first publication date forward in order to beat W. S. Braithwaite's Bostonian and conservative *Poetry Journal*. William Marion Reedy, like other editors, was overwhelmed with unsolicited verse contributions; he expected, he says, to get a sheaf of sonnets any day from Bryan or Woodrow Wilson.[2]

Harriet Monroe, a spinster of excellent standing in Chicago social and conservative artistic circles, was a strange leader for revolt. She had been born into the Chicago uplift of the last generation. As a young girl, dressed in white, she had recited her official ode at the opening of the Fair. Her program was reasonable and simple. Poetry was to get a share of the subsidy given drama and painting, and Chicago was to make a place for itself on the poetic map. No other program, and perhaps no other person, could have got money for a magazine of new poetry from Pullmans, McCormicks, and Potter Palmers, or from Hobart Chatfield-Taylor, the arch-conservative patron of Chicago's nineteenth-century literary movement.

When her magazine became identified with rebellion Miss Monroe became, incongruously, one of the main defenders of the rebel cause. Though her own poetry was conventional enough, she insisted on the "greatness" of Sandburg and Lindsay, the necessity of treating sordid modern subjects, and above all the duty of writing free verse. Critics ranging all the way from Meredith Nicholson, who deplored the new poetry before the National Academy, to Conrad Aiken, who thought Miss Monroe and her school too cheerful, were vigorously counterattacked. Rival magazines and anthologists were sometimes tartly put in their places, sometimes generously welcomed. Miss Monroe's courage brought her the respect of many who seceded from her patronage: her greatest achievement was to have started more than she could finish.

Harriet Monroe was proudest of her two early discoveries, Vachel Lindsay and Carl Sandburg, and these with Edgar Lee Masters seemed at the time to epitomize Midwestern verse. All three poets

[2] Edgar Lee Masters: *Across Spoon River* (New York, 1936), p. 349.

belonged to the older group of writers who found the Rebellion, and were found by it, only after years of spiritual wandering. All were believers in the doctrine of spontaneity, and all prided themselves on their native American manner, though all were crucially influenced at some point by literary tradition. All wrote their best poetry within a decade of their encounter with the Rebellion, and lost their influence on poets almost as soon as they acquired a public reputation. In these ways only they were similar; otherwise they could hardly have been more different, as poets or as men.

Lindsay was the most original. Almost his whole impetus came from the widespread, largely inarticulate religious discontent with the blandness of American life. Brought up in Springfield, in the sectarian, prophetic, revivalistic Campbellite communion, he spent his life trying to put together a religion of his own, a pantheistic and prophetic creed of beauty and holiness. His wide reading led him not to the iconoclastic writers of the day but to Ruskin as critic and the great seers whom he chose for his masters: Jesus, Swedenborg, Tolstoy, St. Francis, Whitman, Emerson, and Shelley.

After studying art in Chicago and New York, Lindsay became a poetic pilgrim. In 1912 he walked from Springfield to New Mexico, begging his way, reading his poems in farmhouses and saloons, and issuing manifestoes about the dawn of Religion, Equality, and Beauty.

This trinity defined his hopes. His Map of the Universe, with its amaranth vine growing from Earth to Heaven, seemed the basis for a new prophetic sect, another of the obscure revelations so frequent in American religious history. The new change of heart was to begin in the little towns. Lindsay preached not the rebellion from the village, but the rebellion of the village. He called for a new kind (really an old kind) of socialism, and his manifestoes urged the Kansas farmers (who must have been surprised) to sing the Psalms of David instead of the Internationale.

In 1912 Miss Monroe requested Lindsay to submit some poems, and *Poetry* for January 1913 opened with "General William Booth Enters into Heaven." From this point on Lindsay was, for the public, the revivalist of the new verse. His shouting and chanting, particularly of "The Congo" with its "Boomlay, Boomlay, Boom" resounded in lecture halls and New York apartments for the next twenty years. The Rebellion lionized Lindsay; the twenties were sure that he had been rescued from the village just in time, and turned toward fruitful social themes and jazz rhythms. Lindsay hated jazz, and was uncomfortable in the Jazz Age. Recently critics have turned away from his popular "Callyope Yells," back to his earliest, simplest quatrains, written when he still expected the prairies to flower with a new religion. The Rebellion discovered Lindsay; it also damaged him.

Carl Sandburg's "Chicago" outraged the city's polite aesthetes in *Poetry* for March 1914. Because Sandburg, instead of declining after the war, evolved from rebellious poet into biographer and national sage, his image is familiar. He is, most obviously, the epitome of the revolt against formal literary convention, the heir of Whitman, the prophet of common speech. According to Harry Hansen, one of Sandburg's favorite remarks in early Chicago days was "Think what Shakespeare could have done with the emotion behind the sonnets if he had been free, not bound by any verse form." [3] A political as well as a literary rebel, the early Sandburg was the militant socialist, the Swedish spokesman for the immigrant, the friend of the bum, the enemy of the preacher and the plutocrat.

It is not really surprising that Sandburg grew up not in a forlorn immigrant community but in Galesburg, seat of three colleges, one of the many Athenses of the Midwest. He was turned toward writing by a professor at Lombard College who preached Ruskin and Morris. Sandburg himself, in much the same manner as La Follette or Bryan in their college days, gave the college Erosophian Society an oration on "Ruskin, a Man of Ideals." Fortunately Sandburg, like Anderson, encountered the Rebellion and was liberated by it from Ruskin and in part from Whitman, another dangerous master. Some of his short poems—fragile, direct, condensed—are

[3] Hansen: *Midwest Portraits*, p. 61.

clearly affected by Imagism. It is not altogether surprising that he and Pound admired each other during the brief period when both appeared in *Poetry*.

Edgar Lee Masters, "missed" by Miss Monroe to her permanent regret, was neither a revivalist preacher nor an immigrant socialist, but the son of the mayor of Lewiston, Illinois. He was educated in traditional literature to the point of pedantry, and was probably a more secure classicist than Ezra Pound. By the time he achieved his sudden poetic success he was thoroughly established as a Chicago lawyer, forty-three years old, prominent in local Democratic politics, the author of several volumes of prose and conventional verse.

Yet Masters like the others reflected nineteenth-century native rebellious undercurrents in Midwestern culture. His father, a freethinker and anti-Prohibitionist, had been attacked by the forces of small-town moral censorship, and Masters hated "Puritanism" well before the young rebels had discovered it. At Knox College, where Spencer and Huxley had hit him hard, his nickname had been "the Atheist." He had been the law partner for eight years of Clarence Darrow. Thus, despite his prosperity, he had been living close to the center of Chicago radicalism. He was a defender of social, religious, and still more insistently of sexual freedom.

In 1914 three things happened to Masters. He discovered the young and bubbling Chicago Renaissance, a visit from his mother recalled his small-town childhood, and some of his conventional poetry was rejected by William Marion Reedy. Under the name of Webster Ford, Masters sent Reedy a series of short poems about a village, in free verse heavily influenced by the concise epitaphs translated in the Mackail *Greek Anthology*.

Most of Masters's poems about Spoon River, like Anderson's short stories, painted a dark picture of village lusts and hates and ironies. Yet the book contained some of the Rebellion's favorite affirmations also. Pettit, the poet, was taken to task for writing villanelles and rondeaux while "Homer and Whitman roared in the pines." Lincoln, an important symbol to Lindsay and Sandburg, was treated reverently by Masters in the poem about Ann Rutledge's semi-mythical sacrifice. And an occasional salty native character like Lucinda Matlock expressed from the grave her confidence in the Life Force: "It takes life to love life."

Well beyond the circles that read the little magazines, Masters, widely reprinted, was praised as a new Whitman and denounced as a pessimist. Floyd Dell, the voice of cheerful youth, drew a precise line between the younger rebels and nineteenth-century iconoclasm. He admired Masters, but thought his pessimism cut him off from appreciation of "perhaps the most fundamental and characteristic thing in America, . . . a gay and religious confidence in the goodness of things." In a *Forum* symposium on Masters, Willard Huntington Wright pontificated in the pretentious accents of *fin-de-siècle* aestheticism. *Spoon River* was cheap, superficial, and, still worse, typically Anglo-Saxon in its "hypocritical Freudian reaction to a zymotic puritanism." Bliss Carman, survivor of an earlier rebellion, could only put a question:

> . . . Am I still living in the world in which I was born? Or am I, too, as dead as all these people in the green Spoon River Cemetery? A relic of another age walking around like a ghost? Very likely.[4]

It is not surprising that this reception was too much for Masters's always slender stock of self-criticism. (He discusses, in his memoirs, the relative difficulties faced by Mark Twain, Whitman, Keats, Shelley, and himself.) For the rest of Masters's life he wondered why his earlier and later books did not get as exciting a reception as the *Spoon River Anthology*. Like *Winesburg, Ohio*, this had been the product of an instant and a series of lucky encounters.

Chicago poetry seemed to have arrived by the time of the famous dinner for William Butler Yeats on March 1, 1914. Miss Monroe, somewhat aflutter at the prospect of entertaining the distinguished

[4] Dell's review was in the *New Republic*, April 17, 1915, p. 15. The remarks of Wright and Carman were parts of a symposium in the *Forum*, LV (1916), 109–13.

and formidable Irish poet, invited the wealthy backers of *Poetry*, the established figures of Chicago's polite art world, and all available poets. She paid Lindsay's fare from Springfield, and saw that recent numbers of *Poetry* were placed by Yeats's bed.

Yeats began his banquet speech by praising the "strange beauty" of Lindsay's work, and he read two poems of Pound as examples of fruitful experiment. Lindsay responded by reading, or rather shouting, his new poem "The Congo," and the whole evening left Miss Monroe glowing.

Yet Yeats had raised a divisive issue. Usually, he said, when he opened an American magazine, he found the sentimentality, rhetoric, and moral uplift that had dominated English poetry in the heyday of Tennyson. This archaism existed:

> Not because you are too far from England, but because you are too far from Paris.
> It is from Paris that nearly all the great influences in art and literature have come, from the time of Chaucer until now.

Alice Corbin Henderson, Miss Monroe's principal assistant, answered this part of Yeats's speech in *Poetry*. American poets did not need any outside help. She had already pointed out that Poe and Whitman were the sources of modern French poetry; we could go to them directly.[5]

The same issue, involving in the long run far more than the relative merits of Whitman and the French, had been raised by Ezra Pound as soon as he received Miss Monroe's prepublication circular. "Are you," he asked, "for American poetry or for poetry?" If the latter, he went on, he would like to be foreign correspondent. Evidently she satisfied him; he became foreign editor.[6]

Pound, the most baffling and the most important figure in the

[5] The Yeats speech and an account of the circumstances are in Harriet Monroe: *A Poet's Life* (New York, 1938), pp. 336–8. Miss Henderson's comments on the speech are in *Poetry*, IV (1914), 105–11, and her statements about American influences in France in *Poetry*, I (1912–13), 87–9.

[6] D. D. Paige, ed.: *Ezra L. Pound: Letters, 1907–1941* (New York, 1950), 259–60.

history of recent American poetry, illuminates the Rebellion chiefly by his battles against its main doctrines. He fought everybody he met, and all the time he fought himself. The sources of his tensions lay deeper than ideological differences. All innovating writers resent public hostility; most people who try to be teachers of their times feel occasionally the teacher's desire to hit his students over the head. Pound had been cross-grained, however, before he had become a poet or critic. William Carlos Williams in 1904 had written home from the University of Pennsylvania about his new friend, Ezra Pound:

> He loves to be liked, yet there is some quality in him which makes him too proud to try to please people.[7]

This could serve as an analysis of his style. Even in his earliest poems one can find his unparalleled verbal and rhythmical felicity and delicacy. One can find also the strained locutions and angry, often irrelevant argumentation which were always to spoil much of his work.

On an obvious level, part of Pound's running battle with himself and others was about America. In the midst of the patriotic uplift of *Poetry's* first number, Pound addressed Whistler in startling terms:

> You and Abe Lincoln from that mass of dolts
> Show us there's chance at least of winning through.

In 1914 *Poetry* published his "Pact" with Whitman, whom he approached "as a grown child who had had a pig-headed father. . . ." Already, in 1909, he had put this still more strongly in an unpublished essay:

> Mentally I am a Walt Whitman who has learned to wear a colar and a dress shirt (though at times inimical to both). Personaly I might be very glad to conceal my relationship to my spiritual father and brag about my more congenial ancestry—

[7] John C. Thirlwall, ed.: *The Selected Letters of William Carlos Williams* (New York, 1957), p. 6.

> Dante, Shakespeare, Theocritus, Villon, but my descent is a bit difficult to establish. And, to be frank, Whitman is to my fatherland (Patriam quam odi et amo for no uncertain reasons) what Dante is to Italy. . . .[8]

That Pound hated and loved his fatherland became more obvious all through his tragic career.

Pound's principal patriotic duty, as he saw it, was to insist on the excellence that America, his sloppy, fecund, intensely interesting country, had always neglected. The way to achieve excellence was to apply a few simple principles. First came work: a writer must work as hard as a musician. Here Pound was fighting not only Chicago but the period's widespread overconfidence in the Life Force. Second, a poet must study the sources of the poetic tradition. Pound, as his critics have pointed out, was a shaky and sometimes pretentious, though always an intense scholar. One must study the classics, or at another point in his career the troubadours, or the modern French, or the Chinese. His real point was a sound and necessary one: that the nineteenth-century Anglo-American canon was not ultimate. Finally, the poet must always find images or symbols with which to state his emotions; he must abolish abstraction, rhetoric, and uplift.

Largely because Pound was there, the first rival to Chicago as capital of American poetry was neither New York nor Paris but London. In 1909 the poet from Hailey, Idaho had arrived to begin the siege of the imperial capital. A surprising number of young American writers, ranging all the way from Van Wyck Brooks to T. S. Eliot, were searching for something—a voice, a literary society, a publisher—in London in the years before the war.[9]

[8] Quoted in Herbert Bergman: "Ezra Pound and Walt Whitman," *American Literature*, XXVII (1955–6), 60.

[9] Robert Frost's first two books were published in London in 1913 and 1914. Frost does not seem to fit easily into any category of poets of his own time. Unlike the Chicago poets, and also unlike Pound and Eliot, he had roots in an old American literary tradition, the tradition of Emerson's poems and of Emily Dickinson, with its combination of homely image and startling metaphysical

This concentration of American poetry in London was not immediately noticed by the English. John Alford, in the December 1913 number of the liveliest English literary journal, *Poetry and Drama,* declared that American poetry did not exist. An angry answer by Louis Untermeyer forced him to make a very slight tactical retreat. Both these antagonists argued for the most part in terms of American poets who have been completely forgotten. Yet even in his first assault Alford had admitted one startling exception:

> Mr. Pound is a unique phenomenon, for he has succeeded in being an American, a man of culture and a poet, all at the same time.[1]

This peak of generous acceptance had not been easily reached. As Pound pointed out in 1916 in letters of advice to a young poet, the English did not willingly accept advice to mend their poetic ways. Mediocre writers were usually the cousins of somebody who must not be offended; even more than in America, criticism of the Elizabethan-Victorian poetic tradition was blasphemy. The Georgians, with their sweet woodland lyrics, were entrenched and well-armed. Yet Pound, despite his mistakes of self-advertisement, had scored. Yeats was with him, so were some of the youngest poets and editors. His *Poetry* editorship helped, and within a few years he had the exclusive entree to several other new magazines in England and America. For a short time he became the one man who could offer a new poet publication on both sides of the Atlantic.

In March 1913, making a decision that must have been long pending, Pound launched in *Poetry* the Anglo-American poetic movement called Imagism, or by him, Imagisme. The principles of this school, announced by Pound and his fellows, were the principles Pound had already been preaching. They were also a description of the poetry that the Imagist group, especially Hilda Doolittle, another American exile, had been writing. They called for intensity, condensation, the use of images rather than abstractions, and

statement. It says much for Pound's catholicity in our period that he heartily praised Frost's work as soon as it appeared.

[1] *Poetry and Drama,* I (1913), 487.

the development of new cadences appropriate to the purpose of the particular poem. As many people have said these are, as far as they go, the principles of all good poetry.

Imagist principles, stated several years before Pound by T. E. Hulme, F. S. Flint, and others, were drawn directly from several of the leading sources of the Liberation. Hulme depended heavily on Bergson. One realm of reality, he said, was beyond human grasp except through religion. The poet should recognize this and confine himself to the immediate. If he did so, he could accomplish exactly the feat which Bergson said was impossible for abstract thought: he could catch small portions of the essential flow of things and fix them, without distortion, in lasting images.

Pound and Flint had dipped, selectively, into the reservoir of recent French poetry. Believers in direct, concrete statement, they were not symbolists. They were not concerned with the paradoxes of Baudelaire or the difficult nuances of Mallarmé or Verlaine. What they found in France was novelty and daring: hatred of rhetoric, precise new images, Corbière's irony, Remy de Gourmont's insistence on sensation and dislike of theory. The French, Pound tirelessly insisted, could teach us to be craftsmen and not moralists.

These principles and tastes could not long live with spontaneity, Whitmanism, and Harriet Monroe. Miss Monroe at first printed the Imagists gladly. Their crisp poems made much of the magazine's content seem vague and sloppy, just as Pound's manifestoes made her own editorials seem pale and timid. Pound's poems were the main target of the magazine's critics, and although she fought for free verse, she did not want to fight for rude language. When she suggested deletions of phrases that might give moral or religious offense, he reacted angrily. Intelligent and fanatical, more than a match for her in critical argument, he could not equal her in generosity, and his answers to her letters grew sharper.

Moreover, he was playing with her rivals. In the winter of 1912 he sent his anthology *Des Imagistes* to Alfred Kreymborg's brand-new and radically experimental *Glebe*; he gained a solid base in

London when his friends captured the suffragette *Egoist*. Finally, in 1917, he committed the unforgivable sin by becoming foreign editor of the *Little Review*.

Long before this, the quarrel had broken out in *Poetry* itself in dramatic form. Since its beginning the magazine had carried on its masthead, below the names of the staff and above the list of rich contributors, a slogan from Whitman: "To have great poets there must be great audiences too." Pound, despite his pact with his admitted ancestor, could stand this slogan no longer. The artist, he insisted, was not dependent on his audience, and no popular audience had ever appreciated greatness. Dante, a greater poet than Whitman, when asked who was wisest in the city, had replied: "He whom the fools hate worst." The few were the only possible audience, and in the long run they prevailed. It is true, he wound up, that:

> The great artist has always a great audience, even in his life time; but it is not the *vulgo* but the spirits of irony and of destiny and of humor, sitting with him.[2]

This was approximately the doctrine of Mencken, and neither Miss Monroe nor most of her prewar contemporaries could tolerate it.

For the moment, a far more promising contender for the leadership of American poetry was Amy Lowell. The sister of the president of Harvard, Miss Lowell was one of those brave, intelligent, and slightly eccentric Boston ladies who have taken up reform causes ever since the days of Eliza Peabody. In her case the energy that might have gone into free nurses or free speech went instead into free verse.

Miss Lowell commanded several kinds of resources that her competitors lacked. She had plenty of money, and the Boston knack of conserving and using it. She had, of course, good connections in publishing and criticism, starting with Houghton, Mifflin and Barrett Wendell. Her position and her eccentricities together opened the headlines to her. Because of a glandular deficiency, she

[2] *Poetry*, V (1914–15), 29–32.

was inordinately fat. Inevitably wounded in adolescence, she defied the world. People knew about her size and unconventional clothes; they soon learned about the seven great sheep dogs who frightened the poets who visited her Brookline estate, the fact that she wrote all night and got up in time for dinner, and above all her cigars. All these eccentricities were cheerfully associated by the newspapers with the new, and obviously crazy, kinds of poetry. With a flair for publicity and tremendous courage, Miss Lowell welcomed this offensive and counterattacked, turning her handicaps into an advantage.

Like Miss Monroe, Amy Lowell espoused radicalism in poetic form only, not in ideas. She detested the tendency of the public to associate free love and free verse, abjured decadent or "sensual" poetic tastes, and thought that the Freudians, in 1917, were running mad on the subject of sex. It is greatly to her credit that she was able to maintain a warm friendship with D. H. Lawrence.

Her colorful poetry and "polyphonic prose" filled the little magazines of the middle teens and the standard anthologies of the twenties and thirties. In the first enthusiasm of his encounter with her, John Gould Fletcher, one of the American members of the original Imagist group, compared her with Shakespeare. Lawrence, in a letter to Miss Lowell herself, made a more lasting judgment:

> How much nicer, finer, bigger you are, intrinsically, than your poetry is.[3]

Amy Lowell, with the confident and unself-conscious patriotism of her kind, saw no reason in the world why the United States either should or should not copy Europe. When she read in *Poetry* the poems of Hilda Doolittle, signed "H. D., Imagiste," she decided she too was an Imagiste, and in that summer she sailed for London with a letter from Miss Monroe to Pound. On this visit and her next in the following summer, she met the Imagists, saw

[3] Fletcher's remark is mentioned in Stanley K. Coffman, Jr.: *Imagism* (Norman, Oklahoma, 1951), p. 32; Lawrence's in Louis Untermeyer: *From Another World* (New York, 1939), p. 124.

the Russian ballet, talked with Hardy and Henry James, discovered Frost, and was introduced by Fletcher and others to the new French poets. For her as for others, these encounters amounted to an intellectual awakening. Her keen intelligence fastened avidly and at once on the new tendencies and she became their eager champion. Pleased with her enthusiasm, and out of rapport with Miss Monroe, Pound asked her to back the movement.

The story of the ensuing quarrel, which dwarfed the Pound-Monroe affair, has been often told. Pound made the mistake of telling Amy Lowell how to manage her financial affairs, and Miss Lowell's publisher made the mistake of implying that she had invented the Imagist movement. The result of the encounter was that Miss Lowell sailed back to America, right after the outbreak of the European war, with a trunkful of manuscripts and the allegiance of all the principal Imagists but Pound. In 1915 she published the first of her own Imagist anthologies with Pound omitted. In the same year, carrying the fight into another enemy's camp, she read some Imagist poems before Miss Rittenhouse's conservative Poetry Society. The uproar which started that night continued for the next two or three years, and Miss Lowell remained at the center of it.

The violence of the opposition to the new poetry and to Amy Lowell as its exponent seems to reflect a growing violence in many areas of American life and thought during these first years of war abroad. Miss Lowell's size, masculine clothes, and cigars were given scurrilous emphasis; her poems were printed incorrectly; she was even called pro-German. Her "Spring Day," which began with a description of a morning bath in the sunlight, was described as a ludicrous and indecent account of the poetess herself in her bathtub. Speaking for the custodians of culture, the *Dial* associated the new poetry with the current inexplicable attack on the moral certainties:

> The real characteristic common to the group is the deliberate abandonment of faith in a type, a law, an ideal—call it what

you will—to which the fleeting momentary experiences caught up by the poet are referred.[4]

Putting pressure on publishers, entertaining and badgering reviewers, above all expounding French poets and new Americans in simple and effective terms, Miss Lowell won her war. With startling rapidity, the walls came down. By 1917 her own poems in the new manner were appearing in the *North American Review*, the *Yale Review*, *Harper's*, *Scribner's*, and the *Independent*. Far more than in embattled England, the new poetry had caught on.

By the period of the Lowell ascendancy, the poetic revolution had grown too big and various to be controlled by anybody. Pound was moving into one of his most violent and abusive episodes with the Vorticist movement. The poets who were to dominate the next decade were nearly all appearing already in the little magazines. Most of these were dedicated craftsmen; many were pessimistic; many were more eccentric than Pound and a few were nearly as brilliant. A little of the spirit of the 1912 rebellion could perhaps be found in William Carlos Williams and Marianne Moore, none in Conrad Aiken, Robinson Jeffers, or T. S. Eliot.

Thanks to Pound, and against her own misgivings, Miss Monroe had let Eliot into *Poetry*. In June 1915 she published "The Love Song of J. Alfred Prufrock," in September 1916 the mature and unforgettable "*La Figlia Che Piange*." Leaders of the Rebellion saw immediately that Eliot represented something new, disturbing, and (their vehemence implied) important. Miss Lowell, Fletcher, and Van Wyck Brooks condemned Eliot's "cynicism" or obscurity. Louis Untermeyer, already fairly well known for his idealistic criticism and socially-conscious poetry, went further. "Prufrock," now a standard anthology-piece read with no great difficulty by college freshmen, was to Untermeyer "the first piece of the English language that utterly stumped me . . . the muse in a psychopathic ward drinking the stale dregs of revolt." Even the brand-new Freudian insights were no help. When Untermeyer

[4] *Dial*, LIX (1915), 28.

read the poem to a mixed group of his friends only one, who was a psychoanalyst, could keep a straight face. He ventured the opinion that a lot could be done for Eliot: ". . . it's a muddled case of infantile repressions and inhibitions." [5]

Apparently an archradical in method, Eliot was already potentially a counterrevolutionary in taste. He never shared the Rebellion's gay confidence in the future; he had learned his skepticism about progress and reform from Irving Babbitt and George Santayana. His hero, like Charles Eliot Norton's, was Dante. Baudelaire, denounced continually by the older generation and so far largely ignored by the Rebellion, was to Eliot neither a destroyer nor a revolutionary, but a preacher to a declining civilization. There is no doubt that Eliot thought that civilization was declining long before the war had suggested this incredible possibility to the rest of his exuberant generation. "Prufrock," his first major poem about paralysis and defeat, had lain in his desk since about 1911.

Neither a decadent nor a rebel, Eliot was eventually to take on exactly the task at which his mentors, the older custodians, had failed, the task of maintaining continuity between traditional culture and modern society. In the teens this was impossible; traditional culture in the current form could not be saved. The order of the day was creative destruction, and Eliot took part in the destructive effort. But he was never cheerful about it; he never shared the exuberant, mystical anarchism of the 1912 Rebellion. By the time Eliot's poetry began to appear, that Rebellion had led to many strange consequences.

To most people who encountered it early, the Chicago Renaissance and the poetic movement which it inaugurated seemed a delightful new chapter, in which daring young people would say new things in a new way. Chicago was the main point of electric contact between new ideas and latent discontents. By 1915 or 1916 the current was running strongly, and most of it was serving to light up New York.

[5] Quoted in Monroe: *Poet's Life* (New York, 1938), pp. 394–5.

III

Intellectuals

New York, when it became the headquarters of the Rebellion, was already the capital of traditional culture, and the chief point of entry for European ideas. These two facts made the New York Rebellion different from the slightly earlier Chicago movement. In New York the intellectual life was older and more taken for granted; fewer of the young rebels came to it raw. It was also more nearly a part of the intellectual life of the Western world.

All the movements coming from Europe in the late nineteenth century had left some effect on New York thought. Naturalism and aestheticism had their active spokesmen, though each seemed a little old-fashioned in the years before the war. Huneker was respected as a veteran defender of artistic novelty. Dreiser, awkward and impressive at Greenwich Village parties, was a symbol to his juniors of battered courage. Mencken was hard for them to understand; clearly not part of the newest movement, he could yet be counted on in a fight against the censors. Young men who were, in the twenties, to revive and carry further the two tendencies of the late nineteenth century were already beginning their work. Carl Van Vechten, who was to write the frothiest novels of aesthetic sophistication, was a music and art critic. Sinclair Lewis had already published several realistic novels, competent but largely unheralded.

The young men of the hour, however, were unlike either their predecessors or their successors. As in Chicago, the main current was neither naturalism nor aestheticism but cheerful, somewhat mystical exuberance. In New York this tendency depended more directly on European sources; not only Wells but Bergson and particularly Freud were major prophets. To the young rebels, psychoanalysis was primarily a way of liberating the emotions. Yet even in the midst of the Rebellion fewer people in New York believed completely in spontaneous, untutored literary expression. The native heritage of revivalist religion was further in the background. New York produced no Vachel Lindsay.

In New York as in Chicago the main means of expression of the Rebellion was literature, but the literary world intersected more often the worlds of the theater, the dance, music, and painting. A number of the young rebels were equipped to dabble at least in several of the arts. Moving back and forth among them, they felt more need of aesthetic theory than the Chicagoans.

In New York, even more often and more importantly than in Chicago, aesthetic criticism was combined with social and political protest. But the kind of radicalism some of the New York rebels brought with them from the colleges was very different from the old Jacksonian or Populist kind. It was different also from the hard-bitten Chicago radicalism of Darrow and Sandburg. New York radicals were more cosmopolitan and more theoretical. They were less insistently equalitarian and more concerned about the problem of leadership. They argued more among themselves about the nature of the coming good society.

The fact that the New York Rebellion came a few years later than the Chicago movement proved to be extremely important, since these few years marked a major turning-point in world history. It is hard of course to date precisely the beginning of any intellectual movement. One crucial New York date was surely February 1913, when the Armory Show opened. The peak of the prewar Rebellion came, however, in 1915 or 1916, with the Provincetown Players, new publishers and magazines, and the full emergence of the younger critics. This meant that in New York, intellectual rebellion was carried on against a background of European war.

We will look closely, later, at the relation between war and Rebellion. At first, the war in Europe seemed to stimulate rather than to halt the exuberance of the rebels. Yet as world disaster gradually, in about 1915 or 1916, came to dominate American thinking, intellectual rebellion became inevitably a more serious matter. The New York Rebellion, partly because it began a little later than that in Chicago, lasted longer. The cheerful prewar Rebellion, though it remains a distinct episode, was continuous at many points with the bigger, louder, richer, and sadder intellectual movement of the twenties.

The difference between the New York and Chicago movements is best conveyed by the difference between their typical products. Chicago's characteristic product was the young poet, New York's the young critic, equipped to attack the dominant credo and culture on the moral, political, philosophical, and literary fronts all at once. At home in painting and music as well as literature, eager to be a part of the European world and yet confident of the prospect of an American renaissance, proud of his sophistication and yet exuberantly optimistic, the New York rebel sometimes was called, and sometimes called himself a Young Intellectual.

The noun was new in America. Its origins were partly socialist; the intellectual to the Marxists was the bourgeois who repudiated his class. William James had proudly taken the word over from the Dreyfusards, who had been attacked as intellectuals by their enemies. As it was used in the teens, the word *Intellectual* associated one with Europe, and particularly with the young heroes of novels from Stendhal to Joyce: the young men from the provinces who had come to the capitals in search of experience and a role in the movement of their time.

The first questions to ask, about New York as about Chicago, are what the insurgents were coming for, and what they were coming from. It is hard today, when New York is a few hours from anywhere and familiar to everybody, at least via television and movies, to recognize what the city meant to the Young Intellectual from the provinces in, say, 1913. First he was struck by its magnificant setting, by the dazzling light reflected from stone and water. If he had read Whitman, as he usually had, the Palisades and the Harbor had heightened meaning. New buildings, like the Gothic Woolworth Tower and the Roman Grand Central Station, both just completed in 1913, spoke so loud of wealth and power that questions about their styles went unasked.

Wealth, unabashed and ostentatious, was all around. The Young Intellectual could see, of course, the Fifth Avenue mansions and the parade of limousines. He could see, as in Chicago, the magnificence of conventional patronage of the arts, in the galleries and the opera. But he might also run into a different kind of philanthropist, the rich radical, the hostess who gave socialist teas, the venturesome backer of avant-garde and radical magazines.

Extreme poverty was also part of the New York scene. Poverty, to the New York Intellectual was a battle cry to reform. It could also be both picturesque and inspiring. He had read Dostoevsky more recently than he had read Zola.

Poverty in New York was closely associated with the city's most advertised characteristic, its foreignness. Exactly for the same reason that Henry James shuddered and conventional middle-class progressives shook their heads, the Young Intellectuals exulted: New York, whatever else it was, was not Anglo-Saxon. This meant more than cheap and good French and Italian restaurants; it meant a serious invitation to attack the dominant conception of culture exactly where it was weakest, in its narrow exclusiveness.

The Young Intellectuals went further than mere tolerance: they turned the conventional hierarchy upside down. Anglo-Saxons, repressed and bigoted, were at the bottom of the scale; at the top were the Italians, the Slavs, and above all, the Eastern European Jews of the East Side. Writers of Puritan ancestry like Hutchins Hapgood, earnest radicals like Ernest Poole, who was studying Yiddish, found an endless satisfaction in the quarter's crowded streets, its theaters, and above all in its Hungarian, Russian, and Polish cafés, where atheist and orthodox, anarchist and socialist, argued endlessly over their glasses of tea. East Side life was beginning to furnish a subject for novels, some by writers like Arthur Bullard who had discovered it in the University Settlement and a few by recent immigrants like Abraham Cahan, the editor of *Vorwärts*, who knew their subject firsthand.

A set of new stock characters was being added to American fiction: the wise and saintly Talmudic scholar, the beautiful young garment worker hungry for life, the heroic union leader, the reckless anarchist, the greedy manufacturer who oppressed his own people to get even with the world. The East Side attracted intellectuals, in this period of halfway rebellions, for two reasons: first because it was so different, and second because its values were the familiar ones, intensified and clothed in new, exciting symbols. On the East Side rebellious men could discover a fierce moral idealism like that they admired in the Russian novels, devotion to an ancient and highly traditional culture, and a struggle for progress against all odds.

In the midst of its cosmopolitan variety New York afforded the Young Intellectuals a quarter of their own, America's nearest equivalent to a Left Bank, the legendary, early Greenwich Village, so often caricatured and imitated and sentimentalized that it is hard to learn what it was really like. Unlike most Bohemian quarters of American cities, the Village had a history. The region of small twisting streets south of Washington Square had long been a quiet refuge from city traffic. The Square itself had been a stronghold of early nineteenth-century aristocracy; the district had housed Irving, Poe, Clemens, and Winslow Homer. In recent times the old, solidly Anglo-Saxon population of the Ninth Ward had been moving out, and a large Italian population had moved in.

To Intellectuals before the war, the Village, as it then began to be called, had the advantages the name implies; quiet, isolation, individuality. One could rent a slightly remodeled stable, or an apartment in an old house with high ceilings and little heat, for about thirty dollars a month, and often the landlord would let one paint the walls. (Black and orange became, for the *Saturday Evening Post* a few years later, a clear sign of sin.) The Italian population was picturesque, and seemed friendly. Actually, it was not: the patronizing manners of the newcomers annoyed it and their free ways scandalized it. It says a lot about the period that the Villagers, mostly from middle-class Anglo-Saxon backgrounds, seldom knew this. In the peace and comfort that comes with escape from home, they could make their quite open experiments in free sexual relations on the idealistic Wells model. Still more daringly, so long as they did not venture uptown the women could smoke and bob their hair with impunity, and the men could wear flannel shirts.

The heyday of the Village, according to its best chronicles, began in 1913, when Henrietta Rodman moved the Liberal Club from uptown to Macdougal Street and Polly Halliday, an anarchist from Evanston, began to run her restaurant on the floor below it. For a while this was the center; it was here that Floyd Dell first staged a Village play, with impromptu lines and no props. To the Liberal Club for arguments and plays and "Pagan Routs," and to Polly's Restaurant and others a little like it—cheap, informal, talkative—several streams of Village immigration began to flow.

Some of the early inhabitants were radicals; after the *Masses* moved to Greenwich Avenue the Village became a center for revolutionary politics, though many socialist stalwarts disliked it as a hangout of anarchists and dilettantes. Writers lived there who had no connection with the Village's much-heralded Bohemian life: Willa Cather for instance lived on Bank Street from 1912 to 1927. Older iconoclasts from Lincoln Steffens to Emma Goldman found themselves at ease there. Even Frederick C. Howe, a typical respectable progressive of Single-Tax leanings, associated with urban reform, feminism, and other solid causes, enjoyed living on West Twelfth Street at the edge of the Village and having "brilliant young people," possible leaders of "an American youth movement," moving in and out of his apartment.[1]

Like all Bohemias, and still faster than many because of the evanescent character of the whole prewar rebellion, Greenwich Village began to decline very soon. By wartime, with some of the

[1] Frederic C. Howe: *Confessions of a Reformer* (New York, 1925), pp. 240–51.

radical discussion cut off and the free Bohemian life a little more subject to criticism, some of the first villagers were already moving to suburban colonies like Grantwood, New Jersey. The extension of Seventh Avenue was threatening the Village's isolation and, still worse, the false Bohemians were swarming in, bringing tea-rooms and expensive restaurants in their wake. After 1917 things were to change very fast: brave ventures in free love were to give way to casual, unhappy promiscuity, radicalism was to turn to ostentatious defiance of convention. The decline was not absolute; as disillusioned early comers moved out, eager new arrivals from the West moved in. But the legends were correct on one point: the earliest period was the Village's creative period, the prewar and wartime years of the *Masses*, the Provincetown Theater, the years associated with Floyd Dell and then with Edna Millay. This was the time when rebels needed each other.

❦

The arts in New York, particularly painting and the theater, were at once a part of the Rebellion's environment and a medium of its own achievement. Through the history of each art in the period runs much the same story, a story similar to that of poetry in Chicago. Spontaneity and self-expression give way to their opposite: intense, devoted technical experiment.

Like the Chicago poets, the painters of the "Ash Can School" believed both in realism and in mystical democracy. Robert Henri, who had started the movement in Philadelphia, expounded Zola and Flaubert as well as Hals and Goya and Daumier. He and his disciples, John Sloan, William Glackens, George Luks, and George Bellows, shared a deep admiration for Whitman, and Whitman's devoted biographer Horace Traubel was a member of their circle.

The Ash Can School painters felt toward the Howard Pyle school of illustration about as the Chicago poets felt toward magazine verse. Like Sandburg, Henri believed that, if one told the truth, technique would largely take care of itself, though of course he respected honest hard work. Like Sandburg and others, these painters insisted on treating butcher boys and tenement women, scenes of the streets and saloons, rather than nymphs and shepherds. Like the Chicago poets, they sometimes sentimentalized their rugged subjects.

Both the Chicago poets and the Philadelphia–New York realistic painters inclined to the political left. Henri and Bellows were attracted by anarchism; Sloan was an active socialist. Like many young writers, these painters faced city poverty with a mixture of indignation and romantic excitement.

The Ash Can School met the literary world at many points. Dreiser was impressed by the subjects of these painters. Lindsay had studied with Henri. Of the New York intellectuals, Van Wyck Brooks encountered Luks and Glackens and Sloan at Petitpas's restaurant, where the conversation was dominated by the Irish painter John Butler Yeats (father of the poet). Cartoons by these painters were the proudest boast of the *Masses*.

Like the heyday of Chicago poetry, the ascendency of the Ash Can School was shortlived. It made its greatest sensation with the "Eight" show in 1908. In 1913 the Armory Show dealt it a blow from which it could not recover. Some of its members were frankly hostile to the new kinds of European experiment; others, like Sloan, tried to adapt their own styles to the new tendencies. The Ash Can paintings remain, probably less dated and more alive than the Chicago poems. But the immediate future of American painting was not with these painters of city scenes.

The opposite camp, the camp of technical, somewhat abstract experiment, was grouped around Alfred Stieglitz, who played at least three roles. First he was a photographer, not only a brilliant creator in this medium himself, but an insistent propagandist for photography as an art. Second, Stieglitz was an innovating exhibitor. In his small and intentionally bare Photo-Secession Gallery at 291 Fifth Avenue, Stieglitz exhibited Matisse in 1908, Cézanne in 1910. Before and after the Armory show he promoted such American experimentalists as Marsden Hartly, John Marin, and Alfred Marner. Third, he was a publisher. His magazine *Camera Work* was the organ, as "291" was the center, of something between a movement and a religion.

Some of the photographs, lovingly reproduced in the magazine, were sharp and incisive renderings of city scenes. Others were nudes, uncomfortably arranged on mountain peaks. Soft flesh and hard granite were the foreground, the background juniper trees or fuzzy distant landscapes.

The text between the pictures was a similarly curious mixture of styles. *Camera Work* printed mystical and affirmative selections from Bergson and Maeterlinck and samples of the work of Stieglitz's friend Gertrude Stein. The magazine's own young critics, Benjamin de Casseres, Sadakichi Hartmann, and Marius de Zayas were unusually given to arty mannerisms reminiscent of the nineties. Devotees of "291" often spoke of it as an "oasis." Stieglitz himself frequently deplored American Philistinism in the manner which was to become more common in the next decade. In the prewar years mysticism, affirmation, and avant-garde aloofness could still be combined. Sherwood Anderson, fresh from Chicago, could feel at home at "291."

The dance, a new and tremendously exciting art form to many young Americans, was still more sharply divided. At one extreme was the Russian Ballet, bizarre and eclectic, linking an old tradition and innovation. At the other was Isadora Duncan, the archfoe of stilted and artificial ballet tradition, whose flowing draperies and bare feet seemed to some people in the period to herald more than a new art. "One must have seen Isadora Duncan to die happy," said Floyd Dell, and when Robert Henri saw her dance he heard "the great voice of Whitman" and saw visions of a new age of "full natural expression" for all people.[2]

With one big exception, the experimental theaters of New York resembled those of Chicago and other cities. The New Theater of

[2] Floyd Dell: *Looking at Life* (New York, 1924), p. 49; Henri quoted in *Literary Digest*, May 1, 1915, p. 1018.

Winthrop Ames, the Neighborhood Theater at the Henry Street Settlement, the Washington Square Players in the Village alternated realism and symbolism like the little theaters of the provinces. A little more venturesome perhaps, they sometimes presented Strindberg or Wedekind shockers as well as the familiar repertory of Ibsen, Chekov, and Maeterlinck.

In about 1910 a small group of artists and writers from New York began spending their summers at Provincetown, Massachusetts. Some came originally from Chicago, others were Easterners. They included, at the start, Mary Heaton Vorse, Hutchins Hapgood and his wife Neith Boyce, Susan Glaspell, and her husband George Cram Cook. Within two or three years these were joined by John Reed, Floyd Dell, Max Eastman, the sculptor William Zorach and others. At first the Provincetown life consisted of writing, swimming, and occasional mild drinking.

Probably the leading spirit from the beginning was George Cram Cook, a somewhat muddled Midwestern idealist of the older generation, a little reminiscent of Sherwood Anderson. Cook had grown up in Iowa, fallen in love with Greek literature and Nietzsche, studied at Harvard and Heidelberg, taught at Iowa and Stanford, tried farming, and settled in Davenport, Iowa as an unsuccessful novelist and small-town intellectual gadfly. In Davenport he met Floyd Dell, a gifted boy who learned what Cook had to teach, then became his patron. Like Anderson, Cook was introduced to the Rebellion by the younger man. When Dell became literary editor of the *Chicago Evening Post* he made Cook his assistant. In Chicago Cook saw the Irish players and Maurice Browne's little theater. In 1913, shortly after his marriage to Susan Glaspell, another Davenport writer, Cook came to Provincetown.

In 1916 the Provincetown group of amateurs was approached by Eugene G. O'Neill, a young man with a single-minded passion for the theater and a trunkful of unpublished plays. O'Neill's life had been more like that of Jack London than like that of Cook. An actor's son, he had gone to sea after a year of Princeton and seen, if not the world, the sailor's world of bars and waterfront slums. He had gone briefly to George Pierce Baker's dramatic workshop at Harvard and experimented with one-act melodrama in a number of styles. O'Neill's early plays nearly always show the influence of Nietzsche, whom he had recently encountered. Sometimes they are realistic in the melodramatic manner of Strindberg, whom he greatly admired; often they are heavily symbolic. They are, unlike most of the Provincetown plays, nearly always tragic.

Opinions of reminiscent Provincetown veterans differ as to who was the principal hero of the Provincetown melodrama. Probably without Cook the group would have amounted to little more than a charming venture in private theatricals; without O'Neill it would have been another little theater, more creative than the others but ephemeral. The first one-act plays, aside from O'Neill's *Bound East for Cardiff*, range from pleasant sophisticated comedy by Dell and Hapgood to social melodrama by Reed, and Louise Bryant's *The Game*, a symbolic drama in Maeterlinck's manner whose characters are Life and Death, Youth and a Girl. In this Greenwich Village group Freud was familiar enough to be the subject of Glaspell and Cook's clever but essentially rather unperceptive sketch, *Suppressed Desires*.

In 1916 the group made the extremely daring decision to take the theater back to New York for the winter, and Cook, with a capital of $245 and much ingenuity, managed to get a building on Macdougal Street. Here this playwright's theater, still with a warm welcome for friendly amateurs, became a major center for all factions of the New York Rebellion. Fairly regular actors included radical writers like Floyd Dell and Max Eastman, and poets like Maxwell Bodenheim and Harry Kemp. Edna St. Vincent Millay, fresh from Vassar but well known for her girlish triumph *Renascense*, turned up in 1917 and immediately became a star. Alfred Kreymborg, who thought the group went in too much for realism and not enough for poetic drama, organized a good-natured secession. One of the early members, Frank Shay, began publishing the Provincetown Plays. A list of those who came and talked and occasionally helped would be a roster of the city's intellectual world, from the *Little Review* writers to the *Masses* staff, from Sherwood Anderson to Emma Goldman.

The fantastic idyll could not last. O'Neill, who was discovering his consistent style, still a mixture of naturalism and symbolic melodrama, naturally wanted wider recognition. In 1917 he sent two plays to the *Smart Set*. With less of the Bergson-Wells kind of uplift about him than most of the young people, O'Neill delighted Nathan, and the *Smart Set* added him to its list of causes. Uptown theaters were becoming interested. With the triumph of *Emperor Jones* in 1920, the period of gay improvisation and shoestring finance was to end. Cook, displaced like many survivors of the prewar Rebellion, left for Greece, and the Provincetown Theater became an institution of the twenties.

New York publishing, with its traditions and taboos, still presented a formidable conservative front in 1912. By 1917 the Rebellion had cracked this front at many points; this may well be the most important evidence of its strength.

From the point of view of publishers, it took courage to break with the practices of the great old houses and at the same time to ignore the get-rich-quick precepts of the Pages and the Harveys. Yet for all kinds of new enterprises, and for publishers in particular, the prewar years were more promising than they looked. Costs were relatively low and stable, the reading public was growing, and there were plenty of manuscripts to tempt the venturesome.

Unobtrusively, B. W. Huebsch had drifted into publishing from printing at about the turn of the century, publishing a book when his interests and friendships suggested it. These interests tended toward the world of genial, unsystematic radicalism. Many of Huebsch's friends were socialists and Single-Taxers. By wartime he was publishing Veblen. Gradually expanding, he had moved into foreign translations with Gorki, Georges Sorel, Artzibashev, Sudermann, and Hauptmann. In 1916 he published both D. H. Lawrence's *The Rainbow* and James Joyce's *Portrait of the Artist.* The most influential literary manifesto of the period, Van Wyck Brooks's *America's Coming of Age,* was accepted by Huebsch after the author's friend, Maxwell Perkins, had failed to persuade William Crary Brownell of its suitability for Scribner's. (Mr. Brownell found the book clever, but "premature" in sweeping the older American writers into the dustbin.) [3]

The New York office of John Lane, an English firm which had been venturesome ever since the *Yellow Book* days, was run by an impressionable young man named J. Jefferson Jones. Influenced by Dell, Mencken, and others, the English house published *Windy McPherson's Son* and other important new American books. In 1916, with memorable consequences, Lane published Dreiser's *The Genius.*

Mitchell Kennerley, more than any other the publisher of the prewar rebels, had come to New York from England with Lane. In 1906 he had started a small firm of his own. His small volumes, distinguished in binding and typography, included some of the early works of Van Wyck Brooks, Vachel Lindsay, Walter Lippmann, Edna Millay and a great many other rebels. In the midteens, Kennerley became president of the Anderson Gallery. Rather suddenly, he stopped nearly all his publishing, cut himself off from many literary acquaintances, and disappeared from the Rebellion scene.

In 1915 *Publisher's Weekly* announced another new venture, the firm of Alfred A. Knopf. The new firm was going to specialize in Russian literature, because "Russian fiction is like German music, the best in the world. . . . America has produced no great work of fiction, Russia at least six." [4] American writers of promise were particularly hard to find in 1915 for a firm that started with a working

[3] John Hall Wheelock, ed.: *Editor to Author: The Letters of Maxwell E. Perkins* (New York, 1950), p. 10.
[4] *Publisher's Weekly,* July 3, 1915, p. 10.

capital of $3,000 and, aside from the founder and his fiancée, one part-time employee as its whole staff.

In 1915 Alfred Knopf was twenty-three. The young publisher was no Young Radical either in his tastes or his political allegiances. He was, however, a graduate of Columbia, and had been influenced by the relatively liberal and cosmopolitan atmosphere of that university. He had studied comparative literature with Spingarn and others, and he had encountered some kinds of recent European thought in the history courses of James Harvey Robinson and Carlton J. H. Hayes. Like a number of his contemporaries, Knopf made a postgraduation trip to England. Already an admirer of Galsworthy, in England he encountered Conrad and W. H. Hudson. He also saw, in the lively circle that frequented Rider's bookstore, what seemed then to many young Americans a brighter literary world. Knopf came home with an admiration for such English publishers as William Heinemann and a determination to enter publishing himself. His first jobs, with Doubleday, Page and then with Kennerley, taught him some of the ropes.

During the first couple of years of the new firm's life, Knopf's novel and conversational advertisements continued to announce Russian and French translations. In 1916 he scored his first major success with W. H. Hudson's *Green Mansions* and began to publish some of the younger Americans. By 1917 the new firm's binding and typography had begun to affect traditional publishers and it had published books by Carl Van Vechten, Ezra Pound, Joseph Hergesheimer, and Henry L. Mencken.

Knopf's preferences, to judge partly from his later lists, were a little less volatile than those of most of his own generation, a little more elegant, and (despite his stature as a publisher of the new writers) traditional. A little more, that is, like the tastes of Spingarn and, still more, Mencken. Most of the story of this firm belongs to the twenties and later, the years of the *American Mercury*, when an extraordinary number of the new authors appeared on its list. Yet in its shoestring origins, its hopes, and some of its methods it reflected the prewar Rebellion.

Albert and Charles Boni, who had two bookstores on Macdougal Street, published such native literary radicals as Kreymborg and such foreign shockers as Wedekind before the war, and in 1917 Albert Boni formed a partnership with Horace Liveright, another newcomer whose name was to become associated with postwar publishing. One of Boni and Liveright's first ventures was the Modern Library, whose small volumes, advertised at sixty cents in "limp croft leather," started the personal libraries of a generation's poor intellectuals. The first choices in 1917 were significant: Number one was Wilde's *Dorian Gray*, and it was followed by Meredith, Shaw, George Moore, Hardy, and an anthology of Russian stories.

Just as the older publishers were pillars of a whole moral and cultural order, the handful of new ones were part of the world of the Rebellion, committed to it, necessarily interested in all parts of it. Huebsch acted with the Provincetown Players; Boni breathed the Village air regularly; Knopf contributed knowledgeable, not particularly radical music criticism to the *Little Review*. According to Alfred Kreymborg, Knopf when he encountered him in 1916 urged him to publish the *Others* anthology, a kind of urging few avant-garde anthologists often experienced.[5] The new publishing, so far, was not a movement but a series of casual events. Its leaders were not especially aware that they were doing anything dangerous or daring. This shows what had happened already to the world of the older critics. By wartime, some of the established firms were cautiously experimenting with innovation.

For foreign literature, provided it did not immediately invite the censors, the bars were fast coming down. Little, Brown's play series included Andreyev, Lawrence, and Schnitzler; Scribner's was competing with Björnson, Strindberg, and Andreyev. The new poetry, after *Spoon River* showed what could happen, was finding publication surprisingly easy. Partly through the august pressures of Amy Lowell, Houghton Mifflin was bringing out several advanced poets a season. Macmillan published Masters and Lindsay; Holt published Frost and Sandburg. Alfred Harcourt, after encountering

[5] Alfred Kreymborg, *Troubadour* (New York, 1925), p. 265.

Sandburg on a trip to Chicago, had had some difficulty persuading Mr. Holt to swallow *Chicago Poems* with its disturbing subject matter, its slangy style, and its "middlewestern atmosphere." [6] Novels, more popular and therefore more likely to produce controversy, often had to wait.

Waldo Frank, one of the Young Intellectuals, says that his *Unwelcome Man* was rejected by fourteen publishers before Little, Brown took it in 1917.[7] The novel begins with an extremely detailed account of the hero's emotions as a baby and goes on, through his battles with a series of philistines, to reach a climax with his decision not to commit suicide. Drawing heavily on Freud as well as Dostoevsky, it is as the author points out the kind of novel that found ready publication in the twenties. It remains true that a conservative publisher finally did take it in 1917; in 1910 this would have been inconceivable.

❦

The magazine world, already shaken to its foundations by the muckrakers, fell much more easily before the assaults of the Young Intellectuals. The *Smart Set* under Mencken and Nathan, not quite of the Rebellion, nonetheless fostered it. In 1914 the *Little Review,* after following Margaret Anderson to San Francisco, had moved to New York, with its special, insistent spontaneity still flowing. The New York Rebellion itself gave birth to three magazines so important in the history of the period that we must discuss each separately: the *New Republic,* the *Masses,* and the *Seven Arts.* There were many others: Alfred Kreymborg's *Glebe* and *Others* published many of the poets who were to dominate the twenties, as well as many never heard of again. The *International,* edited from 1912 by George Sylvester Viereck, had its moments of

[6] Alfred Harcourt: *Some Experiences* (Riverside, Conn., 1951), pp. 18–25; *Illinois State Historical Journal,* XLV (1952), 305–99.

[7] Waldo Frank: *The Unwelcome Man* (2nd ed., New York, 1923), preface, ix–xi.

distinction. Beyond these lay the magazines of the Village, *Bruno's Weekly* (1915), *Rogue* (1915), *Pagan* (1916), *Quill* (1917), and the rest. On the farthest frontier, almost in the forest of Dadaism, were such experimental sheets as *Rong-wrong* (1917). Much the same group of authors, too advanced for the big, or even the bigger little magazines moved from one to the other of these last outposts of revolt.

More important, as a measure of rebellion, than the founding of new magazines was the change that was coming over the world of the revered and long-established organs of standard culture. Most of this world was, as we have seen, relatively intact in 1912, at least on the surface. The *Forum* had changed already, when Mitchell Kennerley became its publisher in 1910. From that time until 1916 it was a stronghold of the Rebellion, an established magazine that acted like a "little" one.

In tone and taste Kennerley's *Forum* was the opposite of the *Smart Set*. It did not altogether neglect the gloomy giants, Nietzsche, Ibsen, and Strindberg, and it occasionally even published a survival of the *fin-de-siècle* like Saltus. Ordinarily, however, it was devoted to the ushering in of a new and freer age; its critics praised Bergson, Freud, and all the principal heroes of the Liberation. Of the foreign Liberators, Wells, Yeats, Maeterlinck and many others appeared in its pages; so did nearly all the leaders of the Young Intellectuals: Walter Lippmann, Harold Stearns, most often of all Van Wyck Brooks. Havelock Ellis and Ellen Key explained the new sexual theories; H. A. Overstreet, an unusually articulate young professor of philosophy, explained how to be just and cheerful without God.

In 1913 Robert Underwood Johnson, who had been prophetically lamenting the troubles of the *Century*, had to retire; the owners decided that culture no longer paid. Steadfast to the very end, in its final volume under the old management the *Century* was still discussing the spoiling of servants and carrying its tradition of military reminiscence to a logical conclusion with a series on "War-Horses of Famous Generals." Nearly at the last moment, in

April 1913 Royal Cortissoz fired from the *Century* some of his famous broadsides at the Armory Show: Cézanne was merely an impressionist who hadn't learned his trade, Matisse and Picasso eccentrics and frauds.

In 1913 and 1914 the *Century* published a little Dreiser, a lot of Wells, drawings in the style of the *Masses* (though with different subjects) by Boardman Robinson, a judicious selection of young poets, costume plates by Bakst, and an article explaining, with tolerance and good humor, "This Transitional Stage in Art." During the next few years it continued along this line, with occasional backward looks, until the war, for it, displaced literary controversy. As Johnson had undoubtedly predicted, even these desperate tactics didn't work: in 1917 as in 1913 people were still gossiping about the *Century's* finances and wondering how long the great old landmark would survive.

In 1914 old readers of the *Nation*, hearing that Paul Elmer More was about to retire, begged the magazine to stand firm against popularizing and sentimentality. For the moment the change was not great: Harold DeWolf Fuller had served on the staff and before that had taught English at Harvard. Yet, in the critical years between 1914 and 1918, the old oracle of the intelligent conservatives lost much of its intellectual consistency and critical bite.[8]

Colonel Harvey, after using *Harper's Weekly* to help elect Wilson in 1912, sold it to the McClure Publications, who made Norman Hapgood, the crusading former editor of *Collier's*, its chief. Norman Hapgood was not, like his brother Hutchins, fully comfortable with the Young Intellectuals. Most of his interest lay in sober social reform, yet he too, in these years of artistic excitement, announced his intention of keeping up with the new movements in drama and art. In the three years of life which remained to it, *Harper's Weekly* like the *Century* published Russian Ballet prints, and it went further: stating specifically that the ultra-radical *Masses* had the best illustrations in the country, Hapgood commissioned

[8] In 1918 the *Nation* was sharply altered. Oswald Garrison Villard made it an organ of political, and then of literary dissent.

magnificent double-spread cartoons of wrestlers, city scenes and similar "strong" subjects from George Bellows and John Sloan.

In September 1916 Frank Harris, the veteran of the Wilde era, became editor of *Pearson's*, which had been a semi-socialist muck-raking magazine. He kept the socialism but added spicy literary gossip. Not an organ of the Liberation, *Pearson's* became none the less its champion, especially in cases of trouble with the censors.

Finally the *Dial*, which had a few years before roundly denounced the new poetry as a blot on Chicago culture, underwent the sharpest metamorphosis of all. At the end of 1916 it was bought by a new group who moved it to New York, announced a staff headed by George Bernard Donlin and including among a number of lively young writers Randolph Bourne, the nearly official voice of the Rebellion. The *Dial's* 1917 manifesto, one of the last manifestoes of the prewar spirit, was one of the most typical:

> It will try to meet the challenge of the new time by reflecting and interpreting its spirit—a spirit freely experimental, skeptical of inherited values, ready to examine old dogmas and to subject afresh its sanctions to the test of experience.[9]

Already this brave promise was becoming in its turn a little obsolete; 1917 was not to be a good year for skepticism and experiment. Yet the troubles soon to be endured by the new magazines could not revive the old; the magazine world of the eighties, still intact in 1912, could never be put together again. Manning the battered defenses were still *Harper's* (monthly), *Scribner's*, Harvey's *North American Review*, and at least on matters of morals and mores, *The World's Work* and the *Outlook*. One cannot help imagining staff conferences in the offices of these survivors, discussing whether or not to let up just a little, and perhaps try one of the new fellows in the next issue. Certainly by the mid-teens the rebels, in the New York magazine world, had all the space they needed and, for a brief moment, most of the morale.

In the publishing houses, on the magazines, still more on the

[9] *Dial*, January 25, 1917, p. 45.

newspapers of the city, young writers who would be heard from later were talking and experimenting. Sinclair Lewis was working for Stokes and Doran, William Rose Benét was an assistant editor of the *Century,* Carl Van Vechten a drama critic, Edmund Wilson after 1916 a reporter. Willa Cather left *McClure's* in 1912 to work on her novels. In her first really characteristic books, *O Pioneers* (1913) and *The Song of the Lark* (1915), she did not seem obviously part of the current Rebellion. Yet her consistent theme, from her first short stories about singers through her Nebraska and Colorado novels was the same as that of the Young Intellectual critics. In different terms she too was dealing with the problem of the rebellious artist in American society.

New York was ready to welcome rebels, and by 1915 they were pouring in fast. They came from two main sources. One was the Midwest, often with a stopover at Chicago. New York lionized the Midwestern writers, and in the process absorbed the Chicago Renaissance as it had absorbed all the provincial literary rebellions of past generations. Floyd Dell quickly captured in New York a position as commanding as that he had left behind; he was at once Villager, playwright, novelist, *Masses* editor, and sexual theorist. Lindsay electrified intellectual young women by sounding his boomlays in New York apartments. Anderson, hailed as a sign of "Emerging Greatness" by Waldo Frank in the *Seven Arts,* turned up in person. The *Seven Arts* staff was astonished to find that he looked like a Midwestern businessman, which he was.

The other main source was the older colleges, and especially Harvard. From the turn of the century on, Harvard turned out a succession of poets including Wallace Stevens, Witter Bynner, Arthur Davison Ficke, Fletcher, Eliot, Aiken, Cummings, and Cowley. The other Harvard contribution to the Rebellion was almost the whole original corps of Young Intellectuals, the new critics who mixed political and aesthetic revolt. These centered around Walter Lippmann, Van Wyck Brooks, and John Reed, but there were many others: Lee Simonson, Edward Eyre Hunt, Robert Hallowell, Alfred Kuttner, Harold Stearns. At Mabel Dodge's salon, on the staff of the *New Republic* and later the *Seven Arts*, Harvard influence was obvious and pervasive.

This fact seemed to some critics at the time, as it seems to some historians today, an anomaly, almost an outrage. Why should the old Puritan college, the center of polite culture and aristocratic pretension, turn out an annual batch of rebels? Actually Harvard rebellion was nothing new; since the days of the Transcendentalists and earlier, angry insurgents from Harvard had denounced Harvard snobbery, indifference, and Philistinism. E. E. Cummings, still in college just before the war, soon to take his place as a rebel of rebels, had actually been brought up in Cambridge. He was the son of a Unitarian minister, Royce and James had both been intimate family friends, and when he was a baby Cummings's mother had knitted him a white sweater with a minute red "H." [1]

Belated Transcendentalism was one source of Harvard rebellion; another was the skeptical, aesthetic tradition inherited from Norton and cherished by Santayana. The *Harvard Advocate* of the years before the war is dominated by a weary Swinburnish tone; beneath a carefully decadent lyric a reader today encounters, startled, a name like John Dos Passos. Malcolm Cowley has described the symptoms in their most acute form:

> Dozens of them were prematurely decayed poets, each with his invocation to Antinous, his mournful descriptions of Venetian lagoons, his sonnets to a chorus girl in which he addressed her as "little painted poem of God." In spite of these beginnings, a few of them became good writers.[2]

There were still other patterns of Harvard Revolt. The University's Poetry Club naturally called in the president's redoubtable

[1] E. E. Cummings: *I, Six Nonlectures* (Cambridge, 1954), p. 25.
[2] Malcolm Cowley: *Exile's Return* (New York, 1934), p. 38.

sister, and some of the young men followed the Lowell wing of poetic rebellion. Political, as well as literary radicalism cropped out in several forms. Since 1909 the Harvard Socialist Club, with Walter Lippmann as its president, had been listening to Wells and Graham Wallas, campaigning in local and state politics, exploring Boston settlements, and even taking up the close-to-home cause of the college servants.

In 1913 Harold Stearns, just out of college, published his "Confessions of a Harvard Man" in the *Forum*, describing among other things an unsuccessful revolt against the Mount Auburn Street clubs. Most of the students, Stearns admitted, were depressingly stuffy, shallow, and Philistine. However, he could not quite refrain from adding, the average was probably even lower at other colleges.

All kinds of Harvard revolt, decadent and radical and ultra-reactionary, apparently helped to free young men from the parental mold. No other college, apparently, could match the strange mixture. At Princeton, a group which included Edmund Wilson, T. K. Whipple, and F. Scott Fitzgerald was discovering the pleasures of pessimism. In 1912 Wilson was reading Wilde and Dowson, Fitzgerald and his friends sampling Dunsany and Swinburne and the purple aristocratic splendors of Compton Mackenzie. The opposite element was lacking; Wilson had not yet discovered the radicalism that was to fertilize his writing. Fitzgerald had not yet run into Mark Twain.

At Yale, some of the faculty and some of the students were worrying out loud about Harvard's literary leadership, but moving very cautiously, frankly fearful of undergraduate opposition.[3] There was no cohesive Yale group, yet Yale graduates of the prewar years make an impressive list: Sinclair Lewis, Waldo Frank, Leonard Bacon, William Rose Benét, Paul Rosenfeld, Cole Porter, Phelps Putnam, Thomas Beer, Donald Ogden Stewart, and Archibald MacLeish.

[3] George Wilson Pierson: *Yale College, An Educational History* 1871–1921 (New Haven, 1952), p. 348.

As sources for the Rebellion, these three colleges had no rivals. Columbia, despite Spingarn and Beard and Dewey, produced few innovators: Paul Rosenfeld, Randolph Bourne and (to the extent that he belongs with this group) Alfred Knopf complete the prewar list. Wartime storms were to stir up another Columbia generation. Very few leaders of the Rebellion were coming yet from the lively University of Chicago or the free, wide-open Western state universities.

Most of the prewar rebels came from one of two opposite environments. One was the village or small town, where latent discontent was suddenly quickened by a refracted ray of new thought. The other was the old, traditional Eastern college, where the ideas of nineteenth-century Europe had made a serious impression. The large important area between these two extremes had not really begun to question Moralism, Culture, and Progress.

Coming eventually to New York, young men from these two sources encountered another pair of worlds, separate but not altogether unrelated. One was the young literary and artistic world which had sprung into existence in the shadow of the old centers of polite culture, a world suddenly complete, with its own theaters, galleries, publishers, customs, and leaders. The other was the world of the American radical movement. At the intersection of these two, the Young Intellectuals created the most typical and important expressions of the prewar rebellion.

IV
Radicals

The spring of 1914 in New York was cold, and the papers were beginning to admit that a business depression was under way. At the beginning of March, Frank Tannenbaum, a young member of the I.W.W., started leading processions of unemployed to the city's fashionable churches, demanding shelter for the night. Some churches argued, a few let the men in. Others, including St. Alphonsus, whose priest was concerned about possible profanation of the sacrament, called the police. About one hundred and ninety men were arrested, but only Tannenbaum brought to trial. He was sentenced to a year in prison and used the occasion, in the manner of the radicalism of the period, for an eloquent speech of defiance. During and after the trial there were further demonstrations on behalf of the unemployed. An anarchist procession followed a large black flag up Fifth Avenue, and a mass-meeting in Rutgers Square was addressed by Bill Haywood, Emma Goldman, Alexander Berkman, Walter Lippmann, Lincoln Steffens, and Hutchins Hapgood.

The whole episode amounted to little, yet the conservative press was disturbed. For one thing, Emma Goldman's was a name that made a good many lovers of peace and property shiver. For another, as the *New York Times* pointed out, New York radicals seemed to be getting a new kind of support. The Tannenbaum trial had been attended by Mrs. Mabel Dodge, a rich woman with a fashionable Fifth Avenue salon. Some of the "extremists" who were taking over the leadership of the pitiable but deluded unemployed were not "the ignorant type" one would expect, but "men of education and culture." Some in fact, were "writers, poets, and artists." Behind the trouble, said the *Times,* were "men and women of that class of 'intellectuals' to which Miss Goldman looks so hopefully." [1]

[1] *New York Times,* March 29, 1914, VI, 2.

In a sense, the *Times*, then a pillar of the social and cultural status quo, was right in its worries. The intellectual radicalism of the prewar years was not immediately dangerous to the social system, but it was dangerous to the dominant set of ideas. The coming together of Haywood, Steffens, Lippmann, and Mrs. Dodge symbolized a mixture of intellectual challenge with some kinds of social discontent, a mixture that proved explosive.

The Tannenbaum affair, with its overtones of direct action and its implied attack on propriety as well as property, was the kind of thing that attracted the Young Intellectuals. Many of these had come to New York from colleges, and especially from Harvard, ready to be radicals and not progressives, and radicals of a certain kind only.

In college the Young Intellectuals had been exposed to nineteenth-century materialism and also to nineteenth-century refutations of it. The result was that most of them regarded Spencer and Haeckel and Marx, and even the more modern materialists, as old-fashioned. At the same time they had ceased to accept, or even to discuss, traditional Christianity. Yet most of them retained a religious habit of mind learned in childhood and were eager for new kinds of faith.

These young men had been deeply affected by pragmatism, and often combined James's wide-openness to emotion and innovation with Dewey's bold belief in social and intellectual reconstruction. They welcomed the more biting dicta of the social scientists; some of them had encountered Veblen's astringent skepticism. Yet Wells, with his optimism and his recent semimysticism was for many of them the most important social prophet. Bergson had given new and welcome support to their confidence in their own intuitions. From Nietzsche and Ibsen and Shaw—for that matter from nearly all the literature they read—they had learned a fierce contempt for nineteenth-century bourgeois morality. Dostoevsky had revived their religious instincts, and Freud had convinced them of the necessity of sexual self-expression. All these influences had combined to produce a new kind of radicalism, passionate yet somewhat imprecise. The Young Intellectuals agreed on at least one point: they were uninterested in any plan for social improvement which was not also a program for spiritual and artistic liberation.

Most of these young radicals came from secure upper-middle-class families, and for this reason were eager to like and admire the poor, especially the urban poor, especially the recent immigrants. From naturalistic novels and muckraking accounts they had learned to feel guilty about the sufferings of the submerged classes, and some of them had seen city poverty at first hand in college settlement work. They did not know or care much about the troubles of the farmer, which they associated with the slightly ridiculous figure of William Jennings Bryan.

The Young Intellectuals regarded the dominant kind of progressivism, with its emphasis on throwing out the crooks and its small-business loyalties, as a bore and something of a fraud. Yet they had been attracted by the Bull Moose Progressive party, as interpreted by Herbert Croly. Its demand for leadership, its occasional use of the language of scientific management, made it seem promising. Few of the Young Intellectuals could altogether resist Theodore Roosevelt's charm and versatility. Wilson seemed at first a little cold and conventional, yet the Young Intellectuals, like everybody else, found themselves impressed by his swift and masterful grasp of power during his first two years as President.

Most of the Young Intellectuals considered themselves socialists of a kind and some of them had been members of college socialist societies. Yet they were not greatly attracted by the more prosaic socialist leaders, the Bergers and Hillquits, or by the routine envelope-addressing work that the party organizations seemed to offer. Some of them had begun to think about socialism as an actual possibility for the future rather than as a set of demands. Wells had stated for them some difficult questions. Would American democratic socialist society, some of them wondered, have a place for *them?*

Where the left wing of American socialism merged with the I.W.W., the Young Intellectuals found a better focus for their loyalty. Syndicalism attracted them because of its appeal for direct action and also its European intellectual prestige. Georges Sorel, its main French prophet, was (as the *Nation* disapprovingly pointed out) a disciple of Bergson. Sorel and other French syndicalists were being translated, American radicals were writing books about sabotage and *la grève générale*, and André Tridon was explaining the successes of the Confédération Générale du Travail. The syndicalist distrust of the state coincided with the teaching of Harold Laski and other English pluralists.

At the same time, the I.W.W. was associated with the Far West, a region as romantic to the Young Intellectuals as Western Europe, and much less familiar. A long series of violent class conflicts brought to Eastern ears such names as Cripple Creek, Goldfield, Spokane, Wheatland, Ludlow. Then in 1912 the I.W.W. invaded the East, with an attack in force on the sick textile industry. At Lawrence, Massachusetts, New England got a demonstration of the new tactics, the songs, parades, and defiant courting of mass arrest. Some intellectual sympathizers helped bring two hundred strikers' children to New York to escape danger and starvation. At Paterson, New Jersey, in 1913, the same drama was repeated within commuting distance; Young Intellectuals could actually hear the fiery speeches of Elizabeth Gurley Flynn; Arturo Giovanitti, the Wobbly poet; and best of all Big Bill Haywood. This hard-bitten, one-eyed veteran of the Far Western labor battles was willing to argue theory and practice with intellectual anarchists and socialists. Upton Sinclair was not the only observer who thought he saw at Paterson something like the dawn of American revolution.

Anarchism, the noblest of radical dreams, attracted many of the Young Intellectuals and their older friends. They did not know much about the older American anarchism, the movement of Josiah Warren and Benjamin Tucker. But anarchism in a general sense was deep in the heritage of the Young Intellectuals. Some of them knew that Thoreau had said that government governs best which governs not at all. Many more knew that their favorite

American older writer Walt Whitman had said he had nothing to do with institutions.

Moreover anarchism had a world-wide literature of great power. Tolstoy's road of renunciation, Kropotkin's distribution according to need, Max Stirner's extreme individualism were specifically anarchist. The anarchist movement, with its drama of bombs and spies, outrage and espionage and persecution, had furnished subjects for Dostoevsky, Henry James, and Joseph Conrad.

In 1886 the Haymarket bombing and its aftermath had given the movement martyrs, and in the nineties a new group of Russian exiles had brought it vigorous leadership. The anarchism of Emma Goldman and Alexander Berkman appealed deeply to the Young Intellectuals. For one thing, Russia, and particularly Russian radicalism, had great prestige. Furthermore, the anarchist leaders hated the halfway measures and compromise goals of current progressivism or majority socialism. Their morality, like their courage, was absolute. They attacked bourgeois culture, marriage, and religion as well as government. In the face of public hatred, they refused to give up their belief in the propaganda of the deed. Destruction must be justified by the establishment of a new reign of individualism and brotherhood, mystically combined. Wildly impractical, yet often enunciating, as Thoreau had, the deepest wisdom, anarchism was at least as much an aesthetic and ethical movement as it was a political program.

Hutchins Hapgood, after living for a while with anarchist leaders, saw this very clearly. Anarchism, he said, was "the fine art of the proletariat." Margaret Anderson suggested in the *Little Review* a similar definition, or way out of definition:

> When "they" ask you what anarchism is, and you scuffle around for the most convincing definition, why don't you merely ask instead: "What is art?" Because anarchism and art are in the world for exactly the same kind of reason.[2]

[2] Hutchins Hapgood: *The Spirit of Labor* (New York, 1907), p. 398; Margaret C. Anderson: "Art and Anarchism," *Little Review*, March 1916, p. 3.

An anarchist cause in which literary intellectuals could take part was the Ferrer School, founded in 1910 and dedicated to the anarchist principles of education: respect for the child's individuality, sex education, and joyful learning. The school's faculty included Bayard Boyesen, the son of Hjalmar Boyesen, the Columbia interpreter of Ibsen and Björnson. Boyesen had himself left a Columbia position to teach at the Ferrer School, where fellow lecturers included Will Durant, André Tridon, Edwin Markham, Clarence Darrow, Lincoln Steffens, and many other distinguished radicals. The art classes were taught by Robert Henri and George Bellows.

Emma Goldman herself was part of the reason intellectuals admired (they seldom joined) her movement. Utterly brave, widely compassionate, she was at her best (among prisoners for instance) a great woman, though a thoroughly shallow social thinker. In a somewhat heavy-handed way, she was seriously interested in literature, as part of the culture which all people must some day inherit with their liberation. One of her favorite lecture subjects was the Modern Drama. Her favorites, of course, were the realists, beginning with Ibsen, Strindberg, Hauptmann, Sudermann, and Shaw, yet she managed to find a good word for everybody who had criticized any aspect of bourgeois culture, and that meant every playwright from Rostand to Maeterlinck.

Emma had been discovered by Margaret Anderson in Chicago *Little Review* days and introduced by her to many of the Chicago writers. In New York she was a friend of Hutchins Hapgood and Mabel Dodge. William Marion Reedy admired her, as did Robert Henri. Even Mencken said in the *Smart Set* in 1913 that he read her with pleasure.[3] With the Young Intellectuals, Miss Goldman went to see the Provincetown Players; in return some of them attended the parties given to raise money for the anarchist magazine *Mother Earth*, especially the famous *Red Revel* of 1915.

Finally, Emma Goldman had long been an exponent, both in theory and practice, of another revolutionary cause which greatly interested the Young Intellectuals, the revolt in sexual morality.

[3] *Smart Set*, LXIV (1913), 464.

Her lecture topics in 1915, in addition to the drama, Nietzsche, and anarchism, included "The Intermediate Sex (A Study of Homosexuality)," "The Limitation of Offspring," and "Is Man a Varietist or Monogamist?" [4] Like Mencken, she made Anglo-Saxon "Puritanism" a principal target, blaming it for every crime from prostitution to the American Sunday. To anarchists, marriage was obviously and simply a part of the bourgeois conspiracy against the natural freedom and goodness of man. Women, particularly, were condemned by existing mores to a sordid choice between celibacy, prostitution, and slavery.

Neither socialism nor feminism necessarily implied sexual radicalism. Many socialists insisted that their revolution would end vice and establish a purer kind of marriage. Many feminist leaders, long harassed by sneers about masculine women, advertised their belief in family life. Yet the left wing of feminism and revolutionary socialism could come together, in Greenwich Village and elsewhere, to fight the tyranny of convention. Max Eastman was not the only Young Intellectual who felt apologetic when he got married.

For several generations, novelists, playwrights, and poets had been denouncing the sexual mores of the bourgeoisie. Castigators of hypocrisy like Ibsen had recently been joined by cheerful prophets of comradeship like Wells. Those who did not read novels sometimes discussed Ellen Key, the Swedish feminist, who argued mainly that marriage should not be a matter of legal or economic compulsion. Edward Carpenter, the English author of *Love's Coming of Age,* was a little more radical, promising rather vaguely that sexual liberation could bring big new sources of energy and variety. To the left of Carpenter lay the investigations of Havelock Ellis, and for the more precisely curious the technical writings of sexology were translated. The *Little Review* carried a column of advertising for such authors as Krafft-Ebing, Kisch, and Auguste Forel, some of them available only for "physicians, jurists, clergymen, and educators" (one wonders how many of these privileged

[4] These lectures were advertised in the *Little Review,* May 1915, p. 37.

people took the *Little Review*). Simplified manuals of sexual lore, some of them vague and elevating, others precise and practical, were increasingly available. Finally, the spread of Freudian doctrine, however little it was understood, was furnishing the Young Intellectuals with a new and powerful argument against the evils of repression.

For once, American social science seemed to be moving in the same direction as European literature. Lewis H. Morgan, Veblen, even Lester Ward had proclaimed that monogamy and the patriarchal family were temporary stages of evolution rather than parts of ultimate moral law. Here, as often, relativism led in two directions. First, the state should regulate the family and marriage for eugenic purposes. Second, sexual relations should be absolutely free. The latter view was stated in strong terms by Elsie Clews Parsons, a sociologist who spoke the language of the Rebellion. All exclusive groups, she urged in 1915, should be destroyed in the interest of the free personality. Nationality should be a matter of choice; the family should recognize the right of secession. Most important, sex relations should be entirely free from any regulation by society:

> Then at last, assured of privacy and of freedom, passionate love will forget its shameful centuries of degradation to spread its wings into those spaces whereof its poets sing.[5]

Many of the Young Intellectuals went no further toward sexual revolution than to believe in easier divorce or birth control. Of those who advocated free love, Floyd Dell was the most prominent, yet he was untypical. For one thing, his touch was light. There was little frivolity and much high seriousness among the Young Intellectuals who committed themselves to this particular cause before the war. Some of them lived in ostentatiously unmarried monogamy, demonstrating that loyalty did not depend on the force of law. Others preached still wider freedom, applying to sex the favorite doctrine of the Rebellion, that happiness would follow

[5] Elsie Clews Parsons: *Social Freedom* (New York, 1915), p. 31.

complete instinctual self-expression. If they sounded a little shrill and self-conscious when they talked about joy and freedom, we should remember that it took more courage, in the teens, to advocate free love than it took to preach social revolution.

❦

Of all the older dissenters, Lincoln Steffens was most appealing to Young Intellectuals who needed support and encouragement. Most of the muckraking movement no longer interested them, but Steffens was much more than a muckraker. He was sophisticated, he always knew the inside story from Madison or Oyster Bay or Mexico City. His formula, the underlying badness of the good and goodness of the bad, fitted exactly the message of Dostoevsky. Steffens, to the Young Intellectuals, was a major leader of a rebellion *within*, and also *against*, progressivism.

On his part, he was delighted with the new relaxed village way of life, and genuinely interested, as always, in the young. In 1910, searching for a bright young writer to help him on *Everybody's*, he went to Harvard as a matter of course and discovered Walter Lippmann. The father of another Harvard intellectual, John Reed, asked his old friend Steffens to keep an eye on the boy. Steffens fostered the literary career of both these important young men. The house on Washington Square where he lived for a while with Reed became one of the headquarters of gay iconoclasm.

Another older guide and friend of Young Intellectuals was Hutchins Hapgood. Like Steffens, Hapgood was given to turning conventional morality upside-down, but he did so more uneasily. Of Puritan descent, Hapgood was brought up in Alton, Illinois. His father was a leading citizen and a representative of that not uncommon nineteenth-century type, the independent, moralistic small-town atheist. His brother Norman followed a fairly conventional path from this background to muckraking and progressivism, becoming editor of *Collier's* and then of *Harper's Weekly*.

Hutchins Hapgood, temperamentally less activist than his brother, traveled in Europe for a long time after he graduated from Harvard. When he too settled down to a career of liberal journalism in New York, this did not mean that he had conquered his doubts and questions. Like Steffens, he cultivated the company of criminals, prostitutes, and direct-action anarchists rather than that of respectable progressives. Hapgood was looking for copy but also for liberation from prejudices and inner restraints. His goal was something an earlier generation would have called salvation.

Between his ventures into the American lower depths, Hapgood sought answers to his questions in Europe, where he was a friend of the Steins and Bernard Berenson. In Florence he met Mrs. Mabel Dodge, a wealthy divorcee who had interested herself in modern art. Tired of art, Mrs. Dodge asked Hapgood to introduce her to some of the radicals he knew.

Much fun has been made of Mabel Dodge's Fifth Avenue salon, where in her beautiful white room with its Venetian décor socialists argued with I.W.W.'s about the coming revolution. What is hard to understand from her long, frank, and turgid autobiography is what so many able and intelligent men found there. Food, drink, and each other are some of the obvious answers. So was Mrs. Dodge herself. Hapgood understood that she too was a seeker, painfully trying to achieve passionate experience. Margaret Sanger had liberated her, she thought, from taboos. Yet for her and Hapgood's generation, sexual freedom could never be easy and natural. Like art, love affairs failed to fulfill her extravagant hopes. Radicalism was worth trying.

For presiding over a radical salon, Mrs. Dodge had a qualification as important as money and more important than original intelligence. She was open-minded. Believing like all other up-to-date people in the Life Force, she was content to put her evenings in its hands, merely bringing together as many important or exciting people as possible, furnishing plenty to eat and drink, and letting things take their course. Her guests fell, more or less by accident, into several categories. Some were older liberals like Hapgood,

Steffens, Frederick Howe, and Amos Pinchot. Others, the most exciting and the most carefully cultivated, were extreme radicals. Starting with Emma Goldman and her Sasha (Berkman), Mrs. Dodge went on to the Lawrence and Paterson leaders, capturing her biggest lion in Bill Haywood. Of poets, her collection ran from Edwin Arlington Robinson to George Sylvester Viereck (Amy Lowell walked out on one of his readings). Avant-garde artists from the Stieglitz group argued with the radicals that perennial question of the Rebellion: intensive dedication to art against art for the masses. A sprinkling of publishers, editors, and society ladies completed the mixture, except for the most important category: the Young Intellectuals. At the Dodge gatherings Walter Lippmann, Max Eastman, John Reed, and other young men fresh from Harvard met a unique cross-section of American dissent. The press was fascinated: New York had never heard of parties where women in evening dress not only smoked but discussed all sorts of things with roughnecks and Bohemians.

For John Reed, Mrs. Dodge and her parties were an important experience. With him we come to one of the many figures of the period so clouded by legend that it is hard to see him as he was. At Harvard, Reed had not been, like Walter Lippmann, either a radical or an intellectual, but a brash, rather combative boy from the West, fighting snobbery and dividing his time between horseplay and romantic poetry. He still turned out lively occasional verse, political poems in the Kipling manner, and super-Whitman spontaneous chants. Steffens was right about his pupil; he was not a poet, but had the essential qualities of a great reporter: a quick and lively style, more interest in events than analysis, universal curiosity, and courage. Already he was being published in magazines ranging from the *American* to the *Century*. Soon he was to develop his proper role, ranging the world for the *Metropolitan* magazine, which had just been converted to socialism, or for the liberal daily, the *World*, reporting Mexico and Colorado, then France, and finally Russia. When he encountered Mrs. Dodge, however, Reed was still more seeker than radical.

In the Dodge salon, Reed encountered Haywood and the other Paterson strike leaders. Like Lippmann and Mabel Dodge herself, he went to Paterson as an observer. Unlike them, he became passionately involved, making speeches, leading songs, and getting arrested. His reporting was still that of a Harvard man searching for life among the picturesque immigrants:

> As one little Italian said to me, with blazing eyes: "We all one bigga da Union. I.W.W.—dat word is pierced de heart of de people!" [6]

Yet the emotion was a strong one, and Reed determined to do something about it. Calling on his nonradical Harvard friend Robert Edmond Jones, the stage designer, and calling also on Mabel Dodge's resources, he managed the famous Paterson pageant. On the evening of June 7, 1913, several thousand Paterson strikers marched from the Jersey ferries to Madison Square Garden, with red banners flying and the I.W.W. band playing the Marseillaise. On the four sides of the Garden the letters I.W.W. blazed in red lights. Inside, with scenery by John Sloan and direction by Jones, a thousand strikers re-enacted the scenes of the strike: its beginning, the intervention of the police, the funeral of a workingman killed by a police bullet, strike meetings with songs and speeches, the departure of the children, and the climactic promise to stick.

Nearly everybody there was moved: most with the earnestness and genuine emotion of the cast, but some, like Susan Glaspell, with the possibilities suggested for the theater. Mrs. Dodge was fascinated:

> One of the gayest touches, I think, was teaching them to sing one of their lawless songs to the tune of "Harvard, Old Harvard!" [7]

In the long run, as the hostile press pointed out, the pageant failed to make money, the strike was lost, and John Reed left with Mabel

[6] Quoted in Mabel Dodge Luhan: *Intimate Memories,* Vol. III, *Movers and Shakers* (New York, 1936), p. 195.

[7] Ibid., p. 195.

Dodge and others for her Florence villa. Yet the effect on radical intellectuals was great: here was the coming together of art, sacrifice, and the revolution.[8]

❦

The radicalism of the Young Intellectuals reached its fullest expression in three very different magazines, the *Masses*, the *New Republic*, and the *Seven Arts*. The character of the *Masses* was defined by a famous masthead:

> A REVOLUTIONARY AND NOT A REFORM MAGAZINE: A MAGAZINE WITH A SENSE OF HUMOR AND NO RESPECT FOR THE RESPECTABLE: FRANK, ARROGANT, IMPERTINENT, SEARCHING FOR THE TRUE CAUSES: A MAGAZINE DIRECTED AGAINST RIGIDITY AND DOGMA WHEREVER IT IS FOUND: PRINTING WHAT IS TOO NAKED OR TRUE FOR A MONEY-MAKING PRESS: A MAGAZINE WHOSE FINAL POLICY IS TO DO AS IT PLEASES AND CONCILIATE NOBODY, NOT EVEN ITS READERS.[9]

Max Eastman, who with Reed concocted this statement, seemed to many of his friends a strange person to preside over such a sheet. He was the son of *two* Congregational ministers, his mother having taken over his ailing father's pulpit. He had been brought up in Elmira, a home of Beechers and the place which, according to Van Wyck Brooks, had tamed even Mark Twain. By 1912 he had graduated from Williams, nearly completed a philosophy doctorate under Dewey at Columbia, and published a slim volume of poetry with Kennerley. He was working on his *Enjoyment of Poetry*, which turned out to be a reasonably up-to-date survey which thoroughly pleased William C. Brownell. Eastman was to become a well-known opponent of free verse.

[8] A student of this affair who remembers the nineteen-thirties is inevitably reminded of the similar, and probably lesser effect of Clifford Odets's *Waiting for Lefty*.

[9] Quoted in Max Eastman: *Enjoyment of Living*, p. 421.

True to his origins, Eastman spent much of his youth worrying—about dependence on his mother, sexual success, and religious doubt. He was troubled with backache and insomnia. A radical feminist, he fell in love for a while with Inez Milholland, the most handsome of the militant suffragettes. He managed to replace his lost religion with a painfully worked out personal philosophy. This combined Dewey's kind of pragmatism, a determined belief in the enjoyment of living, and a sense of social duty Eastman called "hard-headed idealism." In 1912 he decided he was a socialist, and as a matter of course sided against the bureaucrats and with the party's extreme, revolutionary left wing.

Handsome, well dressed, well mannered, well connected, respected in academic circles, Eastman had some of the same advantages for editing a rebel publication as Harriet Monroe. He was able to get financial support not only from Mrs. O. H. P. Belmont, the feminist society leader, but from such moderate progressives as Amos Pinchot and E. W. Scripps. As he says himself, he was instinctively rather reticent, even prudish, and bold as the *Masses* was he managed to keep it from becoming as eccentric as the *Little Review* or as extreme on sex matters as some of the Village would have liked.

When Eastman was persuaded in December 1912, to take over what had been an unremarkable socialist magazine, he was able to collect a brilliant staff. John Reed served for a while as managing editor; Floyd Dell as associate editor. Dell, as well as Eastman, gave the magazine its special interest in nonpolitical causes like feminism, psychoanalysis, and free speech about sex. Thc magazine was run at first by a free and easy system of mutual agreement. It paid nothing, but could accept from well-paid writers the things nobody else dared take.

For its pictures, the *Masses* drew on the best of the Ash Can School and the best of newspaper cartooning. The one and two-page spreads by Sloan and Bellows spoke the language of Daumier; Boardman Robinson, Art Young, Robert Minor, Cornelia Barnes, and Maurice Becker were sometimes almost as brilliant. Unlike most radical cartoons, the *Masses* cartoons were both moving and funny. The rich and respectable looked silly rather than wicked; the Negro, the immigrant, the down-and-outer were human beings, not stock symbols. A famous cover showed two pathetically homely, wretchedly dressed girls from Hoboken, New Jersey. One was saying to the other: "Gee, Mag, think of us bein' on a magazine cover!" The *Masses* could even laugh at itself. A Sloan cartoon showed two avant-garde parlor socialists, sprawling in a comfortable apartment with a Japanese print on the wall, and wishing that the strikers would "do something—let a few of them get shot, and it'll look as if they mean business."

The writing was less dependable than the cartoons. The *Masses* published one of Anderson's best *Winesburg* stories, some of Reed's graphic reporting, and a great deal of the period's uneven poetry.

The magazine's main weapon was shock. It supported every really revolutionary cause it could find. It cartooned the Associated Press poisoning the well of truth and stood off a libel suit. One of its special delights was to attack conventional religion in a manner halfway between village-atheist blasphemy and the farthest left wing of the Social Gospel itself. At a luxurious Espiscopalian banquet vulturelike rectors swilled their food beneath a crucifix. Christ, however, was a good radical:

> Thanks to Saint Matthew, who had been
> At mass-meetings in Palestine,
> We know whose side was spoken for
> When Comrade Jesus had the floor.[1]

The *Masses* was not ashamed to be sentimental, especially about children in the slums ("Gee, look, the stars are as thick as bedbugs."). It could be playful. It was in fact, impressionistic, nowhere more so than in its editorial policy. In addition to the Wobblies it published such respectables as George Creel, Walter Lippmann, and Amos Pinchot. Eastman's own editorials veered

[1] This poem, Sarah N. Cleghorn's "Comrade Jesus," is reprinted in Genevieve Taggard: *May Days* (New York, 1925), pp. 116–7.

between revolutionary indignation and progressive moderation. Despite the scorn of more orthodox socialist organs, the magazine could not decide what it thought of Woodrow Wilson.

Serious progressives, serious socialists, and the defenders of traditional culture agreed in their dislike of the *Masses*. It was not the magazine's political radicalism that disturbed some of Eastman's childhood friends, but its "bad taste" and coarseness. Without a touch of the *Smart Set's* rather strained naughtiness, the *Masses* managed to be salty. It drew on the rich underground tradition of popular skepticism, it gave vent to the suppressed humor of newspaper cartoonists, and it gave full scope to the irreverence and taste for novelty fostered by the Rebellion. Its political message was confusing and not very important; its tone unforgettable. By 1916, this tone was changing; the *Masses* had begun to sound a little more cautious. The editors were beginning to face a new kind of problem that even the *Masses* had to treat seriously: the position of radicals during war.

❦

As the *Masses* was the extreme left of intellectual radicalism, the *New Republic*, starting in November 1914, was the movement's sober, thoughtful right. The *Masses* was powerful because it was shocking; the *New Republic* because it was not. It was a bridge connecting the moderate relativism of the older pragmatists to some of the ideas of the Young Intellectuals.

The chief intermediary was Herbert Croly, who was born in 1869 and incarnated the nineteenth-century conscience. Brought up in a particularly strenuous and literal version of mid-Victorian positivism, Croly like many others revolted from this exactly as young men revolt from religion. He emerged from his early intellectual struggles a strange combination of mystic, worrier, and reformer, Hegelian idealist and pragmatist. In 1909 at exactly forty, he wrote a book, *The Promise of American Life*, which may or may not have seriously influenced Theodore Roosevelt but certainly made Croly, for the moment, the leader of the younger progressive intellectuals.

What he demanded was a drastic break with the American progressive tradition. Its insistence on individual rights, its dislike of power, its whole body of Jeffersonian prejudice must be purged away in favor of a new, joyous, "unscrupulous" nationalism. Croly abandoned the small businessman, mainstay of traditional progressivism, and offered little to the farmer. Neither the trust nor the labor union was to be broken up; both should be disciplined and used. In the seat of power should be not the politician, but the disciplined and trained intellectual, the superior man.

This program, keenly attractive to young rebels, was drawn from many sources, including Scientific Management, recent social science, and H. G. Wells. Efficiency was its watchword, yet it was never unmoral. Not a hint of cynicism or aestheticism crept into Croly's sober program. Social reform was to produce an artistic renaissance, but it was to be a "masterful and jubilant intellectual awakening," in the service of "moral and social regeneration." Croly spent the rest of his life watching for the dawn of this particular new day.

He and his friends thought they saw it in the Bull Moose movement, which they vigorously supported. The outcome disappointed them, but their efforts attracted the interest of Willard and Dorothy Straight, who wanted to back a new magazine and had the money. (Mencken, who knew the problems of editors, referred bitingly to the "kept idealists of the *New Republic*.")

To help him edit the *New Republic*, Croly found two men. One was Walter Weyl, a veteran progressive of his own age. Weyl, who came from the social settlement movement, took a careful, scholarly interest in economic problems and gave expert study to such measures as wage-and-hours legislation. The third member of the group, and for Young Intellectuals the most important, was Walter Lippmann.

Lippmann, at Harvard a few years before, had been tempted and educated by Santayana's skepticism. His most important master, however, was James, who had lodged in his mind once and for all the principle that thought must take account of will and emotion.

Lippmann had already run through most kinds of socialism. In the Harvard Socialist Club, he had acquired some experience of both practical politics and social-Christian settlement work. Graham Wallas, who visited Harvard in 1910, became a close friend; at this point Wallas was insisting that socialists and others learn to deal with the new theories of human nature. On graduation Lippmann had served briefly as secretary of the Socialist mayor of Schenectady. This experience with municipal socialism had confirmed for Lippmann a favorite lesson of the Rebellion, distrust of reformers and political machinery.

All Lippmann's European masters of this period were those who joined the later James in attacking sterile rationalism. Lippmann admired and quoted Bergson; he was interested in Sorel. He frequently referred to Wells's recent writings, with their substitution of "poetry" for the inadequate "mental instrument." Finally Lippmann, as Freud himself pointed out, was the first American to incorporate into political thought the insights of psychoanalysis. In the summer of 1912 Lippmann made a trip to the Maine woods with his Harvard classmate Alfred Kuttner, who was then working on the translation of *An Interpretation of Dreams.* Like many others at the time, Lippmann found with delight that Freud was going his way; whether he was going Freud's was another matter. Freud, and all the rest of Lippmann's early masters led him to demand that political thought harness, for the purposes of intelligence, instinct and passion. These were the very qualities Lippmann himself was always accused of lacking.

In 1913 and 1914 Lippmann almost became a radical. He attended Mabel Dodge's salon, looked on in Paterson, and wrote occasionally for the *Masses.* By the time of the founding of the *New Republic* however, he had rejected the Dodge-Reed circle, and it him. Stung by the criticism of those who called him prematurely old and wise, he retaliated with a waspish, patronizing sketch in the *New Republic* of "The Legendary John Reed," whom he made into a callow dilettante:

> He wrote stories about the night court and plays about ladies in kimonos. He talked with intelligent tolerance about dynamite, and thought he saw an intimate connection between the cubists and the I.W.W. He even read a few pages of Bergson.[2]

Lippmann himself was done, remarkably early, with these delights of the Young Intellectual's salad days. From this point on he turned more and more toward pragmatism of the less irrationalist kind, toward Dewey, toward Brandeis with his special version of scientific management, and briefly toward practical Wilsonian politics. It was, however, in his most radical period that he wrote his most arresting book. Freud, Bergson, and Wells, perhaps even Reed and Mabel Dodge, inform the pages of *A Preface to Politics*, published by Kennerley in 1913.

The *Preface* was the most smashing blow yet received by American progressivism of the dominant variety, the kind that was still part of the national faith. Some of the indictment was familiar to readers of Croly. American politics were dominated by obsolete institutions like the two-party system and dead issues like the tariff and the trusts. Progressive politicians clung to a Jacksonian belief in nose-counting democracy, and a rural suspicion of the educated expert. But Lippmann's criticism went deeper than this.

The real trouble with American progressive politics, he said, lay in its concentration on abstract goals, its moralism, and its confidence in old-fashioned reason. Instead of talking about good and bad, instead of prohibiting prostitution or trusts, progressives must learn what Lippmann had learned from "the Freudian school of psychologists." This was that "crime and civilization, art, vice, insanity, love, lust, and religion" sprang from the same sources. Only training and opportunity decided whether these drives should

[2] Lippmann: "The Legendary John Reed," *New Republic*, December 26, 1914, pp. 15–16.

emerge in "civilized," or in "barbaric or morbid" forms. Properly channeled, sexual passion and aggressive egotism, the vigor of the business leader and the courage of the syndicalist, could make a richer civilization.

This led Lippmann to one of the most genuinely and deeply radical statements of the Rebellion. To channel these rich and dangerous instincts, he said, we must rely neither on conventional morality nor classical reason, but on will, invigorated by instinct:

> No moral judgment can decide the value of Life. No ethical theory can announce any intrinsic good. . . .
>
> This amounts to saying that the goal of action is in its final analysis aesthetic and not moral—a quality of feeling instead of conformity to rule.[3]

Lippmann's second book, *Drift and Mastery* (1914), stated much the same doctrines in milder form, and applied them more closely to the contemporary scene. The two books made exciting reading; they still do. At last, it seemed, political thought had caught up with psychology and literature; at last it was dealing with reality and not abstraction. This was to some extent true. The problems which Lippmann raised were so real that they have never been solved. The rich insights he described were so alien to the spirit of most American progressivism, with its built-in rationalism, its pervasive moralism, that most progressives have ignored them. Walter Lippmann in 1913 was not able to reconcile progressivism, relativism, and psychoanalysis. He could not bring together reason and emotion. He could not explain how human intelligence, itself at the mercy of complex and mysterious forces, was to use and redirect human instincts. He was admirably fitted, however, to bring these paradoxes, long emergent, fully into view.

Naturally, Young Intellectuals turned first to Lippmann's articles and not to Croly's or Weyl's when they bought their *New Republic*. The rest of the staff was closer to Lippmann's generation than to Croly's. At least six of the staff members and recent contributors

[3] *Preface to Politics* (New York, 1913), p. 200.

were Young Intellectuals fresh from Harvard. Nearly the whole staff came from the Eastern colleges except Francis Hackett, who had done so much to set off the Chicago Renaissance a few years before. For contributors the young men drew on the more advanced older relativists like Dewey, Robinson, and Beard; and on English innovators of such opposite kinds as Harold Laski and Rebecca West. Some of the names of contributors were not yet well known: the reader going back to the prewar files runs into George Soule, Bruce Bliven, Dean Acheson, a little later Felix Frankfurter.

The *New Republic* was every inch an organ of the Rebellion; it called constantly for a national revival in education, literature, and government. Lee Simonson praised modern art; Hackett modern poetry. Yet the magazine was never extreme; it never went far in the directions set either by the *Little Review* or the *Masses.* It was above all a magazine of advanced pragmatism: it called frankly and insistently for an instrumental state run by experts. With the *New Republic,* the Young Intellectuals said good-by to equalitarianism, the agrarian past, and the simple formulas of moral reform. More completely than most of them realized, they cut themselves off from the progressive tradition which still seemed to dominate their time.

The last magazine the Rebellion produced in New York was the movement's pure, distilled essence and also its culmination. For the *Seven Arts,* the American Renaissance was not just on the way; it was here. The two sides of this flowering, literary and political, were represented by two of the magazine's editors, Van Wyck Brooks and Randolph Bourne.

Brooks was the least radical, and in his radicalism the least specific, of the major New York Young Intellectuals. Deeply influenced by Emerson, he remained a transcendentalist at heart. He inherited all of Emerson's optimism, all his impatience of analysis and consistency and earth-bound intellect. With these he combined a little—enough to make him an important writer—of Emerson's gift for sudden, disconnected insights and unforgettable metaphors.

Brooks came, he tells us, from the well-to-do Episcopalian, completely Anglo-Saxon enclave of Plainfield, New Jersey. His family was one of those that traveled back and forth across the Atlantic and Brooks learned early to associate Europe with art, just as he associated America with dullness and security.

At Harvard this association was reinforced. Graduating a few years before the lively period of Lippmann and Reed and their friends, Brooks seems to have encountered at Harvard mainly the surviving tradition of nineteenth-century aestheticism. His friends read Pater and talked about Baudelaire; he went to Norton's Dante evenings. In 1914 he published a book about John Addington Symonds. Like Pound and Frost and others, he headed for London as soon as he could to become a man of letters.

Yet the gospel of art was only one of Brooks's two sides. The other was earnest and reforming. In college he had learned most from Babbitt, with whose strictures he disagreed. Some of Babbitt's moral conservatism was to reappear in the later Brooks. For the moment, however, his search for a new faith centered on socialism. In 1915 he published a book about H. G. Wells, whom he admired both for his socialism and for his repudiation of mechanistic "modernity." In England Brooks taught for nine months at the Workers' Educational Association at Cambridge, and absorbed some of the disciplined ardor of the Fabian movement.

In a series of long articles and little-noticed books Brooks struggled between 1909 and 1916 to reconcile these dilemmas: art and socialism, America and Europe. More than any of his contemporaries he needed the method of the Liberation, the cheerful, modern, mystical reconciliation of opposites. In 1916 he managed, for a moment, to bring his two sides together in a work of prophecy, *America's Coming-of-Age*.

America itself, Brooks argued in this famous manifesto, was divided. Half the national tradition was lowbrow and half highbrow. The distinction was essentially Santayana's; on one side were crudity, greed, and materialism, on the other meaningless idealism and "glassy inflexible priggishness"; on one side "the public that reads Maeterlinck," on the other "the public that accumulates money." Forced to reside in the cold ethereal upper region, cut off from warmth and vigor and the common life, the American writer had always been driven into pale, bloodless sterility.

Going through the standard list of *Our Poets* to demonstrate this thesis, Brooks "ranked" the older Americans in the manner, though by no means in the order, in which they were ranked by conservative literary historians. Longfellow and Lowell were easy to downgrade. Poe was sterile and inhuman, Hawthorne meager and anemic. Coming inevitably to Emerson, Brooks got involved in complex arguments with himself. The real hope lay in Whitman, whom Brooks accepted at face value as a robust common man. Yet Whitman lacked discipline, and discipline as well as joy was necessary to get us out of our doldrums.

Now at last, said Brooks, the hour for regeneration was at hand. It was not clear just what was about to happen: like most prophets Brooks sometimes used confusing metaphors. In the vast Sargasso Sea of America, the fiddles were tuning up.

> A fresh and more sensitive emotion seems to be running up and down the old Yankee backbone, that rarely blossoming stalk.[4]

What was needed was a cause, to release Americans into the middle ground of action, halfway between tenuous idealism and crass practicality. Art, sexual freedom, and brotherhood were all a part of it, and it could be called socialism. Like Lippmann, Brooks expressed a certain contempt for political machinery. His socialism was more like that of William Morris than like that of either Morris Hillquit or Eugene Debs. It was closest to that of Whitman who

[4] *America's Coming-of-Age* (New York, 1915), p. 161.

had said in *Democratic Vistas* that the American regeneration was to be brought about by literature. This was the vision which appeared to all the staff of the *Seven Arts* in 1916.

James Oppenheim, the editor, was a free-verse poet from the Midwest, but his chief assistants were typical Eastern Young Intellectuals. Waldo Frank, the second-in-command, was a Yale graduate just beginning a literary career. Brooks was the most prolific contributor, Paul Rosenfeld covered the arts, and Alfred Kuttner wrote on psychoanalysis. The names of the staff members and contributors are a roster of the Rebellion and its antecedents, ranging from Mencken and Dreiser to Amy Lowell and Robert Frost. One of many still unfamiliar names was that of John R. Dos Passos, identified only as a Harvard graduate. Like the *Masses* and the *New Republic*, the Seven Arts found a backer—Mrs. A. K. Rankine. According to Brooks, she had been persuaded by her psychoanalyst that it would be good for her to back a literary magazine, and had sold her collection of Whistlers in the spirit of Queen Isabella.

The magazine began in September of 1916, not so much in spite of the European war as because of it. Romain Rolland, in a letter printed in the first issue, called on American writers and artists, unhampered by tradition and uncursed by war, to carry on in the spirit of Whitman. Oppenheim fully accepted this mission.

> It is our faith and the faith of many, that we are living in the first days of a renascent period, a time which means for America the coming of that national self-consciousness which is the beginning of greatness. In all such epochs the arts cease to be private matters; they become not only the expression of the national life but a means to its enhancement.

The announcement subscribed to the full theory of literary spontaneity:

> We have no tradition to continue; we have no school of style to build up. What we ask of the writer is simply self-expression

> without regard to current magazine standards. We should prefer that portion of his work which is done through a joyous necessity of the writer himself.[5]

In one of his eloquent editorials, Oppenheim was more acute than he could have known. The period, he said, was one in which people were turning in many directions at once: to mechanistic science, to literary pessimism, to the new mystical optimism. It was, he concluded, a period of adolescence, "adolescence when everything is possible . . . when all is in flux and the next tide may destroy us." [6]

Destruction was at hand in 1917 when Randolph Bourne joined the staff. Like the rest Bourne, since 1911, had been calling for artistic, social, and spiritual revolution. Even Brooks was not as lyrical and unrestrained:

> It is the glory of the present age that in it one can be young. Our times give no check to the radical tendencies of youth. On the contrary they give the directest stimulation.[7]

We are so used to the Bourne of the wartime reminiscences, the heroic Bourne of 1917 to 1920, that it takes a special effort to see the Bourne of 1916 clearly, or to judge the originality of what he had to say. In many ways, one must admit to begin with, he was not very different from the other leaders of the Young Intellectuals.

He had been shaped by the same influences. He was brought up in a prosperous and conservative household, educated in the classics, and indoctrinated permanently with the moral fervor of Protestant Christianity. At Columbia he encountered, and rejected, the simple verities of the custodians of culture. Bourne later wrote acid sketches of President Butler and Mark Van Doren, yet Columbia gave him important help. In 1911 a friendly professor persuaded him to answer an *Atlantic Monthly* article which had criti-

[5] *Seven Arts,* November 1916, pp. 52–3.
[6] *Seven Arts,* January 1917, pp. 267–8.
[7] Randolph Bourne: *Youth and Life* (New York, 1913), p. 25.

cized the younger generation. His answer, expressing the confidence of rebellious youth in its own future, was moderate and not very startling; it launched him as a semi-official spokesman of youth.

During a year of graduate study Bourne came strongly under the influence of John Dewey. A little later he wrote two remarkably sober books advocating advanced progressive education. On a European fellowship in 1913–14 he met the leaders of various kinds of youth movements and acquired the conviction, common a little later but startling in a firm Deweyite, that European, especially Latin civilization was immensely superior to Ango-American.

Like the others, Bourne was a radical. He had been active in the Intercollegiate Socialist Society, he sympathized with the Paterson strike and attended the Madison Square pageant. He leaned already much more toward anarchism than standard socialism: society was to be resisted rather than changed.

Like Brooks and Anderson and many others, Bourne attacked what he called Puritanism as the chief menace to the new spirit. Yet he disliked Mencken and Huneker, rejected Spingarn's impressionism, and seldom talked about art or literature without reference to social regeneration.

Between Bourne and his fellows, there was only one important difference. When this spokesman for life and joy first came to the *Seven Arts* office, Oppenheim tells us that he had to struggle against repulsion. Ellery Sedgwick of the *Atlantic* had had the same struggle several years before, and was sure that God had not forgiven him when he could not bring himself to ask Bourne to lunch.[8] For Randolph Bourne, the most famous symbol of the prewar rebellion and its end, was a hunchback, with a twisted face and a dwarfed body.

Cruelly cut off from normal experience since his birth, Bourne had been through a period, early in his career, of rejection and frustration. Apparently his family had lost its money, and for six

[8] James Oppenheim: "The Story of the Seven Arts," *American Mercury*, XX (1930), 163; Ellery Sedgwick: *The Happy Profession* (Boston, 1946), pp. 223–4.

years between high school and college he had seen life from the point of view of a badly handicapped man looking for routine jobs. His deformity gave Bourne's cheerfulness a heroic quality and also, especially at his most ardent, a touch of something strained and even a little sinister. Beneath his enthusiasm lay a different kind of intensity, not yet demanded by the times.

❦

By the beginning of 1917, the Rebellion had found many eloquent spokesmen. Yet it was never a large movement; a great many Americans must have been ignorant of its existence. The quality of its production was mixed: the word *renaissance*, often applied to it then and later, was hardly justified. The American twentieth century has not yet produced a Dante or a Shakespeare; it has not produced an Einstein or a Freud. Yet the Rebellion in a few years had accomplished a good deal; it had begun a new chapter in the national literature. Nobody who had read *Windy McPherson's Son*, *Chicago Poems*, *Spoon River Anthology*, and *The Song of the Lark* would see American landscapes, towns, or people exactly as he had before.

In the realm of ideas, the Rebellion was more important for its effect than its content. Its power, as well as its most exasperating quality, came from its cheerfulness, its easy reconciling of the most profound contraditions, its simultaneous delight in opposites, its unconsciousness of choices and costs. Only a few of the literary rebels so far realized that their Rebellion, like all successful rebellions, had its tragic side. Mencken, Dreiser, and even Anderson were older than the rebellious generation; Pound, Eliot, and O'Neill important but atypical. Few could have guessed that the remote heirs of the Rebellion would be writers like Faulkner and Hemingway. So far the prevailing ideas of the Rebellion were cheerful and, it must be admitted, somewhat superficial.

Yet, as Bergson had taught this generation, in art and life the whole is more than the sum of its parts. Taken together, the new publishing houses, magazines, theaters, and galleries, the whole new way of life and thought opened to the American intellectual, were more important than any particular achievement. Similarly, Brooks and Bourne were not great critics; what they said mattered less than what they were. They and the rest were primarily openers of doors.

By 1917 the doors were open and, as we look back, it does not seem as if anything very alarming had happened. In fact, if one looks closely at the ideas rather than the metaphors of the leading rebels, they are not very far removed from those of traditional civilization. Neither moralism, progress, nor culture was repudiated. Yet each was drastically redefined, and the stability and certainty on which the whole prevailing credo depended was impaired. The Rebellion was at once innocent and, from a conservative point of view, dangerous. It was this duality that enabled it to triumph, and it was this too that made the prewar movement inevitably a transitory stage in a much larger revolution.

PART FOUR

The End of American Innocence (1914–1917)

1

Cracks in the Surface

The prewar Rebellion, which looks so innocent and cheerful, was the beginning of a long, passionate, and sometimes bitter struggle over the nature of American civilization. In the long run this struggle was to leave the country enriched, but also divided. In its course all sorts of startling emotions were to rise to the surface. To understand how something that started so gaily ended so seriously, one must look at the Rebellion from outside. One must see it through the startled eyes of the unrebellious, in terms of the civilization of 1912.

Though the rebels did not directly repudiate the three main articles of faith which sustained that civilization, their ideas indirectly threatened all three. The harmless mysticism of Bergson or the later Wells, or the exciting, up-to-the-minute pragmatism of the *New Republic*, left little basis for moral certainty. Progress got lip service from the rebels, but when Lippmann or Bourne talked about progress they did not mean the kind of progress most Americans trusted. Significantly, the worst storms rose over culture, the weakest of the major ideals. The new literary and artistic forms, the new primitivism, the extreme belief in spontaneity seemed to make nonsense of standards that had been established and defended by long hard work.

The Rebellion, innocent as it was, aroused old fears that underlay the surface of the dominant civilization. Some of these were fears of ghosts, the surviving specters of nineteenth-century ideas. Still other fears were even older and more mysterious. One of these was the fear of savage human nature. Officially and sincerely, most Americans believed in the goodness of man. But the man they trusted was the educated and civilized man of the nineteenth century. Too much confidence in spontaneous emotion, too much dislike of rules, might rouse passions which should not even be thought about.

During the prewar years, passion and violence seemed to many observers to be rising to the surface in all sorts of inexplicable ways. Before Sarajevo, a sufficiently disturbing picture was presented in American labor struggles, the Mexican Revolution, the Balkan Wars, the suffragette and Unionist furores in England, and the great strikes on the Continent. Up to the middle of 1914, few Americans had changed their belief in a generally peaceful future, but many were somewhat puzzled by events they could not explain.

Fear for civilization was often mixed with concern for the position in American society of the Anglo-Saxon middle class. This class, after all, was assumed by many to have special responsibility for guiding the rest. The Rebellion, seen in conjunction with other changes going on in the prewar years, seemed to threaten the dominant order in its fundamental beliefs, and also in the especially sensitive areas of race, sex, and class.

Sometimes the vague worries of Americans in the prewar period seemed to center in an old complaint: the increasing tempo of life in a mechanized and industrial society. A writer in the *Outlook* in 1912 complained that Americans were becoming a nation of neurasthenics.[1] This fear for the national peace of mind had been recurrent throughout the nineteenth century; it had produced a long succession of mind-cures for the hard-driven. In the prewar years there was plenty of evidence of sharp and sudden change, though no more than at several other points in the past.

Between 1912 and 1917 automobiles, until recently luxuries,

[1] Max G. Schlapp: "The Enemy at the Gate," *Outlook*, April 6, 1912, pp. 782–8.

were beginning to affect the lives of the middle class. From about 1912 on, members of high school and college "fast" sets were beginning to realize some of the possibilities of the automobile, and so were their worried parents. The airplane, with far less concrete importance as yet, was more startling. A fragile thing of wire and canvas, looping the loop at county fairs, it was to some of the younger generation a symbol of almost magical hopes. To some conservatives, man in flight was a disturbing sight: if he could do this, what natural law could he not break?

Because it dealt, or might have dealt, with ideas, the moving picture was alarming in a special way. By 1912 it was no longer a novelty; between 1913 and the war it was fast becoming the main staple of mass entertainment. Movie theaters, originally concentrated in poor districts, were spreading everywhere; it was even being suggested that the movies were respectable.

Naturally many were trying to make the movies, as many made the automobile and the airplane, part of the evidence of progress. The movies, it was claimed, would solve the problem of Scientific Management, they would make education both palatable and easy; the right moral and religious ideas would spread painlessly throughout the world. Edison suggested that within a short time books would be obsolete in the public schools.

William Dean Howells, for one, found it hard to accept this prediction in the right spirit, but he agreed that the movies were powerful:

> The worst of it is that no one can deny the wonder of this new form of the world-old mime. It is of a truly miraculous power and scope; there seems nothing it cannot do,—except convince the taste and console the spirit.[2]

It seemed true that the public did not flock to the more educational pictures. The aging Sarah Bernhardt's gallant ventures before the camera were not really successful; neither were the clas-

[2] Quoted by Brander Matthews: "Are the Movies a Menace to the Drama?" *North American Review*, CCV (1917), 448.

sics, however much adapted. What the public seemed to want, and what it got, was two kinds of picture: melodrama, often about the fall of rural innocence in the city; and custard-pie comedy.

The custodians of culture often worried about the effect on the classic stage, but other Americans were more concerned about morals than culture. What might not happen, they asked, when young people of both sexes, particularly young people of weak standards and little education, sat in darkened houses and watched stories of vice and crime?

Naturally this sort of challenge roused some of the rebels to all-out defense. Vachel Lindsay, in one of his most mystical, Whitmanesque books, hailed the new democratic art as a medium for prophecy. At the opposite extreme of the Rebellion, Sadakichi Hartmann, one of the aesthetes of the Stieglitz circle, insisted in *Camera Work* that the moving pictures had true artistic significance.[3] Randolph Bourne, always honest, described his reactions to the movies in terms that foreshadowed the doubts and fears of the next generation of intellectuals, worried about mass culture and their own relation to it.

Bourne had gone to the movies in the frame of mind of a "would-be democrat," passionately wanting to find the art of the people. What he saw was a didactic and ridiculous "educational film" about tuberculosis, blending stale romance and preachment in about the proportions of the worst muckraking novels. To his surprise, most of the audience, which seemed to represent a cross-section of our great new public, took the film and its message seriously. Bourne, at once a rebel and a passionate democrat, was seriously troubled:

> I feel even a certain unholy glee at this wholesale rejection of what our fathers reverenced as culture. But I don't feel any glee about what is substituted for it. We seem to be witnessing a lowbrow snobbery. In a thousand ways it is as

[3] Vachel Lindsay: *The Art of the Moving Picture* (New York, 1916); Hartmann: "The Esthetic Significance of the Motion Picture," *Camera Work*, XXXVIII (1912), pp. 19–21.

> tyrannical and arrogant as the other culture of universities and millionaires and museums. . . . It looks as if we should have to resist the stale culture of the masses as we resist the stale culture of the aristocrat.[4]

Partly because of the popularity of the phonograph, traditional music seemed to be menaced as seriously as traditional theater. Pious historians of jazz, and no group is more pious, regard the prewar period as the age of the founding fathers. In 1912 W. C. Handy's "Memphis Blues" defied Mr. Crump, in 1914 the St. Louis woman flaunted her diamond rings and store-bought hair. In 1915 New York probably first heard the new instrumental improvising. The great Hegira was under way from New Orleans to Chicago. It is tempting to think of Hamilton W. Mabie listening to the "Yellow Dog Blues." This is chronologically possible but unlikely. Most of respectable America was only barely conscious of jazz and thought of it—quite correctly—as a kind of music that came from Negro brothels.

When the prewar press talked about the new popular music, as it did a great deal, it usually lumped everything together as ragtime. A good many critics defining what they did not like still more loosely, even talked about "cubist music" and "ragtime art."

In 1913 the *Literary Digest* was surprised to find the London *Times* discussing ragtime seriously as an expression of the American character. "America," said the *Digest*, "accepts her ragtime, and dances and sings it, but it is questionable if she has ever attempted to philosophize it." [5] This was already a mistake; the *Digest* had underestimated the young rebels.

In October 1915 Hiram K. Moderwell, the perceptive music critic of the *New Republic*, accused critics and composers of neglecting "the one original and indigenous type of music of the American people." The argument was that of Sandburg for new poetry: ragtime was the only way some new things could be said; it expressed the personality of American city streets, the "jerk and rat-

[4] Bourne: "The Heart of the People," *New Republic*, July 3, 1915, p. 233.
[5] *Literary Digest*, March 15, 1913, p. 574.

tle" that made their sounds different from anything in Europe.[6] This claim drew widespread rejoinders: ragtime was ugly and sordid; it was not true folk song; above all (and here a fighting matter began to well up from below the surface) it was not American at all, but African.

Excitement about ragtime was a minor affair compared to the furor over what went with it: the "Dance Craze" which swept over the country before the war, reaching its height from 1913 to 1915. This episode had two dimensions: in the first place, more people danced at more times. From New York, the dance craze spread to the provinces and even the small towns; from the young it spread to respectable married people in their forties, far past the conventional dancing limit. Second, people danced in new ways. The Turkey Trot, the Bunny Hug, the Grizzly Bear, the more lasting Fox Trot were simple combinations of step, glide, and dip, danced to ragtime. Their chief rival was the exotic and sensuous tango.

The new dances were denounced in press and pulpit, prohibited or carefully restricted in the colleges (Columbia specified six inches between dancers). Even a wave of arrests for indecent behavior seemed only to stimulate the new vogue. To the *Nation* in June 1915, New York was "a city gone mad over the fox trot and the white lights." [7]

The objections were deeper than concern about frivolity or bad manners in themselves. The new dances seemed particularly shocking when they were danced by innocent and well-brought-up young ladies, still more when they brought together young ladies and undesirable types. (Worst of all was the "tango pirate," smooth, sinister, foreign and full of designs.) The dances that were not Latin were of Negro origin. They were, moreover, part

[6] Hiram K. Moderwell: "Ragtime," October 16, 1915, pp. 284–6. Amy Lowell had defended ragtime as "America's first original contribution to the arts" in the *Little Review*, June 1914, pp. 36–7, but because of its source this was little noticed. Carl Van Vechten said ragtime was the only worth-while music being produced in America in his *Interpreters and Interpretations* (New York, 1917), p. 279.

[7] *Nation*, June 3, 1915, p. 614.

of a wave of sensualism and indecency that was sweeping over American society in a way never before dreamed of.

The costumes of 1914 seemed to some the last word in indecency. The ideal conception of American womanhood could hardly survive the hobble skirt, the transparent waist, the increase in the use of cosmetics, the decline of the corset, let alone the degeneration of manners. Many outraged conservatives described the new kind of young woman. H. L. Mencken, who liked her, described her best and with her, her whole milieu. His description brought a new word into public use:

> The American language, curiously enough, has no name for her. In German she is *der Backfisch,* in French she is *l'Ingénue,* in English she is the Flapper. But in American, as I say, she is nameless, for Chicken will never, never, do. . . .
>
> Observe, then, this nameless one, this American Flapper. Her skirts have just reached her very trim and pretty ankles; her hair, newly coiled upon her skull, has just exposed the ravishing whiteness of her neck. A charming creature! . . . Youth is hers, and hope, and romance, and—
>
> Well, well, let us be exact: let us not say innocence. This Flapper, to tell the truth, is far, far, far from a simpleton. . . .
>
> Life, indeed, is almost empty of surprises, mysteries, horrors to this Flapper of 1915. . . . She knows exactly what the Wassermann reaction is, and has made up her mind that she will never marry a man who can't show an unmistakable negative. . . . She has read Christabel Pankhurst and Ellen Key, and is inclined to think that there must be something in this new doctrine of free motherhood. She is opposed to the double standard of morality, and favors a law prohibiting it. . . .
>
> This Flapper has forgotten how to simper; she seldom blushes; it is impossible to shock her. She saw "Damaged Goods" without batting an eye, and went away wondering what the row over it was all about. The police of her city having prohibited

"Mrs. Warren's Profession," she read it one rainy Sunday afternoon, and found it a mass of platitudes. . . . She admires Strindberg, particularly his "Countess Julie." She plans to read Havelock Ellis during the coming summer. . . .

As I have said, a charming young creature. There is something trim and trig and confident about her. She is easy in her manners. She bears herself with dignity in all societies. . . . There is music in her laugh. She is youth, she is hope, she is romance—she is wisdom! [8]

To some, she was decline and collapse. The nineteenth-century attitude toward sex, so strange to Mencken and to us, was sacred to the overwhelming American majority.

❦

Young Intellectuals constantly attacked Puritanism; actually, nineteenth-century Anglo-Americans were stricter about sexual morality than their Puritan ancestors. Liberal religion, giving less emphasis than its predecessors to the theological virtues, gave more to some kinds of conduct. In 1912 religious liberals, respectable freethinkers of the Ingersoll kind, and staunch evangelical Christians still saw eye to eye about sexual morality.

Chastity was, whether by divine precept or common consent, as absolute a good as honesty, and (this was tacitly admitted) far more difficult. Not all Americans agreed with Billy Sunday about the reality of a personal devil, but most had reason to believe in temptation. Paradox lay at the root of the matter: sexual intercourse in marriage was a sacred duty, romantic love the most beautiful thing in life, and sexual lust evil. Since women, except the depraved few, were naturally pure, it was best that they have jurisdiction over the whole field of sexual relations. The duty of

[8] Mencken: "The Flapper," *Smart Set*, XLV (1915), 1–2. Quoted by permission of Mr. August Mencken.

men was to make every effort to grow up pure, and especially to avoid the debilitating dangers that arose from evil thoughts. The crown of the whole civilization was the American family, with the father supreme in the economic sphere but the mother, freer and more respected than the women of other countries, in special charge of morals.

The millions of people who believed in this code and tried to live by it knew of course that it was continually broken. Lapses could be forgiven; outright defiance was far more serious. From Shelley to Sarah Bernhardt distinguished foreigners had flouted the code; now there were Americans who openly repudiated the customs of their own country. The mores of the Luhan circle, the noble and impractical sexual theories of the anarchists, the emancipated attitude of Dell and his friends were only beginning to receive wide circulation. Every now and then a member of the conservative middle class discovered that some people actually advocated and practiced what sounded to him like sheer deliberate wickedness. He was not surprised when such people turned out to be avant-garde artists or writers.

Women's rights were sometimes a corollary of nineteenth-century moral progress, yet some kinds of militant feminism could be disturbing. To some American males it was disquieting in itself to find the weaker sex taking on the roles of athlete, professional, or political agitator. Sexual defensiveness was not far below the surface of some of the ridicule directed against allegedly mannish feminists and their effeminate male defenders.

One of the most logical ends of female equality, and one of the most disturbing, was the demand that women take control of their own most important function: childbirth. In 1913 Margaret Sanger, according to her own account, coined the term birth control for a movement that had a long subterranean history. Mrs. Sanger was not hard to connect with the rebellious intellectuals. She had been brought up a socialist and influenced by Emma Goldman, she had contributed to the enlightenment of Mrs. Dodge, and she had summered at Provincetown. Yet she was inescapably respectable, the wife of an architect and the mother of two children. Her interest in the problem had begun in a way the period approved. As a nurse in the New York slums, she had been horrified by abortion, the death of mothers, and the neglect of children, just as other reformers of the period had been horrified by tenement sanitation.

On her lecture tours, in her editorial and clinical work, and during her trial and imprisonment in 1916 Mrs. Sanger obviously ran into a complex whirlpool of public emotions. Expressions of horror and outrage were many; to some her purpose seemed an almost unbelievable apology for lust. Yet there was clearly another side. Many respectable feminists shared her view that motherhood must not be brought about by uncontrolled male passion, and some sociologists believed that the poorer classes at least must be helped to restrict their offspring. Mrs. Sanger's admirers extended far beyond the desperate and frantic women from the slums who saw her as a personal deliverer from slavery and death. The press noticed that limousines drew up outside her Western lectures. The government, goaded by Comstock and others into persecution, handled Mrs. Sanger with obvious gingerliness and timidity.

Dangerous thoughts about birth and marriage were not the whole trouble; the statistics too were alarming. Since 1867 the national birthrate and the average size of families had been declining. As an endless succession of books and pamphlets was pointing out, the decline was sharpest among the well educated, especially those of native New England stock. Divorce was going up. In 1914 the number of divorces first reached a round hundred thousand. This meant about one per thousand in the population; in 1867 the rate had been .35; in 1920 it was to reach 1.6. President Roosevelt, who had frequently denounced divorce in the press, considered the national sin of "wilful sterility" and the menace of "race suicide" serious enough as early as 1905 to give them considerable space in a message to Congress.[9]

[9] Fifth Annual Message, December 5, 1905, J. D. Richardson, Comp.: *Messages and Papers of the Presidents* (Washington, 1910), XIV, 7048. See also

Here too public emotions were divided. It was, after all, a progressive era, and a large and respectable minority thought the family should change with the times. Many sociologists, a sprinkling of liberal ministers, and several of the muckraking magazines agreed that marriage itself needed overhauling. This was the message of William E. Carson's *The Marriage Revolt*, a popular summary of liberal doctrine published in 1915. To Carson the divorce rate and the wide uneasiness about marriage did not mean a spread of evil ideas. It meant that people were finally learning to see marriage not as an unchanging ordinance, but as a custom that could be altered for human happiness. To real moral conservatives, no suggestion could have been more shocking.

The sharpest indication of sexual malaise was the white-slave panic, which reached its unaccountably hysterical peak in the peaceful prewar year 1913. It apparently started with the muckrakers, who had turned to the enticing subject of prostitution as early as 1907. Their attitude was a familiar one: the "Daughters of the Poor" were innocent victims; the real criminals were members of a secret, mysterious white-slave trust. In 1910 Congress attacked this trust with the Mann Act, designed to end the interstate white-slave trade. In the same year the New York Grand Jury, with John D. Rockefeller as foreman, started an investigation, and in 1911 the Chicago Vice Commission issued its famous report. Within three or four years most of the nation's states and cities conducted some sort of inquiry.

Inevitably, the cause was taken up by sensationalists on the borderline between evangelism, muckraking, and pornography in a number of lurid books about "The Girl Who Disappears." Novelists seized on the subject; the movies devoted a number of full-length features to "The Traffic in Souls." Any girl, it seemed, who said hello to a stranger in a large city was likely to be pricked with a poisoned needle and spirited away. She would wake up, helpless, in the brothels of Rio or Constantinople. A corre-

Roosevelt's *Autobiography* (New York, 1913), pp. 176–84 for discussion of this and similar subjects.

spondent of the *New York World* said that his wife believed fifty thousand women disappeared from Chicago and New York every year, and that more than half the men in the country were working night and day in an organization more formidable than the Steel Trust. Frederick C. Howe, Wilson's liberal Commissioner of Immigration, found himself on Ellis Island the custodian of hundreds of alien men and women, seized on flimsy evidence as prostitutes or procurers. Howe, describing the excitement later, compared it in intensity to the Pro-German hysteria of 1918 and the Red Scare of 1919–20.[1]

By 1913 and 1914, when the panic reached its height, a counteroffensive got under way. Mencken, among others, jumped with delight on this new, superb example of Puritan gullibility. Sober newspapers assured their readers that the poisoned needle was a myth. In a strange backwash of emotions, the censors started to object to white-slave films and novels. In 1913 *Current Opinion*, seizing a phrase of William Marion Reedy's, lamented that it seemed to have struck "Sex O'Clock" in America. Our reticence about sex was yielding, it said, to a frankness that would have startled Paris, and the center of the trouble was the constant discussion of prostitution.[2]

All these and other fears lay behind the reaction of conservative America to the essentially innocent ideas of the Rebellion, and to its favorite literature. No literate American could manage by the mid-teens to ignore Ibsen, Wells, and Dreiser entirely. To many, the solution seemed simple, to tighten the existing censorship. The *Dial*, in 1912, four years before it deserted to the rebels, stated exactly the point of view that the Freudians and others found most abhorrent:

> Now reticence may possibly go too far, but no sane person can deny that there are ugly things in life that had better be kept in the dark corners of consciousness.[3]

[1] Howe: *Confessions of a Reformer*, pp. 272–88. The *World* reporter's statement is discussed in *Current Opinion*, LVI (1914), 129.
[2] *Current Opinion*, LV (1913), 113–14.
[3] *Dial*, editorial, January 16, 1912, pp. 39–40.

Ever since the seventies, Anthony Comstock, for one, had been trying to keep them there, and his activities seemed to be reaching a wild crescendo just before his death in 1915. Armed with the federal and state laws which his efforts had secured, commissioned as a special agent by the Post Office Department, backed by his own New York Society for the Suppression of Vice and a network of similar societies in other states, Comstock was a formidable figure. Since he believed deeply in the pervasive, infectious power of evil thoughts, Comstock drew no lines between deliberate pornography, European classic art, and factual reports of vice commissions. In 1912 he attacked and made famous a painfully decorous picture which had won the medal of honor at the Paris Spring Salon; it was called "September Morning." In 1914 he went after the February issue of the *Chautauquan*, which had on its cover a photograph of a Greek faun recently dug up by a University of Pennsylvania expedition.

To publishers, and especially to new, daring, and vulnerable publishers, Comstock was not by any means a laughing matter, and neither was his slightly less spectacular successor as Secretary of the New York Society, John S. Sumner. Those who defied him might find their books denied the mails and boycotted by booksellers, themselves in court facing an inflamed and hostile jury. In 1913 Comstock led a dramatic raid on Mitchell Kennerley's office and brought the publisher to trial over the novel *Hagar Revelly*. In December 1915 Knopf, barely started, was threatened with attack over Przybyszewski's *Homo Sapiens*. In 1917 Sumner attacked Appleton for publishing *Susan Lenox*, the famous, impeccably uplifting, white-slave novel of the muckraking novelist David Graham Phillips.

The climax of prewar censorship battles, and the prelude to many celebrated engagements of the twenties, raged round the battered head of Theodore Dreiser. In July 1916 the Western Society for the Prevention of Vice, aroused by a Cincinnati minister, attacked *The Genius*, got it removed from the bookstores, secured a temporary cessation-of-circulation order from the Post

Office Department and filed a complaint with its New York counterpart, Sumner's famous Society. Sumner, following the usual procedure, persuaded Lane to withdraw the book pending a court contest and managed to get it banned throughout the country.

This time, however, Sumner ran into a fight. Despite Mencken's correct warnings that anti-German sentiment would be brought into the contest, Dreiser refused to compromise, and Mencken roused a public protest. He failed to get help from Howells, Brander Matthews, and most of the other custodians of culture. Yet he was able to line up a formidable list of libertarians: in England Arnold Bennett, Hugh Walpole, and Wells; in this country Amy Lowell, Robert Frost, Edwin Arlington Robinson, Willa Cather, William Allen White, Knopf, Huebsch, and many others. The book remained substantially suppressed until 1923, but the defenders of intellectual freedom were aroused to battle as never before.

In this battle, and in the whole war that was opening, both sides were serious. To the intellectuals, censors were nasty and cruel old men, inflicting on others their own frustrations, denying to America the possibility of free and joyous self-expression. To some of the conservatives in the prewar years, a strange flood of filth was welling up from mysterious sources. Erotic plays and books, divorce, free love, lascivious dances, birth control were menacing not only American culture but the possibility of moral restraint, the sheet-anchor of any and all civilization.

The *Nation,* balanced and serious as usual, presented a picture of the situation in 1913 which was fairly accurate, given the *Nation's* assumptions. All was not lost, despite:

> Tango, eugenics, the slit skirt, sex hygiene, Brieux, white slaves, Richard Strauss, John Masefield, the double standard of morality . . . a conglomerate of things important and unimportant, of age-old problems and momentary fads, which nevertheless have this one thing in common, that they do involve an abandonment of the old proprieties and the old reticences. . . .

One must distinguish, said the *Nation,* between the fluttering tastes of the half-baked intellectuals, attracted by all these things, and the surviving soundness of the great majority. It was still only revolt, not revolution.[4]

❦

When racial fear was mixed with sexual uneasiness, cultural civil war seemed to come a little closer. In the swelling uneasiness of the immediately prewar years, these two currents often mingled. Most of the white slavers were assumed to be foreign; from 1911 on, the international white-slave trust figured prominently in the famous and biased investigations of Senator Dillingham into the evils of immigration. Race suicide was blamed on the despair of the pure-minded Anglo-Saxons, who knew they could never compete with lustful, prolific South Europeans. Sometimes sexual and racial fears seemed to flow temporarily in opposite directions, for instance when easy divorce, eugenically regulated marriage, and birth control for immigrants were urged as methods of preserving the race, and yet condemned as breaches of sexual morality.

In the midst of the apparently peaceful prewar years, when the dominant attitude toward immigrants was one of patronizing uplift, racial fear was present beneath the surface. One of the curious racial panics that mar the American record of assimilation was to reach its peak between 1917 and the early twenties. Knowing this, one can see the signs of its beginning in the prewar years.

Part of the reason for increasing tension was, as in earlier crises, economic. The depression of 1914 revived labor's fears of foreign competition, and decreased the employer's interest in a steady flow of immigrant workers. Lawrence and Paterson presented to newspaper readers the picture of the dangerous alien immigrant. And every time anybody, for any reason, worried about the preservation of old ways, he was likely to glance, with alarm, at the annual inflow of half a million newcomers.

[4] *Nation,* "Is There a Public?" September 4, 1913, p. 205.

New allies came to the aid of the immigrant-haters in their hard fight against the traditional doctrine of the open door. Eugenics, once a Utopian design for improving the race, developed a less benign negative program for weeding out the unfit. Its teachings mixed easily with those of an older and still more dubious science, the study of racial differences. For a long time students of race had started with minutely careful skull measurements and gone on to ponderous discussions of innate moral differences. Now eugenics, racial science, and popular prejudice mixed to produce a new kind of popular "scientific" doctrine, powerful, simple, and destructive.

For a century or more the message of science had been principally encouraging; now it was apparently moving toward pessimism. The melting-pot was a lie; the power of education and political democracy a dangerous delusion. Head-shapes of immigrants might alter in the New World, instincts could not. This was not, perhaps, the fault of immigrants; most of their traits had been determined several generations earlier. None the less, it was necessary in self-defense for Americans to cast aside old scruples about individual liberty; drastic action was necessary to save the race.

The loudest sounder of alarm was Madison Grant, whose *Passing of the Great Race*, published in 1916, added to the message of science a rehash of nineteenth-century racist history. Nordics had been even more responsible for social advance than most Americans had realized: Jesus, for instance, had really been a Nordic, probably a Greek. Yet the worst disaster in history had been the spread of the Christian, democratic, sentimental doctrine of human brotherhood. This had led to the two disastrous errors: freeing the slaves and trying to uplift the immigrants.

Even hysterical fanatics like Grant were widely praised, but racial fear probably received more important support from the works of well-intentioned, progressive social scientists. Edward A. Ross, for instance, admired the spirit of the immigrants struggling upward, and conceded that many individual immigrants had fine qualities. The mass, however, could do nothing but harm, and Ross felt it his duty to overcome the sympathy he felt. Posterity was more important. Ross, a Wisconsin progressive, believed as strongly as Barrett Wendell that the best American qualities had been inherited from the Puritans. These qualities must be saved at all costs from further adulteration.[5]

This sort of moderate statement, backed by misleading but impressive figures about crime and vice and illiteracy, occur very frequently in the period's textbooks on the "immigration problem." "Problem" was the key word: immigration and racial decline were one of the challenges which we could meet, now that we were free from the false doctrines of nineteenth-century laissez-faire. This was a typically progressive doctrine, yet at its base lay racial determinism, sharply hostile to the most fundamental progressive assumptions. One could improve social arrangements, but one could not make good citizens out of "bad" stock.

The same sort of "realism" was invoked more harshly against the Negro. In April 1916 a writer in the Archives of Psychology put his conclusions in terms of statistics:

> pure negroes, negroes three-fourths pure, mulattoes and quadroons have, roughly, 60, 70, 80, and 90 percent, respectively of white intellectual efficiency.[6]

This kind of "scientific" support had long been invoked by historians, dealing with the folly of abolition and the horror of Reconstruction. The tragedy of the attempt at Negro equality was a favorite theme of romantic novelists. In 1915 D. W. Griffith's "Birth of a Nation" used a more powerful medium to drive home the same lesson.

One can see indications of tightening racial feelings in many concrete events: in the 1915 demand for a literacy test, barely defeated by Wilson's veto; in the Wilson administration's own action two years before that in formalizing segregation in many gov-

[5] E. A. Ross: *The Old World in the New* (New York, 1914) *passim.*

[6] George Oscar Ferguson, Jr.: "The Psychology of the Negro," *Archives of Psychology*, XXXVI (1916), 125.

ernment offices; in the continued enactment of minute, insulting discriminatory laws in the South. Sometimes racial feeling erupted in violence, and the violence was not all directed against Negroes. Two Italian miners were lynched in Pennsylvania. In Georgia in 1914 Leo Frank, a Jewish manufacturer accused of the sex murder of a female employee, was killed by a mob after a state-wide emotional storm. The storm of hatred that burst in 1917 and 1918 against the German-Americans, the race riots of 1919, the xenophobia of the early twenties, did not come out of a really clear sky.

The Young Intellectuals, rejecting many parts of traditional ideology, turned against the doctrine of Anglo-Saxon superiority with special delight and enthusiasm. For them the only hope for American culture lay in the influx of cheerful Italians and soulful Slavs. For opposite reasons, many of them agreed with the extreme racists in disliking the idea of the melting-pot. Immigrant cultures must be preserved to leaven the solid Anglo-Saxon lump. Disregarding sociologists like Ross, the Young Intellectuals turned instead to the Boas school of anthropology. From it they learned, with pleasure, that there was no sound reason for assuming that any one culture was superior to another.

As the defenders of the Anglo-Saxon ascendancy became less complacent and more shrill, the rebels became angrier. Their generous enthusiasm for the underdog sometimes became a positive preference for whatever was most alien or primitive. Sometimes it was to seem that any set of customs could be tolerated but one's own. And the crime of racial snobbery was added, sometimes justly and sometimes not, to the indictment against the Puritan bigot. In their turn the younger generation were accused of racial treason, almost as serious a charge as moral revolution.

The angriest denunciation of the younger rebels did not come, at first, from those benign and complacent dignitaries, the custodians of culture. These had changed little since 1912. In 1915 Robert Underwood Johnson was absorbed in a new cause, obtaining official immortality for the Academy of Arts and Letters through passage of a Congressional act of incorporation. Unfortunately, stubborn congressmen from the West and South found the Academy's membership too Northeastern. "Is it not," asked Johnson, "a trivial objection that the Academy, based on large achievement, has no representative of certain states where less attention is given to literature and the arts? So much more do they need the help of such an organization." [7]

The greatest official synthesis of the American literary past, the *Cambridge History of American Literature*, was being written before and during the war. Published belatedly from 1917 to 1921, it spoke with the unaltered tones of 1912. Most of it could have been written much earlier still; the rating of the standard authors was the familiar one; the new literature and new viewpoints that had appeared in Chicago and New York drew only the barest and most disapproving mention. In 1917 William Dean Howells's eightieth birthday was celebrated in New York. This time, Howells himself could not make the trip from the South; President Wilson was too busy for more than a written tribute; the affair stayed on the inside pages.

Secure in their own standards and confined to their own circles, some conservative critics were slow to see that the Rebellion existed. In November 1914 the *Dial*, which had been loudly denouncing its neighbor *Poetry*, deplored the fact that no younger literary generation seemed to be in sight.[8] When the rebels did, as they soon did, make their presence impossible to ignore, they were not always spanked. It is easy to find plenty of conservative wowsers, but it is easy also, especially in the years before 1915, to find tolerance and even generosity. The defenders of tra-

[7] Johnson to Representative Ferris, February 12, 1915, quoted in *Literary Digest*, March 20, 1915, pp. 610–11.

[8] *Dial*, "The Younger Generation," LVII (1914), 323–5.

dition, like all American conservatives, were hampered by the fact that the tradition they were defending included a commitment to progress and free speech as well as standards.

The *Atlantic*, in 1912, invited Randolph Bourne to speak his piece for his generation and the next year the *Nation*, commenting on Bourne's intense and not always very original early essays, characterized the new generation with some penetration:

> It appears here to be a little deficient in gaiety of heart, unduly confident in the strength of its insight, and amazingly disrespectful of its elders. In compensation it is fearless, honest, and terribly serious.[9]

This tone, just, patronizing, and untroubled, would have been the most effective one for the defenders to adopt. It demanded, however, more security than they commanded. Gradually and reluctantly, some of the custodians of culture were losing their own serenity.

In 1917 William Crary Brownell, like several other old-line critics, published a book which was a little more defensive and a little less urbane than his earlier works. Brownell admitted he was deeply disturbed by careless, formless poetry, by postimpressionist art and its defenders, by changes in dress and manners, by social violence, and by the general "ferocity modified by fatuousness" of the young. Once, he said, America had had a stable, discriminating minority, an entrenched group almost like that which arbitrated artistic controversy in France. Now this was gone: democracy had enlarged the "intellectual and aesthetic electorate" until it was useless to hope for standards. Yet—here was the dilemma of American conservatism—Brownell refused to abandon democracy. The Puritan doctrine of the saving remnant, he said, had its place in art and letters but could not be accepted in the social and political sphere. This dual program, Brownell undoubtedly realized, was hopeless.[1]

[9] *Nation*, May 29, 1913, p. 550.

[1] Brownell: *Standards* (New York, 1917), esp. pp. 37–8. Another good ex-

The most consistent and intellectually firm opposition to all kinds of novelty at once came from the two humanists, Babbitt and More, who were not hampered by prejudices in favor of democracy. These two men, as we have pointed out earlier, were not really defending the American culture of the nineteenth century, but much older forms and beliefs. This is one reason their conservatism survived the overthrow of the culture of 1912. When Wilsonian idealism perished, the Greek and French classics were not much affected.

More, looking back at the decadence of the nineties which he had detested for its perversity and prurience, found it preferable to the insane optimism and confused spirituality of the current Rebellion. The young admirers of Dostoevsky, he said, were asking us to accept vice not in Oscar Wilde's childish spirit of paradox, but as the road to redemption:

> Filth, disease, morbid dreams, bestiality, insanity, sodden crime, these are the natural pathway to the emancipation of the spirit.[2]

Unlike Brownell, More was as rigidly opposed to social and political as he was to literary rebellion. All kinds of innovation came from the same source, sentimental contempt for standards. Ben Lindsey and Jane Addams, appealing for sympathetic understanding of criminals, were really breaking down individual responsibility; their "new morality" was "an ulcerous evil," part and parcel of the prevailing sensuality of 1913. In 1914, when the National Guard in Colorado burned the miners' tent colonies, killing women and children, and the radicals of the day exploded with indignation, More stood firmly beside John D. Rockefeller. While he could not of course condone violence from any source, the rights of property, More said, were sacred even when they were abused. Going further than American conservatives had often

ample of increasing tension on the part of an important custodian of culture is Brander Matthews: "The Tocsin of Revolt," an essay of 1917 published in a volume of the same name (New York, 1922).

[2] More: "A Naughty Decade," *Nation*, May 21, 1914, p. 600.

wanted to go, More said flatly that they were more sacred, with the civilization that depended on them, than life itself. This statement, much quoted by the intellectual rebels, More never repudiated.[3]

When the war came, More and Babbitt, the most extreme opponents of intellectual innovation, were far more moderate and controlled in their emotions than most of the custodians of culture. Since their ideas all rested on a belief in the evil of man's nature, they were not entirely surprised by this revival of barbarism. Modern culture, to them, was not a triumph of progress and peace, but a long decline. Though both preferred the Allies to the Germans, both objected to current stereotypes. The cause of the Allies was not divine, and we could not afford at this point to read Germany out of European civilization. Despite her serious faults:

> There is nevertheless a touch of the irrational and the indecent in our frenzy of bitterness towards that country, and in readiness to gloat over every tale of brutality. This is particularly the case in academic circles.[4]

Here More was quite right, and nobody furnished a better example than his own pupil Stuart Sherman, who was both more optimistic and less profound than his master. Most of the custodians of culture, beset already by intellectual attack and worried by signs of sexual, racial, and other kinds of insurrection, linked the Allied Cause with the defense of all they valued, and thereby added the last element needed to produce a really big explosion.

[3] More: *Aristocracy and Justice* (*Shelburne Essays,* IX, Boston, 1915), p. 141.

[4] *Unpopular Review,* III (1915), 14. Babbitt expressed somewhat similar views in the *Nation,* June 17, 1914, pp. 677–80, and June 24, pp. 704–6.

II

"She Can Do No Other"

On March 4, 1913, Woodrow Wilson stated the lofty purposes of his administration, committing it to the twin standards of progress and eternal moral values:

> We have made up our minds to square every process of our national life again with the standard we so proudly set up at the beginning and have always carried at our hearts. Our work is a work of restoration.[1]

This inaugural marked the beginning of a period which was the peak of progressive accomplishment. It marked also the beginning of the tragedy of Woodrow Wilson, one of the few perfect tragedies of history, a story in which nobility of purpose combined with spiritual pride were cruelly punished by the gods.

Through the war and its outcome, through the cycle of hope, hatred and disillusion, the credo which Wilson embodied was discredited and torn apart. The principles of moralism, progress, and culture, already linked disastrously to snobbery, racial pride, and prudery, were linked now to the Wilsonian version of the Allied cause. Inevitably, the country was to turn against both. The war brought about the victory of our intellectual rebellion, and in so doing, changed its nature.

In 1913, when Wilson moved briskly into command, even his admirers were surprised. Idealism had been expected by all; only

[1] R. S. Baker and W. E. Dodd, eds.: *Public Papers of Woodrow Wilson, The New Democracy* (New York, 1926), p. 3. Other Wilson speeches quoted and referred to can be found here and in other standard collections.

a few had expected Wilson's superb vigor, political astuteness, iron will, and even (though sometimes the public smile creaked a little) geniality. Wilson was always at his most charming in times of victory. Defeat, as some people at Princeton already knew, could bring out another and less lovable set of qualities.

Progressives, members, that is, of the amorphous American majority, could hardly believe their good fortune; in the first two years many who had voted for Roosevelt and some who had voted for Debs rubbed their eyes and decided to follow the new leader. Marshaling and badgering and cajoling the professional politicians, this amateur managed in 1913 to solve the two immensely complex problems of banking and tariff reform, problems which had stymied every president since Lincoln, even since Jackson.

Nobody was more delighted with the great accomplishments of Wilson's first two years than the custodians of culture. More than had ever seemed possible even to the most optimistic, the people had surpassed themselves, electing a man of the right kind, in fact of the highest type.

One of Wilson's first acts had been to press the British embassy on Charles W. Eliot. Eliot had declined the London post, as Meredith Nicholson of the Indiana literary school had declined Lisbon and Dean Harry Fine of Princeton, Berlin. But at least three of Wilson's diplomats were perfect representatives of progressive culture. Henry Van Dyke went to the Hague, Brand Whitlock, the progressive novelist and reformer, to Brussels. Walter Hines Page, the personification of robust literature and respectable reform, finally accepted London.

Delighted as they were with tariff reform and some other domestic accomplishments, the custodians of culture and morality were even more thrilled by Wilson's opening moves in foreign policy. The principles, stated again and again, were simple and clear. A nation must act in practice, even under the temptations of the wicked international world, exactly according to the very best standards of private morality, and even of gentility. The United

States must maintain the most spotless honor, but at the same time she must lead. Without interference in the affairs of others, she must promote constitutional democracy everywhere; without the slightest taint of self-interest, she must help the backward nations to advance economically. Wilson's enemies sneered at his incessant and somewhat bookish enunciations of these principles: yet in his first year and a half in office he seemed actually, unbelievably, to be putting them into practice.

To Robert Underwood Johnson of the *Century*, who represented the elevated taste of the 1880's with complete accuracy, the most important problem facing the nation was that of the Panama Canal tolls. The United States, bound by treaty with Great Britain to accord equal treatment to foreign vessels, had decided by Act of Congress in August 1912 to exempt from tolls American coastwise vessels going through the Canal. Johnson led a protest in the name of honor and Anglo-American relations. Now the president-elect, fighting Irish Anglophobia, widespread Democratic nationalism, and even the platform on which he had been elected, forced the Congress to repeal the tolls exemption in the name of honor. At last a nation, commented much of the respectable press, had shown that it could act like a gentleman.

In the Far East the administration moved toward Philippine independence and, more important, toward recognizing the special moral significance of China. Wilson denounced the six-power "consortium" formed during the previous administration for the purpose of making railroad loans to China. He easily persuaded American bankers to withdraw on the ground that the project might lead to violation of China's sovereignty. Against the advice of his experts, he hurried to recognize the new Chinese republic, hailing the dawn of free government in China as the greatest event of the age.

Mexico, where American investments amounted to a billion dollars, offered the hardest test of all for the policies of altruism. Since 1911 she had been torn by revolution. The world of power politics would have approved American intervention in the interest of financial stability. A policy of strict nonintervention seemed the only possible alternative. Wilson chose neither. Instead, he brought American power to bear on the side of revolution, trying to direct its energies into constitutional channels but giving little attention to immediate American economic interests.

Wilson's Mexican policy, the extreme example of idealism in foreign affairs, hardly worked as he had hoped, at least in the short run. At times it seemed to be uniting Mexicans against him. Yet the President's many critics could not budge him. They represented, he insisted, those "material interests" which were the chief enemy of progress even at home. His Mexican policy, he explained, was designed to educate and uplift the downtrodden; it offered an altruistic example to the world. Many were stirred; despite its lack of immediate success Wilson's Mexican policy was supported by the Midwestern progressives, by many of the custodians of culture, by Lincoln Steffens and Max Eastman, and probably by most of the people.

The keystone of the new foreign policy was of course world peace, and the Secretary of State, William Jennings Bryan, was perhaps the only consistent, dedicated Christian pacifist ever to be foreign minister of a great power. Ignoring the sneers of the sophisticated, Bryan served grape juice at banquets, delivered at Chautauqua an oration about "The Prince of Peace," and negotiated an impressive series of arbitration treaties. Despite the mounting petty violence in some quarters, Wilson himself said in December 1913 that the world seemed to be entering a period of settled peace. So far the record demonstrated that it was possible to pursue at once peace, world progress toward free government, and American national honor. Foreign policy could at last become a counterpart of domestic reform, conducted with full regard to moral principle.

In 1914, all at once, a whole mass of heavy clouds rolled across this glowing sky, and the administration never encountered really clear weather again. At home, the year was one of gathering depression, of bitter labor war in Colorado, of mounting demands for immigration restriction. In Congress, the year was chiefly taken up by a battle over regulation of big business. Here Wilson eventually scored a qualified success, but the struggles over the Clayton and Federal Trade Commission Acts revealed the ideological divisions among progressives. Confronting this difficult issue, the administration could no longer bring together the Jeffersonian Southern Democrats, the trust-busting friends of little business, and the young, hard-boiled believers in expert administration. From 1914 on, as Arthur Link, Wilson's leading modern biographer, has made clear, the administration veered back and forth between different groups of its supporters. Sometimes the *Nation*, with other spokesmen of traditional morality, was worried about tendencies to demagogy and class legislation. At other times, to Walter Lippmann and the *New Republic*, the administration seemed to be reverting to Jeffersonian platitudes, forgetting altogether the modern conception of the scientifically administered state. In 1914 the administration, and progressives generally, suffered a sharp setback in the congressional elections.

Other political crises brought to light the period's rising tensions. In 1915 Wilson, consciously defending nineteenth-century American tradition, vetoed a bill providing a literacy test for immigrants. All his prestige barely prevented the Congress from overriding the veto.

In 1916 many of the subtle divisions in American society were suggested by the storm over the appointment of Louis D. Brandeis to the Supreme Court. When Wilson submitted this appointment to the Senate, protests poured in from Boston, Brandeis's home. Such predictable objectors as President Lowell, a bevy of former Bar Association presidents, and Charles Francis Adams were joined by Moorfield Storey, Boston's favorite reformer.

Storey's participation helped the opponents of Brandeis to insist that anti-Semitism was not an issue. It was hard for them to explain just what was at stake. Brandeis was a leading proponent of Scientific Management and a believer in the application of social science to law. These opinions, while disturbing to conservatives, were hardly in themselves plausible grounds for rejection. Pushed to explain further, the objectors alleged that Brandeis as a lawyer had strayed from strict devotion to the interests of some of his clients; he had, that is, acted too much like a judge. If he had not been unethical, he had been accused of being unethical, and this made him too controversial for the bench. He did not see enough of other leading Boston lawyers, or consult them sufficiently on ethical matters. Both the *New Republic*, Brandeis's devoted defender, and the *Nation*, a stronghold of the opposition, saw what the issue really was: Brandeis was not the kind of man who had usually been appointed to the court.[2]

In April 1914 the Administration's Mexican policy involved it, at Tampico, in something that looked like the worst of old-fashioned imperialism. To avenge a petty insult to American troops an admiral, fully backed by Washington, demanded under threat a punctilious salute to the American flag. This incident was followed shortly by American military occupation, against resistance, of Vera Cruz. Much of Latin America was furious, and a Wilsonian solution nowhere in sight. Observers noticed that the President, hit hard by American deaths in action, stiffened his policies instead of changing them.

Then, in August, an obscure chain of events which almost no Americans had closely followed brought war on an infinitely greater scale in Europe. At the same time tragedy struck the White House itself. On August 5, the day after Britain declared war on Germany, Mrs. Woodrow Wilson, a charitable, gracious, rather retiring woman, died in the White House with the President at her bedside. Wilson, shattered and almost paralyzed with grief, had to turn his attention to a kind of problem neither he nor his country had really been able to imagine.

[2] *Nation*, March 9, 1916, pp. 272–3; *New Republic*, March 11, 1916, p. 139.

Few Americans could grasp, and fewer still could admit, all that the outbreak of World War meant to them and their ideas. Frank H. Simonds, in the *New Republic*, came as close as any contemporary to seeing in 1914 the dimensions of the disaster. "Is it not a possibility," he asked, "that what is taking place marks quite as complete a bankruptcy of ideas, systems, society, as did the French Revolution? . . ." [3]

The nineteenth-century view of history as progress, accepted in one form or another by nearly all Americans, received a shattering blow. Perhaps the most important victim of war was practical idealism, that loosely formulated set of assumptions on which Americans had come to depend so heavily. After 1914 it became increasingly hard to argue that the essential morality of the universe could be shown in the daily course of events. Still more obviously challenged was the special prophetic vision of Social Christianity: the gradual dawn, here on earth, of the kingdom of peace and love.

In the perspective of world catastrophe, nineteenth-century positivism and up-to-date social science seemed remarkably similar, in their fundamental assumptions, to liberal nineteenth-century religion. Everybody, from Charles W. Eliot to James Harvey Robinson, who had predicted the steady, successful application of scientific method to social problems, had some rethinking to do. Either this whole picture was mistaken or—a far more common conclusion in all camps—some particularly powerful, reactionary force had been overlooked. This left the question: what was such a force doing in the twentieth century?

As 1914 wore on to its end, the news from Belgium seemed to challenge not only the progressive view of history, but an assumption still more deeply rooted in dominant American ideology, the fundamental decency of modern, civilized human nature. Americans were not particularly gullible, as later critics have implied, when they believed the atrocity stories. For one thing, atrocities

[3] Frank H. Simonds: "1914—The End of an Era," *New Republic*, January 2, 1915, pp. 12–13.

occurred, as they do in all wars. As Max Eastman shrewdly pointed out, what was really shocking was war itself. Many practices justified by the code of an invading army—the shooting of civilians caught with arms, the exaction of collective penalties, even the taking of hostages—were almost incredibly brutal to Americans, who had forgotten Tennessee or Georgia in the Civil War.

A picture that was shattered past repair in 1914, and a picture that had been more deeply imprinted on the American consciousness than most Americans realized, was the picture of a united European culture. Europe, as we have seen, was a necessary backdrop to American cultural disputes. To some it was a civilization which could be contrasted to American crudity, to some it represented aristocracy or decadence. To still others European culture was a rival which we must equal and surpass. Now it was no longer there: in 1914 European civilization tore itself apart in public.

In October, ninety-three German intellectuals published a famous manifesto defending the "pure cause" of the fatherland against the lies of the West.[4] Germany had tried to avoid war; she had been fully justified in invading Belgium; her soldiers had behaved with uniform excellence despite the cruel atrocities of the Belgians; the Allies were calling in the yellow and black races and the barbarous Slavs against the home of Goethe and Beethoven. Americans did not recognize all the names on the list of signers, but many had heard of the dramatists Hauptmann and Sudermann, the director Max Reinhardt, the gentle idealist philosopher Eucken, the grand old naturalist Haeckel (who had recently protested against nationalism on eugenic grounds), the physicist Max Planck, or the chemist Wilhelm Ostwald, or Wilhelm Wundt, the grandfather of most American psychology. On the other side much the same

[4] This manifesto, much quoted in the American press, was published complete in France. Auguste Picard, ed.: *Les Versions Allemande et Française du Manifeste des Intellectuels Allemands* (Paris, 1915).

line-up took place with a little less organization and precision. Anatole France renounced his pacifism; H. G. Wells was converted to patriotism and religion at once. Only an occasional Bertrand Russell remained a pacifist, only a very rare Romain Rolland tried to keep alive the idea of European intellectual unity.

The old picture of the world was gone, and Americans had to construct a new one. Meanwhile in the years of argument over American action, they had to draw on whatever emotions and ideas were uppermost in their minds. Inevitably, their attitudes toward the war were affected by their positions in the current cultural controversy. It is with this aspect, and this aspect only, of the argument over intervention that we are concerned.

Those who made the Allied cause most passionately their own from the beginning were not, as one later legend said, the business interests. These moved rather cautiously. Nor was the heart of interventionism a realistic sense of American interest in the Atlantic barrier or the balance of power. The earliest and most consistent supporters of the Allies were the beleaguered defenders of nineteenth-century tradition, and particularly the professional custodians of culture. Conversely, those who were doubtful about the sanctity of the Allied cause were often those who had been involved, before the war, in some kind of intellectual revolt.

Nearly all the leading men of letters, the college presidents, the old-line publishers, the editors of standard magazines, and their friends knew where they stood from the start. Only a very rare member of this group, like Oswald Garrison Villard, let inherited pacifism outweigh other considerations. Most of the older idealists were not as bellicose as Roosevelt and his immediate followers like Lyman Abbott. Their feelings did not center in hatred, but in hope and exaltation. Instead of seeing the war as the doom of their culture, they believed it would bring about its revival: the war was a severe but necessary lesson in moral idealism.

To construct this mental picture of the war, it was necessary for the custodians of culture and their friends to change a little their traditional picture of Europe. The easiest job, strangely enough, was to rule Germany out of the camp of idealism and culture. The manifesto of the German intellectuals helped here a great deal; it seemed to demonstrate that the Germany of philosophy, of music, and of science had been entirely subverted by Prussian militarism. Psychoanalysis and other recent tendencies linked Germany with decadence. Most useful of all was Nietzsche, who became the subject of innumerable sermons and speeches. It was vain for his defenders to point out, as they did, that Nietzsche had expressed contempt for Germany. He could be quoted as glorifying war and apologizing for brutality. Also, he was linked with the recent upsurge in America of moral skepticism, particularly with H. L. Mencken.

France, the home of licentious literature and futurist art, seemed to present a more difficult problem, but a formula was quickly developed. The fires of war were purging the French soul; soon aestheticism, eccentricity, and even Voltairian skepticism would be forgotten. In the future, the older literary journals proclaimed over and over with the greatest confidence, the true France would be reborn, the France of Joan of Arc, of religion, patriotism, and ordered beauty. Bergson, the most famous Frenchman of the day, assured the American press that the war was a contest between material and spiritual strength. From Belgium the voice of Maeterlinck, the favorite modern writer of the older critics, called for help.

Naturally the sympathies of American men of letters centered, as they always had, around England. Henry James, without fanfare, took in 1915 the logical step of becoming a citizen of the country he lived in. He meant it, he said, as "a simple act and offering of allegiance and devotion, recognition and gratitude," [5] but the press took it as an interventionist gesture.

Britain seemed to need regeneration a little less than France, yet Wells's conversion was warmly welcomed and Shaw's continued iconoclasm deplored. (Shaw did not oppose the war, but in March 1917 he drew delighted laughter from a soldier audience by saying that what Europe wanted was "an early and dishonorable peace.")

[5] Percy Lubbock, ed.: *Letters of Henry James* (New York, 1920), II, 479.

Rupert Brooke, one of the first of the many English literary losses, became the favorite young hero of the older American critics. Superbly handsome, both conventional and skillful as a poet, Brooke had indulged before the war in mild Cambridge cynicism. In the year between the outbreak of war and his death, he had said a ringing good-by to his doubts:

> Now, God be thanked Who has matched us with His hour,
> And caught our youth, and wakened us from sleeping. . . .
>
> Glad from a world grown old and cold and weary,
> Leave the sick hearts that honour could not move. . . .

Barrett Wendell, who had been worried about British intellectual tendencies for some time, could hope only that the great tonic of war had not come too late.[6]

As early as 1914 President Hibben of Princeton expressed the fear that the postwar world might see Europe chastened and purified while America, denied the great experience, weltered in materialism. Robert Herrick, in his "Recantation of a Pacifist," was sure that "The youths whose graves now dot the pleasant fields of France have drunk deeper than we can dream of the mystery of life." [7] Others recalled the Civil War which, according to the New England tradition enshrined in Lowell's "Commemoration Ode," had been a similarly ennobling experience.

Young acquaintances of these elder idealists were early in the field. The older colleges and the more exclusive prep schools contributed far more than their share to the volunteer units. The first American ambulance corps in the French army was organized by the son of Charles Eliot Norton, and Henry James busied himself to raise money. The older generation itself found an emotional outlet in the preparedness movement of 1915. Some of the needs satisfied by war were indicated by Ralph Barton Perry's comment from the Plattsburg training camp:

[6] Howe: *Wendell*, p. 359.

[7] Hibben in *Literary Digest*, October 17, 1914, p. 741; Herrick: "Recantation of a Pacifist," *New Republic*, October 30, 1915, p. 329.

> There is a fine restraint in military ceremony that enables the purest product of New England self-repression to *feel*—without awkwardness or self-consciousness.[8]

The custodians of culture and their friends knew that their unqualified commitment to the Allied cause put them in a minority; they were used to being the leaven in the lump. Many were impatient with Wilson, whom they had admired in 1913–14, but who had never, as a Democrat, been entirely acceptable. Nearly all the opposition to the Allied cause came from sections of opinion they had always distrusted. In January 1916 George Edward Woodberry, rejoicing in the emergence of a firmer pro-Allied tone, was sorry he could not call it national:

> Thank God that it is Eastern, at least—ashes, at least of the old powers of devotion and insight still warm in the old soil.[9]

In March 1916 Barrett Wendell saw a little more virtue in Wilson, who was fighting hard against the proposal of Western Congressmen to prohibit American travel in armed belligerent ships.

> But I had not before quite understood the disloyalty to national spirit—the profound Bryanism of his party; nor the degree to which, in other parts of America than this, the traditional dislike of England has prevented the vulgar from admitting to themselves the full monstrosity of Germany.[1]

For the custodians of culture the primary issue was not American interests, not neutral rights, not even the rescue of England and France. The ideals they wanted to defend abroad were to them the same as those they had long been defending at home. England, France, and Belgium came to embody all that they believed in, Germany and her apologists all that they hated and feared. Their whole view of life and history seemed to lead toward this conclusion. If

[8] Perry: "Impressions of a Plattsburg Recruit," *New Republic*, October 2, 1915, p. 231.

[9] Woodberry: *Letters*, p. 160.

[1] Howe: *Wendell*, p. 272.

the war was not caused by the special wickedness of Germany, it would have to be accounted for in more general terms. This would suggest that all nineteenth-century civilization must be a sham and a failure.

Even if the war had come in earlier and more confident days, the custodians of culture might have interpreted it in this way. Yet one cannot help suspecting that the extremes of simple and disastrous emotional response were related to prewar tensions. The custodians of culture knew that their ideas and their position were under attack from many quarters. It was all too easy to lump together all kinds of loyalty on one side, and all kinds of skepticism on the other. The war provided outlets for angry emotions, already running high against scoffers and cynics, against moral, sexual, and racial insurrection.

❦

The groups that opposed American intervention with real fervor all clearly came from outside the dominant minority, and they knew it. To German-Americans, ranged solidly behind the beleaguered and misunderstood Fatherland until 1917, and to the more militant Irish-Americans, pro-Allied sentiment was part of a familiar Eastern, Anglophile conspiracy to distort the truth. To extreme radicals, the war in Europe was obviously a product of declining capitalism, and those who idealized it in America were playing the game of the munition-makers. The I.W.W. and the anarchists forthrightly and solidly condemned both sides, and refused to have anything to do with bourgeois war, before and after 1917.

These groups were clearly outside respectable America; as we have seen the larger Socialist Party was not quite sure whether it was or not. Beneath the intraparty battles of the prewar years lay the unsettled question, was American socialism a part of progressive America and of practical idealism, or was it part of an international revolutionary movement, uninterested in bourgeois reform?

Even before the outbreak of war, the Wilson administration was drawing some of the right wing out of the Socialist camp; this was clear in the elections of 1914 and 1916. During the first years of European war another group left the party over the war issue, and still more split away when the test of American entry came. The majority, in the famous St. Louis convention of spring 1917, declared its undying opposition to American participation.

The prowar Socialists included most of the prominent recruits from well-to-do Anglo-Saxon reform circles: William English Walling, J. G. Phelps Stokes, Robert Hunter, Charles Edward Russell, and many more. Gustavus Myers, the socialist historian, suggested in the spring of 1917 another way to classify the seceders: it was the idealists who were leaving the Socialist Party. The war he said (and Russell said the same thing a little later) was proving the inadequacy of a philosophy based on sordid materialism.[2] Myers was right; the faction which was leaving the party was the faction which shared the emotions and ideas of the American credo, the section which took seriously such matters, bourgeois abstractions to their fellows, as international law, neutral rights, and the self-determination of small countries. The remaining socialist party was much more influenced by its left wing; it was on balance a tougher, more skeptical, and more alienated group that passed through the wartime ordeal. This changed the course of radical history in America; it also contributed to the coming together of moral and political orthodoxy in 1917.

At the opposite extreme from the militant socialists, but equally militant and equally outside prewar American society, were the religious Fundamentalists, and they too contributed to the wartime opposition. The war seemed to some Fundamentalists to prove what they had always known: that modern liberal culture was a failure. Some of them were able to support the Allies, since Germany was the chief home of biblical criticism. For others, however, Sodom was fighting Gomorrah, and the place for the justified mi-

[2] Myers: "Why Idealists Quit the Socialist Party," *Nation*, February 15, 1917, pp. 181–2.

nority was outside this worldly battle. To the premillennialists particularly, war for democracy made no more sense than progressive reform. Nothing could save the world from the coming Judgment, least of all war. Some of the stoutest opponents of the war came from Adventist groups and tiny Holiness churches.

To the more liberal majority of American Christians, Fundamentalist pessimism was embarrassing and annoying. With a few prominent exceptions, the Social Gospel leaders strongly supported the Allied cause. Many went far toward identifying victory with the coming of Christ's Kingdom. Some leading social Christians sharply attacked Fundamentalist leaders for lukewarmness toward the Allies. When war came, almost no spokesmen of liberal Christianity protested against the savage sentences given Russellite and other millennialist preachers for condemning war on traditional Christian grounds. A good many spokesmen of dominant church opinion actively approved such suppression, of Fundamentalists and radicals alike.

Fundamentalists, already alienated from progressive civilization, were deeply angered by attacks on their patriotism, especially from quarters they regarded as fundamentally disloyal to Christian tradition. Their hopes renewed by the failure of progressive civilization, they began sounding the call for a counteroffensive. This militant movement was to break out, to the amazement of the liberals, after the war. To some, the destined leader was already at hand. In 1917 William Bell Riley, one of the most prominent Fundamentalist leaders, predicted that American opinion would turn away from Wilson toward the peace-loving, God-fearing leadership of William Jennings Bryan.[3]

Finally, a few American intellectuals, some of German stock and some not, took a strongly anti-Allied position because of their admiration for German culture. These included such diverse figures as John W. Burgess and Simon Patten, and H. L. Mencken. Menc-

[3] William Bell Riley: *Daniel vs. Darwinism* (Minneapolis, 1917), pp. 89–90. I am indebted for this reference, and for much of my information about prewar Fundamentalism, to Carroll E. Harrington (see Bibliographical Essay, II, 1).

ken's position on the war, like many of his more extreme attitudes, was explained in large part by what he was against. The Puritans, the Nietzsche-haters, the preachy critics, the Anglo-Saxon bigots were leading the pro-Allied camp. According to their own statements, they wanted to make the world over into a moralistic, American-style democracy under Wilsonian leadership. He could hardly have found any prospect more appalling. In the *Smart Set,* he increased if anything his use of German words and phrases, his praise of German music, literature, and wine. In the *Baltimore Sun* he positively gloated over the successes of German arms. This, as Mencken probably realized, was asking for trouble, and trouble came.

Most Americans in 1915 and 1916 were slowly making up their minds, not yet committed to either extreme view of the war. The progressive majority, moderately idealist but practical, was not prepared to follow the custodians of culture into a sacrificial crusade. Neither was it altogether skeptical or hostile to the Allied cause. Progressive emotions pulled both ways, against Kaiserism and yet for peace.

Everybody knew that the line which divided progressives was partly geographical. Despite many exceptions, it was clear that most progressive opposition to war came from one huge Western area, bounded roughly by Robert M. La Follette and William Jennings Bryan. The geographical line was partly a moral one; as we have seen, Western and Eastern progressivism had always been a little different. Western progressives thought of themselves as practical, equalitarian, and nationalist. Some of them had long thought of progress as something that had to be achieved against Eastern opposition; others thought, like E. A. Ross, that Eastern progressives were addicted to "investors' idealism." Now many believed the Hearst press when it said that war talk came from Anglophile bankers and profiteers. Other Western progressives were simply not much interested. The Non-Partisan League, for instance, was too busy fighting bankers and millers to fight Germans. Even after 1917 the villains in *Non-Partisan Leader* cartoons wore silk hats more often than spiked helmets.

It would be wrong to exaggerate, as some worried Easterners exaggerated, the antiwar tendencies of the West. Nobody was more active or fervent in the Allied cause than the Indiana novelists Booth Tarkington and Meredith Nicholson. In every Midwestern city and college town it was the local defenders of culture who felt most keenly the duty of fighting provincial backwardness, and sometimes the fight was extremely bitter on both sides.

The crucial section of opinion was the middle class of the northern Mississippi Valley, a group which considered itself the real backbone of American civilization. One immediate reaction of this section to the war was the hope that it would end, once and for all, the European nonsense of kings and aristocracies and military pomp. This might, for Europe, be worth all the fighting. When it came to America's role, few in the Midwest outside the circles of leading citizens wanted to go to war to defend either England or the tradition of Western European culture. If war became necessary for the defense of American rights, that would be different.

The events of 1915–17, with war alternately coming closer and receding, made the West impatient. The tendency that gained most from this impatience was neither isolationism nor interventionism but nationalism. By the spring of 1917 most Midwesterners apparently concluded that there was nothing left to do but beat the Germans and get it over with. Once in the war, the Midwest was determined to show what it could do. It became even more impatient with dissent than the East. But this determined nationalism was by no means the same thing as the fervent belief of the custodians of culture that war would restore the authority of their tradition. The country became united for war, but those who thought that the West had finally accepted Eastern views were due for a series of postwar shocks.

Progressives were divided on ideological as well as regional lines. Those who took the strongest pro-Allied position were those who believed most completely in the whole of the dominant credo, those to whom moralism and culture were inseparable from progress. To those who were used to interpreting events in moral terms, Wilson's or even Roosevelt's attitude toward the war made sense. To those who were devoted to Anglo-Saxon culture, it was obviously more likely that wickedness should stem from Germany than from England.

Pragmatic progressives faced a more difficult problem. Obviously the spokesmen of relativist social science and philosophy could not make up their minds about the war by simple moral generalizations. Much depended, for his many admirers, on the decision of John Dewey in particular.

Clearly, to Dewey the war could not mean the revival of idealism. In fact he thought one kind of idealism had had a good deal to do with starting it. In 1915 Dewey, who had long been moving farther and farther from his Hegelian origins, published a brilliant and hostile sketch of *German Philosophy and Politics*. The villain's role was given to Kant, who had taught the Germans to separate the spheres of general ideas and practical affairs. This to Dewey was the cardinal intellectual sin, and it was this dualistic habit of thought that permitted the Germans to be at once idealistic and brutal, to be scientists and philosophers and yet give disciplined support to the military state.

Inclined to dislike the German Empire, Dewey was also inclined to dislike pacifism, which he found tiresomely "Tolstoian" and absolutistic. Yet war was hard to reconcile with the "method of intelligence." Like other Americans, Dewey had to make a difficult break with his past assumptions in order to deal at all with this great crisis, and the easy emotional responses of many of his contemporaries were ruled out by his principles. Wrestling with this hard problem, writing more than usual about concrete political matters, Dewey gradually worked out a position. Perhaps his decision was right; even his admirers have seldom found his statement of it altogether satisfying.

In two articles of 1916, one in the *New Republic* and the other in the *International Journal of Ethics*, Dewey stated his conclusions on the problem of force. Force, and in this term Dewey here included physical power of all kinds, making no separation between accomplishment of work and coercion of people, was ethically neutral. When it was harnessed efficiently for purposes, it was energy; when it ran wild and was not related to ends, it was violence. The question of its legitimacy, he said over and over, was purely a question of efficiency.

Obviously commenting on conventional pro-Allied rhetoric, Dewey deplored the fact that men justified war in behalf of emotionally charged words like "honor, liberty, civilization, divine purpose and destiny." War had "concrete results on earth," and had to be condemned as mere violence unless it could be shown to be "the most economical method of securing the results which are desirable with a minimum of the undesirable results."

This meant that approval of war was at least conceivable, and Dewey showed marked and increasing impatience with pacifists. "Squeamishness about force," he said, was "the mark not of idealistic but of moonstruck morals." Pacifists were wrong from the beginning because they believed the origins of war to lie in man's nature rather than in objective causes. Absolutistic libertarians were as misguided as absolutistic patriots or pacifists. Like the question of war

> the question of the limits of individual powers, or liberties, or rights, is finally a question of the most efficient use of means for ends. That at a certain period liberty should have been set up as something antecedently sacred per se is natural enough. . . . But it is as an efficiency factor that its value must ultimately be assessed.[4]

[4] Dewey: *Characters and Events*, II, 789.

In the Spring of 1917, just before Congress declared war, Dewey decided that the intelligent decision was to support, and thereby try to use for good, American intervention. Announcing this decision in the *Seven Arts,* he spoke of the war and the Germans in remarkably Wilsonian terms:

> As I write, we seem to be on the point of arriving at the conclusion that we cannot aid, by means of a passive compliance, the triumph of a nation that regards its triumph as the one thing so necessary that all means whatsoever that lead to that triumph are not only legitimate but sacred.

Yet Dewey insisted that even with participation our "national hesitation" must not be ended; we must force the Allies to fight on our terms for (one is a little surprised to encounter these terms in this connection) "Democracy and civilization." [5]

This decision, and the grounds on which it was made, were deeply disturbing to many radicals and pacifists who had admired Dewey. Jane Addams, taken to task personally, though not impolitely, by Dewey in the coming months, was to express her feelings only much later. Nearly all her generation of progressives, she had said, had admired the great leaders of pragmatism. Now however, Dewey's position seemed to make impossible all determined resistance to the course of events. Miss Addams could neither abandon her own pacifism, nor defend it, in the midst of wartime hysteria, on the ground that it would influence events. She had to search for other grounds.[6] Her decision may have been hasty; in the long run pacifism may have been effective. But at the time it seemed to many that in this profound crisis, Dewey's method of making choices had proved emotionally and intellectually inadequate.

Dewey's reasons for supporting the war differed from those of the Wilsonian idealists; Thorstein Veblen's differed still more. Veblen, like Dewey, made up his mind with some difficulty. Imperial Ger-

[5] Dewey: "In a Time of National Hesitation," *Seven Arts,* May 1917, p. 6.

[6] Addams: *Bread and Peace in Time of War* (New York, 1922), esp. pp. 141–51.

many, he pointed out in detail in his book of 1915, was at once more efficient than capitalist England and more alarming: its way of thought and life were deeply permeated by barbaric survivals.

Yet patriotism, to Veblen, was dangerously anachronistic and preparedness a serious form of sabotage of production. He seriously considered the relative economic advantages of surrender to Germany. Finally he decided that the disadvantages of such a course would be decisive. Under German rule insubordination, in which he placed his hopes, would be more difficult. Full of doubt, and surrendering little of his status as an iconoclast, he inclined to the Allied side.

One more figure with some following among the Young Intellectuals took a position hostile to Germany, but not pro-Allied. George Santayana in 1917 lambasted *Egotism in German Philosophy* more strongly than Dewey. Yet toward the war Santayana retained a position of almost inhuman detachment. Neither side, as he said in private letters from the beginning, offered much hope for the survival of the mature, classic Europe which had all his allegiance.[7]

To the young rebels, as to everybody else, the outbreak of war was a severe shock. It did not lead them to abandon rebellion; on the contrary, the collapse of European culture seemed to some of them to make their own activities more important. Only in America could youth and joy and art survive. To Susan Glaspell and George Cram Cook, their mission was "to keep alive in the world the light of imagination," and they could fulfill this mission best through the Provincetown Players.[8] The *Seven Arts* staff listened gladly to Romain Rolland urging them to keep the arts alive and also to throw off European convention, now more than ever discredited.

[7] Daniel Cory, ed.: *The Letters of George Santayana* (New York, 1943), pp. 138–9.

[8] Glaspell: *Road to the Temple*, p. 267.

This is what the *Seven Arts* Group had intended to do anyway.

For much of the Rebellion the war, after the initial horror of its outbreak, stayed in the background. Anguish over distant events, no matter how terrible, is a hard emotion for most people to sustain. The current controversies were close at hand. The year 1915, when submarine warfare first brought the shadow of actual involvement to America, was also probably the peak year of the prewar Rebellion, the year of *Spoon River*, the Provincetown Players, and *America's Coming of Age*. The year 1916, when the nation first drew closer to war and then seemed to back determinedly away, saw a slight decline in cultural controversy. Yet this was the year of *Chicago Poems*, *Windy McPherson's Son*, and the *Seven Arts*.

Sooner or later, everybody had to take some sort of a position with regard to the war, even if it were to be one of determined aloofness. When the time came to decide, many of the Young Intellectuals found their emotions very complex.

Obviously the extreme pro-Allied camp represented everything the Rebellion disliked most. When the custodians of culture talked about a revival of patriotic idealism, they seemed to Young Intellectuals to be using terms almost unbelievably obsolete. When they hoped that the war would purge Europe and America of decadence and irresponsibility, they were asking for an end of all that the Rebellion most admired.

At the other extreme, some of the ardent opponents of war were persuasive. Few of the Young Intellectuals, admirers of Wells and sometimes of Nietzsche, were pacifists, and yet Jane Addams was not a figure they could altogether ignore. On Henry Ford's much derided peace ship, the sailing list included such interesting figures as Ben Lindsey, the innovating judge; Inez Milholland, the beautiful and advanced feminist; and B. W. Huebsch, one of the Rebellion's favorite publishers. Mencken's steadfast skepticism became more compelling when Mencken was attacked. Some Young Intellectuals read *Pearson's*, where Frank Harris continued as long as he could to contrast socialized Germany with arrogant, aristocratic

England, the country which had persecuted Wilde and scorned Shaw.

The daring of the I.W.W. leaders and Emma Goldman, roundly condemning all war, could not help being impressive. Whether or not the Young Intellectuals accepted their whole case against war, they instinctively agreed that pro-Allied and patriotic slogans, like other old-fashioned moralistic slogans, smelled of decay.

And yet the pull was not all one way. It is very important to remember that the prewar Young Intellectual, cynical as he was about the official uplift sponsored by the older custodians, was himself full of both idealism and optimism. Sacrifice for a cause was not, in itself, unattractive to these young believers in the claim of the emotions. It was not easy to resist the call of beleaguered France. European culture was not all old-fashioned, and France, as much as any country, represented what was new.

The older American leaders whom the Young Intellectuals most respected inclined, for the most part, to a cautious and complicated support of the Allies. Dewey, Veblen, and Charles Beard all came down on this side. Hating war, hating still more surrender to old-fashioned leaders and old-fashioned emotions, yet stirred and pulled like everybody else, the leaders of the Rebellion reacted to war in a number of ways, nearly all leading in the long run to unhappiness and alienation.

Only a very few became, before 1917, fervently pro-Allied. Amy Lowell, between battles in the trenches of poetry, served like other women of her class in Allied bazaars. Naturally, by 1917, she was saying that the idealism of the Allied cause had been prefigured in the idealism of the poetic revival. A little later she was writing poems about poisoned candy that Germans gave children. To some irreverent young poets, all this simply proved what they had suspected, that the official leader of the new poetry didn't belong in the movement.[9]

Some young writers felt an emotion which seemed to their elders

[9] Damon: *Lowell*, pp. 447, 717–21.

to be enthusiasm for the Allies and was really something quite different: enthusiasm for war as a personal test. Alan Seeger, a Harvard poet and an acquaintance, at least, of some of the Young Intellectuals, enlisted in the French army as soon as he could. His youthful and moving letters are full of love of the French country and peasants, concern about gallantry under fire, and general exuberance. He repudiates, however, any dislike of Germans and says practically nothing about war aims.[1] Though Seeger became, with his death, one of the first American war heroes, his set of emotions had little in common with official stereotypes.

Younger than the youngest generation of the prewar Rebellion, a group of enthusiastic adolescents was finding its way straight from college, or even high school, into the French or Italian ambulance corps. Some of these were as idealistic about the war as their elders expected them to be, but many were interested in experience rather than in a cause. Living longer than Seeger, some of these young veterans eventually combined nostalgia and disillusion, respect for wartime heroism with hatred of civilian heroics. "I was always embarrassed," one of these men made his hero say later, "by the words sacred, glorious, and sacrifice, and the expression in vain." [2]

Still smaller than the fervently pro-Allied group among the Young Intellectuals but more conspicuous was the pro-German coterie. George Sylvester Viereck became such a fervent and official advocate of Germany that in later years his earlier reputation as a poet of sex freedom was almost forgotten. Like the most extreme German intellectuals he wrote odes to the Kaiser and songs of hate against England.[3] A few others were so rebellious against official Anglophilia that they followed Mencken into admiration for the other side. Willard Huntington Wright, who was conducting a not unjustified campaign against the *Encyclopaedia Britannica* for its neglect of modern continental art and literature, was perhaps the second most conspicuous example. To the champions

[1] Alan Seeger: *Letters and Diary* (New York, 1917), p. 141 and *passim.*

[2] Ernest Hemingway: *A Farewell to Arms* (New York, 1929), p. 196.

[3] Viereck's wartime poems, as well as his others are quoted in *My Flesh and Blood* (New York, 1931).

of idealism and war, these few examples of "decadence" and pro-Germanism laid the basis for a stereotype.[4]

Ludwig Lewisohn represented a somewhat larger group: those who were not pro-German, but were suspected of being so and thereby forced into some degree of disaffection. Lewisohn, who had written about modern German literature, was teaching his subject at Ohio State University. Like some other Midwestern universities, Ohio State was full of militant champions of the Allies, eager to atone for the shortcomings of the region. Persecution led Lewisohn to contrast German art and literature more sharply than ever with American, and especially Midwestern, materialism and Puritanism. His wartime experience lent a bitter tone to his important postwar critical work.[5]

The most common reaction of the literary rebels to war in Europe was not primarily a preference for one side or the other, but sheer dismay. As William Carlos Williams put it, "everything I wanted to see live and thrive was being deliberately murdered in the name of church and state." Naturally the most hopeful and the least cynical were hardest hit. Vachel Lindsay's war poems, denouncing war propaganda as the ultimate sin and calling on his pacifist heroes, Buddha, St. Francis, Tolstoy, and Christ, are full of suffering.[6] They are not good poems; the spontaneous, mystical enthusiasm of Lindsay and many other Chicago poets was not a method that could be used to deal with complex tragedy.

The war strengthened the few important figures within the Rebellion who had never shared the movement's optimistic mood. Pound was already so hostile to contemporary society that war could hardly deepen his alienation. Writing to Harriet Monroe in 1914, he found on both sides of the war only "atavism and the loathsome spirit of mediocrity, cloaked in graft," and thought the war only "a symptom of the real disease" of civilization. The loss of

[4] Willard Huntington Wright: "England's Intellectual Colonization of America," *Seven Arts*, February 1917, pp. 395–401.

[5] See his *Upstream* (New York, 1922), *passim*.

[6] Williams: *Autobiography*, p. 158; Lindsay: *Collected Poems* (New York, 1925), pp. 375–90.

his sculptor friend, Gaudier-Brzeska, seemed to him more serious than the destruction of Rheims cathedral. He disliked England in wartime so much that he left it as soon as he could. Yet Pound, more than most prewar writers, retained in a strange way a kind of balance, a kind that he was to lose in a later war. At the time and afterward, he remained convinced that a Hohenzollern victory would have been the worse of the two alternatives.[7] And unlike most prewar poets, he was able fairly early to master his hatred of the war sufficiently to express it in poetry.

Lacking the resources of pessimism, valuable resources in time of catastrophe, many of the leaders of the rebellion floundered around in search of escape. Some simply moved out of town, and away from constant war talk. This motive had something to do with the establishment of the poetic colony at Grantwood, New Jersey, and also with Provincetown. Others had to turn inward for relief. Mabel Dodge went from radicalism to psychoanalysis; Sherwood Anderson felt "compelled to little playful things." John Gould Fletcher repudiated all mechanical civilization and turned toward the contemplation of nature. (He had started on a road that was to lead to a variety of Southern agrarianism.[8])

That portion of the intellectual rebellion which was specifically concerned with politics as well as art had to face the problem of war directly. The *New Republic* followed a somewhat shifting course roughly parallel to Dewey's. It opposed both pacifism and uncritical, emotional patriotism, was calm and skeptical about atrocity stories and opposed to any suggestion of war for abstract principles rather than concrete purposes. Staggered by the world-wide explosion of violence, the editors none the less pinned their hopes bravely in the power of human reason:

> We cannot abandon the labor of thought. However crude and weak it may be, it is the only force that can pierce the agglomerated passion and wrong-headedness of this disaster.[9]

[7] Quoted in Hoffmann: *The Twenties*, p. 167.

[8] Luhan: *Movers and Shakers*, p. 303; Sherwood Anderson: *Letters* (H. M. Jones, ed., Boston, 1953), pp. 28–29; Fletcher: *Life*, pp. 260–1.

[9] *New Republic*, editorial, November 7, 1914, p. 7.

Yet the *New Republic* was too sophisticated in the ideas of the Liberation, in the anti-rationalism of Wells and Bergson and even Freud, to sustain its hope that reason could prevail. A Lippmannesque editorial of 1915 described the appeal, to these activists, of colossal action:

> That calm moral grandeur in which we revelled a year ago, when it seemed as if we were destined to be the arbiter of nations, is no more. It has given place to a strange restlessness and discontent. Instead of the thankfulness that we are providentially escaping the storm, one finds on every hand the sense that we are missing something.[1]

In war as in peace, the *New Republic* wished to channel and direct, not to repress, emotion. What was needed was to abandon old-fashioned isolationism and undertake bold and active leadership for peace. Neither the magazine itself nor Lippmann and Weyl in their wartime books found it easy to explain just what this meant. All advanced countries, including Germany, should join in a League which would administer the backward areas of the earth. When Wilson's policies seemed to include this plan, the *New Republic* veered to his support, only to court disillusion.

The *Masses*, contemptuous of involved argument, expressed its feelings about war in graphic symbols. Christ was in jail, greedy profiteers were celebrating. A carload of virgins, leaving for inland strongholds to avoid rape by possible invaders, cast interested glances behind them. Max Eastman himself, after a brief visit to France, announced that the war was a bore, and that he personally cared more about being allowed to lie on a bench in Washington Square when he was tired than about being allowed to ride on a British vessel through the submarine zone. This was no use: Eastman could never overcome his ministerial inheritance enough to be as irresponsible as he wanted to be. Neither he nor the *Masses* could sustain the tone of radical gaiety.

In 1916 Mitchell Kennerley, who published many of the writings of the anti-interventionists, persuaded Eastman to write a book

[1] *Editorial*, "The Reality of Peace," October 30, 1915, p. 322.

called *Understanding Germany*.[2] A little didactically, Eastman announced in the introduction that he did not feel patriotic toward any country, and planned to explore the emotions of war with the help of William McDougall and Sigmund Freud. Using Dewey and Veblen as well, Eastman tried to explain how Germany had become what she was, and why there were atrocities on all sides. Whatever was the right policy it was not, he was sure, preparedness. We must fight warlike feelings in ourselves by learning the mechanism of the emotions. Yet Eastman had said consistently in the *Masses* that he was in favor of a German defeat.

Bewildered and unhappy, at once skeptical and idealistic, saddened by the threatened interruption of their renaissance, repelled by the moralistic bloodthirstiness of their old opponents, the Young Intellectuals had no answers whatever for the problems of war. Eager to resist pressures, they were yet very conscious of the pull of emotions toward participation in a great experience. Some turned entirely inward or back toward the gospel of art, a few finally crossed the line into committed antiwar radicalism. Many, probably most, turned for a while, full of misgivings, toward the leadership of Woodrow Wilson. He was, at least, an intellectual, though not a Young Intellectual in any conceivable sense, and he was resisting the Roosevelts and Abbotts. In 1916 Eastman and even Reed supported him for re-election, deserting their socialist commitments. The *New Republic* conscientiously labored to destroy its old picture of Wilson, the old-fashioned moralist, and to construct a new picture of Wilson, the intelligent, astute leader of realistic action in the cause of peace.

❦

It is not part of our purpose to say which of the conflicting pictures of Wilson is the true one; the argument will never be settled, and it cannot even be entered without a detailed examination of

[2] Eastman: *Enjoyment of Living*, pp. 541–2.

the mountainous evidence, month by month and week by week. Here, it is enough to say that most contemporary pictures and some later ones were ridiculous: Wilson the trembling pacifist, Wilson the sly and unscrupulous warmonger, Wilson the masterly, confident leader. He was a far more complex person than he seemed.

As much as any Young Intellectual, Wilson had always felt the tug of emotion against the strong leash he had learned was necessary. With the custodians of culture he shared, at least from 1915 and probably earlier, the almost instinctive certainty that the cause of the Allies was that of civilization. They knew this, they knew that he believed in punishing the guilty, and that he felt the conduct of the Germans inexcusable. This belief that he must really agree with them was what made them so angry at his hesitations. Yet he sounded sometimes like a pacifist, had real and deep pacifist inclinations, and at times could not restrain his dark insights into the consequences of war for the kind of civilization he treasured. Most consistently he cherished the old dream of keeping American leadership utterly clean, unstained by blood and passion, ready to exert the leadership for which the nation's whole history prepared her.

The result of Wilson's internal divisions was that he was eloquent, sincerely eloquent, in favor of several successive incompatible policies: neutrality in thought and deed, punishment of the transgressors, being too proud to fight, strict accountability for American lives lost, a peace of compromise, and commitment to Allied victory. On the surface, and in support of several of these positions for a short time, he seemed determined and confident. Yet he was always tortured by doubts before a major decision, and had to search within for certainty that was not easily forthcoming. When after contemplation, often after a brief move in an opposite direction, he committed himself to a course, it could never be merely the best bet in a difficult situation. It had to be absolutely right, in both immediate and ultimate terms. Like many of his countrymen, Wilson demanded both practical results and a clear conscience.

In the spring of 1917 the inevitable answer to the problem of intervention seemed to reveal itself with unusual clarity. On January 22, Wilson made his strongest demand for a peace of conciliation and was hailed by doubters and pacifists as their champion. Then a week later the German government announced, with the full realization that it would mean American entry into war, the resumption of submarine warfare against belligerent and neutral alike. In March a huge ambiguity was removed from the Allied cause by the Russian Revolution. As Wilson explained, voicing the current myth about Russia, the Russian people, always "democratic at heart," had moved "in all their naïve majesty and might." Finally Germany was disclosed to be plotting, in case of war, combined action with Mexico and Japan, as the *Omaha World-Herald* put it "to turn loose upon the United States—our own country—the hordes of alien and inferior civilizations." [3] Yet Wilson still hesitated, while ships were sunk and passions mounted.

By the time the president called a special session of Congress at the beginning of April, the emotions of the most respectable citizens had reached a dangerous pitch. The clergy were already condemning pacifists from the pulpits. In New York the Mayor's Committee announced that it had secured a million signatures for its giant pledge, a pledge not only of unconditional loyalty to the country but of support for the President. Everywhere public-spirited citizens were warning the police to be ready for huge demonstrations by pro-German pacifists. In Baltimore, the day before Wilson's war message, rioters broke up a meeting at which David Starr Jordan was to talk under the auspices of the American League against Militarism. The *New York Times*, ardently interventionist, noticed that the mob was led by "men socially prominent," including "college professors, students, bankers and lawyers." [4]

In contrast to the high pitch of popular emotion, Wilson's speech to Congress was perhaps the least bellicose war speech since Lincoln. It was a genuinely great and stirring expression of the best qualities of the civilization Wilson so completely represented, the

[3] Quoted in *Literary Digest*, March 17, 1917, p. 689.
[4] *New York Times*, March 3, p. 6; April 1, p. 2; April 2, p. 1.

civilization of the United States in the recent past. It was, the President said, "a distressing and oppressive duty," a "fearful thing to lead this great peaceful people into war." Not only did he twice insist on the country's friendly feeling toward the oppressed German people, he demanded that this friendliness be demonstrated in American treatment of German-Americans, always excepting the very small hostile minority. The solemn choice, he insisted,

> must be made with a moderation of counsel and a temperateness of judgment befitting our character and our motives as a nation. We must put excited feeling away.

We were, as other countries were becoming, responsible to the familiar and simple moral code:

> We are at the beginning of an age in which it will be insisted upon that the same standards of conduct and of responsibility for wrong done shall be observed among nations and their governments that are observed among the individual citizens of civilized states.

Finally, in his majestic peroration, echoing perhaps unconsciously his first inaugural, Wilson told his listeners that our war aims were simply our old ideals:

> We shall fight for the things which we have always carried nearest our hearts, for democracy, for the right of those who submit to authority to have a voice in their own Governments, for the rights and liberties of small nations, for a universal dominion of right. . . .

In such a cause "America is privileged to spend her blood and might. . . . God helping her, she can do no other."

The war message, like several of Wilson's great war speeches to come, tugged at the emotions even of those who hated the prospect of war. Obviously these were the words of a man of peace. For the moment only the most strong-minded and the most completely disaffected pessimists could altogether resist the hope held out.

Those who had long thought of the war as America's destiny found Wilson for once exactly the leader the country needed: Barrett Wendell's doubts were almost overcome; Senator Lodge shook Wilson's hand; Theodore Roosevelt called the speech a great state paper.

It was more; it was an enduring monument to a whole passing period of American civilization. Its assumptions and its purposes embodied the country's conception of itself and of the world. Unfortunately they had little to do with the particular war Wilson was talking about, and, in their most literal aspects, little to do with history itself. The most famous phrase, for instance, asserted that the world must be made safe for democracy. For a long time, a great many different people had demonstrated that the world was not and never would be safe for anything, let alone that precarious product of hard work and good fortune, democracy. This phrase, within a decade, was to be quoted very frequently as an example of all that was most facile and obsolete in the credo of Wilson's generation.

Since Wilson was unaware of much that had been happening to American civilization, he could not have foreseen, even in his keenest flashes of insight, what the war would bring; division and disaster to the old American civilization, and to the many sided rebellion against it, at once victory and unhappiness.

III

The War and After

The chapter of intellectual history that began in April 1917 is a separate subject, too interesting to be treated summarily. Yet no break in history is complete, and it is necessary to carry forward a few threads in order to complete the pattern.

The response to Wilson's speech was a great outpouring of energy and sacrifice and then, after a few months of curious calm, a mighty outburst of emotion. Idealism and Utopianism about the war went beyond all limits, and so, despite Wilson's warnings, did hatred. For this, contrary to some postwar legend, the administration itself was not directly responsible. Even the much-maligned Committee on Public Information tried to stimulate enthusiasm and still discourage undue vindictiveness or suspicion. As Wilson had apparently foreseen, this proved impossible. If, as he now told the country, the Allies and their cause were entirely good, the enemy must be entirely bad. In the world Wilson's wartime speeches painted, only the Germans and their sympathizers stood in the way of the millennial, world-wide triumph of American ideas.

Historians during two waves of revulsion against war emotions have described what happened with almost loving completeness. The actual violence can be exaggerated, though ugly incidents occurred when war gave authority to the psychopathic few, as it did for instance in some federal prisons. But the mental debauch is hard to overstate. Not only were radical and pacifist tendencies fairly thoroughly suppressed, but the lukewarm, the reticent, or the unpolitical were often hounded and pilloried. Teaching the German language, speaking it, retaining souvenirs of the old country were forbidden in German-American areas by official and unofficial action. Respectable people, of kindly emotions and gentle manners, repeated atrocity stories, full of detailed invention with obvious sexual overtones. Liberal ministers preached the *jehad* with the full accompaniment of promised salvation to killers of the infidel; pulpits rang with denuciations of pacifists, radicals, moderates, and, not least, those who supported the war but refused to make this a matter of religious faith.

Discussion of the war and its causes had been freer in the Civil War, it was to be far freer in World War II, it was less sharply restricted in 1914–18 in England or Germany. Hysteria of this kind is a complex and puzzling phenomenon; it cannot be explained with a few simple references to propaganda.

Part of the explanation lies in the story we have been telling: America went into the war in a period of apparent complacency and underlying, sharply increasing tension. Enemies of the war were often in fact, and were always believed to be, opponents of the dominant American civilization on other counts. Some were radicals, some were foreigners, some were believers in new ideas. The *Saturday Evening Post* urged that the "scum of the melting pot" must now finally be cleaned out of the schools, the press, and the government and insisted that those who defended German music must belong in one of two well-known categories, radicals or half-baked dreamers.

The outpouring of hate was matched by an equally irrational crescendo of hope. The war, according to many editors and critics, was not only going to bring back idealism here and in Europe; it was going to give rise to a purer religion. Some went further; quite a few were certain that the sacrificial atmosphere of the camps and trenches was going to turn our youth away from sexual impurity. One point more, implied since 1914, was now made explicit: the war was going to produce in America and the Allied countries a new and noble literature. Joyce Kilmer, who had denounced modern poetry for several years, came to this cheerful conclusion in the trenches; Stuart P. Sherman was able to reach it at home.

The period is full of irony, and there is much irony in the fact that Sherman, more than any other person, riveted together wartime political orthodoxy and conventional literary taste. Sherman had never been quite able to subdue his own impulses toward tolerance and even skepticism. In May 1917 he wrote in strict confidence to his mentor Paul Elmer More that he hated the war and doubted whether any abstractions were really worth fighting for. Brooding about bloodshed had made him suspect even that "there was something rotten in our damned ideals." [1] In a letter from Sherman to More, the language was as striking as the sentiment.

In 1915, however, Sherman had written a hostile series of articles for the *Nation* about different kinds of realism. He had pitched into Dreiser particularly hard, and had pointed out obliquely that his novels and characters were not only amoral but non-Anglo-Saxon.

> I am greatly impressed by them as serious representatives of a new note in American literature, coming from the "ethnic" element of our mixed population which, as we are assured by competent authorities, is to redeem us from Puritanism. . . .

When half the world, Sherman went on, meaning the Kaiser's half, accepts a theory which makes human behavior simply animal, it is reassuring that "the other half arises in battle. And so one turns with relief from Mr. Dreiser's novels to the morning paper." [2]

This attack, associating Dreiser with the Germans, had come just before the assault of the censors on *The Genius*. Naturally the Young Intellectuals, not all admirers of Dreiser but all enemies of suppression, sailed in to counterattack not only the Vice Society but also Sherman. They were reinforced by an older and more skillful literary battler, H. L. Mencken. In an article on Dreiser published in the *Seven Arts* in August 1917, in the same issue with the famous rejections of the war by Bourne and Reed, Mencken handled Sherman with a most effective type of contemptuous patronage, treating him not as a serious antagonist, but as an inflated,

[1] Sherman to More, May 1, 1917, in Jacob Zeitlin and Homer Woodbridge, eds.: *Life and Letters of Stuart P. Sherman* (New York, 1929), I, 315.

[2] Stuart P. Sherman: "The Naturalism of Mr. Dreiser," *Nation*, December 2, 1915, pp. 648, 650.

didactic, academic young fool. This article was reprinted in 1917 in Mencken's *A Book of Prefaces.*

In November of that year, Sherman, full of complex wartime emotions and also of personal pique, gave his cause away in a *Nation* review of *A Book of Prefaces.* Imitating Mencken's own manner, Sherman reviewed his adversary's preferences in continental literature, commented on his habit of using German phrases, reminded his readers of the book on Nietzsche, and accused Mencken, accurately, of sympathy with the German cause. But this was not all: Sherman listed all the iconoclasts he could think of, all the people in any way associated with the literary rebellion, who had central European names, including Huneker, Lewisohn, Untermeyer, Viereck, Otto Heller, and Knopf. His peroration was as Menckenesque as he could make it:

> (Mencken's) continuous laudation of a Teutonic-Oriental pessimism and nihilism in philosophy, of anti-democratic politics, of the subjection and contempt of women, of the Herrenmoral, and of anything but Anglo-Saxon civilization, is not precisely and strictly aesthetic criticism; an unsympathetic person might call it infatuated propagandism.[3]

This not very distinguished polemic accomplished two things: it helped to make the war years unpleasant for Mencken, and it made him far more than before the favorite champion of the younger generation, whose major organs and leading spokesmen rallied angrily to his defense.

Sherman denied that he had meant to attack anybody on the basis of nationality. This was not the last time, however, that he linked together non-Anglo-Saxon origins, pro-German sentiments, and dangerous literary tastes. In a speech of December 1917, reprinted and very widely circulated as an official release of the Committee on Public Information, Sherman pointed again to the literary enemies of the republic. Along with the well-known activi-

[3] Sherman: "Beautifying American Literature," *Nation*, November 29, 1917, p. 594.

ties of actual spies there existed he said, "an anti-American campaign of a more insidious character," conducted "ostensibly" by American citizens in the English language. Their method was to praise everything German and, especially, to attack everything of English origin in America, including moral and humanitarian reform, the recognized classics of American literature, and "the Puritans who since the seventeenth century have constituted the moral backbone of the nation." What these enemies especially singled out for praise was the decadent literature of Berlin and Vienna, "especially that nastiest part of it which they are certain will offend what they scoffingly call the Puritanical sensibilities of Americans." [4]

Not alone, but together with others who hinted the same things, Sherman had linked together the different components of two stereotypes. For some of his readers, he had inked in the image of the immoral, subversive, polyglot, materialist, decadent, pro-German intellectual. For others, probably for more in the long run, he had created the opposite image of the racially prejudiced, sexually timid, pro-Comstock, politically reactionary Anglo-Saxon believer in prohibition and righteous bloodshed, the fanatical defender of James Russell Lowell and Woodrow Wilson. Neither of these sitting ducks existed in literal fact, both drew heavy fire in the controversies of the twenties, and neither is quite dead yet.

❦

Despite Sherman and its other enemies, the diverse literary revolution survived the war; it was in fact entering its most brilliant and diverse phase. Yet one phase of this revolution, the gay and innocent prewar Rebellion, was over. One can see this change in magazine history; some of the Rebellion's most characteristic organs were early casualties of the war years.

[4] Sherman: *American and Allied Ideals: An Appeal to Those Who Are Neither Hot nor Cold* (War Information Series No. 12, Washington, D.C., 1918), p. 7.

Kennerley's *Forum* might have gone down even without the war; it did not make money in its brilliant rebellious period. In 1916 it went back to the family of its former publisher, Isaac Rice. Literary radicalism was immediately eliminated, and so was the magazine's tendency toward skepticism of the Allied cause. In its first issue under the new management the *Forum* adopted the two slogans "Public Service" and "America First," and printed a super-orthodox attack on those who would tolerate radical dissent.

The *Masses*, despite its intermittent Wilsonian tendencies and its increasing caution, could not survive the change of climate; its death and the bare escape of its editors from jail sentences became part of radical legend. Its spirit could never be revived; the end of its breezy defiance signaled the loss of much that had been most fresh and original in American radicalism. Literary rebellion and the political left, although they were to come together again, never met in such a free and unforced union. The *Seven Arts*, most ardently American of the prewar little magazines, sure of a swelling American renaissance, full of poems to Whitman and Lincoln and even apostrophes to Wilson, refused to suppress the outspoken, wholehearted rejections of the war contributed by John Reed and Randolph Bourne. Its sponsor, frightened, withdrew its subsidy, and this last and best representative of the prewar Rebellion went down with all its flags flying.

There were of course rebellious magazines left. The *New Republic* continued to argue with itself about literature and art as well as the war. The *Little Review* published a blank page headed "The War" in its April, 1917 number and went on its insouciant way. New allies of the rebels appeared from unlikely quarters. To the horror of its old readers, Villard's *Nation* veered sharply left. The *Dial*, recently converted to the new literature, was revamped again in 1918. With a brilliant staff and frequent articles by Thorstein Veblen, it skirted the limits of wartime radicalism. By the early twenties a whole new crop of rebellious magazines was ready to take over.

All that was gone was the special flavor of a brief episode: the prewar mixture of exuberant innovation, cheerful mysticism, insistent spontaneity, and certainty that everything was turning out superbly. This could hardly have lasted; it was a program for revolution without cost.

❦

The war and its emotions passed with extraordinary suddenness. To see the full meaning of the story that ended in 1917 it is necessary to look beyond the wartime enthusiasm and beyond the complementary, savage disillusion of the postwar years. At some time long after the Armistice whistles had stopped blowing, it became apparent that a profound change had taken place in American civilization, a change that affected all the contenders in the prewar cultural strife. This was the end of American innocence. Innocence, the absence of guilt and doubt and the complexity that goes with them, had been the common characteristic of the older culture and its custodians, of most of the progressives, most of the relativists and social scientists, and of the young leaders of the prewar Rebellion. This innocence had often been rather precariously maintained. Many had glimpsed a world whose central meaning was neither clear nor cheerful, but very few had come to live in such a world as a matter of course. Exceptions to innocence had existed in all camps—they had included unhappy elder thinkers like Henry Adams, rueful naturalists like Dreiser, and vigorous skeptics like Mencken. None of these had yet deeply affected the country's image of itself; all, including Henry Adams, who died in 1918, were to become influential in the twenties.

This change, on the way for a long time and precipitated by the war, is worth looking at very briefly as it affected several segments of the increasingly divided nation. The most obvious aspect of change was the complete disintegration of the old order, the set of ideas which had dominated the American mind so effectively from the mid-nineteenth century until 1912. The heresies of the nineties had undermined this set of beliefs; the Rebellion had successfully defied it; the twenties hardly had to fight it. After the war it was hard to find a convincing or intellectually respectable spokesman for the prewar faith. The old moral idealism had become a caricature of Woodrow Wilson; the old culture was an inaccurate memory of Howells.

Progress, right after the war, seemed to be equally shattered, and various types of reaction, long present beneath the surface, thrust militantly into the open. Racial violence reached an all-time high; the Fundamentalists made their most extreme and pathetic efforts to crush the liberalism which had seemed to them oppressive. A little later, in the mid-twenties, something else which had been latent before the war reached a position of great power: the ultra-practical, anti-intellectual, pseudoidealistic gospel of Prosperity First.

Yet many have denied that progressivism perished completely. Certainly it would be foolish to say that Americans lost their capacity for social innovation: in different ways both the twenties and the thirties saw more changes than the century's first decade. What was gone was the prewar *kind* of progressivism with its supreme confidence. This had been closely linked to moralism and culture; it could not survive without them.

Later political history was to make this change and some of its meaning clear. In the twenties, a number of promising attempts to form a progressive coalition failed. Most of the components, including liberal leaders and several kinds of articulate discontent, were present. What was lacking was the old idealistic cement, the thing that had made representatives of opposing interests sing hymns for Roosevelt or wipe their eyes over a Wilson peroration. Even the New Deal, much more thorough in its innovations than prewar progressivism had ever been, suffered from a serious—in the long run, perhaps a disastrous—lack of ideology.

The general belief in progress as the direction of history suffered quite as much as political progressivism. In the twenties and after, progress in this sense was repudiated by many of the most admired American novelists and poets. Before the war, most of the literary rebels had believed in progress as strongly as their opponents, though they had defined it differently. After the war, typical attitudes of writers ranged from Eliot's religious conservatism to Jeffers's naturalistic despair. The precise moment of change can be seen in one famous case, the wartime metamorphosis of Randolph Bourne. Bourne did not move all the way, before his death in 1918, to pessimism. He did, however, lose completely his confidence in the state. Formerly an exuberant, mystical, somewhat naïve insurgent, he became in his last essays a sharp, courageous, profound inquirer, a defender of freedom in what he had learned was a hostile world.

Bourne's change symbolized the decline of literary optimism; it also demonstrated the failure of pragmatism to produce a new consensus. Before the war Bourne, like many other intellectuals, had combined an allegiance to John Dewey with a number of incompatible elements. When Dewey announced his support of the war and began his attacks on pacifism, Bourne renounced pragmatism in a series of stinging essays. Its values, he charged, had depended on the easy consensus of a peaceful period. Under fire, its insistent practicality and emphasis on the possible deterioriated too easily into shallow opportunism.

Somewhat angrily, Dewey continued to attack impractical idealists and pacifists and during the war moved still further toward support of the Wilsonian program. Disillusioned in 1919, he turned against Wilson and the League, explaining his wartime position in terms that sounded almost apologetic.

Dewey and his followers went on after the war to some of their most important work, and to a new height of prestige in some circles. Yet for some kinds of people who had once admired Dewey, Bourne's wartime questions remained moot. Rejecting far more than pragmatism alone, Bourne had helped to drive a wedge between the values of art and those of practical betterment.

> Is there something in these realistic attitudes that works actually against poetic vision, against concern for the quality of life as above machinery of life? [5]

Despite several generations of serious and sometimes promising effort, this question has not been answered. Pragmatism became one of a number of contending views and not what its founders still hoped it might be: the basis of a new, progressive "common faith."

The Rebellion, in its innocent prewar form, was over. Having helped to destroy the nineteenth-century credo, it perished with its old opponent. In a more general sense, the American intellectual revolution was only beginning. This has moved in so many directions that its later history cannot even be suggested here. One thing that happened after the war was the re-emergence with new prestige of the two main nineteenth-century heresies, extreme naturalism and extreme aestheticism.

In the new, more complex, and less cheerful climate of postwar dissent, nearly all the chief leaders of the prewar movement found themselves feeling strange and uprooted. The Chicago poets, the first generation of Greenwich Villagers, the *Masses* radicals, the original New Republicans all felt disoriented after the war in the presence of their juniors. Some disappeared, some like Dell wrote well only about their prewar experiences, some like Brooks and Lippmann moved slowly into very different careers. Two things seemed to bother them in the world of Fitzgerald, Hemingway, and Faulkner: real frivolity and real pessimism. The only prewar writers who were really comfortable later were those who had belonged from the start to the nonexuberant minority, those who had centered their method not on spontaneity but on craft. Chief among these were Pound and his young protégé of the prewar years, T. S. Eliot.

Finally, since Americans of all generations retain some tendency to moralize, it is impossible to refrain altogether from passing some judgments. The prewar Rebellion is not hard to assess. It was fragile,

[5] Bourne: "Twilight of Idols," *Seven Arts*, October, 1917, pp. 695–6.

contradictory, and usually shallow. Yet it was immediately very valuable, and in the long run its consequences were complex and momentous. It protested effectively against both rigid materialism and meaningless moralities. In its time, it won victories that could not have been won by a more consistent and penetrating kind of insurrection. Even at its shallowest, it taught the truth that all romanticism teaches and that Americans had been forgetting, the truth that the world cannot be reduced to simple formulas. It produced some excellent work in its own day, and it introduced a period of artistic and intellectual achievement that lasted and flowered for two decades.

The old culture is harder to come to terms with, since it lasted longer and ran deeper. In the nineteen-fifties nostalgia comes easily. It is not hard to see the uses of unquestioned moral consensus in a world too shaken to be even rebellious. The kindness and cheerfulness of prewar America at its best are more than attractive. Most of us feel that we cannot get along if some vestiges of these qualities do not survive.

Yet the civilization of 1912 condemned itself. It failed to carry out its own evolutionary precept of adaptation to conditions. It shut its eyes to some glaring flaws in the general success of American society. It allowed itself to become closely linked with a hopeless program that contradicted its own best insights: the dominance of a narrow class and a minority "race." It became blind even to its own heritage, the best of the American past.

These mistakes were not accidents, neither were they parts of some mysterious, inevitable cycle of maturity and decline. They were the results of a permanent flaw in American nineteenth-century thought: its inveterate optimism. Peace, economic expansion, and a large measure of general content were facts of the American scene most of the time. These had become confused with inevitable upward evolution and even with the coming of God's kingdom on earth. The American culture of 1912 fell into pieces not because it was attacked but because attack, combined with the challenge of events, brought to light its old inadequacies.

Since this happened, American civilization has been less happy, less unanimous, and more precarious. Off and on, it has also been more interesting. Its least successful periods have been those like the immediate present, times of false complacency that caricature the old confidence. Its best periods have been those when it has most nearly come to terms with an unfriendly world.

The end of American innocence was part of a great tragedy, but it was not, in itself, an unmitigated disaster. Those who look at it with dismay, or those who deny that it happened, do so because they expect true stories to have a completely happy ending. This is a kind of innocence American history must get over.

Afterword

By Henry F. May

In my brief comments I will make use of the helpful framework provided by David Hollinger's Introduction. Hollinger first presents the argument of the book, then summarizes recent scholarly criticism of it, and finally treats it as "a product of its own time and place" (and of its particular author).

Hollinger's summary of the book's thesis and content is generally accurate and perceptive. *Innocence* is the study of a transitional period in the thought and feeling of the educated middle class in America. The emphasis is on literature and politics more or less equally, and on the informal but deep moral assumptions and preferences that underly both. In my opinion, the most interesting as well as the most difficult subject for cultural historians is to define and describe those assumptions which in each period are so generally taken for granted that they do not always need to be specifically expressed.

The book locates the transition between what have come to be called "Victorianism" and "modernity" in the years 1912 to 1917, spending a good deal of time on the nineteenth-century intellectual tendencies that led toward this brief transitional period. Hollinger understands, as some readers have not, that my purpose was by no means to diminish the importance of political history but rather to give more depth to the study of prewar Progressivism and the First World War itself by presenting both against a background of growing cultural division.

It is certainly questionable, as many critics have suggested, how seriously such claims about decisive transitions should be taken. Perhaps I made a mistake in using in my title and subtitle two overly portentous phrases, "the end of American innocence" and "the first years of our own time." One could easily argue that American innocence ended at a number of other points—for instance, as Perry Miller suggested, in the late seventeenth century, or in the doubts and disillusions of the years after the Revolution, or in the years of Reconstruction when racial equality was taken off the American agenda. Probably it would have been better to state clearly what I always meant to imply: that American innocence had never existed at all outside certain powerful national images and beliefs. Obviously the "first years of our own time" referred only to my own perception about the beginnings of *my* time, and could not play this role in the consciousness of younger critics.

I could easily dispense with these phrases, but I could not as easily give up my perception that the years 1912–1917 had their own distinctive character, a perception that I had acquired the hard way. I had spent some years trying to write a book about the nineteen-twenties, which everybody knew were the crucial years of cultural change. Working on the previous period as background to *that* time of change, I found that the prewar period was itself a time of growing moral and literary rebellion. The rebel movement of this early period, however, though it was full of vitality, could not escape the pervasive optimism of a time of apparent peace, progress, and prosperity. The young intellectuals tried to proclaim their rebellion against official rigidities while also resisting the pessimistic conclusions of some of their nineteenth-century predecessors—the grey deterministic naturalism of some and the frightening moral nihilism of others. The center of the prewar intellectual rebellion, running through its philosophy, politics, and art, was a sort of open-ended vitalism, invoking indeterminism and instinct against both depressing determinism and arid rationalism. This is why the French philosopher Henri Bergson, for instance, was not only a major influence on American intellectuals like William James, but was also a big figure for the middlebrow magazines and a hit with New York society. This is also why the ideas of the Young Intellectuals proved to be a fragile mix when the time came to deal with the tougher challenges of the war, of the failure of Wilsonian hopes, and of threatening social and ethnic conflict in the immediate postwar years.

It is only right that in the last thirty-four years younger scholars have looked at my book through their own experience and opinions. I am gratified that they have looked at it at all. I accept Joan Shelley Rubin's complaint that there is not enough in the book about women and their struggles. In my present opinion the deficiency is not primarily in my treatment of various kinds of radical feminists like Emma Goldman and Margaret Sanger. These important figures are indeed treated briefly, but so are almost all individuals. And a good many other interesting women are presented: doubtless I could have found many more. A more important fault in the book is that in my presentation of the reigning official culture I did not give a sufficient treatment to the many and severe limitations placed on women's activities and expression by that culture. I come closest to this topic in my brief treatment of Ellen Glasgow, who had to deal with the especially narrow limits prescribed for a Southern lady. In my recent writing I have tried to deal with this the damaging limits placed on women's behavior by nineteenth-century culture, especially in my treatment of my own mother in my autobiographical *Coming to Terms*.

I accept also a similar criticism regarding my lack of emphasis on black Americans. They are there, but the interesting and complicated relation between their struggle for equality and the general movement of cultural liberation is not sufficiently explored. I especially regret this, since one aspect of my enterprise was to explore the always complex and difficult relation between social reform and artistic innovation.

The suggestion that my treatment could be enhanced by more discussion of the marketplace aspects of public expression seems fruitful. If I had continued my study into the twenties this would have been even more essential. In that period some of the anti-Puritan revolt of the young intellectuals and their older patron H. L. Mencken became confused with something quite different, the equally anti-Puritan but also vulgar and promotional hedonism of consumer culture in the allegedly Golden Twenties.

Finally, I come to the charge that I treated the Innocent Rebellion in too patronizing a manner. This may well be just, and it is always foolish and mistaken to condescend to the past. I continue however to find a certain moral superficiality in the work of Sandburg and Lindsay, most of the New Poetry sponsored by Harriet Monroe, and the criticism of Van Wyck Brooks. The rebellious intellectuals of this short period, like the people who proclaimed a new dawn of history in France in 1789–91, found themselves in the enviable position of proclaiming their rebellion and heralding great changes while still taking for granted the normal functioning of society. "Bliss was it in that dawn to be alive;" later things got tougher. In Randolph Bourne, however, I saw a special case. If one reads his earlier work, he sounds much like his young contemporaries, though his writing is already more disciplined and acute than theirs. In wartime, however, he was able more than most spokespersons of the Innocent Rebellion to rise to a more severe challenge. His wartime writings show a sharp increase in courage and maturity.

For obvious reasons, I find most interesting the last of Hollinger's three topics, his remarkably perceptive effort to consider *Innocence* as "a historical artifact, a product of its own time and place," and therefore necessarily of my own actual experience. He gathers correctly from my *Coming to Terms* that I saw genteel nineteenth-century culture as that of my father, who was born in 1860. He is right, I hope, that I treat my father in that book in a loving manner. He is also right about the ambivalence I felt. By the time I wrote *Innocence* I had consciously—and no doubt a bit pompously—rejected many of his opinions and, I thought, much of his culture. The key figure here was his major hero Woodrow Wilson. I pretty well accepted the picture of liberal failure presented by John Chamberlain in *Farewell to Reform* (1932) and was considerably influenced by John Dos Passos' sketch of "Meester Veelson" as an idealistic and phony sellout in *1919* (also 1932). I had gotten over some of this conventional disillusion, but only some of it, by the time I dealt with Wilson in *Innocence*.

In college during the thirties, I was powerfully affected by both the bohemian libertarianism which was left over from the twenties and the current vogue of Marxism. By 1959 I had only very recently thrown off the latter. Perhaps that is why, according to Hollinger, my treatment of the older culture has held up better than my treatment of the rebellion against it. With the first, I knew where I stood even if the stance was ambivalent. With my own version of liberation I was still struggling.

One more important movement was to affect my life and opinions a few years later. To all Berkeleyans, the sixties obviously began with the Free Speech Movement in 1964. This movement, eventually more important for culture than politics, went through a bewildering series of metamorphoses during the rest of the decade and affected everybody who lived, as I did, in the middle of it. If I had written *Innocence* after 1964, it would doubtless have been different. I doubt, however, whether my assessment of the Innocent Rebellion of 1912 to 1917 would have been much altered. The beginning of the movement of the sixties was not altogether unlike the movement of 1912. The original rebels of 1964, at least in Berkeley, were rigorously sincere moralists, motivated by devotion to freedom and hopes for a future society of love. As in the earlier case, the movement became tougher and harsher, perhaps also more realistic, as it developed, partly once more under the pressures of war. My attitude toward this and earlier revolutions could not, at this time in my development, have been other than ambivalent. Sometimes revolutions have to happen, but they never turn out as their makers had hoped. No doubt this conclusion is related to the growing tendency among historians and others in the fifties toward an emphasis on ambiguity, irony, paradox and so forth. There is also no doubt that this "Niebuhrian" consciousness carries with it its own dangers of complacency and acquiescence. In any case, it is clear and by no means to be deplored that my younger critics reacted differently than I did to the events of the sixties, and therefore to rebellions in the past.

Another kind of history, or perhaps historiography, must also be invoked to explain *Innocence* as a product of its time. As Hollinger suggests, intellectual history was still on the defensive in history departments in 1959. I felt under some pressure to show that my kind of work was real history, just as factual and thoroughly researched as any other. This explains why there are so many publishers, magazines, and biographies in the book; if I were writing it now I might well leave some of these in my notes and state my general conclusions without piling up instances.

This determination to be thorough also partly explains my principal method of research. I took on the job, among others, of turning through all the major magazines. In the early twentieth century, more I think than in any other period and much more than at present, every shade of American opinion and every level of culture had its magazine. Many of these, from the austere and conservative *Nation* to the genuinely daring and innovative *Masses* and *Seven Arts*, or even the popular and muckraking *McClure's*, were excellent of their kind. Among them they covered, seriously and remarkably fully, European and American politics, literature, philosophy, social theory, science, and art. I tried to read every book, European and American, that was given major attention by reviewers. This endeavor had its disadvantages, aside from the long effort it demanded. It also had its advantages, among them that my conclusions seemed to come right out of the evidence. I say "seemed," because I take it for granted, and did then, that all apparent deductions from the "facts" come also from the experience and emotions of the historian. It certainly seemed to me at the time, however, that my general conclusions were not predetermined but forced themselves upon me as I worked. Among these were the tripartite ideology of the old culture, the vitalist essence of the Rebellion, the defensiveness of both these opposing parties against 19th-century varieties of materialism and nihilism, and the effects of cultural division on attitudes toward the War.

When I finished the book I was tired, and especially tired of the sources and the people with whom I had been working for about a decade. I had lots of notes and lots of opinions about the twenties, and had expected (and was expected by others) to write a sequel about the postwar decade. Instead I turned my own efforts and my seminar toward the late eighteenth and earliest nineteenth century. Partly from fatigue, but partly also for positive reasons, I put aside my notes on the twenties and plunged with real excitement into what turned out to be more than a decade of retraining and retooling before I felt ready to write anything in the new period. The sources and techniques were very different, but the issues were less so. Perhaps I originally thought I was looking for the beginnings of American innocence, but I soon found that the Age of the Enlightenment was by no means that simple. Something more like American innocence came out of the evangelical and egalitarian movement of the early nineteenth century. The Genteel Tradition that I had tried to describe in *Innocence* was forged in the literary efforts to deal with these forces in the era of Oliver Wendell Holmes, Sr., and James Russell Lowell.

I have never in the least regretted this decision to work in a new period. It did, however, damage in a way my book on the early twentieth century. Neither the prewar establishment nor the prewar rebellion could be fully described without a careful comparison with its postwar successor. This comparison, in my 1959 book, was only hinted at. I hope somebody decides to undertake, in his or her own terms, this interesting task.

Bibliographical Essay

The sources for any book which deals with the cultural history of a period are impossible to limit precisely, and it would be useless to try to list the works I have consulted. My principal single reliance has been on a fairly systematic coverage of the period's very diverse and lively periodical press in all relevant fields. I have read as much as I could in the books which were influential, directly and indirectly, on the intellectual developments I have described. I have discussed the period with people who remember some of its events and personalities. I have benefited greatly, and obviously, from the work of a great many historians and literary historians who have dealt with portions of the subject. The following essay deals only with the less obvious and most directly useful works.

PART ONE. THE NINETEENTH CENTURY INTACT

II. Practical Idealism

The starting point for American idealism is Santayana's unfair but illuminating discussion of "The Genteel Tradition" in *Winds of Doctrine* (New York, 1913), supplemented by several chapters of his *Character and Opinion in the United States* (New York, 1920). The various histories of American philosophy mostly treat recent idealism rather perfunctorily. Two summaries of the state of philosophic opinion at the time I am discussing, useful here and later, are Ralph Barton Perry: *Present Philosophical Tendencies* (New York, 1912) and the article on "Metaphysics" by Thomas Case in the 1911 edition of the *Encyclopaedia Brittanica,* XVIII, 225–53. Josiah Royce: *Lectures on Moral Idealism* (New Haven, 1919) discusses authoritatively the relation of German and American idealism. A representative attitude toward science is that of G. H. Howison: *The Limits of Evolu-*

tion and other Essays (New York, 1901). A representative figure for the development of liberal religion in relation to evolution is Lyman Abbott, whose views can be studied in his works, in the *Outlook,* and in Ira V. Brown: *Lyman Abbott, Christian Evolutionist* (Cambridge, 1953).

III. A Nobler Future

The bibliography on Progressivism is enormous and well known. My treatment of the subject, here and later, has been influenced considerably by Richard Hofstadter's *Age of Reform* (New York, 1955), and by David W. Noble's often illuminating series of articles on progressivism, now collected as *The Paradox of Progressive Thought* (Minneapolis, 1958). The problem of the progressive constituency is helpfully discussed by George E. Mowry in *The California Progressives* (Berkeley, 1951), pp. 86–104; and Alfred D. Chandler: "The Origins of Progressive Leadership," in Elting E. Morison et al., eds.: *The Letters of Theodore Roosevelt, VIII* (Cambridge, 1954), pp. 1462–5.

IV. Custodians of Culture

For this chapter particularly, and for the whole of Part I, valuable background is provided by Walter E. Houghton's magnificent survey of English nineteenth-century culture, *The Victorian Frame of Mind* (New Haven, 1957). The transmission of Victorian culture to America needs much further exploration. John Henry Raleigh: *Matthew Arnold and American Culture* (Berkeley, 1957) makes an excellent beginning and is one of the few good treatments of American conservative culture. Lionel Trilling's *Matthew Arnold* (New York, 1939) is also helpful. Charles Eliot Norton's Letters (2 Vols., Boston, 1913) are supplemented by Edward H. Madden: "Charles Eliot Norton on Art and Morals," *Journal of the History of Ideas,* XVIII (1957), 430–8. William Allan Neilson: *Charles W. Eliot* (2 Vols., New York, 1926) includes much source material. The most perceptive treatment of the period's attitude toward immigration is in John Higham's general history of the subject, *Strangers in the Land* (New Brunswick, N.J., 1955). In my opinion both this book and Barbara Salomon's *Ancestors and Immigrants* (Cambridge, 1956) somewhat overstate the hostility of the New England gentry toward immigrants.

A very able contemporary summary of the state of historical thought is C. W. Alvord's article on "The New History" in the *Nation,* May 9, 1912, pp. 457–9. My treatment of textbooks in history and literature rests on a systematic sampling. For this purpose the following two summaries furnished useful bibliography: W. C. Bagley and H. O.

Rugg: "The Content of American History as Taught in the Seventh and Eighth Grades," University of Illinois School of Education, *Bulletin*, No. 16 (Urbana, 1916); Bert Lewis Dunmire: "The Development of American Literature Textbooks" (MS, Ph.D. thesis, University of Pittsburgh, 1954). Howard Mumford Jones: *The Theory of American Literature* (Ithaca, 1948) offers some helpful comments on the development of American literary studies.

V. Fortresses

My main sources for this chapter are periodicals and the works of the men discussed. For the Eastern colleges, Henry Seidel Canby's *Alma Mater* (Boston, 1936) is superbly evocative. For Boston and New York publishing I have relied principally on *Publisher's Weekly* and on the numerous publishers' autobiographies and commemorative house histories. The standard work on the subject, Hellmut Lehman-Haupt: *The Book in America* (New York, 1939), is supplemented by the two excellent chapters by William Charvat and Malcolm Cowley in R. E. Spiller and others: *Literary History of the United States* (3 Vols., New York, 1948). Donald Sheehan: *This Was Publishing* (Bloomington, 1952) is one of the few good monographs in the neglected field of publishing history. None of the histories of magazines covers the prewar years adequately. The fourth volume of Frank Luther Mott's thorough *A History of American Magazines* (Cambridge, 1957) brings his account up to 1905. However, each of Mott's volumes includes histories of individual magazines founded in the period covered, and these individual histories deal with the magazine's entire career. Raleigh: *Arnold in America* is good on Brownell and Sherman.

VI. Culture and the Continent

This chapter is heavily influenced by Henry Nash Smith: *Virgin Land* (Cambridge, 1950) and has profited from standard works on literary regionalism. Eastern influences are discussed in Louis B. Wright: *Culture on the Moving Frontier* (Bloomington, 1955), and D. R. Fox, ed.: *Sources of Culture in the Middle West* (New York, 1934).

Two immensely illuminating works on the South are W. J. Cash: *The Mind of the South* (New York, 1941) and C. Vann Woodward: *Origins of the New South 1877–1913* (Baton Rouge, 1951); Allen Tate: "The Profession of Letters in the South," an essay of 1935 reprinted in his *The Man of Letters in the Modern World* (New York, 1955) exemplifies a very different modern attitude toward the Southern past. Edmund Wilson: "The James Branch Cabell Case Reopened," *The New Yorker*, April 21, 1956, pp. 129–56, offers some extremely interesting comments on the South in our period. A typical contemporary account of Southern literature is Montrose J. Moses: *The Literature of the South* (New York, 1910).

The fundamental book for early California literature is Franklin Walker: *San Francisco's Literary Frontier* (New York, 1939). Much of the literature on Far Western cultural history is ephemeral, but some biographies are helpful. Josiah Royce has some shrewd insights in "The Pacific Coast," an address reprinted in *Race Questions* (New York, 1908). The nature and quality of California writing in the period is conveyed by Ella Sterling (Cummins) Mighels: *Literary California* (San Francisco, 1918). For Eastern knowledge of the Far West, Earl Pomeroy: *In Search of the Golden West* (New York, 1957) is highly interesting. Interesting observations on Far Western culture are contained in Frederick Bracher: "California's Literary Regionalism," *American Quarterly*, VII (1955), 275–84. Southern California literature is carefully and rather indulgently chronicled in Franklin Walker's *A Literary History of Southern California* (Berkeley and Los Angeles, 1950). This is informatively supplemented by Lawrence Russ Veysey: "Southern California Society, 1867–1910" (M.A. thesis, Chicago, 1957).

For the Indiana writers an excellent brief summary is Richard A. Cordell: "Limestone, Corn, and Literature," *Saturday Review of Literature*, December 17, 1938, pp. 3–4, 14–15. Two unusually helpful biographies are James Woodress: *Booth Tarkington, Gentleman from Indiana* (Philadelphia, 1954) and Richard Crowder: *Those Innocent Years*, about James Whitcomb Riley (Indianapolis, 1958). There is much material on the village in Lewis Atherton: *Main Street on the Middle Border* (Bloomington, 1954). Merle Curti and Vernon Carstensen: *The University of Wisconsin* (2 Vols., Madison, 1949) offers a way into the sources about that institution. For Chicago, Bernard Duffey: *The Chicago Renaissance in American Letters* (East Lansing, 1954), an unusually fine monograph, is one of the few books which gives the movements of the prewar period an historical background in depth. The civic histories and some biographies offer some information on Chicago developments.

VII. The New Augustan Age

My interpretation of Roosevelt and Wilson owes a great deal to the familiar and excellent secondary literature on both men. A helpful recent addition is Merle Curti: "Woodrow Wilson's Concept of Human Nature," *Midwest Journal of Political Science*, I (1957), 1–19. For my purposes Wilson's *Mere Literature* (Boston, 1896) is particularly illuminating.

PART TWO. OLDER INSURGENTS AND INVADERS

I. Outsiders

The sources of this chapter are in part fragmentary. The degree of racial and class exclusiveness is suggested by some of the literature on immigration mentioned under Part V and by recent sociological work, though the latter is seldom chronologically organized.

The most suggestive account of farmer resistance to progress is in Samuel P. Hays: *The Response to Industrialism, 1885–1914* (Chicago, 1957), pp. 110–115. My treatment of conservative Christianity is influenced by the reinterpretation of American religious history now under way. The most important recent contribution to this reinterpretation is Timothy L. Smith: *Revivalism and Social Reform in Nineteenth-Century America* (New York and Nashville, 1957). This offers a salutary but unduly sweeping correction to the secular emphasis of previous books. A synthesis is badly needed. For fundamentalism and revivalism specifically I am indebted to the unpublished research of Lynn Marshall and Carroll E. Harrington. The latter's study of "The Fundamentalist Movement in America, 1870–1920" is far the fullest available. The standard works deal almost entirely with the postwar phase of the movement. William G. McLoughlin, Jr.: *Billy Sunday Was His Real Name* (Chicago, 1955) is a brilliant study. For guidance in the voluminous sources on business thought and scientific management I am indebted to Samuel Haber, whose study of the latter subject will be wide-ranging. Milton J. Nadworny: *Scientific Management and the Unions, 1900–1932* (Harvard, 1955) is the fullest recent published account.

II. Questioners

Morton G. White: *Social Thought in America: The Revolt Against Formalism* (New York, 1949) treats American relativism in illuminating fashion; I think, however, that it connects political progressivism too closely with pragmatic philosophy. Philip Wiener discusses with keen insight *Evolution and the Founders of Pragmatism* (Cambridge, 1949). Good summaries of the development of both philosophy and social science in the period will be found in Merle Curti, ed.: *American Scholarship in the Twentieth Century* (Cambridge, 1953) and May Brodbeck et al., eds.: *American Non-Fiction 1900–1950* (Chicago, 1952). A new and interesting interpretation of the whole history of American thought which appeared too late to be heavily used here is Stow Persons: *American Minds* (New York, 1958).

The literature on James and Dewey is summarized and listed in the standard histories of American philosophy such as those by Herbert Schneider and W. H. Werkmeister. One of the outstanding lacks in American studies is an intellectual biography of Dewey comparable to Ralph Barton Perry's magnificent *Thought and Character of William James* (2 Vols., Boston, 1936). For Dewey's educational thought in relation to other subjects I have found considerable help in several articles by Lawrence Cremin, especially "The Revolution in American Secondary Education, 1893–1918," *Teachers College Record,* LVI (1955), 295–308. Existing works on the history of American social science badly need bringing up to date. Summaries of developments in this period are E. C. Hayes, ed.: *Recent Developments in the Social Sciences* (Philadelphia, 1927); and some of the chapters in the Columbia commemorative *A Quarter Century of Learning* 1904–1929 (New York, 1931). My comments are, however, based primarily on my own sampling of social science literature. The most helpful of the many treatments of psychology is Edna Heidbreder: *Seven Psychologies* (New York, 1923).

The history of the economic thought of the particular kind relevant here is best discussed by Allan G. Gruchy: *Modern Economic Thought, The American Contribution* (New York, 1947). There is a considerable amount of recent writing on Mitchell, most of which is listed in Arthur F. Burns, ed.: *Wesley Clair Mitchell, The Economic Scientist* (New York, 1952). The tendencies in economics important for our subject are summarized by Mitchell himself in "Human Behavior and Economics: A Survey of Recent Literature," *Quarterly Journal of Economics,* XXI (1914–15), 1–47. L. S. Mitchell's *Two Lives* (New York, 1953) is useful at several points in this book. For political science, C. E. Merriam and H. E. Barnes, eds.: *A History of Political Theories, Recent Times* (New York, 1924) is source material for our period, and Dwight Waldo: *The Administrative State* (New York, 1948) a highly sophisticated re-examination. The literature on American historical relativism and the recent discussion of Beard are well known to historians. The influence of Robinson on teaching is documented in Luther V. Hendricks: *James Harvey Robinson, Teacher of History* (New York, 1946).

III. Scoffers

The topic of naturalism in America is treated very briefly by Harold A. Larrabee in Yervant H. Krikorian, ed.: *Naturalism and the Human Spirit* (New York, 1944). Stow Persons: *American Minds,* treats this subject at length and interestingly.

For scientific thought, which I have had to approach in this and other chapters from a background of scientific ignorance, I have received more help from J. T. Merz: *History of European Thought in the Nineteenth Century* (Edinburgh, 1903), II, than from any other account. Two philosophical discussions of scientific naturalism and its limits that have influenced my attitude greatly are Morris Cohen: *Reason and Nature* (Glencoe, Ill., 1931); and Alfred North Whitehead: *Science and the Modern World* (New York, 1925). Wiener: *Evolution* classifies the varieties of naturalism helpfully.

I have profited from Lucille Birnbaum's "Behaviorism in the 1920's," *American Quarterly*, VII (1955), 15–30, and from Mrs. Birnbaum's unpublished researches on behaviorism. William H. Hay: "Paul Carus: A Case Study of Philosophy on the Frontier," *Journal of the History of Ideas*, XVII (1956), 498–510 is a useful short account of a rather neglected figure.

For the naturalism emanating from radical quarters, the best approaches are the radical press and radical autobiographies. My treatment of divisions within socialism owes a lot to the recent historians of socialism, particularly David Shannon and Daniel Bell. A study of Steffens that adds to the standard sources is Irving G. Cheslaw: "An Intellectual Biography of Lincoln Steffens," (MS, Ph.D. thesis, Columbia, 1952).

For literary naturalism and also for the topics discussed in the next chapter, Oscar Cargill: *Intellectual America, Ideas on the March* (New York, 1942) is the most ambitious account. There are many helpful studies of the influence of particular authors. See also B. Q. Morgan: *A Critical Bibliography of German Literature in English Translation* (2nd ed., Stanford, 1938). My main source for statements about availability of foreign authors is my study of periodicals and a systematic check of American and English translations.

IV. Amoralists

The following two interpretations of European decadent literature are extremely helpful: Edmund Wilson: *Axel's Castle* (New York, 1931), and Marcel Raymond: *From Baudelaire to Surrealism* (New York, 1950). Roger Shattuck: *The Banquet Years* (New York, 1958) is a new and fascinating survey of extreme avant-garde movements in France from 1885 to 1918. American imitations of European decadence are dealt with by Bernard Smith: *Forces in American Criticism* (New York, 1939), pp. 266–89, and Harry T. Levin: "The Discovery of Bohemia," in Spiller et al.: *Literary History*, II, 1065–79.

Among helpful studies of individuals are: Edgar McKitrick: "Edgar Saltus of the Obsolete," *American Quarterly*, III (1951), 22–35; J. B. Pritchard and J. M. Raines: "James Gibbons Huneker, Critic of the Seven Arts," *American Quarterly*, II (1950), 153–61; G. B. Munson: "A Forgotten American Critic" (on Pollard), *Freeman*, II

(1920), 135–6. I have learned a lot about Reedy from Fred W. Wolf: "William Marion Reedy, A Critical Biography" (MS, Ph.D. thesis, Vanderbilt, 1954). The Nietzsche movement in America is dealt with very briefly by Benjamin de Casseres, *The Superman in America* (University of Washington Chapbooks, No. 30, Seattle, 1920). The secondary material on Mencken is well known and not very satisfactory. My interpretation is affected by one of the earliest essays, Edmund Wilson, Jr.: "H. L. Mencken," *New Republic*, June 1, 1921, pp. 10–12.

PART THREE. THE INNOCENT REBELLION

I. Liberators

General books which deal with some part of the material of this chapter include Alfred Kazin: *On Native Grounds* (New York, 1942); Van Wyck Brooks: *The Confident Years* (New York, 1952); and, briefly but well, H. S. Commager: *The American Mind* (New York, 1950), pp. 120–40. Probably the two best contemporary accounts of this whole tendency in Europe and America are Santayana's brilliant *Winds of Doctrine* (New York, 1913) and Floyd Dell's highly impressionistic but acute *Intellectual Vagabondage* (New York, 1926).

Approaches to the history of science accessible to the layman are mentioned in this Essay under Part II. The Columbia lectures are particularly helpful, and are supplemented by reviews of the recent history of each field in the September 1950 number of the *Scientific American*. For popular scientific thought periodicals are helpful, especially, on their two levels, the *Nation* and the *Literary Digest*.

The contemporary American literature on Bergson, in books and periodicals, is so large that it is surprising his influence has not been more noticed. A good start is offered by Santayana's hostile essay in *Winds of Doctrine* and E. E. Slosson's admiring presentation in *Major Prophets of To-day* (Boston, 1914).

For irrationalist political theory the following serve as an introduction: Cohen: *Reason and Nature*; Merriam and Barnes: *History of Political Theories, Recent Times*; and W. Y. Elliott: *The Pragmatic Revolt in Politics* (New York, 1928).

For the influence of Freud, I used profitably John C. Burnham: "Freud Comes to the United States" (MS, Ph.D. thesis, Stanford, 1957). Freud's own brief account in his history of the psychoanalytic movement (quoted in the text) is essential, and there are occasional mentions of American reception in Ernest Jones's colossal biography of Freud. For Freud's literary influence, Frederick J. Hoffman's *Freudianism and the Literary Mind* (Baton Rouge, 1945) is the most thorough study, and Lionel Trilling's brief *Freud and the Crisis of Our*

Culture (Boston, 1955) is extremely penetrating. W. David Siever: *Freud on Broadway* (New York, 1955) seems to me to extend the influence of Freud on the theater too far. For Freudian influence on American social science see *The American Journal of Sociology*, entire number for November 1939, and several essays by A. Kroeber in *The Nature of Culture* (Chicago, 1952). Important evidence of the nature of Freud's first reception is in G. Stanley Hall: *Life and Confessions of a Psychologist* (New York, 1923); and even more in J. H. Putnam: *Human Motives* (Boston, 1915). A subject that needs investigation is the comparative *lack* of influence of C. G. Jung, whose approach was obviously more acceptable than Freud's in some quarters. It seems probable that he failed to achieve some of the medical and psychological approval that with Freud supplemented other support.

In my opinion, far the best account of Freud's early reception in America is in the unpublished treatment by Frederick Matthews, to which I am greatly indebted. A brilliant interpretation of Freud's place in intellectual history, published just too late for use here, is Philip Rieff, *Freud, The Mind of the Moralist* (New York, 1959).

For the European Literature of the day the *Nation, Dial,* and *Forum* are particularly helpful. Good contemporary summaries of the "new theater" are Sheldon Cheney: *The New Movement in the Theater* (New York, 1914); Thomas H. Dickinson: *The Insurgent Theater* (New York, 1917). For Wells, Van Wyck Brooks: *The World of H. G. Wells* (New York, 1915) exactly expresses the sentiments of the contemporary American intellectual. For France, some sources are indicated in the footnotes. For Germany, see Ludwig Lewisohn: *The Spirit of Modern German Literature* (New York, 1916); for Russia, Royal A. Gettmann: "Turgenev in England and America," *Illinois Studies in Language and Literature,* XXVII, 2 (Urbana, Ill., 1941) documents the shift of taste to Dostoevsky.

For the graphic arts, excellent starting points are Oliver Larkin: *Art and Life in the United States* (New York, 1949), pp. 360–7; and Milton W. Brown: *American Painting from the Armory Show to the Depression* (Princeton, 1955), pp. 3–67. An illuminating essay on the Armory Show is Meyer Schapiro: "Rebellion in Art," in Daniel Aaron, ed.: *America in Crisis* (New York, 1952), pp. 202–42. For the Russian Ballet in America a number of descriptions in autobiographies are supplemented by accounts in the *New York Times,* January 25 and 26, 1915. On new influences in music, see Jerome Mellquist and Lucie Wiese: *Paul Rosenfeld, Voyager in the Arts* (New York, 1948). Some of Rosenfeld's important prewar essays are included in his *Musical Chronicle* (New York, 1923). H. Stuart Hughes: *Consciousness and Society* (New York, 1958), an important work dealing with much of the subject-matter of this chapter, appeared just too late for me to use.

II. Poets

The whole literary history of the prewar period receives brief treatment in a great many books, of which the most illuminating is Kazin: *On Native Grounds*. Howard Mumford Jones: *The Bright Medusa* (Urbana, Ill., 1932) is partly firsthand. Lloyd R. Morris: *The Young Idea* (New York, 1917) prints artistic credos by a number of the new writers. Morton Dauwen Zabel: *Literary Opinion in America* (rev. ed., New York, 1951) gives very useful insights into changing literary opinions. For its special subject, Frederick T. Hoffman, Charles Allen, and Carolyn F. Ulrich: *The Little Magazine* (Princeton, 1946) is indispensable. There is a good deal of material on the prewar period in Hoffman's literary history *The Twenties* (New York, 1955). Reminiscences are many, and the period has already been subjected to intensive study in periodicals of American literary scholarship.

For the Chicago movement in particular, Duffey's brilliant *Chicago Renaissance* is as useful for this as for the previous period. This book will serve as a guide to other accounts and sources. The best account of St. Louis in this period is in Orrick Johns: *Time of Our Lives* (New York, 1937). On Dell and Anderson, most of the material is well known. The following were particularly helpful: William L. Phillips: "How Sherwood Anderson Wrote Winesburg, Ohio," *American Literature*, XXIII (1951–2), 7–30; *Newberry Library Bulletin*, Second Series, No. 2 (1948), *Sherwood Anderson Memorial Number*.

The sources for the rebellion in poetry can be found in the standard literary history bibliographies. I found the autobiographies especially useful here, and among them particularly those of Harriet Monroe, William Carlos Williams, Richard Aldington, and John Gould Fletcher. Foster Damon: *Amy Lowell* (Boston, 1935) is a detailed and excellent history of all the movements in which Miss Lowell took part. Horace Gregory: *Amy Lowell* (New York, 1958) is an entertaining critical sketch. Stanley K. Coffman: *Imagism* (Norman, Oklahoma, 1951), is informative about the sources of that movement. Of the very large and controversial literature on Pound, the well-known reminiscenses by contemporaries are useful, and his influence is well summed up by Ray B. West, Jr.: "Ezra Pound in Contemporary Criticism," *Quarterly Review of Literature*, V (1949), 102–200.

III. Intellectuals

A good evocation of New York in this period is Lewis Mumford: "The Metropolitan Milieu," in Waldo Frank et al., eds.: *America and*

Alfred Stieglitz (New York, 1934). For the fascination of the East Side, see the autobiographies of Hutchins Hapgood and Van Wyck Brooks, cited elsewhere, and Ernest Poole: *The Bridge* (New York, 1940). Caroline F. Ware: *Greenwich Village 1920–1930* (Boston, 1935) adds some solid social history to the flood of romantic reminiscences. Albert Parry: *Garrets and Pretenders* (New York, 1933) discusses the history of Bohemianism. Floyd Dell: *Love in Greenwich Village* (New York, 1926) is obviously authoritative for its subject.

The references for the arts mentioned above (for Part III Chapter 1) are useful here too. Van Wyck Brooks: *John Sloan, A Painter's Life* (New York, 1955) is excellent for the Ash Can School. Frank: *America and Alfred Stieglitz;* Dorothy Norman, ed.: *Stieglitz, A Memorial Portfolio* (New York, 1946); and the files of *Camera Work* convey excellently the atmosphere of this group. The most helpful book on the Provincetown Theater is Helen Deutsch: *The Provincetown* (New York, 1931). See also Susan Glaspell: *The Road to the Temple* (New York, 1927) and the autobiographies of early Provincetowners.

For beginnings of the publishing revolution, a subject which needs full-length study, I have used the sources mentioned in the earlier section on publishing, plus a few short accounts by participants including Alfred Knopf and B. W. Huebsch. Additional information on Knopf can be found in the profile, "Publisher," by Geoffrey Hellman, *New Yorker*, November 20, 27, December 4, 1948, pp. 44–57, 36–52, 40–53. I have learned most from extended conversations and correspondence with Mr. and Mrs. Knopf and correspondence with Mr. Huebsch. My account of magazine changes comes largely from the magazines themselves.

For Harvard, references used in Part I were useful. Donald Hall, ed.: *The Harvard Advocate Anthology* (New York, 1950), is a most interesting selection. For Princeton, see Edmund Wilson: "Thoughts on Being Bibliographed," *Princeton University Library Chronicle,* V (1944), 51–61 and Henry Dan Piper: "Fitzgerald's Cult of Disillusion," *American Quarterly,* II (1951), 69–80. A full account of the Yale "Literary Renaissance" is given by George Wilson Peirson: *Yale College, An Educational History 1871–1921* (New Haven, 1952).

IV. Radicals

The general flavor of the kind of radicalism discussed here is better conveyed by Lillian Symes and Travers Clement: *Rebel America* (New York, 1934) than by any other secondary work. Biographies previously mentioned are helpful, and also Granville Hicks's heroworshipping *John Reed* (New York, 1936). On anarchism, the unpublished work by Richard Drinnon on Emma Goldman adds a lot to Miss

Goldman's autobiography and the other standard sources. Sources for sexual radicalism in general are discussed under Part IV, Chapter 1. Especially relevant here are the works of Floyd Dell: *Homecoming, Love in Greenwich Village*, and *Women as World Builders* (Chicago, 1913). The Cheslaw thesis on Steffens, mentioned under II, 3, was again useful here. For Hapgood, his autobiography and other works offer a great deal of information on many subjects. A brilliant caricature of the Mabel Dodge salon is presented in Carl Van Vechten: *Peter Whiffle* (New York, 1923), pp. 121–45.

On the *Masses* and its group, a number of autobiographies and biographies contain useful reminiscences, beginning of course with Max Eastman: *Enjoyment of Living* (New York, 1948). On the *New Republic*, standard sources are importantly supplemented by Charles Budd Forcey: "Intellectuals in Crisis: Croly, Weyl, Lippmann and the *New Republic*, 1900–1919" (MS, Ph.D. thesis, University of Wisconsin, 1954). I am particularly indebted to Mr. Forcey for his discussion of the precise influence of Freud on Lippmann.

The *New Republic* is also discussed very intelligently by David Noble in two articles: "The New Republic and the Idea of Progress, 1914–1920," *Mississippi Valley Historical Review*, XXXVIII (1951), 387–402; and "Herbert Croly and American Progressive Thought," *Western Political Quarterly*, VII (1954), 537–53. This period of Lippmann's life is covered by Heinz Eulau in "Mover and Shaker, Walter Lippmann as a Young Man," *Antioch Review*, XI (1951), 291–312; and the same author's "Man Against Himself: Walter Lippmann's Years of Doubt," *American Quarterly*, II (1954), 291–304. See also D. E. Weingast: *Walter Lippmann* (New Brunswick, New Jersey, 1949).

Van Wyck Brooks's several autobiographical works are supplemented by unpublished research by M. E. Harriman. For Bourne, I have relied considerably on Louis Filler: *Randolph Bourne* (Washington, D.C., 1943). Laudatory writings on Bourne since his death form a study in themselves, which would have to begin with Brooks's introduction to Bourne's *History of a Literary Radical* (New York, 1920). Oppenheim wrote two accounts of the magazine, one in the *American Mercury*, cited in the footnotes, and one in the preface to Bourne's *Untimely Papers* (New York, 1919).

PART FOUR. THE END OF AMERICAN INNOCENCE

I. Cracks in the Surface

For changes in mores in this period, the following offer a beginning: Cargill: *Intellectual America*; H. V. Faulkner: *The Quest for Social*

Justice, 1898–1914 (*A History of American Life*, XI; New York, 1931), and best, Mark Sullivan: *Our Times* (*The War Begins, 1909–14*, IV, New York, 1932). I am particularly indebted for work on some of the elusive subjects discussed in this chapter to the graduate students at the University of California, listed in my Acknowledgments.

Much more work needs to be done on the history of American sexual mores. There is a beginning in Cargill: op. cit., and Sidney Ditzion: *Marriage, Morals and Sex in America* (New York, 1953). Oscar Handlin: *Race and Nationality in American Life* (Boston, 1957) has some perceptive suggestions about the relation between racial and sexual fears.

Statistical information is available in the census and in a number of textbooks such as E. W. Burgess and H. J. Locke: *The Family from Institution to Companionship* (New York, 1945). Of the immense literature discussing changes in customs in our period, the best single sample is William E. Carson: *The Marriage Revolt* (New York, 1913).

For birth control, the best single account is Margaret Sanger's *Autobiography* (New York, 1938). An approach to the history of censorship is made by Kimball Young: *Bibliography on Censorship and Propaganda* (University of Oregon Publications, Journalism Series, I, 1, Eugene, Oregon, 1928). Most of the books on this topic are polemic rather than historical, but Heywood Broun and Margaret Leech: *Anthony Comstock, Roundsman of the Lord* (New York, 1927) is an objective and even sympathetic treatment. There is a full account of the *Genius* episode in Robert H. Elias: *Theodore Dreiser, Apostle of Nature* (New York, 1949).

For racialism, Higham: *Strangers in the Land* (New Brunswick, 1955), is the best beginning, and points out the *prewar* increase in tension. Handlin: *Race and Nationality* gives some emphasis to social science, and both these books discuss the eugenics movement briefly. A full-length study of this extremely complex development would be interesting. A sample of the sometimes neglected kind of "objective" and "scientific" discussion that associates foreigners with almost every kind of vice and crime is J. W. Jenks and W. Jett Lauck: *The Immigration Problem* (3rd ed., New York, 1913).

II. "She Can Do No Other"

Wilson, public opinion, and the war have become one of the half-dozen major themes of American historians. Like all recent students, I have been influenced here by the careful and informative work of Arthur Link. Works which give significant attention to the relations of political and cultural history include Harley Notter: *The Origins of the Foreign Policy of Woodrow Wilson* (Baltimore, 1937); William Diamond: *The Economic Thought of Woodrow Wilson* (Baltimore, 1943); and Robert E. Osgood: *Ideals and Self-Interest in America's Foreign Relations* (Chicago, 1953). John A. Garraty's very brief treatment in his *Woodrow Wilson, A Great Life in Brief* (New York, 1956) seems to me fresh and illuminating.

The fact that defenders of the older culture almost always were strong partisans of the Allied cause is well known, though it has not received much analysis. Of the major custodians of culture treated by me in Part I, I am only able to find one exception: William Lyon Phelps, who remained doubtful well into 1917. Opinion of this group and of other groups, on particular European countries or events is drawn largely from periodicals.

For the gradual change in public opinion and its relation to cultural divisions the most suggestive single book I have read is Cedric C. Cummins's monograph on *Indiana Public Opinion and the World War 1914–1917* (Indianapolis, 1945). Mr. Cummins is far more sensitive to religious, cultural, and class differences than the authors of other state monographs and similar works on the subject.

Most, though not all, of Dewey's extraordinarily interesting statements about the war, suppression, the peace, etc., are collected in his *Characters and Events* (2 Vols., New York, 1929). His attitude is critically discussed in Morton White: *Social Thought in America*. Veblen's opinions can be found in his *Imperial Germany* (New York, 1915), *Vested Interests and the Common Man* (New York, 1919), and his *Dial* essays.

A few more names could be mentioned among people who took some part in the new literature and strongly supported the Allied Cause, including such opposites as Gertrude Stein and Willa Cather. Charles A. Fenton: "Ambulance Drivers in France and Italy, 1914–1918," *American Quarterly*, III (1951), 326–43 demonstrates that many of the very youngest group of volunteers did not share the disillusioned attitude of some famous ambulance drivers. But it is difficult to find anybody centrally associated with what I have called the Rebellion who was not either opposed to participation, doubtful, or indifferent. My list of those who have recorded such attitudes could be considerably expanded.

For the *New Republic*, the *Masses*, and the *Seven Arts*, during the approach to war and after, see references mentioned in previous chapters. Additional insight into the self-questionings of the *New Republic* group can be found in the wartime books of Weyl and Lippmann and in Heinz Eulau: "Wilsonian Idealist: Walter Lippmann Goes to War," *Antioch Review*, XIV (1954), 87–108.

III. The War and After

Of the works on wartime hysteria, the most relevant for my purposes, since it links opinion on the war with other allegiances, is Ray H. Abrams: *Preachers Present Arms* (Philadelphia, 1953).

Further evidence that members of the prewar Rebellion found themselves ill at ease among their juniors in the immediately postwar world will be found in the autobiographies, cited earlier, of Brooks, Johns, Dell, Fletcher, and others. The relation between the pre- and postwar literary movements is brilliantly treated in Malcolm Cowley: *Exile's Return* (New York, 1934). For brief comments on postwar divisions of opinion, mostly continuations of prewar tendencies treated in this book, see my article "Shifting Perspectives on the 1920's," *Mississippi Valley Historical Review*, XLIII (1956–7), 405–27.

Index

Index